# Homo Mimeticus
A NEW THEORY OF IMITATION

# Homo Mimeticus

A NEW THEORY OF IMITATION

by
Nidesh Lawtoo

Leuven University Press

This project has received funding from the European Research Council (ERC) under the European Union's Horizon 2020 research and innovation programme (grant agreement n°716181).

Published with the support of the KU Leuven Fund for Fair Open Access

Published in 2022 by Leuven University Press / Presses Universitaires de Louvain / Universitaire Pers Leuven. Minderbroedersstraat 4, B-3000 Leuven (Belgium).

© Nidesh Lawtoo, 2022

This book is published under a Creative Commons CC BY-NC-ND 4.0 Licence:
https://creativecommons.org/licenses/by-nc-nd/4.0/

Attribution should include the following information:
Nidesh Lawtoo, *Homo Mimeticus: A New Theory of Imitation*.
Leuven: Leuven University Press, 2022. (CC BY-NC-ND 4.0)

ISBN 978 94 6270 346 9 (Paperback)
ISBN 978 94 6166 477 8 (ePDF)
ISBN 978 94 6166 478 5 (ePUB)
https://doi.org/10.11116/9789461664778
D/2022/1869/57
NUR: 730

Layout: Crius Group
Cover design: Anton Lecock
Cover illustration: *Drawing Hands* (1948) © M.C. Escher

> We remain unknown to ourselves,
> we seekers after knowledge, even to ourselves:
> and with good reason. We have never sought after ourselves
> —so how should we one day find ourselves?
>
> Friedrich Nietzsche, *On the Genealogy of Morals*

# CONTENTS

Introduction: Drawing Mimetic Studies — 9

## PART 1 — GENEALOGIES: FOUNDATIONS — 41
Chapter 1: Birth of Homo Mimeticus — 43
Chapter 2: *Vita Mimetica* in the Cave — 69
Chapter 3: Sameness and Difference Replayed — 93

## PART 2 — AESTHETICS: CASE STUDIES — 127
Chapter 4: The Plasticity of Mimesis — 129
Chapter 5: On Animal and Human Mimicry — 157
Chapter 6: The Human Chameleon — 191

## PART 3 — POLITICS: MIMETIC *RE*-TURNS — 225
Chapter 7: Banality of Evil/Mimetic Complexity — 227
Chapter 8: Vibrant Mimesis — 255
Chapter 9: The Age of Viral Reproduction — 277

Coda: The Complexity of Mimesis: A Dialogue with Edgar Morin — 301

Notes — 321
Bibliography — 337
Index — 351

INTRODUCTION

# DRAWING MIMETIC STUDIES

It's only a reproduction and you have probably seen it many times before, perhaps in passing. It's a familiar image and, at first sight, doesn't appear new, let alone original. But have you taken the time not only to see it but also to experience its power of affection? Absorb this book cover long enough, and sooner than you would think, it will start making an impression on your senses. If you persist for a little longer, you might even feel the hands becoming strangely animated, three-dimensional, and embodied—emerging, phantomlike, from the flat surface. Perhaps, in a mirroring move, these hands even start pulling you in a spiraling loop that defies linear logic, yet strangely affects us nonetheless. This paradoxical pull, as you have already intuited, is playing on the unconscious register of a *homo mimeticus*, whose moving contours we will draw and redraw in the pages that follow.

The mimetic experience I have just invited you to partake in is so ordinary that it tends to go unnoticed, and thus unthought. It thus requires artistic originality to make it perceptible. This is, indeed, what M. C. Escher does in one of his most often reproduced lithographs, aptly titled *Drawing Hands* (1948):[1] he delineates with his inimitable artistic craft an aesthetic paradox that throws a wrench, or rather, two pencils, in the traditional laws of mimetic realism, allowing a different, more complex, and dynamic conception of mimesis to emerge—that is, a drawing of homo mimeticus crossing the boundaries between art and life, animating this picture's affective and logical powers. Since *Drawing Hands* generates a spiraling loop that is constitutive of the paradoxical movement this book will repeatedly outline, in guise of introduction, I invite you to take a second look at the book cover. This time, pay closer attention not only to what you *see* but also to what you *feel*, not only to the image outside the book but also to the affect inside yourself—if the two can, by now, even be dissociated.

As mimesis tends to generate shared experiences, I'll join in this little aesthetic experiment as well. At a first, distracted sight, the picture appears clear enough. As the title already indicates and the content of the work immediately confirms, *Drawing Hands* seems to objectively represent two hands drawing on a piece of paper with two pencils. It's a black-and-white drawing, perhaps done with the same kind of pencils the hands hold, and the drawing is pinned in an aslant, casual position, as you sometimes see on pinboards hanging in public spaces, say a café, a university, or a museum. Even the style seems to conform to the traditional laws of mimesis understood as a straightforward imitation, copy, or representation of realty. You can try it out for yourself: take a white piece of paper and two pencils in your hands; place the right hand on top and the left hand below; and, voilà, you will see something that appears to approximate *Drawing Hands*.

But as often with appearances, similarities can be deceptive. As the title makes equally clear, the hands are not simply drawn. They are actually *drawing*. And this inversion changes everything. In fact, as we follow the movement of the drawing hands, an imperceptible magnetic and spiraling pull immediately doubles the distance of the visual experience via a strangely embodied, affective experience. This happens in a few seconds, in a subliminal way that escapes full conscious control, yet operates in the gray zone between logic and affect, mind and body, art and life. *Nolens volens*, we are now caught in a counterclockwise, circular, or rather spiraling movement that makes us see and feel the initial impression had, indeed, been deceptive all along. The first sight that turned the hands into a passive object of visual representation is redoubled and overturned by a second, more complex sensation that the hands are active subjects in the process of drawing—or better, they are drawing each other, generating a self-reflexive, paradoxical loop that turns an aesthetic object into a mimetic subject, passivity into activity, the hands drawn into the *drawing hands* that the title had, after all, foregrounded all along.

Caught in this spiraling loop, the mirroring hands, whose realistic three-dimensionality stuck out from the beginning, feel increasingly animated. Well before the invention of three-dimensional simulations, they already transgress the traditional laws of representation. At one further remove, we might even participate in the process of drawing, an imitative process that can now, in any case, no longer be contained within the autonomous sphere of art but is constitutive of the life of an embodied, affective, and imitative species. This creative, sometimes maddening, and often dizzying paradox that turns passivity into activity, a static image into a dynamic imitation, a mimetic object into a mimetic subject, hands drawn into drawing hands, *is* the fundamental paradox at play in the different manifestations of the protean phenomenon we struggle to take hold of in this book.

From imitation to identification, affective contagion to mimetism, suggestion to hypnosis, embodied simulation to influence, mirroring reflexes to algorithmic spells, the protean phantom of what the ancients called, enigmatically, *mimēsis,* is back. Reloaded by the digital age, mimesis is currently generating a spiraling vortex that can no longer be framed by the traditional logic of visual representation; nor can it be considered a reflection that falls neatly within the dominant philosophical conception of an autonomous, self-possessed, and fully rational subject qua *Homo sapiens*. On the contrary, this phantom brings us back in touch with the embodied, relational, and affective dimension of a homo mimeticus whose protean transformations are still in urgent need of philosophical, aesthetic, and political delineations.

In an elegant, seemingly effortless, and original aesthetic gesture, the artist already succeeds in capturing, via an impressive image, if not the essence, idea, or form, certainly the movement, *dunamis*, and power of a paradoxical subject that will animate the pages that follow. He also provides a blueprint to delineate a picture of homo mimeticus whose hands are already in the process of drawing, or redrawing, its own moving contours. My general goal? Opening up a new transdisciplinary field of inquiry I propose to call, *mimetic studies*.

## Mimetic Studies

For some time, an old yet always changing phantom has been haunting, animating, or perhaps reanimating the humanities, generating new critical twists and original theoretical turns that are currently opening up new areas of inquiry across a variety of disciplines. From the affective turn to the cognitive turn, the new materialist turn to the ethical turn, the neuro turn to the digital turn, the posthuman turn to the environmental turn, it is well known that a number of future-oriented turns led by some of the most influential and creative thinkers writing today in what are still nostalgically called the "humanities" are currently redefining the contours of what it means to be "human" in the twenty-first century.

Less known is that, more recently, some of the very same thinkers have been engaging in collaborative, dialogic, and transdisciplinary efforts that mark a return of attention to the affective, embodied, and relational side of a mimetic phantom in the process of being theorized anew. From continental philosophy to literary theory, political theory to feminist and decolonial theory, new materialism to posthuman studies, among other emerging perspectives,[2] there is now significant evidence that a plurality of voices is currently rethinking mimesis from the angle of aesthetic, philosophical, and political differences rather than reducing it to the logic of a metaphysics of sameness. In the process, they are contributing to a mimetic turn that, via a spiraling feedback loop, now *re*-turns to put the ancient realization that humans are imitative animals to new critical and theoretical use.

A *re*-turn differs from yet another turn in the sense that it looks back, genealogically, to influential precursors in order to generate repetitions with a difference internal to a concept that spans nothing less than the history of western civilization. At the most general and foundational level, our drawing of mimetic studies finds in classical antiquity an unavoidable genealogical starting point. At the dawn of philosophy, in fact, Plato and Aristotle disagreed radically about the evaluation of mimesis understood as a representation or imitation of realty, and this disagreement is often stressed. In the *Republic* (ca. 375 BC) Plato, let us briefly recall, violently critiqued literary representations like Homeric epic, comedy, and tragedy for at least two reasons: for generating false "appearances," "shadows," or "phantoms" (Plato 1963, 514a–516a) of reality he relegated to the bottom of a mythic cave at "the third remove from truth" (602c) (epistemic and ontological reasons), but also for staging bad models of behavior that generate an irrational affect, or *pathos*, in the soul of citizens playing social roles within the city or *polis* (psychological and pedagogical reasons). On the other hand, in the *Poetics* (ca. 335 BC), Aristotle, contra Plato, defended poetry by restricting mimesis to a dramatic "representation of an action" (Aristotle 1987, 37) (aesthetic reasons) structured upon rational laws of necessity and causality he considered universal, thereby concluding that mimesis or "poetry is more philosophical and serious than history" (41) (logical reasons). The agon, or opposition, at play in these competing evaluations of mimesis defined as an artistic image, mirror, or aesthetic representation of realty could thus not be more fundamental. The *Republic* and the *Poetics* delineate two antagonistic philosophical hands drawing opposed pictures of mimesis, so to speak, an opposition that would likely have led to antithetical evaluations of *Drawing Hands* as a pictorial representation of what reality really is, or is assumed to be.

And yet, as often with inversions of perspectives, this agon might not be as clear cut as it appears. I call it a *mimetic* agon because, despite their conflicting evaluation of mimesis qua representation, Plato and Aristotle fundamentally agreed on a more archaic, anthropological, but also philosophical point:

namely, they put pencil to paper to jointly draw a picture of humans as imitative animals—or homo mimeticus. This second, perhaps less discussed, but more ancient and in my view, far-reaching definition of mimesis, is the one I take as my genealogical starting point to launch the field of mimetic studies. Its general goal is to redraw the boundaries of subjectivity, aesthetics, and politics for contemporary times—while sitting, so to speak, on ancient shoulders.

As Aristotle famously put it in chapter 4 of the *Poetics*, overturning Plato's negative evaluation of mimesis while echoing a lesson he had indeed learned from his teacher:

> There is man's [*sic*] natural propensity, from childhood onwards, to engage in mimetic activity (and this distinguishes man from other creatures, that he is thoroughly mimetic and through mimesis takes his first steps in understanding). (Aristotle 1987, 34)

The founders of philosophy agree, then, that humans remain, for good and ill, all-too-mimetic creatures. This does not mean that nonhuman animals do not imitate, or that imitation cannot be used to generate irrational misunderstandings, or that mimesis cannot be even more thoroughly and effectively at play in new techniques of digital simulation. Far from it. *Re*-turning to an ancient insight does not entail a simple repetition of ancient lessons. Rather, it involves re-evaluating them in light of contemporary insights, historical contexts, and emerging problems that necessarily introduce significant differences and call for both theoretical innovations and creation of new concepts on which a new transdisciplinary field can grow.

What founders of philosophy indicate, for the moment, is that since time immemorial, humans have imitated other human and nonhuman animals with their bodies first, often in ritualized, affective, participatory, not fully conscious, and mirroring ways constitutive of the very origins of the concept of *mimēsis* itself. It is thus useful to recall at the outset that the verb *mimeisthai*, to imitate, comes from *mîmos*, whose meaning is already double, as it signifies both the actor or mime and a type of dramatic performance.[3] From its inception in pre-Platonic times, mimesis is indeed tied to aesthetic ritual practices that are more invested in a moving body than in a static image, more attentive to dramatic action than visual reproductions, more sensitive to spellbinding gestures than to visual resemblances. What is at stake in the practice of the *mîmos* is thus not an ontological distinction between art and reality, truth and falsity, the original and the copy—if only because via gestures and impersonations, the mime would perform actions for spectators to both see and feel. Consequently, in its process of emergence as a prephilosophical concept, mimesis is more entangled with bodies moving than with bodies represented, with mirroring gestures more than gestures mirrored; or, if we return to our matrix image, mimesis was more sensitive to drawing but also mimicking, playing, dancing, and thus moving hands to be intimately felt, than to static hands drawn to be seen from a distance.

While the western founders of competing theories of mimesis attempted to stabilize this destabilizing dramatic concept via different notions of representation—a speculative mirror for Plato, a dramatic plot for Aristotle—they remained nonetheless fundamentally aware that, in its prephilosophical origins, the all-too-human tendency to imitate with one's body manifested itself via a plurality of performative practices that did not rest on an abstract binary logic opposing fiction to reality, origin to copy, truth to falsity, ideal worlds to illusory afterworlds. On the contrary, the affective drive, power—or as we shall call it, convoking an ancient concept, *pathos*—at play in mimetic activities was experienced with both body and soul, individually and collectively, for good and ill.

Mimesis was in fact dramatized in protean ways not confined to the side of fiction, for it affected and infected individual bodies as well as the body politic. It also crossed the fiction/reality, aesthetics/politics divide via chameleonlike transformations that, perhaps more obviously than ever, continue to reach into the present: from mimicry to mimetism, dance to ritual, tragic dramas to comic spectacles, enthusiastic recitations to theatrical dramatizations, imitation of bad models to imitation of good models, crowd behavior to public behavior, and, more recently, cinematic identifications to new digital simulations, video games to algorithmic social media, among other avatars of mimesis. Indeed, the human propensity for imitation remains inscribed in our contemporary "mimetic condition."[4] It is this all-too-mimetic, or as I call it, hypermimetic condition that now urges us to *re*-turn to a long genealogy of thinkers that go from antiquity to modernity, from philosophy to aesthetics, politics to ethics, psychology to a plurality of disciplinary perspectives I draw from to inaugurate the field of mimetic studies.

The goal of this study is ambitious but pluralist in orientation. As the title says, it aims to develop a new theory of imitation to jumpstart a transdisciplinary field of inquiry that cannot be restricted to a universal and transhistorical mimetic theory. On the contrary, it traces the movement of a chameleon concept that is informed by the historical, aesthetic, and political backgrounds from which it emerges. I thus propose to call this new field of inquiry mimetic studies precisely to emphasize its pluralist, heterogeneous, and perspectival approach. And since mimesis is an ancient concept currently reloaded by new media, we could qualify it as *new* mimetic studies to stress the urgency to account for the contemporary manifestations of mimesis.⁵ The book's telos is thus Janus-faced: it looks back to theories and practices of mimesis of the past from which mimetic studies emerged to better delineate new manifestations of homo mimeticus that go beyond ancient quarrels between philosophy and art in the present and future.

## Beyond Ancient Quarrels

Precisely in light of this ancient genealogy, the close link between philosophy and mimesis might continue to surprise. It thus still requires a word of explanation as we set out to join philosophy and the arts, supplemented by the social sciences, to launch a transdisciplinary field focused on the protean manifestations of homo mimeticus. Since the origins of western thought, there is, in fact, a complex, sometimes agonistic, at times defensive relation between philosophy and the dominant medium at the time—namely, poetry, or as we call it today, literature, which now includes film, TV and new media as well.

This ancient quarrel starts in classical antiquity with Plato's critique of mimesis and Aristotle's defense of it and traverses the history of western thought and art. Under a different mask, it concerns the imitation of artistic precursors at play in modern *querelles* between advocates of classical imitation, on the one hand, and of romantic innovation, on the other. In the modern period, these two opposed hands set up perhaps too simplistic a binary between *les anciens et les modernes* that does not take into account what the French philosopher Philippe Lacoue-Labarthe calls, via an oxymoronic-sounding title, *L'Imitation des modernes* (1986). At one further remove and closer to us, the quarrel between philosophy and literature does not consider that mimesis informs a "mimetic unconscious" that turns the modernist ego in what I call, in a Nietzschean title, *The Phantom of the Ego* (2013). For both the moderns and the modernists, the subject or ego is not a self-contained, autonomous, and fully rational or intentional subject. On the contrary, it is a phantom ego who is easily possessed by others, affected by crowds, manipulated by leaders, and now dispossessed by a plurality of social media that catch homo mimeticus in spirals of becoming other.

My first step for the new theory of imitation articulated here emerges in the wake of a genealogy of what I called the "imitation of the modernists" (2013,

288). It was articulated precisely at the crossroads where philosophy and literature meet, face each other, and reflect critically and creatively *on* one another. A number of critical and theoretical steps have expanded the *re*-turn to mimesis since, and at a growing speed. But despite numerous efforts to go beyond disciplinary quarrels on the contested topic of mimesis, to this day, the dominant academic stance on this ancient Janus-faced concept is to split it in philosophy and literature departments that, at least in Europe, often rely on external EU funding, transdisciplinary seminars, and somewhat clandestine back-and-forth exchanges across faculties in order to share insights, dialogue, and go further.[6] Hence the need for a transdisciplinary field in order to catch up with transgressive manifestations of mimesis in the twenty-first century.

A degree of specialization is obviously necessary for scientific knowledge to advance. As the reader will see, this book is far from inimical to specialized training, as each chapter brings the mimetic turn to bear on specific disciplines, from philosophy to literary studies, from film and media studies to political theory, among others. Still, this old academic, and thus Platonic, split between philosophy and literature is determinantal to an adequate theorization of the transdisciplinary concept of mimesis and, by extension, of the plurality of mimetic and hypermimetic problems that are now at play in the contemporary world. Again, a look back to the ancients can give us the necessary genealogical distance to move beyond academic walls that were not yet solidified as mimesis was first theorized, and now need to be bridged to face interdisciplinary problems that redraw the very boundaries of this protean concept.

For instance, let us recall when Plato, in book 10 of the *Republic*, asks, under the mask of Socrates, to his brother Glaucon: "Could you tell me in general what imitation is?" In asking this question, Plato is the first to foreground the difficulty of capturing this concept via his philosophical *logos*. In a characteristic avowal of ignorance, Socrates candidly admits, "for neither do I myself quite apprehend what it [mimesis] would be at" (Plato 1963c, 595c). If our knowledge of what initially appeared as a familiar and stable notion is already a bit troubled by now, there is thus nothing to worry about: we're actually in good philosophical company. Socrates, then, proceeds to famously state that there is an "ancient enmity" (607c) between philosophy and poetry for the epistemic and metaphysical reasons already mentioned: mimetic poets represent illusory phantoms, not true reality as he defines it. Granted. But it is also true that the quarrel might not have been as ancient and oppositional as it is often believed to be, at least if we recall Plato's earlier realization in book 3 of *Republic* that mimesis is at play in dramatic spectacles that, via mythic figures, have what he considers a pathological effect on the education of the Greeks living what I call a *vita mimetica* (chapter 2). As we shall see, this is, indeed, a lesson inferred from theatrical performances more than from dialectical reflections, from the dramatic sphere of myth (*muthos*) more than from the abstract sphere of reason (*logos*).

There is thus a fundamental paradox at the very origins of mimetic studies that may, in a different form, still be our paradox. On the one hand, Plato excludes figures like poets and rhapsodes from the ideal city for spreading lies, miseducating the Greeks, and for their irrational or pathological effect on the life of the polis; on the other hand, with Socrates as an alter ego, he borrows a number of mimetic strategies himself from his main rival, Homer, including dialogues and allegories, heroic protagonists and spellbinding myths, where "he," Plato, puts the affective powers of mimesis to good educational use.

This conflict, or agon, reveals a fundamental debt to the artistic figure the philosopher opposes. Hence the need to qualify Plato's quarrel with Homer as a mimetic agon insofar as the opponent is also a model from which Plato borrows the tools to set up an opposition in the first place. Somewhat revealingly, then, a clear-cut dualistic distinction between philosophy and literature is even inadequate to account for the philosophical-literary qualities of the most famous Platonic account of mimesis, a dialogic account born, paradoxically, out of a myth: namely, the "Allegory of the Cave." This is an example we discuss in more detail in our genealogy of mimesis in part 1. Still, it is a foundational example for mimetic studies, old and new, that provides a methodological hint we shall follow throughout: namely, to adequately account for a Janus-faced concept that is born out of a mimetic agon between philosophy and literature, we shall have to join rather than oppose these competing perspectives, which are both constitutive of our mimetic education today.

Since classical antiquity, literary and philosophical authors agreed, in fact, that mimesis is central to education. This should not come as a surprise. As any teacher or student knows from direct experience, education relies heavily not only on repetition and representations of objects but also on memorization, imitation, and last but not least, identification with influential models or subjects. It is in fact a good mimesis with selective models or subjects that often guarantees a successful education in selective disciplines or objects of inquiry.

If we now consider another exemplary reference on the side of literature that serves as a precursor and agonistic companion to Plato's *Republic*—namely, Homer's *Odyssey*—we notice that it stages an exemplary character embodying qualities like perseverance, justice, and cleverness that, despite some patriarchal, territorial, and warlike dispositions characteristic of Homeric times, provides lessons that may still be worthy of imitation today. For instance, in one of the most memorable chapters of the *Odyssey*, devoted to the cyclops, Ulysses and his men are captured in yet another dark cave, where lessons on the *vita mimetica* tend to originate, as Plato will be quick to sense. And asked by Polyphemus about his identity, this exemplary mythic figure provides his famous and much-repeated reply: "My name is nobody [*outis*]" (Homer 1991, 135). This hero far from home is thus a mimetic subject who is nobody.[7] But precisely because of his ability to evade the question of personal identity, this founding scene and the journey that follows dramatizes a plurality of exemplary experiences that go from the affective to the psychological, the mythical to the religious, the political to the ethical, the pedagogical to the educative, among other concerns about mimesis that will become proper to philosophy as well.

No wonder that in another dialogue, Plato sides with Odysseus to defend what he will call a noble lie.[8] The philosopher certainly learned a few lessons from his literary precursor. And yet, to this day, literary and philosophical texts, when and if they are read or taught, tend to be split in separate and often competing disciplines with methods of analysis that artificially divide a focus on narrative and affect, on the one hand, and a focus on concepts and arguments, on the other. What we learn from classical literary and philosophical examples, instead, is a suspicion concerning clear-cut oppositions that reach, via education, into the present. Once uncritically passed down to younger generations at an age in which their character is "best molded and takes the impression that one wishes to stamp upon it" (Plato 1963c, 377b), the ancient quarrel between philosophy and literature in particular, and the ensuing fragmentation within the humanities in general, continues to carve out hyperspecialized territories that are inadequate to account for a homo mimeticus in search of an identity that, as we shall repeatedly confirm, is indeed no(t) one.[9] Hence again the need to develop a diagonal field of studies that draws on both philosophy and art to account for both the affective and conceptual manifestations of imitation today.

Closer to us, we could say that mimesis continues to manifest itself as a complex concept in the specific sense the transdisciplinary thinker Edgar Morin gives to it. Bringing yet another classical image to bear on the complexity of the present, Morin reminds us that complexity comes from *complexus*, "interwoven" (*tissé ensemble*) (Morin 1999, 43), as a tapestry or text is composed of different yet interwoven threads. If we begin, not unlike Penelope at night, to disentangle these threads, a movement more than a form begins to emerge from these knitting hands. This movement is indeed complex, but we can recognize it, for we have encountered it before. Relying on the cybernetic conception of "feedback loop" central to his philosophical anthropology that goes beyond two-culture oppositions, Morin specifies that complex problems generate what he calls a "feedback-loop intellect affect" whereby "the development of intelligence is inseparable from affective development" (21)—for good and ill.

This complex epistemic lesson is particularly relevant to account for a concept like mimesis that goes beyond good and evil. In fact, as we already indicated, imitative activities are vital for rational, logical, and constructive practices, as Aristotle noted, but equally trigger irrational, illogical, and destructive ones, as Plato argued. Morin thus urges us to go beyond ancient quarrels, as he states that "affectivity can both prevent [*étouffer*] and promote [*étoffer*] knowledge" (21). To put it in a figurative language, the affective hand of homo mimeticus draws the logical hand as much as the logical hand redraws the affective hand, generating paradoxical loops that can be both disabling and enabling, deformative and transformative. Both sides are under the lens of mimetic studies. In the process, as Escher's *Drawing Hands* already suggested, such studies on homo mimeticus can affectively implicate the subject in the object that is drawn, thereby going beyond the subject-object divide.

## *Sapiens, Ludens, Mimeticus*

So far, so good. But how should we study a phenomenon in which all humans are, to different degrees, affectively involved? Our drawing of homo mimeticus presupposes that the affective tendency of humans to imitate is not in opposition to their cognitive or rational side, just that the *homo* is not intended to single out humans as an exceptional species driven by "culture," opposed to nonhuman animals driven by "nature." On the contrary, it is precisely such traditional binaries such as rational/affective, mind/body, nature/culture, human/nonhuman, but also individual/collective, biology/technology, embodied/virtual, online/offline, among others, that the mimetic turn or *re*-turn challenges, as it reveals them as complexly interwoven.

Our goal, then, is not so much to deconstruct binaries that are obsolete in the present century but, rather, to reconstruct *both* the affective *and* rational principles constitutive of a species that was perhaps too unilaterally called *Homo sapiens*. In fact, as Johan Huizinga perceptively argued in *Homo Ludens* (1938), a book that bears a family resemblance to our own: "we must be more than rational beings, for play is irrational" (2016, 4); and he adds: "the Aristotelian *animal ridens* characterizes man as distinct from the animal almost more absolutely than *homo sapiens*" (6). What we must add to Huizinga is that the Platonic/Aristotelian view of *animal imitans* is not only central to the play element of culture, as Huizinga defines it—namely, as a disinterested, often agonistic, and eminently social activity "distinct from 'ordinary' life" (9); it is also at play in the daily practices of ordinary everyday life, which, from birth onward (and probably already prior to birth) tie humans to others—the mother *in primis*—via affective forms of unconscious imitation that are constitutive of culture, aesthetics, and politics at large.

The scope of *Homo Mimeticus* is ambitious and might initially recall popular accounts of the history of *Homo sapiens*, which it aims to supplement from a different and so far untraveled perspective. Historian Yuval Harari, for instance, argued in his widely popular history of mankind, *Sapiens* (2014), that "Many of history's most important drivers are inter-subjective: law, money, gods, nations" (132). I not only agree with this point; I also argue that the underlying principle that allows intersubjectivity to emerge in the first place is rooted in a mimetic drive. In fact, if Harari rightly stresses the role of "fiction" for sapiens to "cooperate successfully by believing in common myths" (30), we shall see that mimesis is not only the aesthetic cave out of which fictions and myths are born; it is also the affective mechanism that ties humans to a shared belief, again, for good and ill. Moreover, if Harari recognizes that the task of the humanities and social sciences is to explain "exactly how the imagined order," such as mythology, politics, or culture, "is woven into the tapestry of life" (127), I add that imitation is one of the main imperceptible threads that stiches the tapestry of life together across the ages, individually and collectively.

Humans become *sapiens* because they are *mimeticus*; imitation is crucial to the history of who we are and can potentially become. This, at least, is the thesis *Homo Mimeticus* aims to develop. I do so not so much by adopting a fictionally omniscient point of view to map the continuous historical development of humankind via a series of "revolutions" (cognitive, agricultural, scientific, digital, etc.). Instead, I rely on a more modest and avowedly partial and perspectival genealogical method that engages with rigor and specificity some of the most penetrating thinkers of mimesis over the ages (Plato, Nietzsche, Arendt, Girard, etc.) in view of developing a new theory of imitation that accounts for intersubjective processes (language, consciousness, politics, pandemics) at play in our hypermimetic age as well.

One of the fundamental assumptions of the new theory of mimesis we outline is that the protean phenomenon under consideration cannot be treated only from a safe rational distance by a disinterested and detached scientific observer—though a degree of distance is vital to notice the phantom of mimesis and its movements across fields, periods, and media in the first place. Rather, genealogical investigators are themselves affectively entangled in the pathologies of homo mimeticus they delineate, prone to identification, open to mirroring reflexes, vulnerable to affective contagion, sensitive to natural and technological influences, among other contemporary manifestations of mimesis. And yet, precisely for this embodied reason, they can paradoxically develop a (self-)critical approach that is as attentive to the interior dynamic of affects as to their exterior logical manifestations. New mimetic studies emerges from this double perspective.

The subject *of* mimesis is, indeed, Janus-faced: it is as much turned toward the mimetic *phenomena* it aims to draw (objective genitive) as to the mimetic *subject* who is drawing (subjective genitive). This also means that there is no necessary contradiction between a subjective and objective approach, just as there is no reciprocal exclusion between an affective and a conceptual perspective. On the contrary, it is precisely because homo mimeticus is driven by both affect and reason, body and mind, nature and culture that an immersion in the shared pathos of mimesis—as in sympathy or *sym-pathos* (feeling with) can serve as an embodied source of inspiration to develop a critical discourse or *logos* on the dynamic of mimetic affect or *pathos*. I call this method of analysis "patho-*logy*" to indicate the dynamic and spiraling interplay between affect and reason, body and mind, *pathos* and *logos*, animating the two sides, or drawing hands, of homo mimeticus.

We are now in a position to see and feel that, as I turned to a drawing for aesthetic inspiration, I did so to implicitly suggest that philosophy and aesthetics, concepts and affects, theorists and artists, can no longer be simply opposed in the twenty-first century. On the contrary, not unlike Escher's *Drawing Hands*, both sides are part of a paradoxical feedback loop outlining the same picture of a homo mimeticus in its dynamic process of emergence. Speaking of this "strange loop," Douglas Hofstadter considers Escher as the "creator of some of the most intellectually stimulating drawings of all time" (Hofstadter 1999, 10–11), while specifying that his drawings "have their origin in paradox, illusion, or double-meaning" (11).[10] With some genealogical distance, we confirm that these origins accounting for paradox, illusion, and double meaning are interwoven with a complex problematic of mimesis that is still in search of a new theory for the present century. It is, in fact, from the mutual entanglement, reciprocal reconfiguration, and spiraling, looping processes of drawing and redrawing of boundaries that a long-standing genealogy of critical and creative figures join hands in this book to sketch a moving picture of homo mimeticus.

Two mirroring philosophical-aesthetic hands are needed for this. On the one hand, artists are, in fact, endowed with creative insights into the paradoxes of mimesis that tap into the affective sphere, but as Escher's work illustrates, redraw the boundaries of logic as well; on the other hand, philosophers and theorists can help us account for the affective power of mimesis from the distance of a rational discourse—without setting up an artificial binary between these reciprocally drawing and drawn hands. We shall indeed need both philosophical and artistic perspectives at hand—and any other disciplinary hand we can borrow—to draw the picture of mimesis emerging from that singular conjunction of mind and body the ancients called a soul, the moderns called subject or ego, and the contemporaries call consciousness or brain. These are all terms that only do partial justice to a complex subject matter that cannot be reduced to consciousness or the brain, if only because it is driven by unconscious forces that make us largely unknown to ourselves.

The genealogy of mimesis that follows is thus located in the liminal gray zone between philosophy (part 1) and aesthetics (part 2), while also adding politics (part 3), as it expands its diagnostic to imitative phenomena that haunt the contemporary world. These complementary perspectives, not unlike Escher's drawing hands, face and mirror each other in order to better delineate their respective contours. If, broadly speaking, the conceptual hand is drawing the contours of the affective hand while, at the same time, being drawn by it, sketching the process of emergence of homo mimeticus entails paying attention to the complex, reciprocal, and dynamic interplay between two hands that escape a linear billiard-ball causality. Our hypothesis is that affects give form to concepts and, reciprocally, concepts transform affects in a spiraling loop; similarly, consciousness might cast light on the unconscious but the unconscious orients the hand that holds the light of consciousness in the first place. Hence, if we want to have a chance to draw a picture of mimesis in its process of emergence, we need to delineate both sides of this complex mimetic subject.

In sum, as *Drawing Hands* illustrates, a picture of homo mimeticus that is both subject and object, creating and created, drawing while being drawn, does not allow for traditional distinctions between mind and body, reason and affect, thought and thoughtlessness, conscious actions and unconscious reactions. These can be at play in artistic creation and transformation but also subject formation or ethical education, intersubjective communication or collective disinformation, (new) fascist insurrections or totalitarian wars, and including catastrophic climate change in the age of the Anthropocene. In the process, the drawing hands generate spiraling feedback loops in which the human, all-too-human receptivity to affect, or pathos, complicates the traditional picture of a solipsistic, autonomous, and purely rational and ultimately idealist subject qua *Homo sapiens* that is increasingly out of sync with the material reality of the world we inhabit. Instead, they join both *pathos* and *logos* to draw a genealogy of a relational, embodied, vulnerable, and complex subject that, as Morin puts it, is "not only *sapiens*, *faber* and *economicus* but also *demens*, *ludens*, and *consumans*" (Morin 2001, 13).

In the dialogue that concludes this book and thus provides a driving goal or *telos* that informs it from the beginning, Morin and I agreed that we could add homo mimeticus to the list of names as well (chapter 10). Its complex birth had actually been gestating for a while.

## Birth of a Homo Mimeticus

Born out of an interdisciplinary ERC-funded project titled *Homo Mimeticus: Theory and Criticism*, with a tenuous double affiliation in philosophy and arts, this book assembles a cherry-picked selection of numerous essays written over a period of five years, from 2017 to 2022. Some had appeared in specialized journals in disciplines as diverse as continental philosophy, literary theory, film studies, and political theory.[11] Although they all contribute to the same sketch of homo mimeticus, the academic constraints of disciplinary specialization made their genealogical connection difficult or impossible to see or trace for both general and specialized readers. They were each expanded, adapted, and organized as a coherent yet perspectival whole for the present volume. Other chapters on topics such as the *vita mimetica*, vibrant mimesis, viral mimesis, and the final dialogue with Morin, appear here for the first time. Each chapter stands on its own, and for the reader with a specific interest in one facet of homo mimeticus, can be read individually. I tried as much as possible to avoid unnecessary repetitions, but also to recapitulate in each chapter the essential elements of the theory of mimesis I propose, as echoes or refrains. This should allow readers to trace their own trajectory as freely as possible depending on their interests and inclinations while also listening to variations of the same tune.

As my genealogical method assumes that innovation emerges from a confrontation with influential precursors, readers will encounter a number of theoretical hands that contribute to drawing the contours of mimetic studies. We shall begin by disentangling the complex thread of mimesis in dialogic critical conversations with ancient, modern, and contemporary allies. Their names go from Plato to Nietzsche, Roger Caillois to René Girard, Hannah Arendt to Adriana Cavarero, Jacques Derrida to Catherine Malabou, Philippe Lacoue-Labarthe to Jane Bennett to Edgar Morin, among other proponents of the mimetic turn, or *re*-turn, that offer different perspectives on a moving subject. For the reader unfolding the thread beginning, middle, and end, the division in three parts points to the general movement of our trajectory: the chapters are organized to delineate a spiraling design that expands genealogically from philosophy to aesthetics to politics, moving diachronically from prehistoric times to antiquity, from modernity into the present, up to the COVID-19 pandemic crisis. Together, they reveal the centrality of mimesis to a plurality of problems that cast a shadow on the twenty-first century.

I should make clear that in the process of drawing the contours of homo mimeticus, my ambition was not to develop a universal transhistorical theory of mimesis that reduces a protean and constantly changing phenomenon to the same schema, structure, or form. Rather, the book adopts a perspectival approach that is discontinuous and selective in its choice of authors, texts, and problems, but genealogically consistent in the sense that each subsequent chapter picks up and expands the previous one, in a spiraling movement that broadens its complex implications from a different but interwoven disciplinary perspective. It is in fact only by moving and changing perspectives that a new theory of imitation can cast light on phenomena that remain in the shadow of disciplinary-oriented approaches yet cast a growing shadow on contemporary practices.

The book's methodological assumption is that "interdisciplinary" or "transdisciplinary" lenses are not simply a fashionable academic garment to be worn and displayed outside. Adopting these lenses is rather a challenging transversal or, as Roger Caillois calls it, "diagonal" (2003a) practice that entails the quality of a "bridgemaker" more than an "efficient and myopic mole" (344). Hence what Michel Serres says of *Homo pontifex* applies to homo mimeticus as well: "Bridging, in general, becomes an activity so large that it coincides perhaps with the whole human project, in that our very body bridges flesh and word" (in Lury et al. 2018, xxii). Interdisciplinary bridges are vital to tracking a chameleon phenomenon that changes color to adapt to different historical, theoretical, and contextual backgrounds. If this Janus-faced figure has traditionally been split and fragmented in competing disciplinary sides in the past that reduce mimesis to techniques of representation, be they aesthetic, philosophical, or political, my general wager is that these perspectives benefit from being joined in the present to redraw, if not a complete and final, at least a more multifaceted, spiraling, and dynamic picture of mimesis for the present and future. What should appear, in the end, is a singular-plural drawing of homo mimeticus in which a moving whole, not unlike *Drawing Hands*, emerges from the spiraling and dynamic interplay of its constitutive parts. Needless to say, the defining characteristic of a spiral is not its static completion but its progressive widening movement open to future expansions.

This, at least, applies to the general conceptual and affective contours of the picture of mimetic studies we propose to sketch. But what about the color, tonality, and identity of the indeterminate subject who is no one that is drawing while being drawn? This is a crucial question to address at the outset for a genealogical reason that is at least double. First, the notion of *homo* (from Latin, man, human) traditionally conflates the already contested concept of a specifically "human" condition with a problematic and outdated conception of "man" that, under the mask of an abstract, hegemonic, and rather violent universal, has long been traditionally restricted to a white, male, western, privileged, and heteronormative perspective. Dominant until the past century, under pressure from civil rights movements, feminism, postcolonial, decolonial, and LGBTQ+ perspectives, this androcentrism is increasingly outdated in the present century, yet it continues to cast a material shadow on political practices. Second, the shadow of patriarchy is aggravated if we recall that the Greek concept of *homo* (from ὁμο, the same), equally risks reducing the diversity of identities—be they individual or collective, cultural or geographical, racial or sexual, aesthetic or political—to a homogeneous concept that does not reflect or represent the plurality of being human, let alone posthuman in the twenty-first century. If we then couple the traditional etymology of *homo* with an equally traditional concept of *mimeticus* and the sameness imitation also traditionally entails, we are thus at three removes from the plurality of genealogical, aesthetic, and political perspectives this book seeks to affirm.

Why, then, retain the concept of homo mimeticus in the first place? Would it not be more appropriate to erase the traces of a patriarchal, androcentric, phallogocentric, and ultimately metaphysical tradition that is inscribed in the very identity (from Latin, *identitas*, from *idem*, the same) of humans? This would, indeed, be the easiest and most convenient option. Still, it would not remove the problem; if only because, to date, we do not have an alternative name at hand to designate a species whose genus, since Carl Linaeus coined the term in 1758, is still grouped under the rubric of *Homo sapiens*. Rather than denying this genealogy, or pretending it does not inform our (pre)history, I take the risk of provisionally retaining the concept of "*homo*" and for at least two reasons: first, to add a different facet to a traditional conception of *Homo sapiens* understood as fully rational, autonomous, and free by revealing its affective, embodied, and relationally dependent counterpart; and second, because by coupling *homo* with a different, immanent, and antimetaphysical conception of mimesis that is neither simply on the side of sameness nor on the side of difference, but is attentive to the dynamic interplay between sameness and difference (chapter 3), we can continue to decenter and deterritorialize, draw and redraw, normative conceptions of what the human is supposed to be in the present—and can potentially become in the future. Hence the title of this book.

As to the color of our drawing of homo mimeticus, you will already have guessed it. Taking inspiration from *Drawing Hands* on the side of aesthetics, and from the realization that mimesis goes beyond good and evil, on the side of philosophy, I shall further Nietzsche's insight into the privileged color for genealogies. In the preface of *On the Genealogy of Morals* (1887), Nietzsche in fact provides the following advice to genealogists of the future: rather than "hypothesizing *into the blue*," as idealist philosophers since Plato have tended to do, he suggests that genealogists should pay attention to what is "*grey*—by that I mean what has been documented, what is really ascertainable, what has really existed" (Nietzsche 1996, 9).

To be sure, gray may not have the initial attractiveness of the blue sky of abstract, universal, and immutable ideas located in an ideal world "*behind* the world" (*Hinterwelt*) (5). And yet gray comes in different shades that register the changing tonality of immanent and material surfaces in this world. It thus calls for an overturning of perspectives in order to develop a lens attentive to what has really existed and still exists as rooted in this world. As Michel Foucault also recognizes, echoing Nietzsche: "Genealogy is gray, meticulous, and patiently documentary. It operates on a field of entangled and confused parchments, on documents that have been scratched over and recopied many times" (1977, 139). There are thus layers after layers that need to be uncovered from entangled texts for a gray picture of homo mimeticus to reappear from past documents that continue to illuminate present times. But these documents need not to be ancient or modern only; they should include contemporary texts and media as well. In the process, a genealogy of mimesis will pay close attention to the down-to-earth conditions of a *vita mimetica* traditionally confined at the bottom of a mythic cave; despite its darkness and plays of shadows, it reveals nonetheless the immanent gray zones of a sensible, material, and fast-changing world that, despite the growing proliferation of digital shadows on a variety of black mirrors, or perhaps because of it, is still our only world. Hence the urgency to look back to important precursors to better see the phantoms that are up ahead.

## Brief Genealogy of Mimesis

Articulating a genealogy of an existing mimetic species is an ambitious task. While grand historical metanarratives of progress have revealed their limits, genealogy traces selected steps that are documented in the relative short history of human civilization. At the same time, it also looks back to prehistoric times that are partially ascertainable and remain "so difficult to decipher" (Nietzsche 1996, 9), yet might help foresee future destinations. Precisely because of its genealogical origins, my drawing of homo mimeticus shall be necessarily fragmentary, partial, and incomplete; it's part of a process rather than a finished product; it does not aspire to a unitary, transhistorical, and universal form but to delineating a paradoxical movement in which an original species is born—out of mimetic principles.

In this book, I shall thus be more attentive to drawing connections across gray zones of disciplinary knowledge that are often left in the background, while focusing on their movement of emergence rather than on pinning the completed picture of mimesis to the wall in the foreground—a gesture that, as a close reading of Escher already taught us, turned out to be an illusory stabilizing effect anyway. Instead, I aim to capture, via an "art of interpretation" (1996, 10) that Nietzsche considered the soul of genealogy, the different shades of gray that give profundity, material substance, and three-dimensional life to homo mimeticus. This entails drawing on a plurality of disciplinary approaches that blur boundaries in theory to remain faithful to historically documented practices that, step by step, begin to reveal who we are and can potentially become. For as Nietzsche puts it, in the phrase that provides the epigraph to this book: "We remain unknown to ourselves, we seekers after knowledge, even to ourselves: and with good reason. We have never sought after ourselves—so how should we one day find ourselves?" (3)

Homo mimeticus is, indeed, a protean concept that is still in search of an identity that is not one but plural; its contours need to be redrawn as it changes shades and form to adapt to the fast-changing conditions in the twenty-first century. It is particularly plastic, slippery, and protean, since theoretical efforts in the twentieth century started shifting the emphasis from mimetic realism to mimetic subjectivity. Now, if mimesis is the lever, this paradigmatic shift from realism to subjectivity is the fulcrum upon which new mimetic studies turns. Let us briefly retrace important precursors this book aims to supplement in the pages that follow.

On the side of literature, mimesis has long been restricted to techniques of "representation of reality" that in-*form* (give form to) western literature, from Homer to the twentieth century, as Erich Auerbach influentially shows in *Mimesis* (1946). Despite the stylistic sophistication of the close textual readings a humanistic critic like Auerbach performs, this study continues to echo a metaphysics of sameness predicated on the trope of the mirror articulated in "Plato's discussion in book 10 of the *Republic*—mimesis ranking third after truth" (2003, 554). This is an important starting point for idealist and transcendental theories that span western aesthetics up to the nineteenth century. Still, it should no longer be considered the ultimate ontological horizon for embodied and immanent theories attentive to the metamorphoses of homo mimeticus in the twenty-first century.

Conversely, roughly at the same time, on the philosophical side, initial first steps to tilt discussions around mimesis from realism toward a mimetic subject were equally at play. Jacques Lacan, for instance, influentially framed the ego within a stabilizing "mirror stage," representing an ideal image or *imago* that erected itself to the status of an "ontological structure of the human world" (1977 [1949], 2). Despite its innovative reach into an unconscious structured like a language that conformed to the linguistic turn emerging at the time, this ideal image can also be traced to Plato's metaphysics of sameness, or "Platonism,"[12] that is out of sync with more recent, affective, materialist, and digital turns. This does not mean that materialist influences that went beyond human and animal mimicry were not already at play in the mirror stage, informing Lacan's theory, as we shall see via Roger Caillois (chapter 5).

A few decades later, in the wake of structuralism, steps were already underway to overturn theories of mimesis restricted to the logic of sameness that started paving the way for a mimetic turn. A series of transdisciplinary thinkers working at the troubling juncture between philosophy and arts have, since the late 1960s and 1970s, revealed a deconstructive interpretation of mimesis that is not only on the side of difference. Rather, it destabilizes precisely the metaphysical oppositions (copy/model, imitation/original, inside/outside, self/other) mimesis was supposed to uphold, making it "impossible to pin *mimēsis* down to a binary classification" (Derrida 1981a, 186, n14).[13] Despite the differential moves at play in these overturning perspectives that often found in writing the paradigmatic example of a troubling mimesis without proper being, a shared genealogical concern consisted in showing that there is no original without imitation, no model without copy, no metaphysics of sameness without the linguistic difference that brought it into being (chapter 3).

The effects of this overturning poststructuralist gesture were at least double: on one side, the copy was revealed not only to precede but to create the original in a characteristic deconstructive move that was much imitated, repeated, and iterated in theory; on the other side, the mimetic subject restaged in its "original" designation as "mime [*mime*]" (Derrida 1981a, 191), rather than as a mirror or *imago*, turned out not to be simply passive and reproductive but active and productive, a performative mime supposedly without model who had "nothing proper" to itself and for this reason was paradoxically open to a plurality of plastic impersonations of all roles (chapter 4). An alternative genealogy of homo mimeticus was thus beginning to appear on the (predominantly) French philosophical scene, but additional steps were still needed to bring its troubling political insights onto the global political scene.

Furthering this deconstructive genealogy, a performative conception of mimesis linked to theatricality emerged at the twilight of the past century. Its manifestations were plural, but its general goal was to trouble unitary conceptions of the subject internal to debates on identity politics framed primarily in terms of gender, race, and sexuality. A number of dissident theoretical voices continued to pave the way for the *re*-turn to mimesis attentive to a plurality of differences by promoting an antiessentialist, constructivist, and performative conception of mimetic subjectivity that was put to liberating, troubling, and emancipatory purposes.[14] This political move as a segue to deconstruction was much needed. Up to the present, and in the wake of immigration crises that threaten homogeneous notions of national identity, there is, in fact, a long-standing ethnocentric, patriarchal, and violent tendency in western thought and practices that consists in projecting imitative behavior such as mimicry, emotional contagion, hysteria, etc. onto gendered and racial others, often in terms that are derogatory and pathological and that I diagnosed elsewhere under the rubric of "mimetic racism" and "mimetic sexism."[15] In an increasingly polarized political climate haunted by (new) fascist and totalitarian leaders such dominant political pathologies continue to cast a shadow on present generations, reaching via global pandemics (chapter 9) and, more recently, the return of war, including the danger of nuclear war, into the present.

While the focus on the authors I discuss in this book remain primarily within a western tradition that, for better and worse, theorized the Greek concept of *mimēsis* in the first place, an important qualification is thus in order: my attention to homo mimeticus is radically at odds with dominant western tendencies to excoriate imitative subjects outside, or at the margins of the body politic and to project the phantom of imitation onto subordinate "others" under the rubric of suggestibility, hysteria, contagion, madness, among other mimetic pathologies. This critical stance would not have been possible without my prior engagement with feminism, critical race theory, and decolonial perspectives that pave the way for a destabilizing conception of "mimicry" that I furthered elsewhere under the rubric of "postcolonial mimesis."[16]

Awareness of racial and racist oppressions nourishes not only my own thinking about homo mimeticus; it also gave me a language to start bridging my own mixed or hybrid identity that—without ceding to the temptation of autobiography here—informs my personal genealogy as well. This operation sharpened early on my attunement to the role mimesis plays in subject formations, deformations, and transformations. And to this day, it continues to orient my critique of oppressive forms of dominant herd behavior that, more often than not, find in marginalized and dispossessed subaltern subjects privileged victims of the pathologies of mimesis: from mimetic racism to mimetic sexism, mass psychology to contagious violence to (new) fascism, among other symptoms. In short, my attention to differences and the critical distance to the phantom of sameness it entails not only goes back to the genealogical beginnings of my academic career; it also precedes and informs my entry into academia providing it with an experiential perspective that oriented my intellectual trajectory. In its inception, it is perhaps rooted on the side of a *vita mimetica* that provides, if not the inner then the outer experiences that gave this theory of homo mimeticus its "originary" starting point, or *coup d'envoi*.

Over time, moving at the crossroads of disciplines and languages, bridging countries and cultures, while living a nomadic, deterritorialized life familiar to many academics, immigrants, and, in far less privileged circumstances, undocumented immigrants and refugees, I came to sense how deep into the formation of a character, a language, a culture, and a nation the powers of mimesis actually reach. These powers tend to go largely unnoticed by local or native populations, for they have become habitual and second nature over time—part of the mimetic unconscious that constitutes them. On the other hand, nomadic subjects in unfamiliar territories, exposed to different sounds and gestures, opinions and habits, tastes and customs are deeply conscious of being out of sync with homogenized human and nonhuman surroundings; they might thus be inclined to actively draw on the mimetic unconscious to adapt, chameleonlike, to unfamiliar backgrounds if not to fully conform to their surroundings, at least to pass unnoticed. This penchant for mimicry or will to mime can reach pathological proportions, as the case of Woody Allen's *Zelig* (1983) dramatizes (chapter 6). But as the film also reveals, this tendency to conform has already taken hold of the local population as well, at times with horrific consequences, as the case of Adolf Eichmann revisited makes clear (chapter 7).

At the same time, and without contradiction, outsiders who may appear to insiders to be without identity, or no one, are the most sophisticated, attuned, and sensible antennae of the species, who can register the imperceptible powers of mimesis. Being out of sync with stereotypical patterns of behavior that operate on the mimetic unconscious of the native population, they are well placed to notice these patterns from a distance and, if needed, consciously develop techniques of mimicry imbued with destabilizing differences. These chameleon subjects moving across territories, languages, and disciplines soon realize, in fact, that mimesis can also be put to subversive, productive, or patho-*logical* use, generating both critical and affective inclinations that open up subjectivity to the outside. As *Drawing Hands* already suggests, homo mimeticus is both subject and object, acting and acted upon, creating and created. This also means that if one hand is passively subjected to being drawn and potentially deformed by the other, the second hand can actively retroact on the cause, redraw the contours of the drawing hand, and prompt reforms we may not fully master and control but can at least partially influence, correct, and redirect.

What is true for race, then, is also true for gender, sexuality, class, nationality, and other marginalized subjects in the age of the Anthropocene (immigrants, war refugees, and the globally dispossessed): as the Black Lives Matter and #MeToo movements showed, even during the COVID-19 pandemic, victims of mimetic racism and sexism can appropriate the regressive side of mimesis understood as a copy, bad reproduction, or mimicry of an original model (white, male, western, heterosexual, consumer-driven) and put it to creative, productive, and performative use. Central to pluralist philosophical perspectives, this move is currently opening up an emancipatory conception of "mimetic inclinations" (Cavarero and Lawtoo 2021). That is, a relational, affective, and imitative bond that, via a shared affect or *sym-pathos* (feeling with), inclines the subject to share a pathos with the other, thereby challenging the vertical model of *Homo erectus* that continues to cast a long shadow on a plurality of different bodies and souls.[17]

What has perhaps not been sufficiently stressed as yet is that this performative, embodied, affective, relational, and deeply troubling manifestation of mimesis has a genealogy that is much longer and wider in scope, is rooted in the prehistory of *Homo sapiens*, and arguably finds in plural forms of maternal prelinguistic communication a shared beginning. Somewhat surprisingly, this feminist perspective finds in a philosopher who tends to be remembered for his antifeminist, if not downright misogynist views, namely, Friedrich Nietzsche, a genealogical precursor. Nietzsche, in fact, offers an account of the birth of humans out of the reflex of maternal communications that ultimately can be traced back to pre-Platonic times, all the way back to the prehistory of *Homo sapiens* (chapter 1). *Homo Mimeticus*, then, begins by telling the genealogical story of the birth of an original and eminently social species—out of the immanent, affective, and intersubjective reflex of imitation.

In sum, as we trace with our two affective/conceptual hands the genealogy of a plastic, impressionable, and eminently protean subject, it is crucial to bear in mind that mimesis remains rooted in the performative practice of a phantom ego that cannot be framed or stabilized within a mirror representing an ideal image, or *imago*. On the contrary, it goes through the looking glass, so to speak, to affect the body and the mind of the ego staring at the mirror, troubling the image of an autonomous, solipsistic, rationally self-sufficient ideal of a species that, in a moment of hubristic confidence characteristic of the subject of *Aufklärung*, hastily denominated itself *Homo sapiens*.

What emerges from our drawing of homo mimeticus is a different picture. Namely, an immanent conception of subjectivity that is embodied, relational in nature, social in disposition, porous to affective influences, and open to a number of dispossessions, be they human or nonhuman. My wager is that it is this phantom ego that is currently generating a *re*-turn of attention to mimesis in different strands of critical theory. In disciplines as diverse as continental philosophy, aesthetics, literary theory, political theory, as well as in the social sciences and the neurosciences, there is a growing realization that from birth onward, and perhaps since the evolutionary dawn of *Homo sapiens* as well, humans are prone to mimicking others, be they human or nonhuman, individually and collectively, for both good and ill. In the process, they generate spiraling effects that call for a new theory of imitation to face the challenges of the twenty-first century.

Since my goal is to propose new theoretical foundations to account for an impressively plastic, certainly imitative, and perhaps also original homo mimeticus, in guise of conclusion or rather, beginning, let me sketch some of the fundamental concepts that will inform this book, beginning, middle, and end.

## Concepts for New Mimetic Studies

Developing a new theory of an ancient concept that is usually simply translated as imitation or representation might appear paradoxical, and for a number of reasons. First, because the insights that humans are thoroughly imitative animals is, as we noted, as old as philosophy itself; its history, from the dawn of philosophy to the twilight of the twentieth century, has been well documented.[18] Second, because in the wake of structuralism, a mimetic theory that shifted attention from aesthetic realism to imitative behavior, albeit often restricted to desire and violence, already emerged in the transdisciplinary work of René Girard. And third, because arguing for a new, perhaps even original, theory of mimesis to account for a concept that casts the very idea, or ideal, of originality into crisis may appear as a performative contradiction we have long been trained to deconstruct in the past century. What is true of all new critical and theoretical turns is thus triply true for mimetic turns, or *re*-turns: in foregrounding the new, there is always the risk of falling under the shadow of romantic ideals of originality that resurrect the myth of an autonomous, solipsistic, and self-sufficient subject the very concept of homo mimeticus both counters and overturns.

Consequently, in the chapters that follow, I will take care to situate the mimetic turn in a relation of genealogical continuity and discontinuity with important predecessors that paved the way for the current *re*-turn of attention to the different facets of the protean concept of mimesis: from imitation to sympathy, animal mimicry to human mimicry, identification to simulation, mirror neurons to brain plasticity, affective contagion to viral contagion, the perspectives at play in new mimetic studies emerge in agonistic dialogues with ancient, modern, and contemporary theorists of mimesis. A genealogical, transdisciplinary field that does not simply repeat precursors but aims to further their thought via the practice of mimetic agonism generates destabilizing repetitions and differences that defy unitary representations yet are still in need of new conceptual and theoretical supplements to keep up with our fast-changing times.

The driving *telos* of what I group under the rubric of the "mimetic turn," then, consists in giving conceptual substance, genealogical depth, and theoretical momentum to a paradigm shift from a still dominant translation of mimesis as representation of reality—be it aesthetic as in realism or philosophical as in mental representation—which still dominates fields like literary studies and philosophy, toward an alternative conception of mimesis that, with some exceptions, remained in the shadow of academic discourses of the past century, tends to operate below conscious awareness, permeates all aspects of human life—from the neuronal structure of the brain to individual psychology, social behavior to political behavior to online behavior—and has been regaining traction in different areas of critical inquiry since the dawn of the twenty-first century. A genial species that once aspired to be *sapiens* in ideal theories has so far been thoroughly *mimeticus* in historical practices, (hyper)mimetic practices that—from (new) fascism to escalating wars, digital simulations to global pandemics to anthropogenic climate change—make the destiny of human and nonhuman life on earth increasingly precarious and uncertain.

In this historical context, then, it is useful to recall that at the dawn of the twentieth century, Walter Benjamin influentially argued that the use of language and the mediation it entails arguably induced what he calls a "decay of the mimetic faculty" (1986, 334). This may have appeared the case in the early 1930s when Benjamin wrote his short but penetrating essay "On the Mimetic Faculty" (1933). But as we shall repeatedly see, mimesis continues to be, perhaps more than ever, at play in new media generating contagious phenomena of dispossession that are not primarily linguistic but embodied and somewhat magically inform, misinform and transform the digital age. If Benjamin correctly saw that "[c]hildren's play is everywhere permeated by mimetic modes of behavior" that lead them to "become and behave like something [or someone] else" (333), my hypothesis is that this playful drive to become other may be masked in adulthood but continues to orient human behavior in unconscious or semiconscious ways that are more fundamental than often realized. The rise of new digital media is, in fact, currently triggering *an explosion of the mimetic faculty* well beyond linguistic mimesis or familial desires—calling for new concepts to account for our "hypermimetic" condition (chapter 9).

The general theory of mimesis that informs all the chapters that follow aims to sail past the Scylla of linguistic decenterings generated by deconstruction on one side and the Charybdis of violence internal to mimetic theory on the other. (chapter 3) It does so to open up intellectual space for a new theory of imitation that is as attentive to the contemporary pathologies and patho-*logies* of homo mimeticus that are currently transforming what it means to be human and posthuman in the twenty-first century.[19]

Given the emphasis on movement, becoming, and transformation characteristic of our phantom subject, I did not seek to reproduce mimetic theories that focused on deconstructing the metaphysics of presence that in-*form* ontological distinctions between writing and speech, copy and model, shadow and origin—for a poststructuralist tradition has effectively done so from different linguistic, theatrical, gendered, racial, and other perspectives; albeit often within the limits of a linguistic ontology preoccupied by overturning the hierarchy between copy and the original in view of reinscribing mimesis on the side of difference rather than sameness.[20] Nor did I find the starting point of mimetic studies in its restricted relation to desire and the rivalrous struggles for pure prestige characteristic of a Hegelian dialectics of recognition where the desire for the same takes precedence over individual differences—for Girard's mimetic theory has already done so in a mirroring of Oedipal triangles that overturn the structure but tends to leave the ambivalences, rivalries, and sacrificial violence that ensue firmly in place.[21]

Instead, homo mimeticus is grounded on the immanent, relational, and embodied realization that all affects, in their good and evil, logical and pathological manifestations, are imitative. They also spread contagiously from self to others, troubling the boundaries of the individuation of an ego that is no(t) one, for it is a phantom ego open to a plurality of influences that draw its contours while at the same time being endowed with powers to redraw them. Consequently, a plurality of assumptions internal to dominant accounts of *Homo sapiens*, including autonomy, free will, and rational presence to selfhood, need to be revisited in light of intersubjective, social, and largely unconscious transformations that take place in relation of communication between self and others, be they human or nonhuman.

While not forming a universal system, let alone structure, mimetic studies proposes a network of interconnected concepts that theorize the protean transformations of homo mimeticus as it moves against different philosophical, aesthetic, and political backgrounds. Furthering a trilogy of books—namely, *The Phantom of the Ego* (2013), *Conrad's Shadow* (2016), and *(New) Fascism* (2019b)— that paved the way for the mimetic turn in these entangled fields, I now outline the conceptual matrix out of which a transdisciplinary theory of imitation that can move across these fields is born. This entails departing from dominant practices of reproducing concepts passed down from past theories via a form of imitation characteristic of the passive disciple. Theorists of imitation are, in fact, well positioned to see how theories are passed down mimetically from self to others, via a network of educative influences that start in the classroom, continue in manuals and books, are reproduced in exams and, later, academic conferences, and, if one remains long within one field, tend to become second nature over time. The alternative I propose in this book (and there are others) is not only to multiply disciplinary perspectives to avoid seeing the world through homogeneous lenses; it is also to look back, genealogically, to some of the most influential thinkers of mimesis in order to think with and against them in view of creating new concepts from the point of view of the active theorist instead. A major precursor provides a genealogical source of inspiration and a foundation for mimetic studies to build on.

Toward the end of his nomadic career, in an 1885 fragment collected in *The Will to Power* (1901), Nietzsche confirms the importance of rooting philosophy back in the senses, as *Drawing Hands* already urged us to do in aesthetic practice from the beginning. As he puts it, with characteristic ironic distance: philosophers "have trusted in concepts as completely as they have mistrusted the senses: they have not stopped to consider that concepts and words are our inheritance from ages in which thinking was very modest and unclear" (Nietzsche 1968, § 409, 220). We shall see how modest and unclear this prehistoric sensorial and all-too-mimetic inheritance actually is, and how it informs the logos of philosophy shortly (chapter 1). What I now call attention to is how the passage continues. In an arrow directed toward the future and which paves the way for definitions of philosophy that are often echoed yet rarely attributed to their proper genealogical source, Nietzsche adds, with a points of malice towards his contemporaries: "What dawns on philosophers last of all: they must no longer accept concepts as a gift, nor merely purify and polish them, but first *make* and *create* them, present them and make them convincing" (220).[22] A new theory of imitation that aspires to go beyond the traditional confines of the history of philosophy predicated on the repetition of the same, and the diligent polishing of past concepts it entails, then, must create new concepts to address problems that belong to our age. This does not mean that we cannot benefit from precursors. On the contrary, genealogy entails pushing, sometimes agonistically, against the shoulders of influential predecessors of the past in order to better see further ahead into the present and future. I thus propose four concepts that emerge from the practice of mimetic agonism, are constitutive of my genealogy of homo mimeticus, and can now inform new mimetic studies more generally.

First, we have seen how influential theories at the twilight of the past century, like that of Girard, framed mimesis within a triangular structure that found in desire and the rivalries that ensue its privileged starting point. Influential in the past Freudian century, this view implicitly rests on an antiquated account of psychoanalysis as the via regia to the unconscious. It should no longer be simply polished but needs to be updated conceptually for the present post-Freudian century. Desires are now no longer based in a triangular structure but are shaped by an algorithmic network of influences that turn the ego into phantom egos. Similarly, scapegoating mechanisms continue to operate online, generating hypermimetic effects offline that are far from being endowed with cathartic properties. On the contrary, they amplify violence instead.[23] Moreover, since at least the discovery of mirror neurons in the 1990s, it has become once again clear that humans are imitative animals predisposed to unconsciously mirror the emotions of others. They do so via a form of prelinguistic communication that is not moral and mediated by consciousness but neurological and immediate, opening a different door to the unconscious.

Drawing on one of the main advocates of what I call a *mimetic unconscious* that has mirroring reflexes triggered by the sight of movements and facial expressions as a *via regia*, I propose the concept of *mimetic pathos* to account for the relational power of human bodies to be unconsciously affected by human and nonhuman others via a shared sympathy, or *sym-pathos* (feeling with). As Nietzsche's genealogy of language and conscience confirms, the experience of pathos points to ages in which "thinking was very modest and unclear" indeed; he also called for a sensuous, embodied, and relational affective disposition for *Homo sapiens* to be born out of a "pathos" he considers as the "most primitive form of affect" (1968, § 688, 366). As a genealogical step in the never-ending processes of seeking after ourselves, I qualify this pathos as mimetic. And I do so to stress the centrality of a mirroring intersubjective relations to others vital for a relational, embodied, and plastic phantom ego to be born. While desire remains part of the all-too-human affects we discuss in what follows, mimetic desire is now absorbed in the more generalized theory that has *mimetic pathos* as a more ancient yet, as we shall confirm, also more contemporary genealogical starting point.

Second, the paradigmatic shift from desire to the relational power of mimetic pathos to both affect and be affected, provides new theoretical foundations by organizing mimesis around a destabilizing *movement* rather than framing it within a stabilizing *structure*. It is thus historical and attentive to diachronic processes rather than synchronic and restricted to formal interplays, without setting up a rigid binary between the two. Moreover, this movement, as our reading of *Drawing Hands* already intimated, is already at play in immanent bodies that, via mirroring mechanisms first observed by genealogists and now confirmed by the neurosciences, are open by reflex to the mirroring experience of pathos but, at the same time, and without contradiction, also have the capacity to set up a critical distance from mimesis. Homo mimeticus is thus not only passively subjected to the affective experience of imitation; it can also actively resist the powers of imitation and keep them at a distance, at least in theory if not always in practice.

This tension or oscillation between pathos and distance cannot be reduced to the differential movement of a linguistic trace on a chain of signifiers; nor does it conform to the assimilating movement of appropriative desire that reaches for an object framed in a familial triangle. On the contrary, it mobilizes both the affective and cognitive hands to draw a picture of mimesis in its reflex movement of attraction to pathos and critical distance from it. Echoing Nietzsche, I call this constitutive tension between mimetic and anti-mimetic tendencies *pathos of distance* to indicate, with and contra Nietzsche, that even radically individualistic thinkers mostly known for their opposition to different forms of mimesis—from herd behavior to mimicry, from sympathy to crowd behavior—are not immune to the experience of mimetic pathos and the pathologies it generates (chapter 1). On the contrary, as Nietzsche sometimes was the first to admit, the senses can be trusted and put to patho-*logical* use to create new concepts that account for the processes of becoming homo mimeticus in the present century.

Third, to account for a paradoxical diagnostic movement attentive to both the contagious and therapeutic sides of mimesis, I coined the concept of "patho(-)logy," understood both as a sickness caused by mimetic pathos (or pathology) and as a clinical account or discourse (*logos*) that emerges precisely from the exposure to pathos (or patho-*logy*). This is indeed the double-faced perspective characteristic of nomadic subjects who are as attentive to the inner experience of contagious affects as to the exterior discourses that can be used to account for their infective power. As the connecting and parenthetical dash indicates, the interplay between *pathos* and *logos* generates a spiraling movement that can go in opposed direction, for it can be disabling and pathological, as Plato feared, or enabling and patho-*logical*, as Aristotle argued.

The origins of this duplicity go back to the dawn of literature and philosophy in classical antiquity, but the opposed yet interwoven patho(-)logical dynamic is complex in Morin's contemporary sense and can be disarticulated as follows. On the one hand, as an affect retroacts, via a feedback loop, on the rational side of *Homo sapiens*, it can generate disabling irrational effects that dispossess the subject of its proper identity in ways that are disabling and pathological. Crowd behavior, violence, propaganda, (new) fascist insurrections, conspiracy theories, and war are manifestations of what I call *mimetic pathologies*. On the other hand, as Homer taught us, an affective experience with *pathos* that leads a nomadic subject far from home to be no one in particular can serve as the enabling starting point for the emergence of an explorative *logos* that is both informed by *pathos* and, with some powerful allies, is able to navigate its destiny so as to finally come closer to home. The emergence of language and consciousness (out of mirroring reflexes), sympathy, democratic pluralism, communal solidarity, and aesthetic creation are thus manifestations of what I call mimetic patho-*logies*. I stress the plural to indicate the multiple perspectives or discourses—from psycho-logy to anthropo-logy, paleonto-logy to socio-logy, bio-logy to neuro-logy, among others—than can be productively connected in order to further a pluralist account already at play in the protean field of new mimetic studies.

Fourth, at the twilight of the past century, postmodern theorists were quick to proclaim that the digital age generated a world of simulation that had nothing to do with the logic of imitation. The proliferation of "hyperreal simulations" (Baudrillard 1981) that are indeed disconnected from mimesis understood via the logic of representation has increased exponentially in the age of fake news, propelling digital users into what was called, perhaps prematurely, the epoch of post-truth and alternative facts. Yet while referential reality continues to recede behind a procession of simulacra, at least one fact remains: humans remain eminently vulnerable to algorithmic-based digital influences that operate on the mimetic faculty. At the outpost of technological progress, we find a psychological regress all too visible in spectacular capitulations to magical beliefs dominant representatives of *Homo sapiens* tended to project onto "others" in the past, yet are now massively at play in the digitalized western self. I call the power of hyperreal simulations to retroact via spiraling feedback loops on the minds and bodies of homo mimeticus, generating a disquieting tendency to fall under the spell of conspiracy theories, fake news, and algorithmic bubbles, *hypermimesis*.

To be sure, hypermimesis is the product of human technological inventions that started at the dawn of humanity. Our long evolutionary prehistory started over two million years ago and led from *Homo abilis* to *Homo erectus*, from *Homo ergaster* to *Homo neanderthalensis* or *Neanderthal*, among many other human ancestors that eventually paved the way for—and were replaced by— its most recent, perhaps more inventive and collaborative but also more violent and, so far, relatively short-lived descendant, *Homo sapiens*. These evolutionary precursors made it possible to stand where we currently are. Thanks to human verticalization, the liberation of the hand, and the development of an opposable thumb, we can now efficiently manipulate complex tools, including the pencil with which we started this introductory drawing of homo mimeticus and the keyboard on which I'm now typing.[24]

If I'm typing at all, rather than say, playing with my kids, or having a drink on the terrace with my spouse, it is because well before the invention of writing, back in prehistoric times, a prelinguistic form of intersubjective communication based primarily on gestures, facial expressions, and probably grunts, allowed for a characteristically human social ability to understand what other humans think—and care about their thoughts and, above all, actions. Over time, we realized that survival might in fact depend on a correct interpretation of those intersubjective messages. This lead *Homo sapiens* to master increasingly complex forms of verbal communication that expanded humans' cooperative possibilities beyond the familial circle and tribe, traveling, via the invention of writing, in both space and time. And yet it is now strikingly clear that humans are not only typing the contours of their destiny with increasingly sophisticated digital technologies endowed with hyperreal speed and power of dissemination. On the contrary, in a paradoxical loop Escher made us see and feel, the contours of what we call "the human" are increasingly redrawn by technological tools and media of communication of our own creation, about which the least we can say is that they are no longer fully in our hands—which does not mean that it is not our responsibility to keep using them for the better.

In sum, mimetic pathos, pathos of distance, patho(-)logy, and hypermimesis: four interconnected concepts to propose an emerging theory of a homo mimeticus whose drawing hands cannot be distinguished from the hands drawn. How this paradoxical, perhaps maddening, but certainly productive and reproductive spiraling loop continues to draw the moving contours of a *vita mimetica* that is in the process of being redrawn as I write, is what this book now attempts to delineate.

PART 1

# GENEALOGIES
## FOUNDATIONS

CHAPTER 1

# BIRTH OF HOMO MIMETICUS

> From now on therefore, *historical philosophizing* will be necessary, and along with it the virtue of modesty.
>
> —Friedrich Nietzsche, *Human, All Too Human*

Genealogy is suspicious of searches for origins, yet this does not mean that it cannot diagnose specific forms of mimetic communication that gave birth to humans. Despite the conflicting opinions the protean concept of mimesis continues to generate, one point at least is clear: as we enter deeper into the twenty-first century, the ancient concept of *mimēsis* can no longer be confined to realistic representations of reality to be seen from a safe aesthetic distance. Rather, mimesis should be considered as an all-too-human and perhaps also nonhuman and posthuman condition that animates anthropological, aesthetic, social, and political phenomena constitutive of the history of western civilization—and, perhaps, of *Homo sapiens* tout court.

To further the heterogenous history of our all-too-mimetic condition in the twenty-first century, I start by taking a genealogical step back to the *pre*-history of *Homo sapiens* in its auroral phase of emergence. And I do so to leap ahead to the current resurgences of philosophical, aesthetic, and political manifestations of homo mimeticus. While we have no written traces of this long and obscure period, genealogical lenses will allow us to uncover imitative principles that were not yet known in the most informed accounts of the historical vicissitudes of mimesis at the twilight of the last century,[1] yet fully inform the transdisciplinary theory we now propose at the dawn of the present century to open the field of new mimetic studies.

At the most general level, my goal in this first chapter is to unearth a mimetic hypothesis on prelinguistic forms of bodily communication that have been neglected in the past century dominated by linguistic and discursive turns; and yet this hypothesis arguably played a decisive role in the origins of language, consciousness, communication, and by extension, civilization. This opening chapter, then, provides new genealogical foundations consonant with the *mimetic turn*—or *re*-turn of mimesis in philosophy, aesthetics, and politics—that, as the threefold division of this book suggests, provide three related perspectives animating *Homo Mimeticus*.

## Nietzsche's Mimetic Hypothesis

Since Charles Darwin's *The Expression of Emotions in Men and Animals* (1872), the role played by emotions and facial expression in the development of language has fascinated philosophers, anthropologists, and paleontologists. In what follows, I will not reiterate the various hypotheses on such a controversial topic, which traverses western thought and goes from Plato to Locke, Rousseau to Herder, Saussure to Wittgenstein, among others.[2] Instead, I will be strategically selective in my approach by choosing a more specific point of entry. I shall drive a wedge between two of the most influential theorists of mimesis from the end of the twentieth century, to whom *Homo Mimeticus* steps back in order to begin anew: namely, Jacques Derrida and René Girard. Despite their obvious differences, these two French thinkers both posit mimetic principles at the origins of human culture and civilization—namely, writing and scapegoating, or to use their language, the *pharmakon* and the *pharmakos*, with all the similarities these twin concepts entail, as we will see in more detail in chapter 3. But let me start by inscribing my genealogy of homo mimeticus in an untimely figure who has been aligned with the linguistic turn in the past century, yet, at a closer look, develops a hypothesis on the origins of language in line with the mimetic *re*-turn we are currently promoting in the present century: his name, you will have guessed, is Friedrich Nietzsche.

My opening genealogical wager is that Nietzsche's hypothesis on the birth of language and, by extension, consciousness, not only anticipates poststructuralist concerns with the linguistic sign and its "arbitrary" relation to the referential world, nor does it solely provide a genealogical confirmation of the role of violence and sacrifice in the origins of culture and morality, specifically Christian morality—though he does both, thereby paving the way for both deconstruction and mimetic theory.[3] More important for us, Nietzsche also anticipates, by over a century, an evolutionary hypothesis on the origins of language and consciousness that is currently returning to the forefront of contemporary developments in evolutionary anthropology, paleontology, and, more recently, evolutionary psychology as well as the neurosciences. He also provides both philosophical substance and historical perspective to recent returns of attention to affect, performativity, and materiality in different strands of critical theory. Looking back, genealogically, to the birth of human communication will thus bring us back to contemporary concerns with both the mimetic and hypermimetic condition that haunts philosophy, aesthetics, and politics, among other perspectives we shall explore in the chapters that follow.

Due to the spell cast on the structuralist and, later, poststructuralist generation, Nietzsche's theory of language has long been confined within a linguistic ontology not deprived of idealist tendencies—tendencies Nietzsche's immanent thought contributed to overturning. Due to the interpretative brilliance of readers like Jacques Derrida, Paul de Man, and Philippe Lacoue-Labarthe, it is now well known that, in a youthful text published posthumously and previously largely unknown except to Nietzsche specialists, titled "Truth and Lies in an Extramoral Sense" (1873), Nietzsche develops a hypothesis on the origins of language that was taken to anticipate structuralist and poststructuralist insights into the arbitrary nature of the sign. Nietzsche, in fact, conceives of language as a metaphorical process in which "nerve stimuli," as he puts it, are transferred (metaphor, from *metapherein*, to transfer) into an arbitrary "image" and, later into a "sound" (Nietzsche 1992, 635), twice removed from what the stimuli originally signified, generating an arbitrary chain of images and sounds, signifieds and signifiers that constantly differ and defer meaning away from its origins. After a number of iterations, this view eventually led to the foregrounding of a relativist Nietzschean phrase posthumously collected in the fragments of *The Will to Power* (1901) that was repeated like a mantra in the 1980s and 1990s and was taken as a slogan for postmodernism tout court: namely, "there are no facts, only interpretations of facts" (Nietzsche 1968, 481:267).[4]

But is Nietzsche's thought as relativistic as this decontextualized phrase makes him appear to be? What is certain is that genealogy as he practices it fosters what he calls, in *On the Genealogy of Morals* (1887), an "art of interpretation [*das lesen als Kunst*]" that requires, among other things, "an acute sense of discrimination in matters of psychology," as well as "some schooling in history and philology" (Nietzsche 1996, 10, 5). This transdisciplinary, psychologically oriented, interpretative, and qualitative approach leads to a method of reading that Nietzsche will often refer to in terms of "perspectivism," which is not the same as relativism, for it entails a sense of discrimination that is particularly sharp when it comes to diagnosing "mimetic pathologies" turning the ego into what I call, echoing Nietzsche, a "phantom of the ego."[5]

Now, as Nietzsche's perspectival thought unfolds into his middle and more mature period, this self-proclaimed "philosophical physician" (Nietzsche 1976, 35) continues to sharpen his genealogical lenses to reveal how mimesis does not simply take the ideal form of an image or *imago* far removed from material reality—a view that inverts a vertical Platonic ontology to unmask the illusionary and arbitrary nature of the world of ideas (his negative thesis). Rather, his genealogy develops horizontally, on a plane of immanence, by fostering a diagnostic evaluation attentive to "nerve stimuli" that tie humans to other humans in intersubjective, relational, and communicative terms that are far from arbitrary in nature—if only because they are tied to bodily instincts that generate forms of unconscious mimicry out of which *Homo sapiens* is born (his positive thesis).

Consistently in his career, from *Human, All Too Human* (1878) to the fragments collected in *The Will to Power* (1901), Nietzsche pays close diagnostic attention to the involuntary tendency of humans to mimic others with their bodies so as to understand them with their psyches, or souls. To that end, he develops what he calls a "genuine physio-psychology" (Nietzsche 2003, 53) that bridges ontological dualisms that divide the body from the psyche, but also self from others, mimetic *pathos* from linguistic *logos*, animal from human, nature from culture, among other structural binaries.[6] As Nietzsche succinctly puts it in *Human, All Too Human*, it is thanks to an involuntary imitation that mirrors others' expressions and emotions that "the child still learns to understand its mother" (1995, 216:143–144). There is thus a mimetic principle at the origins of individual communication at the level of the development of the child, or ontogenesis. But as the adverb "still" indicates, Nietzsche has a longer genealogy under his lens. Thus, he immediately doubles down on the diagnostic, as he specifies that this is also "how we learned to understand one another" (219).

Understanding without language, you may think: fair enough but how is meaning conveyed? Well, on the basis of what Nietzsche calls "an ancient association between movement and sensation" (1982, 89). For our purpose it is crucial to note at the outset that this association is mimetic without being arbitrary or metaphorical. In fact, it leads a relational, embodied, and porous ego, or "phantom of the ego" (89), to unconsciously mirror the movements seen in the other outside, and by doing so, feel the other's sensation inside. This is one of those philosophical arrows directed toward the future Nietzsche addressed but did not get to see; yet it entails, in embryo, a hypothesis concerning the birth of consciousness of a genial species that is not simply *sapiens* but also *mimeticus*—or better, a species that becomes *sapiens* because it is already *mimeticus*.

For Nietzsche, in fact, imitation is paradoxically central to human originality. Or, put differently, mimesis serves as a relational matrix—or womb—out of which language and consciousness are born, both individually and collectively. As Walter Benjamin also recognized, an account of the human compulsion to imitate must consider ontogenesis but also "presupposes an understanding of the phylogenetic significance of the mimetic faculty" (2007, 333). And confirming Nietzsche's insight, he adds: "Perhaps there is none of his [man's; *sic*] higher functions in which his mimetic faculty does not play a decisive role" (333), including the birth of that higher functions par excellence, which is, of course, language and consciousness.

Nietzsche fundamentally agrees. Contrary to dominant existential interpretations under the spell of death, he is arguably the philosopher who did most to push birth to the forefront of philosophical consciousness. I will return to Nietzsche's account of the birth of the ego out of the "mimetic unconscious" at the level of the development of the child (or ontogenesis) in chapter 3. For the moment, let us look further back and take an additional genealogical step to find out how "ancient" this association between "movement and sensation" actually goes from the perspective of Nietzsche's *relational* psychology. This also means that we need to first consider his genealogy of the birth of an all-too-mimetic species (or phylogenesis).

## Birth of Language: Out of a Mimetic Stimulus

Nietzsche discusses phylogenetic evolutionary processes at different moments in his career, but it is probably in *The Gay Science* (1882) that he goes furthest in his diagnostic. In a brilliant section of book V titled, "*On the 'genius of the species*'" (1974, 354:297–300), Nietzsche makes clear that when he speaks of an *ancient* association between movement and sensation, he means it literally. He was trained as a philologist, after all, but he also goes beyond the temporal confines of his discipline, paving the way for interdisciplinary approaches to come.

Nietzsche's compressed genealogy of the origins of both consciousness and language, in fact, goes back to prehistoric times, to the origins of the species.

That is, an original species whose genius, he argues contra Romanticism, does not stem from a supposed transcendental subject qua genius considered in autonomous isolation—for Nietzsche posits an evolutionary "need for communication" (298) with other human beings at the origins of consciousness. Nor does it rely on a conception of consciousness that frames mimesis as a stabilizing visual representation that realistically mirrors the external ego—for Nietzsche argues, contra idealism, that life is "possible without seeing itself in a mirror" (297), that is, a mimetic device that reflects the stabilizing logic of the same. Rather, both consciousness and language, for Nietzsche, stem from the dynamic—which is also a power or *dunamis* of—involuntary, and in this sense *un*-conscious, imitative relations with other human beings who are part of a social network of prelinguistic, intersubjective, and bodily communications. As Nietzsche makes clear, this hypothesis does not fit within arbitrary conceptions of the linguistic sign caught in what he now derogatively calls "the snares of grammar," or, alternatively, "the metaphysics of the people" (300). Instead, it promotes an intersubjective, and thus relational psychology rooted in a network of mimetic communications as its evolutionary possibility of emergence.

As in "Truth and Lies," Nietzsche's starting point remains immanent and physiological, but the focus is now *not* on mimesis qua arbitrary image far removed from material reality in the abstraction of a linguistic chain. Rather, his diagnostic focus is on mimesis qua physio-psychological instinct that connects humans attempting to survive in the animal and natural world. While Nietzsche's genealogical focus is on the emergence of human consciousness and language, it would be a gross misreading to consider his genealogy as simply human-centered or anthropocentric. On the contrary, his evolutionary perspective transgresses the human/animal opposition, for it goes beyond the nature/culture binary still dominant in the past century but increasingly obsolete in the present century. Hence, Nietzsche clarifies at the outset that "physiology and the *history of animals* place us at the beginning of such comprehension [of the problem of consciousness]" (1974, 354:297; emphasis added). For Nietzsche, then, to begin to comprehend the emergence of *Homo sapiens*' distinctive characteristics (language and consciousness), we need to start with the physiology of animals—including, of course, one of the most thoroughly mimetic animals, which, as Aristotle also saw, is the human animal (Aristotle 1987, 34).

This is not the first time that Nietzsche establishes a genealogical connection between the human and the animal world via the transdisciplinary medium of a behavioral, embodied, and biologically driven mimesis. Already in *Daybreak* (1881), for instance, in a section titled "Animals and Morality," Nietzsche had established a genealogical link between human imitation and animal "mimicry." He did so to diagnose a loss of individuation that is as physiological and biological as it is psychic and moral—thereby anticipating political insights we shall explore in more detail in part 3. For the moment, it suffices to say that Nietzsche establishes an evolutionary "parallel" with ethico-political implications between animal mimicry and human mimetism: just as mimetic animals "adapt their colouring to the colouring of their surroundings" via the "chromatic function" to "elude one's pursuers," he writes, so "the individual hides in the general concept of 'man,' or in society" out of fear and "prudence" (1982, 26:20–21).[7] Paving the way for Roger Caillois's diagonal connection between human and animal "mimicry" (1938) as a pathological condition, Nietzsche considers "what English researchers designate 'mimicry'" (20) purely negatively here. That is, as a dissolution of individuation that renders the ego porous and open to influences that generate a type of psychic and social conformism constitutive of what I call *mimetic pathology*.

Part of a broader unmasking operation whereby the high value of human (Christian) morality is overturned and reframed in terms of low animal (evolutionary) instincts, Nietzsche diagnoses human mimicry as an animal defense mechanism of survival, whereby the singular hides under the general, aggressive personal drives dissolve into fearful gregarious norms. Thus, Nietzsche states: "the animal understands all this just as man does, with it too self-control springs from the sense for what is real (from prudence)" (1982, 26:21). Interestingly, this prudence, for Nietzsche, stretches to in-*form* (to form from the inside) philosophical prudence as well. Thus, he reframes the noble "sense for truth" characteristic of idealist and moral philosophers that dominated western culture in terms of a less flattering material "sense for security, man has in common with the animals" (21). In an arrow directed contra idealism and moralism, Nietzsche's insight strikes a narcissistic blow to the pride of *Homo sapiens*, as he continues: "The beginning of justice, as of prudence, moderation, bravery—in short, of all we designate as the *Socratic virtues*, are *animal*: a consequence of that drive which teaches us to seek food and elude enemies" (21). High all-too-human virtues born out of low animal drives: this is not only how philosophy is born; it is also how herd security is gained and sovereign individuality lost. Subjected to imitative drives, humans become general, average, and lose personal consciousness in pathological terms Nietzsche often associates with "slavery," the "many," or the "herd"—all of which are characterized by a mimetic consciousness. Death of individual mastery, birth of social slavery: this is, in a nutshell, Nietzsche's dominant genealogical perspective on the pathology of mimesis.

And yet Nietzsche's diagnostic evaluation of homo mimeticus is never unilateral for the pathology is always followed by what I call a balancing patho-*logy*: namely, a rational thought (or *logos*) internal to mimetic affect (or *pathos*) that is characteristic of the mimetic turn or *re*-turn this book promotes more generally. Thus, in a characteristic inversion of perspectives, in *The Gay Science*, Nietzsche starts by stressing the formative, rather than deformative, properties of animal/human mimicry. In fact, his focus is now on an evolutionary formation, or better metamorphic transformation that leads to the birth of human consciousness and language. This birth is not individual or autonomous. On the contrary, it emerges out of the womb of intersubjective forms of mimetic communication constitutive of what he calls, not without irony (notice the quotation marks), "the 'genius of the species ['*Genius der Gattung*']'" (1974, 354:297). His evolutionary hypothesis, in fact, goes back, via "whole races and chains of generation" (298) to the dawn of *Homo sapiens*, in order to account for its natural descent—and the cultural ascent of a homo mimeticus whose contemporary implications we have barely begun to evaluate.

At the most general level, Nietzsche provides a patho-*logical* supplement to Darwin's theory of *biological* evolution along *bio-cultural* lines that depart in original ways from universalizing metanarratives of *cultural* evolution that held sway in the twentieth century. Thus, he does not posit a violent murder, or sacrifice, at the origins of culture on the basis of a racist connection between "savages," "children," and "dull-witted people" qua obsessive "neurotics," as Sigmund Freud speculates in *Totem and Taboo* (1940, 15)—a psychoanalytical thesis that neatly fits an Oedipal myth but is hardly considered a hypothesis in the social and evolutionary sciences today. Nor is Nietzsche in line with René Girard's creative reformulation of the Freudian hypothesis of a founding murder in which violence is discharged against a sacrificial victim, or "scapegoat," to put a cathartic end to a "crisis of difference" and install morality, law, and culture more generally, as he suggests in *Violence and the Sacred* (1977, 1–118)—a speculative, ahistorical move central to Girard's mimetic theory yet still in need of a contemporary theory of homo mimeticus rooted in immanent atheological foundations.[8] While Nietzsche is indeed attentive to the violent and unconscious origins of culture, positing aggressive instincts based on ressentiment at the foundations of morality, he also explores a different, less rivalrous and violent, more cooperative and communal, but also more future-oriented route to the origins of consciousness and language. To do so, he zooms in on the role played not so much by mimetic rivalry and sacrificial death but by unconscious mimicry and intersubjective collaboration central for affirming the collective survival of a fragile, precarious, yet eminently social species.

As we now turn to see, it is Nietzsche's cooperative mimetic hypothesis that comes closest to Darwin's evolutionary account of "social habits" such as "language" as a supplement to his main focus on genetic evolution. Darwin had in fact noticed that "the intellect must have been all-important to him [man; *sic*], even at a very remote period, as enabling him to invent and use language, to make weapons, tools, traps &c., whereby with the aid of his social habits, he long ago became the most dominant of all living creatures," while at the same time supposing that "the largeness of the brain in man relatively to the body, compared to the lower animals, may be attributed in part to the early use of some simple form of language" (Darwin 1970, 132–208, 199, 200). While Nietzsche is often critical of Darwin, his analysis of the origins of language both furthers and complicates a Darwinian evolutionary line of inquiry. More recently, it is also receiving the support of new developments in (post-)evolutionary theory that cross the nature/culture divide and span perspectives as diverse as paleontology, evolutionary psychology, and the neurosciences, all of which are embryonic in Nietzsche's genealogy of the birth of consciousness and are constitutive of mimetic studies. Let us take a closer look.

## Genealogy of Consciousness: A Will to Mime

Nietzsche's starting point for his account of the birth of language and consciousness goes beyond nature and culture.[9] It is neither purely biological nor solely cultural but emerges, phantomlike, out of the dynamic interplay of animal physiology and social practices. We could in fact say that he performs what the French sociologist, philosopher, and transdisciplinary thinker Edgar Morin would call a "bio-psycho-social integration" (Morin 1973, 185). Not unlike Nietzsche, Morin, as we shall see in more detail in the coda, also aims to account for a complex process of biological descent and cultural ascent that rests as much on a mimetic *instinct* of survival as on a mimetic *culture* of solidarity.

Specifying the diagnostic, Nietzsche posits the hypothesis that for prehistoric humans "the subtlety and strength of consciousness always were proportionate to man's (or animal's) capacity for communication [*Mitteilungs-Fähigkeit*] […] as if this capacity in turn were proportionate to the *need for communication* [*Mitteilungs-Bedürftigkeit*]" (1974, 354:298). Nietzsche's starting point is as physiological and evolutionary as it is psychological and social. Considering the vulnerability of an animal born too soon, lacking instinctive specialization, and thus radically dependent on others, Nietzsche considers *Homo sapiens*' biological, psychic, and social need to communicate with others to affirm survival as the immanent starting point for what he calls an "extravagant surmise" (297): namely, and this is his main thesis, that "the development of language and the development of consciousness [...] go hand in hand," insofar as "*consciousness has developed only under the pressure of the need for communication*" (298). This may initially sound an extravagant hypothesis indeed, if only because it entails a radical overturning of perspectives that, Nietzsche anticipates, will sound "offensive" to older [read idealist] philosophers" (297). The highest peaks of human achievement—namely, consciousness and language—are here not considered as the *cause* of communication but as their *effect*. It is not consciousness or a rational *logos* that brings communication into being. On the contrary, it is a pre-existing communicative need triggered by affect, or *pathos*, that is the source of our becoming human.

Language, consciousness, communication. How are these concepts genealogically related? And what does Nietzsche mean with "communication [*Mitteilung*]," since it does not presuppose language but is, rather, the fundamental presupposition for both language and consciousness to emerge? Crucially, for the Nietzsche of the middle period, communication is first and foremost *not* a linguistic form of exchange restricted to arbitrary metaphorical signs, words, or *logoi* uttered by a subject considered in isolation; it is rather physiological in origins, intersubjective in nature, and thus eminently social, embodied, and affective in expressive orientation. The physiological dimension of communication, which is expressed in gestures and facial expressions, is particularly important for Nietzsche.[10] Thus, he stresses that "not only language serves as bridge between human beings but also a mien, a pressure, a gesture [*der Blick, der Druck, die Gebärde*]" (1974, 354:299). If such a form of prelinguistic, embodied, and affective communication is still triggered by "nerve stimuli," as in "Truth and Lies," the focus is now no longer on a disinterested autonomous subject who perceives the world in a condition of epistemic isolation, nor is it a question of being caught in the spell of a metaphorical chain of arbitrary associations that lead away from reality, to the creation of ideal worlds "*behind* the world [*Hinterwelt*]" (Nietzsche 1996, 5). Instead, his focus is now on an intersubjective, bio-socio-evolutionary dynamic that ties, *patho*-logically, subjects to other subjects, one gesture to another gesture, one facial expression to another facial expression, via an immanent social network of mimetic communication in which the ego is not autonomous and self-enclosed but is a relational phantom part of a larger cooperative community striving to survive in *this* world.

How does this prelinguistic communication operate? By relying on what nerve stimuli do best: namely, triggering motor movements such as gestures, facial expressions, or pantomime endowed with an affective power, or *pathos*, to bridge the gap between self and others. Nietzsche had already diagnosed this mirroring phenomenon in *Human, All Too Human*, as he writes:

> As soon as people understood one another in gestures, a *symbolism* of gestures could arise: I mean that people could agree upon a language of sound signals by first producing sound *and* gesture (the former symbolically joined to the latter) and later only the sound. (1995, 216:144)

Again, this symbolism is not arbitrary. It is based on a continuity between gestures and sounds, the *pathos* of movements and the *logos* of communication predicated on an unconscious association between *physiological* movements seen outside and *psychic* affects felt inside.

If our deconstruction, to use an old-fashioned word, of mind/body, self/others dualistic binaries, goes beyond linguistic metaphysical principles, it remains firmly rooted in Nietzsche's immanent embodied principles. In fact, for Nietzsche, this *pathos* is nothing less and nothing more than the clearest and most ordinary manifestation of one of his most influential and misunderstood concepts: namely, the "will to power." Why? Because as he puts it in a fragment from 1988, this enigmatic concept goes beyond being/becoming metaphysical binaries to open up a fluid, embodied, and affective drive that opens up the ego to the outside: "The will to power not a being, not a becoming but a *pathos*" (Nietzsche, 1968, 635:339). The foundational concept of "mimetic pathos," which, as we have seen, provides the first step toward the theory of homo mimeticus put forward in this book, finds thus in Nietzsche a privileged starting point. Out of this powerful affect, or *pathos*, then, a new theory, or *logos*, on imitation is born.

Let us be clear: mimetic pathos is not simply pathological for the psychic dissolution of the boundaries of individuation it entails; it is also patho-*logical* in the sense that the will to power of *pathos* triggers a mirroring form of unconscious communication that is not only older than any conscious language or *logos* and the idea of being it entails; it also brings both consciousness and language into an entangled form of evolutionary becoming. Nietzsche specifies this mirroring mechanism in terms of a "psychomotor rapport" in another fragment from the same year central to his genealogy of language, as he writes: "This is where languages originate: the languages of tone as well as the languages of gestures and glances" (1968, 809:428). For Nietzsche, this physiological form of "transmission between living creatures [...] is the source of languages" and goes back to the "beginning" (428); and yet this beginning continues to cast light on the present and perhaps the future as well. In fact, he continues: "even today one still hears with one's muscles, one even reads with one's muscles" (428). There is thus a muscular, physiological, or better physio-psychological form of mimetic communication that provides an embodied medium of expression that underscores, mediates, and renders possible the emergence of linguistic communication. Or, to put it in our language, a mimetic will to power, or *will to mime*, triggers a mirroring form of unconscious communication in homo mimeticus that is not only older than language or *logos*; it is also *patho*-logical, for it brings both consciousness and language into being—out of the powerful stimulus of mimetic *pathos*.

We are now in a position to confirm that, for the mature Nietzsche, communication is not based on arbitrary linguistic signs to interpret from a rational distance; rather, it originates in mirroring bodily movements and facial expressions that convey an unconscious *pathos* as shared affect, or *sym-pathos*. Nietzsche summarizes this dynamic with characteristic succinctness, as he states: "One never communicates thoughts: one communicates movements, mimic signs, which we then trace back to thoughts" (1968, 809:428). This mirroring principle that translates gestures into thoughts via an involuntary psychomotor mimicry is one of the foundational principles of what I call the "mimetic unconscious," a pre-Freudian but also post-Freudian alternative I shall return to.[11] For the moment, suffice it to say that this is a relational, physio-psychological, and thus embodied unconscious that ties the human soul (*psyche*) back to our animal body (*soma*), makes the ego, for better and worse, porous to external influences, renders it plastic and adaptable, and, we now add, emerges from modes of embodied communication that are not based on arbitrary linguistic signs but, rather, on mimicry of physical movements, which are at the origins of psychic sensations and thoughts.

Does this mirroring principle sound familiar? The contemporary reader attentive to recent developments in critical theory that go beyond the traditional two-cultures divide will not have missed the rather astonishing fact that Nietzsche, writing in the 1880s, anticipated *by over a century* what has been hailed as a revolutionary discovery in the 1990s: namely, the discovery of a set of neuronal cells that has triggered renewed interests in mimesis at the dawn of the twenty-first century and that has been grouped under the heading of "mirror neurons." Initially discovered in area F5 of the premotor cortex of macaque monkeys by Giacomo Rizzolatti and his team at the University of Parma, Italy, mirror neurons were later found in humans in the ramified form of a "mirror neuron system" (MNS) (Rizzolatti and Sinigaglia 2008). In a nutshell, mirror neurons are motor neurons, that is, neurons responsible for movement, which activate or "fire" not only as we perform a movement but also—and this is the discovery—as we see others perform a movement, especially goal-oriented movements, such as grasping and holding, but also facial expressions, images, and sounds, triggering an unconscious activation, mirroring sensation, and embodied imitation in the self as well. A genealogy of the mimetic unconscious already showed that this discovery finds important and so far largely unacknowledged precursors in philosophical physicians attentive to the mirroring relation between movements and sensations, what we see and what we feel.

Furthering this emerging line of inquiry, we can now say that Nietzsche, for whom, let us not forget, "the body is a great reason" (2005, 30), already describes this mirroring mechanism with delicate phenomenological precision. His genealogy of homo mimeticus is characteristically Janus-faced: it looks back to the imitative origins of human practices but does so to better look ahead to the future. In *Daybreak* (1881), he unpacks this mirroring communication as follows:

> To understand another person, that is *to imitate his* [sic] *feelings in ourselves* [...we] produce the feeling [of others] in ourselves after the *effects* it exerts and displays on the other person by imitating with our own body the expression of his eyes, his voice, his walk, his bearing (or even their reflection in word, picture, music). Then a similar feeling arises in us in consequence of an ancient association between movement and sensation (1982, 142:89).

This mirroring, nonarbitrary principle allows for an understanding of other minds (or theory of mind) that does not require the rational mediation of a linguistic consciousness (or theory theory). Instead, it perfectly conforms to what has been called "embodied simulation" (or simulation theory), opening up a shared and relational conception of subjectivity Vittorio Gallese designates as the "shared manifold of intersubjectivity" (2003, 171) and I group under the Nietzschean concept of "mimetic communication." This also means that the tradition of the mimetic unconscious on which this mirroring mechanism rests anticipates by more than a century the discovery of mirror neurons, and thus paves the way for it.

This genealogical point is worth stressing in a culture that often thinks the future of original discoveries is primarily on the side of the hard sciences, while the humanities are bound to endless repetitions of past ideas. This is indeed the risk of antiquarian history still dominating many areas in the humanities; yet, for genealogy, tradition and innovation are far from being opposed. On the contrary, what a genealogy of homo mimeticus is beginning to teach us is that revolutionary discoveries might actually turn out to be *re*-discoveries of ancient principles that are now finally confirmed on an empirical basis and contribute to promoting a transdisciplinary re-*turn* of mimesis on the critical and theoretical scene.

But Nietzsche allows us to go further. He also stresses, somewhat paradoxically, that his new genealogical connection is "ancient." His genealogy has thus a broader philosophical point to make. The reflex of mimesis leads back to the *phylogenetic* emergence of *Homo sapiens*, and this step back allows us to leap ahead to more far-reaching hypotheses constitutive of the birth of homo mimeticus. Nietzsche, in fact, adds that human language and consciousness emerged out of an all-too-human dependency on others based on relationality, affectivity, and, above all, prelinguistic forms of communication based on mirroring reflexes constitutive of our species. Mimetic drives, for Nietzsche, are in fact amplified by a constitutive human fragility, dependency, and timidity, which, together, foster relationality, intersubjective communication, and, in the best life-affirmative scenarios, cooperation as well. He clarifies his genealogical hypothesis in *Daybreak* in a passage that continues to account for the birth of the "genius of the species"—out of the "fragility of human nature." It reads as follows:

> If we ask how we became so fluent in the imitation of the feelings of others [*Nachbildung der Gefühle anderer*] the answer admits of no doubt: man [*sic*], as the most timid of all creatures on account of his subtle and fragile nature, has in his timidity the instructor in that empathy [*Mitempfindung*], that quick understanding of the feeling of another (and of animals). Through long millennia he saw in everything strange and lively a danger: at the sight of it he at once imitated the expression of the features and the bearing [*Ausdruck der Züge und der Haltung*] and drew his conclusion of the kind of evil intention behind the features of this bearing. (1992, 142:90)

Fear, timidity, and fragility are thus at the origins of prelinguistic forms of mimetic communication that find in mirroring physiological principles a subtle and quick mode of understanding. How far we are from the caricature of Nietzsche as the unconditional advocate of strong, autonomous, anti-mimetic, but not all that quick-witted, beasts of prey.

This is, indeed, the same hypothesis that informs Nietzsche's genealogy of consciousness and language in *The Gay Science*, where he states: "as the most endangered animal, he [*sic*] *needed* help and protection, he needed his peers, he had to learn to express his distress and to make himself understood" (1974, 354:298). Mirroring gestures and facial expressions allowed for this affective distress (*pathos*) to be communicated quickly, via an unconscious mimesis that paves the way for the emergence of consciousness and language (*logos*). For Nietzsche, then, the speed generated by a reflex sympathy (*sym-pathos*, feeling with) provides the immanent foundation on which dialogue (*dia-logos*, through words) actually rests. Due to their constitutive vulnerability, prehistoric humans turned out to be dependent, relational, and cooperative creatures. Their "consciousness" was thus not monadic, autonomous, and individually self-enclosed; it was rather, from its inception, part of a ramified network of mimetic *pathos*—or will to power—which Nietzsche also calls a "net of communication [*Verbindungsnetz*] between human beings" (298).

Mimetic pathos is at the origins of a communicative network on which the collective survival of *Homo sapiens* depends; our species evolutionary power does not lie in the autonomous ego but in the intersubjective network of communication connecting phantom egos. We can now better understand why Nietzsche says that the "will to power [or *pathos*] is the primitive form of affect, that all other affects are only developments of it" (1968, 688:366). Nietzsche, the philologist, uses the term "primitive" literally and, thus, etymologically (from Latin, *primus*, first) to foster a genealogical insight: namely, that the first mimetic *pathos* ties self to others via an originary *will to mime* that gives birth to an immanent, embodied, relational, and eminently social consciousness. This consciousness is thus not located in a solipsistic ego but in the social network of communication [*Mit-teilung*] that both connects [*Mit*] and disconnects [*Teilung*] self and others in a double movement between mimetic and anti-mimetic tendencies Nietzsche often called, in an oxymoronic and thus agonist phrase, "*pathos of distance*" (1996, 12).

It is my contention that this dynamic tension or oscillation between the unconscious immediacy of pathos and the conscious mediation of distance is the palpitating heart of the mimetic turn, or *re*-turn to an immanent, atheological, and future-oriented theory of mimesis that animates the pages that follow. It also provides the *Stoßpunkt*, or *coup d'envoi*, that sets mimetic studies in motion as a transdisciplinary field attentive to intersubjective, relational, and communicative processes. Time and again, we shall see that homo mimeticus is radically vulnerable to the reflex *pathos* of mimesis, experiences its power with the body, sometimes for the worse, opening up a plurality of pathological perspectives that deserve new attention in the digital age. And yet, at the same time, and without contradiction, this imitative subject can also mobilize all the tools of critical consciousness and the *logos* it entails to set up a diagnostic distance from mimetic *pathos* constitutive of the philosophical physician's patho-*logy*—the clinical *logos* being all the sharper insofar as this mimetic *pathos* is seen outside and experienced inside. Homo mimeticus is thus Janus-faced not only because it looks in two opposed directions, presiding over departures and new arrivals, but also because it relies on both *pathos* and *logos* to chart territories yet to be explored.

There is again a powerful inversion of perspectives, or perspectivism, at play in Nietzsche's Janus-faced mimetic patho-*logy*. The driving *telos* of his genealogy affirms that humans are not social animals because they have individual consciousness. On the contrary, they have a shared consciousness due to their precarious nature that leads them to cooperate, first unconsciously and then consciously, as eminently social creatures. Hence, Nietzsche reiterates the main point of his genealogical inversion, which he considers as nothing less than "the essence of phenomenalism and perspectivism," as he says:

> My idea is, as you see, that consciousness does not really belong to man's individual existence but rather to his social or herd nature; that, as follows from this, it has developed subtlety only insofar as this is required by social or herd utility (1974, 354:299).

For Nietzsche, there is thus a mimetic principle or will to mime at the dawn of consciousness and language characteristic of that original species a.k.a. *Homo sapiens*. I echo that the "genius" of the species was ultimately a mimetic genius, for it was triggered by the unconscious power of mirroring reflexes characteristic of homo mimeticus.

This also means that human power does not stem from a self-sufficient, violent, macho power rooted only in sovereign, patriarchal and rather beastly individuals—though they certainly remain its dominant socio-political manifestation. Rather, it is born from a constitutive, all-too-human vulnerability and dependency to maternal forms of nonverbal communication that opens up the channels of mimetic *pathos* through which will to power flows as a network—inaugurating more collaborative and future-oriented genealogical steps for an ongoing hominization in the future.

## Steps Toward a Hominization of the Future

With few exceptions, Nietzsche's "extravagant surmise" that an unconscious bodily mimesis of gestures and facial expressions lies at the prehistorical origins of human consciousness and language remained in the background of rationalist and ahistorical philosophical trends dominant in western thought. That is, trends that, at one remove, cast a shadow on the (post)structuralist generation as well. For Nietzsche, in fact, it was soon clear that the "original failing of philosophers" is that they tend to consider the concept of "man" as an "*aeterna veritas*" (1997, 2:16). Because philosophers often lack a sense of historical discrimination, he continues, they do not realize that "everything *essential* in human development occurred in primeval times [*Urzeiten*], long before those four thousand years with which we are more or less acquainted" (2:16).[12] To be sure, Nietzsche's hypothesis on the birth of *Homo sapiens* will have to wait until the middle of the twentieth century to find empirical confirmations outside the confines of philosophy. As we have learned to appreciate, his observations often sound extravagant because they are untimely and thus anticipate discoveries yet to come. He might in fact have been offering a genealogical hypothesis to solve one of the greatest riddles in human evolution. Namely, the so-called "great leap forward" that occurred around seventy-five thousand years ago and marked a radical turn in the emergence of *Homo sapiens*.

Let us thus broaden the scope of our genealogy of homo mimeticus.

While paleoanthropologists tend to agree that the human brain reached its present capacity around three hundred thousand years ago, key human characteristics, including symbolic creation, the making of complex tools, cave painting, religious beliefs, music, and language started to appear only much later, around 70,000–50,000 BC. Why so late? A traditional (Darwinian) evolutionary hypothesis would look for a genetic mutation responsible for this leap ahead, but this hypothesis does not account for the speed in which such a human transformation took place and spread across the world. An alternative starting point was suggested by the French paleontologist André Leroi-Gourhan. In his seminal study *Le Geste et la parole* (1964, 1965), he provides evolutionary support in favor of the (Nietzschean) hypothesis that the origins of language cannot be dissociated from gestures and facial expressions. In fact, Leroi-Gourhan argues that the birth of language does not come out ready-made from *sapiens*' brain—like Athena out of Zeus's head, as a "cerebralist" anthropological tradition that goes from Rousseau to Lévi-Strauss suggested. Rather, it has lower, more immanent, and, pace idealist philosophers, modest physiological origins.

If our body is our greatest reason, then, philosophers should start shifting the gaze from the sky of ideas and begin to look at their feet and hands. According to Leroi-Gourhan, humans' capacity for language stems from the foot and the vertical posture (*station verticale*) it allowed, which, in turn, freed the hand for the making of tools and gestures (*le geste*), increased facial exposure via what progressively became a "short face" (*face courte*), which physiologically allowed for the development of facial and eventual oral communication (*la parole*). As he summarizes his untimely thesis: "Vertical posture, short face, free hand during locomotion and possession of removable tools are really the fundamental criteria of humanity" (1964, 33; my trans.). This genealogy of the liberation of the hand attentive to the role of the "tool for the hand and of language for the face" (34), for Leroi-Gourhan, identifies the two main poles potentially responsible for the acceleration of the evolutionary process that led to the full development of *Homo sapiens*' unique capacities, including oral and, eventually, written communication (1964, 33). Thus, Leroi-Gourhan continues by saying that "The prodigious acceleration of progress" characteristic of recent human history, "is simultaneously connected to the channeling of reasoning into technical operations and to the subservience of the hand to language in the graphic symbolism that culminates with writing" (1965, 260). Yes, writing is a foundational genealogical achievement. No one denies it, certainly not people who spend their days writing books.

And yet, before reaching the very recent stage of *écriture* and the externalization of memory it entails that fascinated poststructuralist readers of Leroi-Gourhan (see Derrida 1967, 124–130; Stiegler 1998, 43–179), genealogists of homo mimeticus start from a more modest but foundational embodied premise. It is in fact crucial to stress that it is the interplay of gestures and mimicry that, for the paleontologist, as for Nietzsche before him, led, via a long evolutionary process of hominization, to speech, consciousness, and, eventually, writing. Thus, Leroi-Ghouran specifies:

> this reflective thought, which was expressed concretely in vocal language and mimicry [*langage vocale et mimique*] of Anthropians probably since their origins, acquires during the superior Palaeolithic the handling of representations allowing humans to express themselves beyond the material present. (1964, 270)

Nietzsche would have fundamentally agreed on the original function of mimicry. He might also have added a mimetic supplement: namely, that the fragility, dependency, and lack of specialization of the human animal played a key role in developing relational forms of mirroring communication, sharing, and cooperation that, according to more contemporary hypotheses, turn out to be central to the birth of *homo sapiens-mimeticus*—out of the immanence of mirroring reflexes.

From philosophy to paleoanthropology, let us keep turning the perspectival lens of the patho-*logies* of homo mimeticus. We can now add neurology as well to solve this evolutionary riddle from the transdisciplinary angle of new mimetic studies. Furthering mirror neuron theory from an evolutionary perspective, the neuroscientist V. S. Ramachandran, in a chapter of *The Tell-Tale Brain* (2011) titled, "The Neurons that Shaped Civilization," develops a daring neuro-bio-cultural hypothesis that surprised many but would not have surprised Nietzsche: "mirror neurons play an important role in the uniqueness of the human condition: They allow us to imitate," and Ramachandran adds, "miming may have been the key step in hominin evolution, resulting in our ability to transmit knowledge through example" (2011, 132). Taking his distance from a purely genetic view of evolution to account for a complex *cultural* transformation characteristic of *Homo sapiens*, Ramachandran, like Nietzsche before him, starts by stressing how "utterly depended on round-the-clock care and supervisions" (117) humans are. And he does so to foreground the role of imitation in general and mirror neurons in particular in the development of language and cultural transmission.

Focusing on major technical innovations but also aesthetics, the human ability to read other minds, and self-awareness, Ramachandran builds on Rizzolatti's insight that mirror neurons "may be the precursors of our celebrated Broca's area"—that is, a brain area linked to the "expressive aspects of human language" (123)—to provide a hypothesis for the emergence of language at the dawn of human prehistory. Thus, he argues that a "primitive gestural communication system [read MNS] [was] already in place that provided scaffolding for the emergence of vocal language" (120). This hypothesis allows Ramachandran to move beyond the Scylla of structuralist accounts predicated on language considered as an autonomous system and the Charybdis of universal transhistorical hypotheses on founding sacrificial murders. Instead, he opens up a genealogical hypothesis that relies on the powers or pathos of mimesis and the will to mime it entails for "translating gestures into words" and, more generally, for passing down cultural practices via imitation of examples rather than genetic mutation. Thus, he concludes that "increased sophistication of a single mechanism—such as imitation and intention reading—could explain the huge behavioral gap between us and apes" (134).

More recently, Rizzolatti himself considers Ramachandran's hypothesis "attractive"; he also lends supports to it. Thus, Rizzolatti suggests that, thanks to a genetic evolution that led to a "sufficient number of mirror neurons" in *Homo sapiens*, "humans liberated themselves from the slow Darwinian evolution and were able to set in motion a cultural evolution that rapidly changed the world, carrying us in a very short time to the present world" (Rizzolatti and Gnoli 2016, 182; my trans.). An embodied mirroring communication through mien and gestures might thus have served as a *bridge* between open, porous, and relational subjects on the way to the emergence of language, consciousness, and culture, after all. Perhaps it might even have played a role in the "evolutionary bridge" that made the emergence of the "genius of the species" possible—out of a communicative mimetic pathos, or will to mime. The paradox is not without ironies: imitation turns out to be the source of human originality; *Homo sapiens* is born out of homo mimeticus.

This, I admit, is a daring overturning of perspectives that urges us to rethink the foundations of who we are as a species. Skeptics might worry that it is biased by an excessive faith in mirror neurons. I share this worry. In fact, I have myself been critical of rationalist interpretations of mirror neuron theories that stress perhaps too much their role in understanding other people's actions and intentions at the expense of other, perhaps less based on understanding but equally mirroring, violent, and irrational reactions that can equally be triggered[13]—as we shall have the occasion to confirm with respect to political pathologies in part 3. To be fair to this hypothesis, however, if we keep turning the perspectival lens of our patho-*logy*, we should note that it also finds support in recent perspectives developed independently from mirror neuron theory yet relevant to account for homo mimeticus.

In the field of evolutionary psychology, for instance, Michael Tomasello posits a gestural imitation, or pantomime, as central to *The Origins of Human Communication* (2008). As Tomasello puts it: "my evolutionary hypothesis [is] that the first uniquely human forms of communication were pointing and pantomiming," that is, gestures and expressions he considers central for human "cooperation" based on "shared intentionality" out of which, he adds, "arbitrary linguistic conventions could have come into existence evolutionarily" (2008, 9). While drawing on evolutionary anthropology and comparative studies of great apes and children, Tomasello argues that, philosophically, the "major theoretical arguments" for shared intentionality and cooperative communication are provided by "classic scholars such as Wittgenstein" (334). And rightly so, for Wittgenstein also claims that "'what we call meaning must be connected with the primitive language of gestures'" (in Tomasello 2008, 1; see also Gebauer 2017). Needless to say, the claim that "pointing and pantomiming [...] are 'natural' in the way that 'arbitrary' linguistic conventions are not" (9) finds in another classic scholar, who was also a scholar of classics, such as Nietzsche, an additional source of theoretical arguments on which the mimetic turn, or *re*-turn to mimesis, draws.

Lastly, and to bring us fully into the present, Nietzsche also adds a maternal touch to his genealogy. As his claim on the child understanding the mother with which we started suggests, he was in fact attentive to the birth of language and communication out of maternal influences and collective cooperation along immanent, embodied, and sympathetic lines that resonate productively with feminist philosophers like Adriana Cavarero we shall soon encounter.[14] As the goal of this chapter is to trace as far back as possible the genealogy of the relational foundations animating homo mimeticus, let me turn to an anthropologist and primatologist who shares our mimetic hypothesis and adds a maternal supplement as well. Sarah Blaffer Hrdy is exemplary in this respect.[15]

Building on Tomasello, Hrdy furthers a cooperative account of the evolutionary origins of humans' empathic and relational consciousness that adds yet another confirmation to our genealogy. As the title of her book suggests, Hrdy focuses on *Mothers and Others* (2009) to foreground the "evolutionary origins of mutual understanding" (this being the book's subtitle). She does so by zeroing in on cooperative, predominantly but not exclusively maternal forms of rearing, open to nonparental care (or alloparenting), which resonates directly with Nietzsche's hypothesis of consciousness as a "social network." As Hrdy succinctly puts it: "cooperative breeding came before braininess" (2009, 176). Her evolutionary hypothesis complicates dominant individualistic, violent, or selfish interpretations of human behavior (or genes) by focusing on the all-too-human need for cooperation as *the* source of the development of newborns' mimetic faculty to both feel and think from the point of view of others. As Hrdy puts it: "were it not for the peculiar combination of empathy and mind reading [emerging from the child's bond with a multiplicity of maternal/alloparental relations], we would never have evolved to be humans at all" (28). And in a passage worth reproducing here, she adds in an explicitly mimetic mood:

> Without the capacity to put ourselves cognitively and emotionally in someone else's shoes, to feel what they feel, to be interested in their fears and motives, longings, griefs, vanities, and other details of their existence, without this mixture of curiosity about emotional

identification with others, a combination that adds up to mutual understanding and sometimes even compassion, *Homo sapiens* would never have evolved at all. (28)[16]

Had *Homo sapiens* not been first and foremost *mimeticus*, we would never have evolved to even aspire to becoming *sapiens* in the first place, which does not mean that this ideal has been successfully achieved. Quite the contrary, as we shall see. For the moment, let us register that affectively stepping in others' minds and shoes, emotional identification, compassion, or, to put it in our language, *sym-pathos*, are all part of mimetic forms of communication that most likely gave birth to our cooperative species, allowing for our extraordinary evolutionary expansion on planet earth, for good and ill.

Numerous other recent evolutionary accounts that stress a return of attention to the centrality of mimesis in human development could be mentioned, but these must suffice to make my point.[17] What was true for the latest developments in mirror neuron theory is equally true for the latest developments in evolutionary psychology and anthropology: from the awareness of human dependency and fragility to the centrality of mimicry and pantomime, from the importance of sharing and cooperation to the social nature of human consciousness, these new theories of the origins of communication find in Nietzsche an original and so far largely unacknowledged precursor that reveals the all-too-imitative foundations of a thoroughly innovative species I call, for lack of a more original term, homo mimeticus.

## Beyond Good and Evil Mimesis

Nietzsche, then, encourages genealogists developing new perspectives for mimetic studies to look back to the origins of language—out of mimetic *pathos*. He does so to foster a perspectival critical discourse (or *logos*) that looks ahead to the possible patho(-)logical destinations of homo mimeticus. To pull some preliminary strings that will guide us in what follows, let me schematically outline the relevance of the mimetic turn for an age that is no longer dominated by the primacy of the linguistic turn attentive to the decentering power of language (*logos*), but is entangled in a number of *re*-turns to more embodied, performative, material, relational, yet not less mimetic and contagious affects (*pathê*).

In the past century, Nietzsche's hypothesis paved the way for theories of language and cultural evolution that selectively drew on his genealogical, perspectival, and thus patho-*logical* insights to promote the view that mimesis goes beyond good and evil, for it operates both as a *pharmakon* (poison/remedy) and as a *pharmakos* (scapegoat). This lesson has been immensely productive for linguistic-oriented critical inquiries that, often via the privileged medium of print literature, paid close attention to the texture of texts. They did so not only to disrupt the myth of presence and the (Platonic) metaphysics it entails but also to decenter the subject, reinstate the power of the unconscious, affirm the primacy of the copy over the original, reveal the imitative foundations of human desires, and diagnose a type of sacrificial violence that does not originate in the myth of an ideal, immutable, and fully present rational consciousness.

The theory of imitation we are currently developing on Nietzsche's and other modernist and contemporary shoulders remains genealogically connected to this past tradition of critique, especially when it comes to affirming the pathological consequences of the mimetic unconscious. In fact, in *The Gay Science*, after having stressed the positive role of mimesis in his past-oriented genealogy of language, Nietzsche overturns once again perspectives to diagnose the pathological side of a future-oriented consciousness. He writes:

> Owing to the nature of *animal consciousness*, the world of which we can become conscious is only a surface-and sign-world, a world that is made common and meaner; whatever becomes conscious *becomes* by the same token shallow, thin, relatively stupid, general, sign, herd signal [...] Ultimately, the growth of consciousness becomes a danger; and anyone who lives among the most conscious Europeans even knows that it is a disease. (1974, 354:299–300)

Nietzsche's diagnostic perspectives change over time, but his mimetic patho(-)logies remain double: for him, mimesis not only gives birth to the *logos* of consciousness; the same consciousness born out of the *pathos* of herd-behavior can also spread contagious pathologies that, he warns us a few aphorisms laters, are particularly intense in ages in which "actors, all kinds of actors, turn out to be the real masters" (1974, 356:303). There is thus significant diagnostic potential in a theory of homo mimeticus that draws selectively and genealogically on untimely thinkers attentive to the power of *pathos* to unmask contagious diseases that, in the age of (new) fascist infections amplified by viral infections and new media, contribute to "thorough corruption, falsification, reduction to superficialities, and generalization" (354;300). Welcome to the world of social media.

Mimesis is not a new or original concept; yet the mimetic *re*-turn does not simply echo past linguistic theories that found in literature their primary source of inspiration—though literature continues to remain inspiring to the few. Rather, it introduces repetitions and differences that are constitutive of a digitized, mass-mediatized, and increasingly precarious world traversed by fluxes of (hyper)mimetic contagion that operate with increasing speed and potential of infection. Hence, a new theory of imitation for the twenty-first century cannot be restricted to mimetic *desire* alone. Rather, it must be expanded to consider a (post)human receptivity to the more generalized concept of mimetic *pathos* that includes all affects, good and bad, individual and collective, sad and joyous, pathological and patho-*logical*. It is only on such a dynamic, perspectival, and transdisciplinary base that we can keep up with the transformations of our species in the present and future.

At the same time, on the side of genealogical practices, Nietzsche offers an alternative foundation for mimetic studies. He puts us in a position to see that at the origins of consciousness, language, and by extension culture, is not a cry for murder against a sacrificial victim but a cry for help *not* to be a victim. Nor do we find the primacy of a linguistic trace over the presence of an embodied pantomime but, rather, the speed of intersubjective forms of nonverbal communication animated by a will to mime that bypasses consciousness yet informs, deforms, and transforms the mimetic unconscious nonetheless. Hence, a genealogy of mimesis should not be confused with a hypothesis that hinges solely on scapegoating mechanisms for culture to emerge, as Girard's mimetic theory suggests; nor does it follow the forward movement of a linguistic *gramme* that leads the subject to slide through a chain of signifiers in linguistic terms of appearance and disappearance that supplement the oral presence of speech and gestures, as Derrida influentially argued. Rather, for us following Nietzsche, *Homo sapiens* is born out of forms of preverbal communication that are physio-psychological in origin, relational and intersubjective in nature, and immanent in onto-bio-socio-patho(-)logical foundation. A genealogical focus on mimetic *pathos* and the perspectival patho-*logies* that ensue, then, turns dependency into relationality, individual weakness into social strength, a lack of fixed biological instincts into an excessive power of communication, a mimetic communication that gives birth to language and consciousness—out of unconscious gestures and expressions.

Sitting on the shoulders of a genealogy of thinkers that understood mimesis as a human, all-too-human condition, we have begun to see that this book does not simply advocate a return to the old stabilizing conception of mimesis understood as realistic representation. On the contrary, if we step back to the origins of communication not confined within the boundaries of a conscious *logos*, or a transparent *imago*, it is in order to provide a broader genealogical perspective to recent returns of attention to what I grouped under the ancient concept of mimetic *pathos*. Another genealogist of Nietzschean inspiration, Michel Foucault, usefully specifies that "affection, perturbation, in Greek is called *pathos* and in Latin *affectus*" (2004, 754). Indeed, the recent turn to affect and all it entails—embodiment, performativity, influence, mirroring reflexes, care of the self, inclinations, contagion, etc.—is actually a *re*-turn to ancient principles. This also means that new critical turns as diverse as the affective turn and the neuro turn, the performative turn and the posthuman turn, the ethical turn and the new materialist turn, among many exciting new turns, are currently returning to the ancient realization that humans are, for better and worse, vulnerable to the shared experience of a *mimetic pathos* that distributes consciousness on a network of communication.

In the end, a genealogy of homo mimeticus goes beyond good and evil. The patho(-)logies of mimesis open up complementary possibilities that look simultaneously in opposed directions: namely, both toward social pathologies that trigger violent rivalries, scapegoating, ressentiment, affective contagion, (new) fascism, epidemic contagion and related sicknesses, which, in some cases, can lead to a faith in what is behind the world; and, alternatively, and without contradiction, toward patho-*logies* that strive contra dominant life-negating currents animated by nihilistic forms of ressentiment to promote vital bonds of sympathy, cooperation, public happiness, and joyful inclinations, prompting chameleonlike metamorphoses that aspire to renew our faithfulness to the earth here and now.

This is a decisive, truly vertiginous, and, we are beginning to sense, potentially irreversible crossroads in the labyrinthine process of the becoming (un)conscious of homo mimeticus in the epoch of the Anthropocene. If we want to know whether the Ariadne's thread of our increasingly precarious destiny as a dangerously genial species is still partially in our hands, there is only one way to find out—we shall have to follow it.

## CHAPTER 2

# *VITA MIMETICA* IN THE CAVE

> I divine, he said, that you are considering whether
> we shall admit tragedy and comedy into our city or not.
> Perhaps, said I, and perhaps even more than that.
>
> —Plato, *The Republic*

We saw how *Homo sapiens* came into being as a social, affective, and intersubjective creature, part of a network that ties self to others. Since time immemorial, generation after generation, mimetic forms of nonlinguistic communication enmesh newborns into a network of communal relations that are constitutive of our genealogy of homo mimeticus. Given the central role mimetism plays in the process of all-too-human aspirations to become *sapiens*, we might still wonder: how come, at the dawn of philosophy in classical antiquity, at a key moment in the cultural, social, and political evolution of this eminently relational and gregarious species, when communities of people were beginning to assemble in organized city-states that allowed for imperfect forms of democratic participation among a minority of privileged male citizens—how come, at this crucial turning point in the history of western civilization, a new and emerging discipline known as *philosophia* that aspired to the love of wisdom characteristic of *Homo sapiens* broke with a long-standing oral, mythic tradition that thought it wise to nurture the imitative forms of communication that gave birth to human consciousness?

The story of this quarrel or agon is seemingly well known: the father of philosophy (Plato), under the mask of a fictional dramatization of his teacher (Socrates), set out to violently exclude from his ideal *polis* previously revered arts and the practitioners who dramatized them: primarily poets, rhapsodes, actors, and mimes. That is, the very figures that gave voice to the collective mythic womb that was sensitive to the affective, embodied, and thus social life of a relational species that, as we have seen in the preceding chapter, become *sapiens* by exploiting the relational power of mimetic *pathos* to produce networks of communication.[1] We are thus in a position to recognize that in *Sapiens*, Yuval Harari re-popularizes an ancient idea, as he stresses "that belief in shared myths" is central to building "an astounding networks of mass cooperation" (2014, 117, 115). This is a central historical insight, but it is still in need of a philosophical supplement. Unlike Plato, and later Nietzsche, Bataille and others, Harari does not focus on myth's primary medium of mass communication: namely, mimesis. Hence the need to further complementing the history of *Homo sapiens* with a genealogy of homo mimeticus.

Mimetic studies allows us to revisit an old quarrel from a present-oriented perspective by asking specific questions such as: what reasons or, perhaps, affects motivated this notorious ban at the dawn of western thought? And if Plato's critique of mimesis, as is routinely noted, was paradoxical and self-contradictory, for he fought mimesis with eminently mimetic genres (such as the Socratic dialogue), is there a way to put this ancient paradox to productive contemporary use? At some further removes, could Plato's diagnostic evaluation of mimesis as a patho(-)logy—that is as both sickness and a *logos* on mimetic *pathos*—continue to account for an increasingly digitized society that reloads illusory and spellbinding shadows allegorically projected at the back of a mythic cave in the hypermimetic space of the virtual constitutive of our increasingly digitized caves? These are some of the questions Plato's exclusion of homo mimeticus opens up at the dawn of philosophy and which continue to haunt, perhaps more than ever, our hypermimetic world as well. Hence the urgency to follow up on ancient phantoms reloaded via new media from the pluralist perspective of new mimetic studies.

There is, of course, no single, unitary, and universal answer to these ancient yet still contemporary questions. What our genealogy makes clear is that what the Greeks called, enigmatically, *mimēsis* can no longer be framed uniquely in a stabilizing metaphysical mirror or *imago* that reproduces the logic of the same—though the distinction between truth and lies remains urgent to make in the digital age in order to dispel illusory fables in second lives that may not be disconnected from Plato's idealist metaphysics. But let us start at the beginning.

First introduced in book 10 of the *Republic*, the doubling trope of the "mirror" in-*forms* (gives form to) a dominant idealist tradition oriented toward a vertical hierarchical axis that culminates in abstract, intelligible, and universal ideas posited "*behind* the world"—what Nietzsche, contra Plato, calls "*Hinterwelt*"

(1996a, 5). Pushing against this dominant metaphysical tradition, a genealogy of minor materialist thinkers is currently promoting a *re*-turn of attention to mimesis that helps account for the singular-plural power of affects to both incline subjects and take possession of the ego, from antiquity to modernity, reaching with increasing efficacy into the digital age as well—generating what Nietzsche, this time *with* Plato, calls a "phantom of their ego [*Phantom von Ego*]" (1982, 106).[2] That is, an ego that is immanent, embodied, relational, eminently suggestible, prone to unconscious spells, and easily bound, chained, or spellbound to visual simulations that may be epistemically illusory or false, yet due to a magnetic will to mime, have the power, or *pathos*, to generate material effects in this world as well.

Could it be, then, that it is because in both its phylogenetic and ontogenetic evolution, homo mimeticus is, from birth onward, radically open to mirroring forms of nonverbal communication in childhood that its relational, embodied, and porous ego, both individually and collectively, remains radically open to external influences in adulthood as well, be they real or fictional? This is the genealogical question that I will explore both *with* and *contra* Plato in this chapter. In the process, we shall see that the spell of shadows, be they ancient, modern, or contemporary, have the (will to) power, or *pathos*, to tilt the vertical metaphysics of mimesis framed as a visual phantom predicated on the logic of the same toward relational forms of affective and spellbinding communication that reveal the centrality of otherness in the formation of an ego that is not one—that is, a phantom ego.

## Inclining Mimesis

For this delicate genealogical operation, it is wise to join forces with philosophers who share our attention to mimetic pathos. Furthering a genealogical operation that ties the ancient concept of "mimesis" to the more contemporary concept of "inclinations," I step back to Plato's "Allegory of the Cave" in book 7 of the *Republic* in the company of the feminist philosopher, classicist, and political as well as literary theorist, Adriana Cavarero. My goal is to continue a dialogue on "mimetic inclinations" (Cavarero and Lawtoo 2021) that animate—for better and worse—spectacles that were once staged in oral, theatrical cultures and are now reloaded in digital, audiovisual cultures as well. Perhaps what was true of the shadows in Plato's cave is even truer of the shadows in our digitally connected caves: illusory simulations projected on black mirrors have the magnetizing power to retroact on bodies and souls assembled in the body politic offline, casting a spellbinding effect on the ego that dispossesses it of its proper identity, generating both good and bad inclinations.

Cavarero and I fundamentally agree that since at least classical antiquity, a dominant patriarchal philosophical tradition has tended to restrict, disavow, and project affective inclinations that deprive *Homo sapiens* of rational control over the ideal of the autonomous, rational, and self-sufficient ego onto subordinate, marginalized, and vulnerable "others." This projection of mimesis and all it entails (mimicry, mimetism, affective contagion, hypnosis, dispossession, etc.) onto racial and ethnic minorities is constitutive of what I call elsewhere mimetic racism; it equally applies to the mimetic sexism internal to stereotypically inclined figures who, in the West but not only, are expected to take on the full burden to care for those vulnerable others we all once were, who are the newborns of *Homo sapiens*: namely, mothers.

As Cavarero convincingly argues in *Inclinations* (2016), maternally inclined roles in patriarchal societies are traditionally restricted to women in general and mothers in particular who provide a different ethical posture to care for others. At the same time, we have also noted that different forms of alloparenting central to non-western cultures contribute to complicating this essentialist stereotype. In fact, as Sarah Blaffer Hrdy argues, they open up care to a plurality of inclinations that concerns "mothers and others" (2009), including fathers, uncles, and other caretakers as well. Still, despite the emancipatory progress of feminist movements since the 1960s, the stereotypical figure of maternal inclination is a posture, position, or disposition that continues to weigh heavily on women's shoulders—perhaps because this patriarchal burden is passed down mimetically to girls to reproduce and to boys qua future men to automatically expect, and thus demand or enforce. Moreover, this chain of reproductions is now mediated and amplified via a variety of simulacra (dolls, cartoons, films, YouTube videos, selfies, social media, video games, porn sites, etc.) with intergenerational performative effects that spread contagiously, from generation to generation, via increasingly ramified social networks online that increasingly penetrate the private sphere, generating both repetitions and differences that can congeal in stereotypical behavior offline.

It is well known that stereotypes tend to be reproduced. As the etymology already suggests, *stereos* (solid), *typos* (impression), they also generate solid impressions not only in the mind but also, as we shall see, on the plasticity of the subject that can be imprinted in psychic and bodily dispositions that assume a type as a model. The massive presence of stereotypical differences across cultures is living proof that *all* subjects, to different degrees and irrespectively of their nationality, language, ethnicity, gender, and other differences, are vulnerable to the pression of types. Consequently, it is crucial to pay attention to relational, affective, and embodied dispositions that, since time immemorial, incline not only mothers and women but *Homo sapiens* more generally toward others. This, at least, is true if we want to continue accounting for a relational model of subjectivity that is part of what Nietzsche already called a "net of communication" (1974, 298) that cast a spell on the ego, both individually and collectively. In fact, our genealogy attests to a generalized all-too-mimetic tendency that artists, poets, storytellers, and a tradition of philosopher-poets (Plato included) have long attributed to all humans—for both good and ill.

To schematize things somewhat, on the positive side, mimetic inclinations are at play whenever humans are part of plurality of unique, individual, perhaps even original voices that assemble in the streets to express democratic sentiments on social equality and justice constitutive of what Cavarero calls "surging democracy" (2021); on the negative side, depending on contexts, these assembled voices can also merge into phantom egos who join in a formless group of people traditionally called a mass or mob who can give collective (rather than individual) expression to antidemocratic, violent, and pathological insurrections offline we will discuss more at length in part 3 and are constitutive of what I call "(new) fascism" (2019).

Building on these Janus-faced perspectives, this chapter explores the heterogeneous affects internal to the immanent, relational, and magnetizing power that, for both good and ill, inclines the subject toward others. Such mimetic inclinations are at play in our private homes but also in public streets and increasingly in virtual spaces animated by digital simulacra that connect users online—part of a maddingly indeterminate patho(-)logical power that continues to find in mimetic *pathos* its primary inclining force. That is, a (will to) power endowed with *both* liberating, affective, and logically grounded aspirations to be in common, on the one hand, *and* a violent, imprisoning, and pathological potential to be dispossessed, on the other. Both sides, as we turn to see and feel, are internal to forms of contagious communication that continue to shift the focus of attention from the solipsistic and purely rational and self-contained individuality of *homo erectus* toward the relational, embodied, and affective disposition of homo mimeticus.

The powers of mimesis, then, cannot be reduced to the metaphysical logic of the same, if only because they generate differential effects depending on the pathos involved, the bodies at play, and the degrees of distance it allows. While in her more recent work, *Surging Democracy* (2021), Cavarero has tapped into the democratic potential of affective inclinations that culminate in a plurality of distinct voices constitutive of what Hannah Arendt calls the *vita activa* (Arendt 1998), like Arendt before her, Cavarero remains equally worried about the dangerous inclinations that lead a plurality of people to fuse in what a long tradition in crowd psychology calls a "mass" (*massa, Masse, foule*) (Cavarero 2021, 59–70). My wager is that from the liminal space between the *vita contemplativa* that, since Plato, orients philosophical thought (*logos*) toward abstract and universal ideas, on the one hand, and the *vita activa* characteristic of political action (*praxis*) based on the exposure of one's uniqueness to otherness, on the other, the patho(-)logical shadow of a *vita mimetica* driven by a destabilizing interplay of both *pathos* and *logos*, uniqueness and dispossession, and above all, attentive to the power of aesthetic shadows to form and transform both thoughts and actions, informs two radically antagonistic ways of being in common today: this agon confronts the pathology of fusion characteristic of masses under the spell of (new) fascist leaders, on one side, to its patho-*logical* counterpart that gives birth to the singularity of unique plural voices that animate surging democracy, on the other. Whether these two antagonistic concepts define opposite manifestations of the *vita mimetica*, or whether a destabilizing mirroring interplay could exist between mass and plurality (or both), is what this chapter sets out to explore.

Following our genealogical orientation, let us start by stepping back to that *locus classicus* of both philosophy and aesthetics that is Plato's "Allegory of the Cave"—in order to leap further ahead.

## Homo Mimeticus in Chains: From *Ion* to the Cave

As any minimally attentive reader of Plato soon realizes, despite the apparent brutality of the exclusion of the poets from the ideal city, his critique of mimesis in the *Republic* rests on a complex patho-*logical* operation in which his philosophical *logos* remains nonetheless deeply entangled in the mimetic *pathos* he critiques. In fact, "he" (Plato), never speaks in his proper name. Instead, he speaks under the mask of his dead teacher (Socrates) via a dramatic impersonation that informs his dialogues. This also means that "he" (Plato) relies on a first-person mimetic speech "they" (Plato-Socrates) condemn in theory but actually enact in practice. This paradox is indeed constitutive of what Nietzsche calls, oxymoronically, "the pathos of philosophy." To be sure, on the side of philosophy, Plato's dialogues generate original thoughts on science (*episteme*), the nature of the mind or awareness (*nous*), and a reason (*logos*) oriented toward intelligible forms or ideas (*eidos*) located in another world; at the same time, on the side of *pathos*, he also dramatizes mythic tales, characters, and exemplary heroes clearly intended to serve as affective models for imitation in this world. Philosophy may thus aspire to the contemplation of abstract ideas driven by a rational logos in theory, but as it is enacted in practice, it cannot shed the shadow of the pathos animating homo mimeticus—which includes, nolens volens, the philosopher's pathos.

Genealogical lenses urge us to take this aporia seriously. My goal, however, is not to deconstruct once again Plato's paradox, which has received enough attention so far.[3] Rather, it is to reconstruct the affective logic of Plato's patho-*logical* thought, which, as we shall see, both confirms and furthers the genealogy of homo mimeticus we have been uncovering so far. In fact, since the dawn of philosophy, Plato's critique of mimesis cannot be confined to epistemic concerns with visual representations or simulations far removed from an ideal, universal, and intelligible truth that finds in the vertical specularity of the mirror in book 10 of the *Republic* the paradigmatic trope. That is, a mirroring trope that sets up binary oppositions between origin/copy, model/shadow, universal/particular among other vertical hierarchies that led idealist philosophers to turn away from the world of sensible impressions in order to become "enraptured" by universal theoretical abstractions characteristic of the *vita contemplativa* (Arendt 1998, 303–304). Nor can mimesis be solely locked up, or rather, locked down, at the bottom of a metaphysical cave where shadows are continuously projected on a dark wall, preventing prisoners qua spectators under the spell of simulations to actively participate in civic plural actions of public appearance and exposure to others constitutive of the *vita activa* (14–17)—though it is clearly both, as Hannah Arendt, whose *anti*-mimetic categories I have been borrowing, convincingly shows in *The Human Condition* (1958).[4]

Mimesis is also, and perhaps above all, an affective, embodied, relational, and magnetizing force, power, or *pathos* that may not always be fully visible, for it operates on an imperceptible, unconscious register that can be oral and is difficult to theorize (from *theōrein*, to see, or look at). Yet mimesis literally animates the Platonic dialogues, generating both echoes and reflections that, like a magnetizing atmosphere, or hypnotizing bond, align mimesis, contagion, and the madness (*mania*)[5] it generates with both pathological and logical properties constitutive of the origins of philosophy. On both these patho(-)logical fronts, Plato relies on dialogues to develop a *dia-logos* within a mind vertically oriented toward the ideal abstractions of the philosopher's ontological fixation on the *vita contemplativa*. At the same time, he also consistently aligns mimesis with more relationally inclined figures like poets, rhapsodes, actors, or mimes, from which mimesis, as we recalled in the introduction, derives its conceptual identity (*mimēsis* from *mimos*, actor, and performance) and other practitioners of the *vita mimetica* attentive to the power of aesthetics to operate on the impressionable senses of homo mimeticus. Plato's Janus-faced perspective *with* and *contra* mimesis, then, stages a kind of double life out of which philosophy is born. At some removes, this double life might continue to inform contemporary mimetic studies as well.

Here is a Nietzschean question for idealist philosophers: who can seriously claim to have risen above the shadows of the contemporary avatars of mimesis—from film to TV, social media to the Internet—in order to contemplate the splendor of a "true world—attainable for the sage, the pious, the virtuous man" (Nietzsche 1954, 485) while leaving shadows behind locked down in mythic caves? If humans never relinquished mimetic spectacles in the past, it is highly improbable they did so during pandemic lockdowns in the present as I write. It is also increasingly unrealistic they will do so, as we sail deeper into a turbulent environmental world outside toward a future redoubled by idealized second lives inside our digital caves projecting a world behind this world. Hence the urgency to account for the ongoing relevance of Plato's untimely dialogues on the spellbinding powers of mimesis that, perhaps more than ever, chain homo mimeticus to all kinds of visual simulations.

To re-evaluate these powers from the joint perspective of both affect and reason, *pathos* and *logos*, constitutive of Plato's patho-*logy*, it is important to recall that the "Allegory of the Cave" is not the only myth in which Plato ties the affective powers of mimesis to the allegorical trope of an enigmatic "chain." In a minor but, for our genealogy, crucial dialogue titled *Ion*, Plato had already made clear that there is a subtle magnetic and highly contagious power at play in professionals of theatrical impersonation, or rhapsodes, who specialize in oral recitation. His target is a rhapsode named "Ion," who has just won a prize for his oral recitation of Homer. He did so not because of any artistic knowledge, or *tekhnê*, in general, Plato argues (under his Socratic mask), for Ion can recite well only Homer and cannot transfer his skills to other poets.[6] Rather, Ion's gift in impersonating different Homeric characters makes him what Plato calls (drawing on a Homeric analogy) a bit like "Proteus" who "twists and turns" (Plato 1961a, 541e), eluding the philosopher's grasp.

This protean power, Socrates presses on, tightening the grip on this chameleonlike character, stems from a divine inspiration or possession that renders Ion "enthusiastic," for he becomes *en-theos* when he recites, or in the god. As Plato puts it: "this gift you have of speaking well on Homer is not an art [*tekhnê*]; it is a power divine" that generates "enthusiasm" (533d) through which "it is the god himself who speaks" (534d). A character who does not speak in his proper name; someone who is skilled in agonistic contests; a reliance on Homeric myths; the use of mimetic speech…notice how, so far, these moves define Ion as much as Plato.

Still, Socrates does not register the aporia. Instead, to explain this confusion of identities, he convokes the trope of a magnet he borrows from Euripides: namely, a magnetic stone (or "Stone of Heraclea") that "does not simply attract the iron rings, just by themselves; it also imparts to the rings a force enabling them to do the same thing as the stone itself" (533d). Within this vertical concatenation of magnetically connected but still divided rings, then, Ion is framed as a "middle ring" in a "mighty chain" (536a) that goes from Apollo to the Muses, from Homer to the rhapsode, who in turn casts a magnetic spell that charms the audience in the theater, rendering them "enthusiastic" and "possessed" (534a) as well.

What, then, is this mysterious, magnetic, spellbinding, and highly contagious power? Informed voices have addressed this question before. In an admirable account of *Ion* that resonates in many ways with our genealogy of mimesis and informs Adriana Cavarero as well, Jean-Luc Nancy rightly notices that "magnetism is here the enigma" (Nancy 1982, 61).[7] Hence, he starts by taking the metaphor of magnetism literally as he notes: "the characteristic of magnetism […] is that is that it communicates its force" (61). This is a communicative force that reaches, through what Nancy calls a "sharing of voices [*partage des voix*]" (68) into the present. But then again, what force allows for such a *partage* (sharing/dividing) that is as much a sharing in the same flow of magnetic contagion as a division in uniquely separate rings—a *con*-division that might as well be animating the *vita mimetica* of relational, embodied, and affective subjects?

Cavarero, not unlike Nancy, but from a different perspective, has an attuned ear to register the sharing of voices at play in this long chain. In our dialogue, a shared concern with Ion's power of dispossession already implicitly informed our account of what we started to call "mimetic inclinations." That is, affective, embodied, and relational inclinations that find in a nonvisual, oral, and affective mimesis the force that opens up the ego to the other. For instance, joining forces to tilt mimesis from a purely visual model of representation or realism toward an embodied and relational *pathos* internal to homo mimeticus, Cavarero starts by recalling that poetry "charms [*incanta*]" (from *canto*, song) (Cavarero and

Lawtoo 2021, 185). She does so to give a specific oral dimension to the spell of poetry that is not simply read but, rather, as *Ion* also suggests, recited and sung, as rhapsodes and lyric poets launch into "harmony and rhythm" (534a). Speaking of the "Allegory of the Cave" but convoking the trope of magnetism at play in *Ion*, Cavarero also specifies that "there is a magnetic field of attraction/fascination" (185) that is perhaps invisible, imperceptible, and thus not suitable for contemplation or *theōria:* from *theōrein*, to look at.

And yet the powers of mimesis already incline, chain, and magnetize those poor prisoners "squatting" in the infamous cave. If the cave is indeed an allegory of the Greek city or *polis* still under the spell of what Eric Havelock in *Preface to Plato* (1963) influentially calls an "oral culture" in which poetry in general and dramatizations of Homer in particular served as an "encyclopedia" that educated the Greeks inducing an "oral state of mind," we may ask: how does this strange power or force of incantation operate, as it magnetizes the prisoners, both physically and psychically inclining them toward moving shadows that may be illusory, for sure, yet are endowed with an all-too-real binding pull?

If we follow the rings back to their magnetic source, this state of being enthusiastic originates in Apollo, the god of Music who presides over the Muses. Once mediated by that "winged thing" who is the poet and echoed by the rhapsodes who are "interpreters of the gods, each one possessed by the divinity to whom he is in bondage" (Plato 1961a, 534e), this state of Apollonian dispossession also flows down to the audience to generate a bondage that is mimetic in the sense that it is highly contagious, spreads from self to others, and generates an intoxication Euripides famously linked to Dionysus in *The Bacchae*. Thus, Plato specifies, always under the mask of Socrates, once in this state of "enthusiasm" (533d), the theatrical audience is not unlike the "worshiping Corybantes [who] are not in their senses when they dance," and "are seized with the Bacchic transport, and are possessed—as the bacchants" (534a). Although this divine genealogy is not frequently noted, there is a revealing magnetic, contagious, and dispossessing power, or force, that is shared between two gods—namely, Apollo and Dionysus—with a number of mediating rings in the middle. Important for us to note is that this contagious, and in this sense mimetic, power is not simply linked to visual representations; it also triggers a Dionysian form of intoxication that is commonly attributed to Nietzsche's youthful artistic metaphysics in *The Birth of Tragedy* but is already embryonic in Plato's metaphysical poetics at play in *Ion*.[8]

Now, Cavarero offers important steps to further this genealogical connection beyond Ion by taking us to the very allegory that provides a mythic origin, or womb, out of which a theory of homo mimeticus is already developing in embryo, waiting for a push to be born. In an inspiring essay titled "The Envied Muse," for instance, the feminist philosopher convincingly argues that the magnetic chain that ties the Muses to the rhapsode to the audience in *Ion* is not without a strange family resemblance to the famous chain in the Platonic cave. This leads Cavarero to perceptively suggest that the chained prisoners "allude to the Muses' enchanting power" (2002, 52), if only because those shadows explicitly allude to that crowd of simulators Plato groups under the rubric of *mimētēs*: primarily poets, actors, and rhapsodes.

On the shoulders of Nietzsche, I fundamentally agree. To put it in his (anti-)Platonic language, the mimetic power of visual Apollonian representations projected on a wall cannot be detached from the embodied *pathos* of Dionysian intoxication. This also means that, in the shift of perspective from the magnetic *pathos* at play in *Ion* to the visual *dispositif* that in-forms the "Allegory of the Cave" in *Republic*, there is an important difference in the binding powers of mimesis to be registered: if the epic poet par excellence Ion excels in reciting, namely Homer, enchants through the invisible medium of voice, meter, and rhythm, generating a state of enthusiastic dispossession Plato compares to the Dionysian Maenads when they dance, the "shadows cast from the fire on the wall of the cave that fronted them [the prisoners]" (514c) enchain visually, not orally, via what Cavarero calls "projection of visual tricks" (2002, 55), whereby "the bearers of simulacra [*eidola*]" turn the wall of the cave into "a projection screen" (48).[9]

This is a crucial point in our genealogical reframing of the affective powers of mimesis. The agon confronting Plato and Homer not only stages philosophy contra poetry, the power of intellectual abstraction contra the affective power of enchantment—though it does that; it is also redoubled by a second, less perceptible, but not less fundamental agon that opposes an oral mimetic culture against a visual mimetic culture. The *pathos* of oral mimesis contra the *logos* of visual mimesis; or, to put it in a Nietzschean language arguably inspired by this founding *agon*, the oral *pathos* of Dionysian intoxication contra the visual power of Apollonian representations. This is, in a nutshell, the genuine *mimetic agon* that both opposes and connects Plato to the Homeric culture he is up against.

## Mimetic Agonism and the Sharing of Voices

I call this agon *mimetic* because Plato not only violently opposes Homer but also admires him and thus copies him—the opposition being all the more radical to counter the magnetic power of attraction of his antagonistic model. If Plato's opposition to Homer is most visible and often noted, the mimetic continuities are loud and clear, at least to genealogists. Still, the agonistic mimetic logic, or patho-*logy*, that both opposes and connects them, is still little understood: Plato, in fact, like Homer before him, invents mythic characters, narrates allegories, speaks in mimetic rather than diegetic speech, stages heroes and models to imitate, generating in the process mirroring inversions that destabilize the clear-cut opposition between poetry and philosophy he appears to work hard to set up—with and against Homer and the poetic culture he represents. The agon is thus mimetic because Socrates, and at one remove, Plato "himself," as Jean-Luc Nancy also specified, "envies not so much the prize but the art of the rhapsode himself" (1982, 55)—a point that Cavarero shares with Nancy, as she speaks of Plato's "envy" for the power of the Muse that inspires this art or techne.

Envy is based on imitation, as Girard saw, but mimetic agonism should not be confused with mimetic rivalry. In the former, in fact, the opposed poetic figure (Homer) is not simply a model turned rival for a contested object of desire that leads to violence—though a scapegoating exclusion does ensue, at least in that utopian philosophical fiction that is the *Republic*. Rather, the antagonist is an admired model who generates a paradoxical form of imitation I call patho-*logical*, for the pathos of envy is not simply rivalrous or destructive but is put to creative, productive, and logical use. To borrow once again from Nietzsche's categories, this time from a youthful text titled "Homer's Contest" (1967), we could say that the mimetic agon, or Homeric *contest* Plato stages is not based on what Nietzsche calls, thinking of Hesiod, a "bad Eris [strife]," driven by sad, rivalrous passions like "resentment" (1996b, 3). Rather, it is reproductive, heroic, and creative, for it is mediated by a "good Eris" that incites the opponents to a "contest [*Wettkampf*]" that is heroic in its Olympic nature. Thus, Nietzsche specifies, that by a sort of positive contagion internal to the logic of the contest: "Every great Hellene passes on the torch of the contest; every great virtue sets afire new greatness" (4). This applies to a Greek culture under the spell of Olympic contests. It also applies to cultural contests at play in oral recitations, tragic/comic dramatizations, and philosophical contestations as well, as Nietzsche's colleague in Basel the historian Jacob Burckhardt also noted.[10]

In my interpretation of this mimetic agon, then, the torch is passed on, from generation to generation, via a paradoxical movement in which the opposed model provides both the conceptual and technical tools to promote a new discourse or *logos* that sets new greatness on fire—by pushing with and against the shoulders of influential predecessors already invested with the force of mimetic *pathos*. That *logos* born out of a mimetic agon with the pathos of poetry or myth is now known under the rubric of philosophy. As Jean-Pierre Vernant recognizes, myth means that "formulated speech" "belongs to the domain of *legein* [...] and does not originally stand in contrast to *logoi*" (1980, 187). On the contrary, we are arguing that myth makes the development of logos possible. And if philosophy is born out of a mythic womb, this also means that the paradoxical logic of mimetic agonism destabilizes the opposition between poetry and philosophy via the very concept (mimesis) that apparently sets up the all-too-visible opposition in the first place, yet in reality was channeling imperceptible continuities instead. Contrary to romantic models of originality based on an Oedipal anxiety of influence, then, the ancient but also modernist logic of mimetic agonism provides a productive starting point that continues to inform the sharing of voices animating mimetic studies as well.

Nancy comes to similar conclusions via his concept of sharing/dividing, or *partage*. In an evaluation of the enthusiastic poet who is "dispossessed" of "proper" qualities, Nancy speaks of a "*partage* of poetic and philosophical genres" (1982, 66) that are both divided and shared, shared-divided (*partagées*) precisely on the improper question of mimesis. This is indeed the *partage des voix* that obviously divides Ion and Socrates, the specialist of *pathos* and the technician of the *logos*. But, as Nancy also shows, this agonistic strife also implicitly connects the shared voices of the philosopher and the poet, Plato and Ion, Socrates and Homer. How? Via the mimetic agon that connects seemingly opposed figures—not unlike *Ion*'s chain con-divides different yet connected rings. If we now enter into the patho-*logical* flow of conjunctive-disjunction at play in *Ion*, we can say that this *partage* is generated by an improper figure like Ion who, Nancy specifies, "has nothing proper to its own [*rien en propre*]" (1982, 66). And paradoxically, precisely because of this "absence of proper capacity" or "*dépropriation*" (66), this (dis)possessed figure enters into an enthusiastic state of creative receptivity that is both passive and active, restricted to copying a model (Homer) and re-productive of a magnetic spell that generates (Dionysian) bonds. There is thus an implicit mimetic paradox at the heart of the sharing of voices that has so far gone unheard, and that our genealogy allows us to make audible.

This is the moment to register that the *partage des voix* Nancy theorizes at the level of his *logos* is redoubled by a shared mimetic experience that generates revealing echoes that resonate throughout the different chapters, or rings, of this book as well. In his hermeneutical practice, Nancy is in fact clearly echoing a voice with whom he has much more in common than is often realized. Who is this secret sharer Nancy is giving voice to? A colleague in Strasbourg where they both cotaught for their entire careers, a coauthor of numerous books, a philosopher-poet, and above all, an intimate friend, sharer of communities, as well as one of the most profound late twentieth-century thinkers of mimesis, this secret sharer is no one else than the French philosopher, literary theorist, and professor of aesthetics, Philippe Lacoue-Labarthe.[11]

As we shall see in more detail in chapter 4, Lacoue-Labarthe made an original interpretation of mimesis without proper models the throughline, or *fil conducteur*, of his entire career. His account of the "impropriety" of the mimetic subject, its plastic malleability, and radical openness to both restricted (or passive) mimesis that is internal to the "imitation of the moderns," and finds in Plato a key genealogical starting point, is clearly echoed in Nancy's interpretation of *Ion*. It is thus no accident that Nancy not only quotes Lacoue-Labarthe a few pages later (1982, 74, n. 52); he also leans on him to give mimetic specificity to his genealogy of shared mimetic voices. Nancy speaks, for instance, of "the singularly complex problematic of mimesis" (70) at play in the rhapsode, a complex mimetic disposition that puts Ion in a passive and receptive position in which he is not properly "himself," for he is dispossessed by a divine and magnetic power; and yet, paradoxically, this dispossession also puts this improper mime in a position to re-*produce* a "creative mimesis" characterized by what "he," Nancy, calls an affective "participation" or "*methexis*" (71).[12] Nancy even opens up the hypothesis that "mimesis could be the condition of this participation" (71) in the first place, thereby entangling mimesis and methexis in the sharing of voices he performs philosophically.[13]

This is a significant supplement to traditional conceptions of mimesis restricted to representation constitutive of *Homo sapiens* but no longer adequate to account for the side of humans that is also *demens*, *ridens*, and *ludens*. If, in his influential account of *Homo Ludens*, Johan Huizinga relied on classical scholars like Jane Harrison to claim that play is "*methectic* rather than *mimetic*" (2016, 15), a philological supplement from *Homo Mimeticus* could help clarify an opposition that is not one. Harrison herself, as a classicist, had in fact duly noted: "We translate mimesis by 'imitation,' [or representation] and we do very wrongly" (1913, 46). Recalling the genealogy from which we started, Harrison adds: "The word mimesis means the action or doing of a person called a *mime*" (47)—and what does a mime do if not rely on mimicry to elicit an affective identification, participation, or *methexis*? Homo mimeticus in its multiple dramatic manifestations, be they ordinary or extraordinary, serious or ludic, sympathetic or agonistic, logical or pathological is thus animated by the dynamic interplay of mimesis and methexis characteristic of a mime who may lack a proper identity yet can impersonate a plurality of roles.

It would be useless to deny it. There is, indeed, a mimetic phantom animating the paradoxical voice (passive/active, dispossessed/possessed, copying/creative, reproducing/producing, etc.) of that *mime de rien* who is Ion, which accounts for the paradox that directly concerns us as well: Ion's recitation of Homer is, in fact, both unique (he just won a prize in a Homeric contest), and he can control the emotions he triggers in spectators from a *distance*. Contradicting Socrates's thesis, Ion knows very well what he is doing, as he masters the *techne* of recitation via a patho-*logy* that makes him observe the audience's *pathos* from a critical distance. Ion observes:

> As I look down at them from the stage above, I see them, every time, weeping, casting terrible glances, stricken with amazement at the deeds recounted. In fact, I have to give them very close attention, for if I set them weeping, I myself shall laugh when I get my money, but if they laugh, it is I who have to weep at losing it. (Plato 1961a, 535d–e)

Socrates appears to dominate Ion, but at a closer hermeneutical look, the mimetic agon is more balanced than it appears to be. It is in fact clear that Ion balances the magnetism of pathos with the mastery of his techne of interpretation, or *hermeneia*, a techne Socrates tries to wrest from poetry to hand on, like a torch, to philosophy. This poetic *hermeneia* rests on a pathos of distance, entailing the reading of human faces from a distance that fail to trigger any mimetic responses in the rhapsode. Quite the contrary: the opposite pathos emerges. Thus, in a mirroring inversion, weeping triggers laughter, laughter triggers weeping. And yet, at the same time, Ion also admits to being possessed by a magnetic power that is not proper to him and dispossesses him of his proper being, generating a magnetizing *pathos* that conveys an enthusiastic intoxication in the audience.

Already for Plato, then, or perhaps especially for Plato, mimetic *pathos* and philosophical distance, but also orality and writing, the danger of fusion and the unique gift of inspiration, passive reproductive mimesis and active productive mimesis, may not be as stable a binary, as his idealist aspirations make it seem to be. As Nancy puts it in a chiastic mirroring phrase that sums up the paradox of shared voices at play in Ion and perhaps in "his" shared voice as well: "a philosophical rhapsody allows for a philosophy of rhapsody" (1982, 79). Who is the rhapsode, and who is the philosopher here? In the alternation of voices, it is indeed no longer clear who speaks. Still, this shared singular-plural voice has mimetic properties nonetheless.

In this mirror game interesting inversions begin to appear. The mimetic agon between philosophy and poetry is entangling the philosopher in the very pathos that he aims to exclude. Conversely, on the side of poetry, an affective, participatory, and paradoxical mimesis is revealed at play in the magnetic chains characterized by a "communicability and transitivity" that turns "passivity" into "activity" (Nancy 1982, 62) and vice versa. In this process of mimetic communication, a long chain of rings is formed that goes not only from the Muses to spectators but also connects, like a magnetic flow, distinct dialogues like *Ion* and *Republic*. Already for Plato, then, the chain is already shared.

So far, so good. But why does Plato insist in the "Allegory of the Cave" on foregrounding *visual* mimesis, given poetry's predominantly *oral* powers? If the magnetizing powers of Ion's chain are oral, why are the shadow's powers visual, since the same mimetic agon with and contra Homer animates both dialogues? Picking up this specific question from the point of view of the Muses' enchanting power, Cavarero has an interesting answer: she argues that Plato's speculative focus on a visual culture out of which philosophical speculation is born leads him to invent, as a counterchange, so to speak, visual "tricks and devices" intended to displace the oral power of Homeric poetry, now "replaced by an artificial harnessing of the gaze" (2002, 63).[14] Philosophy contra poetry, vision contra orality, mimesis contra mimesis: this is, in a nutshell, the mimetic agon animated by a Platonic good Eris with and contra Homer, which literally in-*forms* the Platonic dialogues. As Cavarero succinctly puts it, confirming Nancy: "Plato imitates the fascinating effects of the Muse because he envies her" (64). The father of philosophy is thus skilled in the poetic craft he denounces in his opponent, because, in the practice of mimetic agonism, the opponent to displace is also a model to imitate. Hence, in a mirroring overturning, Plato counters oral mimesis with visual mimesis, the magnetizing pathos of sound with the stabilizing image of the shadows, later stabilized by the speculative trope of the mirror. The mimetic agon is thus not simply reproductive but re-*productive*—if only because philosophy is born by mirroring, if not echoing, the song of the Muse.

This mirroring overturning of perspectives at the origins of philosophy fits in well with the spirit of our theory, whose goal is to go beyond simple oppositions between philosophy and literature in order to recuperate an oral, ritualistic, and embodied conception of mimesis. At the same time, the opposition between oral mimesis and visual mimesis might not be clear cut. Recall that, at the same time, and without contradiction, Plato is not only addressing a culture that is still dominated by Homeric recitations and practices of memorization that enchant orally; this culture is also under the spell of theatrical spectacles such as comedies and tragedies that rely on *both* orality *and* vision in order to spellbind what Plato calls "the nondescript mob assembled in the theater" (1963c, 604e). And what is a theater if not a *théatron*, a place for viewing (from *theáomai*, to see, to watch, to observe)? The agon between philosophy and poetry, then, technicians of *logos* and specialists of *pathos*, also stages *theōria* against *théatron*, and this mimetic agon is inscribed in the shared genre of the dialogue (from *dia* through and *legein* to speak) that both Platonic dia-*logues* and theatrical *dia*-logues have in common.

This is a point Philippe Lacoue-Labarthe, in a dialogue with Nancy that informs the latter's conception of shared voices, clearly hears, as he observes to his philosophical alter ego: Plato's "choice of the dialogue attests to a severe rivalry and *agôn* vis-à-vis tragedy" (Lacoue-Labarthe and Nancy 2013, 80; my trans.). The mimetic agon between philosophy and literature, in other words, is given voice by the mimetic lexis (*lexis mimētikē*), or the "mode of enunciation" (75) they have in common, or share (*partagent*).[15] This is not entirely unlike what Plato's whispers between the lines that animate his allegorical cave. After all, in his mimetic agon with Homer, he stages, via the mode of the dialogue, a sharing of voices that make fascinating shadows speak, generating a magnetic spell on the bound prisoners who both see and hear them from a visual distance.[16] Perhaps then, it is arguably this interplay of orality and vision, phonic *pathos* and visual *distance*, that is constitutive of the magnetizing power of those talking shadows—Homeric rhapsodes, but also actors and mimes—giving voice to a blind poet by impersonating roles at play in epic, but also tragic and comic spectacles.

Having listened carefully to the Muses and felt and seen their spellbinding powers at play, let us now return down to the cave with this double audiovisual mimetic hypothesis in our minds and ears attentive to the echo of the shadows "themselves."

## The Echo of the Shadows

On the double shoulders of Nancy's interpretation of the sharing of voices in *Ion* and furthering Cavarero's oral account of the "Allegory of the Cave" in the *Republic*, I propose a Janus-faced genealogy of both Apollonian (visual) and Dionysian (oral) mimesis, which should put us in a position to both see and hear the binding power of those enigmatic chains at the dawn of philosophy. The paradoxical logic of mimetic agonism attuned us to the fact that a mirroring interplay between oral and visual mimesis, the pathos of voice and the distance of the eye, activity and passivity, is jointly responsible for the powers that magnetize spectators in the Platonic cave in classical antiquity. At two removes, it equally in-*forms* a paradox of mimesis constitutive of the imitation of the moderns. At a third remove, so to speak, it might continue to cast a spell on homo mimeticus in the digital age as well.

It is in fact crucial to recognize that Plato—via his alter ego, Socrates—specifies that the projection screen in the cave is not based on the spell of visual simulacra alone. True, the specular shadows are the most visible phenomena in the cave and in-*form* the speculative metaphysics the allegory clearly alludes to: the shadows stand for the artistic reproductions of the sensible, phenomenal world, presumably represented by the material shapes simulators hold up in front of the fire—though this redoubling, as we shall see, lends itself to more than one interpretation of the *vita mimetica*. Shadows are thus far removed indeed from the intelligible, abstract, universal, but also blinding truth symbolized by the sun outside the cave, standing for the world of ideas in general and the idea of the Good in particular—what the philosopher aspires to via the dialectical ascent to a *vita contemplativa*. As Plato specifies in book 10 via the specular/speculative trope of the mirror, artistic shadows and the "imitators" that give form to them are "at three removes from nature" (1963c, 597e), by which he clearly means the intelligible nature of ideal Forms. Less perceptible to what Plato calls the "most sunlike of all the instruments of sense" (508b), namely vision, but audible nonetheless in the affective and communal sphere of myth, we should also register that a visual mimesis is both redoubled and amplified by an acoustic mimesis that resonates throughout the cave, generating not only a visual but also a sonic doubling effect. There is, in fact, an echo that supplements an auditive dimension to the projection mechanism that is not visible, and thus has tended to elude speculative theorists fixated on, or perhaps spellbound by, the *vita contemplativa*; and yet it is audible enough if one takes the trouble to interpret the myth. As we shall hear, this echo has wide-ranging theoretical implications for our genealogy of a *vita mimetica* open to the pathos of mythic fictions.

This echo's origin is illusory and, in this epistemic sense, false, for it appears to emerge as an original voice from the shadows themselves. Still, it is operative on the senses of homo mimeticus via Dionysian powers of the false that generate an affective bondage nonetheless. Originating from the voices of the carriers of simulacra at the back of the prisoners, the echo generates a confusing yet eminently effective redoubling that alters the visual shadows in front. The echo, not unlike in the myth of Narcissus, follows its illusory visual counterpart, or shadows, yet it has mimetic powers of its own: in fact, it radically amplifies the visual spellbinding powers of the shadows in the foreground by generating a simulation of *talking* shadows with confusing but also spellbinding effects. Thus, Socrates asks his interlocutor who, in yet another doubling, happens to be Glaucon, Plato's brother: "if their prison had and echo from the wall opposite them, when one of the passers-by uttered a sound, do you think that they would suppose anything else than the passing shadow to be the speaker?" (1963c, 7.515b) This is a rhetorical question if there ever was one. "By Zeus, I do not, said he" (515b), echoes Glaucon. The doubling trick is not specular and thus does not lend itself to univocal theoretical speculations. If it risks going unheard, and thus unthought, by unilateral speculative thinkers focused only on what they see, it deserves an attentive ear to capture its patho-*logical* implications for Janus-faced thinkers who both see and hear.

The echo of the shadows is both deviously deceptive and magnetically effective, for it operates on both the *logos* and the *pathos* at play in the *vita mimetica*. On the side of *logos*, the shadows' echo generates an epistemic confusion that leads the prisoners to mistake the identity of the speaker and attribute the voices behind their back to the illusory "shadows of artificial objects" (1963c, 515c) in front— an epistemic confusion that is de rigueur in metaphysical discussions of mimesis, is concerned with the unconcealment of truth, or truth as unconcealment qua *aletheia*, and has already received much attention among influential advocates of the *vita contemplativa*.[17] On the other, less-attended side of *pathos*, the echo also generates a troubling confusion of identity that has destabilizing and rather spellbinding powers on the embodied psyches of the prisoners living a *vita mimetica* through their senses—an affective confusion that was once central in ethico-political concerns with education or *paideia* in oral cultures and that, albeit via different media, continue resonate with digital cultures as well, with amplifying effects.

Thanks to the echo, in fact, the illusory shadows appear to speak. This is an epistemic illusion the philosopher unveils, of course. But my point is that this audiovisual illusion is powerful, affective, and spellbinding and generates a suspension of disbelief. Why? Because the shadows become *animated*, both in the ancient sense of being given a voice and thus a soul (*anima*), and in the modern sense of a visual animation. The echo of the shadows, in other words, urges us to overturn perspectives and change the orientation of the philosophical gaze by attending to the magnetizing field of the cave itself: if a dominant tendency in western philosophy privileged a visual mimesis to be theorized form a *distance* along a vertical and increasingly disembodied axis that leads outside the cave toward imaginary speculative *Hinterwelts* characteristic of the *vita contemplativa*, our driving *telos* is the opposite. Thus, we reenter the immanent audiovisual sphere of a *vita mimetica* under the magnetic spell of participation with animated shadows that need to be experienced with *pathos* with our audiovisual sensorium first, in order to subsequently re-evaluate the communal bondage they generate.

Despite the abstraction of the dialectical machinery, or rather because of it, the specular patho-*logical* illusion is easy enough to see, and thus to theorize. It generated the speculations that set up a vertical hierarchy subordinating art and sensible phenomena to an idealist and fabulous metaphysics based on binaries (truth/falsity, original/copy, reality/illusion, etc.) Plato inaugurated and, for over two millennia now, informed religious beliefs in a "true world" behind the world. This *Hinterwelt*, as Nietzsche provocatively noted at the twilight of metaphysics, turned out to be "unattainable, indemonstrable, unpromisable [...] At any rate, unattained. And being unattained, also *unknown*. Consequently, not consoling, redeeming, or obligating" (Nietzsche 1982, 485). There are ample reasons to abolish this fable, for the metaphysical shadows it casts are still with us in the digital age, as we shall see and feel. But if we listen carefully to the voice of *muthos*, the allegory also tells a different story that is not deprived of truth. This audiovisual *dispositif* is staged to make readers feel, via an interplay of Apollonian simulation and Dionysian contagion, the talking shadow's disconcerting magnetic power of attraction, a mimetic will to power that, I suggest, echoing and amplifying a long chain of minor voices in the philosophical tradition—from Nietzsche to Lacoue-Labarthe, Nancy to Cavarero—inclines the vertical ideal of *Homo erectus* toward the embodied, relational, and immanent reality of a homo mimeticus both possessed and dispossessed by fictional others.

If we now return one last time to the "Allegory of the Cave" via the double lens of our mimetic patho-logy attentive to both vision and orality, a fundamental re-evaluation is needed. This requires readers to engage with the art of interpretation, rumination, or *hermeneia*, for what we are reading is, after all, a myth. We can summarize its main insights in the *vita mimetica* as follows. The magnetizing powers of artistic representations are not purely visual nor solely oral but rest on a dynamic interplay of a mutually reinforcing audiovisual mimesis. Fictional characters staged in the theater animated via the middle rings of rhapsodes or actors impersonating epic or tragic/comic heroes, played on both a visual and an oral mimesis to magnetize and chain the audience to spell-*binding* spectacles.

How does the spectacle bind or chain the prisoners? Via a Janus-faced spell. Its phenomenology operates as follows: the mimetic pathos of such talking shadows, in Plato's diagnostic view, orients the audience's gaze in the dark to such talking and moving shapes; such a fixation narrows the field of vision, fixates it so to speak, preventing the spectators qua prisoners to look around. In the process, it generates a light hypnosis that dispossess the audience of its ability to think rationally while under such mesmerizing spell. And this spell is shared in a way that is double: all the prisoners are simultaneously tied to the same mesmerizing spectacle above, but also to each other horizontally; they feel the pathos of the animation directly, but they also sense that other spectators feel the same pathos. This double bond has self-reinforcing properties built in it that are hard to break loose from. In such a vertical/horizontal double bond amplified by a double visual/oral mimesis, the animation does not appear to be real. It *is* real. It operates on our sensorium and affects how we feel, how we act, and what we think. The magnetic spell of the double bonds is complete, and the chain is locked—welcome to the *vita mimetica*!

Having patiently reconstructed the audiovisual projection machine that animates the shadows in the cave, endowing them with a magnetic-hypnotic-contagious will to power, a last narratological supplement is still needed to come to grips with this contagious power of talking simulations. A mimetic narratology is in fact internal to the echo of the shadows, waiting for an interpretation to make it apparent. As Plato/Socrates had already specified in book 3 of the *Republic*, when the concept of *mimesis* was first introduced on the philosophical scene, what matters in questions of dramatic recitation or impersonation is not only *what* is said at the level of content (*logos*) but also *how* it is said at the level of enunciation (*lexis*). When Marshall McLuhan famously stated that "the medium is the message" (1964, 23), he was echoing an ancient lesson that needs to be reloaded for new mimetic studies as well.

The dialogue between Socrates and Adeimantus is worth relistening. It goes as follows: we are "done with the 'what' of speech and still ha[ve] to consider the 'how'" (1963c, 394c). Hence having considered "the topic of tales," Socrates picks up "that of diction [*lexis*] [...] so we shall have completely examined both the matter [*logos*] and the manner [*lexis*] of speech" (392c). Thus, Socrates sets out to distinguish between tales that proceed "either by pure narration [*haple diegesis*] or by narrative that is effected through imitation [*mimēsis*] or both" (392d). Adeimantus can follow the philosophical argument contra mimesis focused on the content or logos but has trouble following this fundamental formal distinction. Philosophers spellbound by metaphysical Forms might have the same problem. Still, Adeimantus deserves credit, for he starts by candidly admitting: "I don't understand what you mean by this" (392c). Hence, the philosopher-poet who, in his youth is said to have burned his poems but channeled his poetic drive, or will to mime, in the writing of philosophical dialogues, takes up, once again, the paradigmatic example of his nemesis, Homer—for not only the content of Plato's myths but also the form of his dialogues remain chained to his mimetic antagonist.

Plato's example is classical. The beginning of *The Iliad*, as every educated Greek would remember, relies on an interplay between mimetic and diegetic speech, or mixed style. Echoing the opening lines, Socrates makes the following narratological point: when it comes to mimetic speeches, for instance when the priest Chryses of Troy asks the Achaeans for the release of his daughter, the speaker (imagine a rhapsode like Ion) "tries as far as may be to make us feel that not Homer is the speaker but the priest" (393b). You might say that the rhapsode speaks with the voice of the priest, or better, impersonates or animates the old priest for the spectators to hear and see on the stage. In the context of Plato's poetics in book 3, which precedes and thus in-*forms* the "Allegory of the Cave" in book 7, then, we find once again a confirmation that spectators are tricked by a technically crafted mimetic *pathos* (affect) perhaps more than by the *logos* (content) of poetry. Socrates, in fact, specifies that contrary to diegetic speech (*diegesis*), in mimetic speech (*mimesis*) the rhapsodes or actor do not speak in their own proper voice but, rather, in the voice of another.

## Reanimating the *Vita Mimetica*

Do you hear the echo? Can you see the animation? This is also the narrative situation in the cave, where the shadows speak with the voice of others who animate them. A sharing of voices, we are now in a position to both hear and see, is not only problematic for epistemic reasons concerned with knowing who speaks as philosophers routinely assume.[18] Everyone knows by the fourth century BC, even the cavemen, that Homer is dead. This sharing is problematic above all for the affective power to give voice and body to the pathos of the priest Chryses. How? Not only by *what* the actor or mimos says but by *how* he says it. That is, by "likening oneself [via a mimetic *lexis*] to another in speech or bodily bearing" (1963c, 393c). Plato is insistent on the audiovisual power of this dramatic posture. There are indeed dramatic contagious effects on the audience that ultimately rest on the rhapsode's/actor's "imitation in voice and gesture" (397b)—or, if you prefer, orality and vision, echoes and shadows.

The electrifying power of mimetic speeches dramatized by actors that cast a magnetic spell on spectators is now revealed in its *patho*-logical implications, which, at the dawn of philosophy, are perhaps more psychological and pedagogical than epistemic and metaphysical. In fact, in book 3 Socrates had already specified that this impersonation onstage has the disconcerting magnetic power to generate spellbinding "imitations, [which] if continued from youth far into life, settle down into habits and second nature in the body, the speech, and the thought" (1963c, 395d). Among other things, it generates stereotypical impressions that cut deep in the delineation of homo mimeticus, in bodily positions, but also linguistic and above all mental dispositions, generating a pathos that cuts across the mimetic agon between philosophy and poetry. It is in fact Socrates who, in the end, confirms our genealogical suspicion that the simulators on theatrical stages the shadows in the cave obviously allude to are not only problematic because of the illusory nature of the educative content (*logos*) of their tales—though they remain that too; they are also, and perhaps above all, dangerous for the magnetizing feeling (*pathos*) of participation (*methexis*) generated by mimetic speeches and gestures at the level of poetic diction or form (*lexis*). In sum, what we hear from the shared voices internal to Plato's patho-*logy* of mimesis is a diagnostic indication that it is this audiovisual confusion of identity that is endowed with a magnetic-hypnotic-contagious *pathos* that spell-*binds* the audience qua prisoners in ways that deprives them of a proper identity and is constitutive of the *vita mimetica* in the immanent sphere of the cave qua polis.

While form and content cannot be dissociated, when it comes to mimesis, the how in the end might have more power than the what; the medium might be even more important than the message. And if this is obviously true for poetry, it might be equally true for philosophy as well. No wonder that Plato dramatizes dialogues to counter the power of the mimetic poetry he is up against. While a sacrificial exclusion from the ideal city might be a fictional solution at the end of the *Republic*, the scapegoating mechanism not only failed to work in theory; the narrative strategy of the opponent was also deftly assimilated by Plato in his dramatic practice and is constitutive of the birth of philosophy: out of the pathos of mimetic agonism.

At one remove, when it comes to the art of interpretation, our genealogy of the *vita mimetica* suggests that philosophical attention to *logos* alone is radically insufficient to get hold of that protean figure who is homo mimeticus. Even for the father of philosophy, or rather, especially for him, a techne of the logos must be doubled and redoubled by genealogical diagnostics attentive to the power of mimetic *pathos* in view of generating patho-*logies* that speak to the contemporary human condition and are constitutive of mimetic studies, old and new.

Since the dawn of philosophy, it was clear that *Homo sapiens*' fascination for mythic fictions not only created solid bonds of communal solidarity on which the life, identity, and unity of the polis rested for the better; they also generated spell-binding effects that took possession of *Homo sapiens*, dispossessing *homo mimeticus* of its individual identity and rendering it easy prey to the magnetizing powers of myth for the worse. In the end, Yuval Harari was right to stress that "myths, it transpired, *are* stronger than anyone could have imagined" (2011, 115), at least among mainstream social scientists in present times. Still, a genealogical perspective shows that ancient philosophers not only could imagine their strength; they also provided, between the lines, insights that account for this power or *pathos* in the first place, pointing to therapeutic patho-*logies* as well. Hence the importance of supplementing the history of *Home Sapiens* with a genealogy of *Homo Mimeticus*.

This Janus-faced insight at the dawn of aesthetic theory remains an untimely insight to take hold of by new generations. That humans continue to remain under the spellbinding effects of audiovisual simulations projected on a variety of black mirrors is clear enough.[19] A magnetic chain continues to generate phantoms in the egos too, that reach, via different and increasingly spellbinding media, from antiquity into modernity, animating the *vita mimetica* in the contemporary period. Perhaps never before has *Homo sapiens* been so constantly under the spell of magnetizing fictions that fixate our gaze, affect our thoughts, and orient our actions from the dark, mesmerizing and increasingly ubiquitous encaved space between the *vita activa* and the *vita contemplativa*. Whether a chain of thinkers that follow these shadows can help us put the pathos of philosophy to productive use to generate patho-*logies* that prove adequate to capturing the protean transformations of homo mimeticus in the present century is what our genealogy still needs to find out.

CHAPTER 3

# SAMENESS AND DIFFERENCE REPLAYED

> The shadow, the "genealogy,"
> and the empty spaces are Nietzsche's [paths].
>
> —Richard Macksey and Eugenio Donato,
> *The Structuralist Controversy*

The "Allegory of the Cave" continues to cast a long shadow on our *vita mimetica*, a hypermimetic life that, perhaps more than ever, informs, disinforms, and transforms daily practices in the digital age. And yet, before we look more closely into present pathologies, genealogical lenses urge us to take another step back to theoretical precursors of mimetic studies who rethought mimesis in past century and still need to be supplemented by a theory of homo mimeticus for the present century.

Although the Platonic dream of leaving the cave behind to contemplate the blinding light of the sun via a *vita contemplativa* still dominates traditional philosophical trends out of touch with the magnetizing sphere of pathos, the immanent foundations of mimetic studies remind us that a plurality of shadows continue to be cast on all-too-human lives nonetheless, including philosopher's lives. This is perhaps most visible at the very birth of a transdisciplinary type of philosophical discourse at the margins of institutional power that, starting in the 1960s, became paradoxically central in the Anglophone world and now, with a spatiotemporal deferral, returns to haunt the foundations of continental philosophy in Europe and around the world as well.

That the shadow of mimesis cannot be dissociated from the birth of what became known as "poststructuralism," "French theory," or more generally, "theory" can be traced back precisely in space and time. As the literary critic Richard Macksey put it to the distinguished French scholars who had crossed the Atlantic back in 1966 to participate in a transdisciplinary symposium held in the then newly founded Humanities Center at Johns Hopkins University and organized with the intention of introducing a new method of interpretation in the humanities known as "structuralism" in the United States: "There is no Symposium without its shadow" (1972, 319). With these ominous words, Macksey, in the company of the co-organizers Eugenio Donato and René Girard, drew the legendary Johns Hopkins symposium, The Languages of Criticism and the Sciences of Man, to a close. A lot of water has flowed under the bridge since this event shook the foundations of what the humanities are, or were supposed to be, back in 1966. And in the meantime, the human sciences, as well as the humanities centers that host them, have continued to move even farther to the margins of institutional power—thereby remaining truthful to the decentering trajectory that was already at play in that founding theoretical event that was the symposium.

And yet, the shadow of what became known as *The Structuralist Controversy* (1972), continues, to this day, to haunt, phantomlike, the heterogeneous world of theory, philosophy, and the arts, generating doubling effects that transgress the arbitrary walls that so often still divide the human sciences in an increasingly specialized, territorial, and precarious academic world. It is, I believe, this spirit of affirmative transgression, playful intellectual freedom, and rather tenacious resistance to power that, fifty years later, led me to join a plurality of scholars and return to that mythic liminal space which was then still called the Humanities Center, and where the theory of homo mimeticus originated in the first place.[1] I did so to retrace the moving contours of a shadow that—attempts of violent exclusions notwithstanding—continues to animate what we still call "the humanities," despite the awareness that the centrality of the human has long been decentered, destabilized, and deterritorialized by nonhuman forces we shall attend to as well.

Having been haunted by shadows, phantoms, and related figures for some time, I could not resist the temptation to outline, in broad and admittedly partial strokes, the silhouette of the shadow of the symposium by asking a double-faced question. At the most general level, and at the risk of schematizing the outline somewhat, this question could be formulated in the following, paradoxical terms: could it be that the 1966 Hopkins symposium was an event that cast a shadow so long on the present and future of the humanities because, in the space between spectacular presentations, it silently contributed to transforming our understanding of a concept that defined the languages of criticism since their beginning in classical antiquity: namely, *mimēsis*? And if this genealogical hypothesis is correct, which remains to be proved, what form, or perhaps movement, does this shadow trace in the contemporary moment? Answering these questions in light of our genealogy of the *vita mimetica* urges us to evaluate the powers of mimesis that, over two millennia later, re-*turn* to haunt not only philosophy but the humanities, opening up the transdisciplinary field of new mimetic studies.

How does mimesis haunt the present? Via shadows that continue to give theoretical substance to homo mimeticus and we shall have to trace to the end.

## The Mimetic Re-*Turn*

A shadow is a classical mimetic trope, but since its contours are, by definition, moving and destabilizing, we should be careful not to offer a unilateral answer at the outset that would fix, once and for all, mimesis in an immutable form. The shadow of the symposium was obviously not one but plural in its manifestations. It can thus not be framed in terms of a classical aesthetic conception of mimesis restricted to aesthetic realism and the representation of reality it entails—let alone as a degraded mirroring representation far removed from ideal Forms.

After all, Ferdinand de Saussure's insight into the arbitrariness of the linguistic sign that informed structuralism in its different disciplinary manifestations marked a radical break with a type of criticism confined to what Roland Barthes, in his contribution to the *Structuralist Controversy*, called "the totalitarian ideology of the referent" (1972b, 138) central to realism. Despite the controversy the symposium generated, the participants tended to agree at least on one point: namely, that what were then still called—in a patriarchal language soon to be decentered—the "sciences of man," could no longer rest on a stabilizing, homogeneous, and transparent rendering of mimesis understood as representation, copy, or mirror of reality that dominated the language of criticism from classical antiquity to, say, the nineteenth century. And yet, this does not mean that a minor conception of *mimesis*, already at play in heterogeneous, destabilizing, and shadowy manifestations, was not secretly replayed with significant differences. A genealogical concern with the *vita mimetica* was in fact already implicitly informing the participants' theoretical engagements with the human and social sciences, establishing different, perhaps more playful, certainly more unstable, protean, and transgressive models of mimetic criticism for the twilight of the twentieth century—now stretching to the dawn of the twenty-first century as well.

During the symposium, mimetic appearances were masked but manifold: from Roland Barthes's account of structuralist activity in terms of a "*homology*" (1972b, 136), predicated on what he called an "activity of *imitation*," or "*mimesis*" (1971, 1197), to Jacques Lacan's psychoanalytic conception of the subject as a "divided essence," which is the effect of a "repetition of [...] symbolic sameness" (1972, 192); from Georges Poulet's phenomenological account of "mimetic criticism" (1972, 65), attentive to what he calls a "possession of myself by another" (61), or, alternatively, "*mimesis*" (65), to Jean-Pierre Vernant's classical concerns with the "ambiguity of the pharmakos" (1972, 277) that centers on a dramatic actor, or *mimos*, from which *mimēsis* derives its conceptual identity; from Guy Rosolato's reframing of myth not as "representation, a sort of copy of the outside world" but, rather, as a "duplication" of "sender" and "addressee," *destinateur* and *destinataire* (1972, 202), to other supplementary doublings and redoublings that troubled the stability of an original and autonomous form or identity, introducing heterogeneous differences in place of homogeneous sameness, it would be possible to show that the problematic of *mimesis* did not only follow, shadowlike, most of the presentations; it also preceded them, informing and transforming the different and still original challenges to the metaphysical "*status of the subject*," which, as Macksey recognized, was a "recurrent preoccupation" during the symposium (Macksey, Girard, and Hyppolite 1972, 319–320).

The shadow of mimesis looms large on the decentering of the subject at play in *The Structuralist Controversy* in general and what become known as poststructuralism in particular. But given my genealogical focus, I would like to retrace its emergence from a specific perspective partially in line with the phantom of homo mimeticus that, as we saw and heard in preceding chapters, is currently returning to reanimate the contemporary theoretical scene, albeit under different masks and conceptual personae. After stepping back to the origins of consciousness and language with Nietzsche and then re-evaluating the dawn of philosophy with Plato, read along with Nancy and Cavarero, I will now take my cue from two participants who, in many ways, were located at the structural antipodes of the controversy and occupied opposed, agonistic, perhaps even rivalrous theoretical positions. They provide, in fact, the Scylla of sameness and the Charybdis of difference my theory of homo mimeticus pushes against—to gather speed to sail toward future-oriented destinations. The names of these precursors, you will have guessed, are René Girard and Jacques Derrida.

## Enemy Brothers

At first sight, the differences between these two French thinkers far outplay the similarities. Starting from their respective contributions, "Tiresias and the Critic," that prefaced the symposium, and "Structure, Sign, and Play in the Discourse of the Human Sciences" that marked its culmination and launched deconstruction on to the international scene, Girard and Derrida not only consistently promoted opposed languages for criticism; they also developed radically divergent methods of interpretation that split their respective theories in competing, antagonistic, and seemingly incommensurable sides: if mimetic theory centers human subjectivity in general and desire in particular within a triangular structure Girard will defend to the end, deconstruction decenters the all-too-human desire for such structures from the beginning; if Girard believes in violent sacrificial referents that always rest on a metaphysics of presence, Derrida sets in motion the play of signifiers that are already absent, thereby unmasking presence as a metaphysical illusion; Girard is looking back to the origins of culture, Derrida looks ahead to the forward movement of the trace; the former is a theological literary critic with philosophical reach, the latter is an atheological philosopher with a literary sensibility. In short, as the slogan goes, mimetic theory focuses on imitation and sameness; deconstruction, the counterslogan echoes, is attentive to writing and difference.

Either way, the opposition could not be more clear-cut. It opens up a binary that, to this day, tends to generate antagonisms that continue to latently structure debates on the relation between mimesis, language, and culture. And yet one of the major lessons of the symposium was that, as always with such oppositions, a closer diagnostic look reveals that underneath the first layer of straightforward discontinuity, underlying continuities begin to appear, shadow-like, from the interstices of competing theoretical positions. Rather than dismissing such appearances as an illusion, I would like to replay these competing accounts of sameness and difference in slow motion, as one replays scenes from two radically different but equally classic movies of the same period. My goal is to see and feel, from the shadows reflected on the screen, if two traditionally opposed conceptions of mimesis can paradoxically be used to supplement one another in view of furthering new mimetic studies in the twenty-first century.[2]

I suggest that looking back, genealogically, to both Girard's and Derrida's contributions to the symposium and related texts of that period reveals that these opposed figures are theoretical doppelgangers, perhaps even "rival brothers"

(McKenna 1992, 12), whose agonistic stance reveals important continuities characteristic of mimetic agonism. If these precursors find in a Janus-faced conception of mimesis an original starting point for their critical and theoretical languages for the human sciences that was influential for the (post)structuralist turn informing French Theory in the 1960s and 1970s, I argue that they still provide genealogical steps to further the mimetic *re*-turn half a century later in the 2010s and 2020s. My wager is that once provisionally joined via a genealogical operation that is attentive to what Nietzsche calls "a knowledge of the conditions and circumstances of their [values but also theories] growth, development and displacement" (1996a, 8), Girard's and Derrida's mimetic reflections generate a series of destabilizing redoublings that not only provisionally bridge the gap that divides their critical languages; they also pave the way for double-faced diagnostics of the all-too-human tendency to imitate relevant for our contemporary, hypermimetic times.

From the empty spaces in between sameness and difference, then, we shall see that a humanities center once opened up transdisciplinary perspectives that now tend to be disseminated at the margins of an increasingly specialized academic world. And yet contemporary problematics that tend to spill over disciplinary boundaries—from the rise of conspiracy theories to (new) fascism, brain plasticity to cultural adaptations, gender and racial oppression to the need for nonhuman sympathy in the age of the Anthropocene, among other perspectives explored in this book—cast a shadow on the contemporary human and social sciences, projecting the silhouette of a constantly changing figure of homo mimeticus each generation of critics and theorists must retrace for their own times. But let us start our genealogy with a double conception of criticism first.

## Mimetic Criticism: Two Interpretations of Interpretation

Unlike many of his generation, René Girard never shared a preoccupation with the linguistic sign as such. He was more interested in the referential reality of mimetic desire and the violence it generated than in arbitrary relations between signifiers and signifieds. Yet, already at the time of the symposium, which he co-organized with Richard Macksey and Eugenio Donato, Girard's theoretical foundations were clearly grounded in synchronic and diachronic presuppositions he directly inherited from structuralism.[3]

Starting with his contribution to the structuralist controversy titled "Tiresias and the Critic," Girard, in fact, frames his account of the subject within a triangular conception of mimetic desire, which, as his title makes clear, finds in Sophocles's *Oedipus Rex* a synchronic, universal, or, as he puts it, "coherent structure" or "*structural model*" (1972, 19, 20). As he explains: "What Oedipus needs, is to do away with both his *Self* and his *Other*—equally imaginary, at least in part—through an abandonment of their sterilizing interplay in the constantly reforming structure of his relationships" (17). Imaginary oppositions, sterilizing interplay, structure of relations: the critical language Girard mobilizes clearly bears the traces of structuralist influences but also introduces a hierarchy that orients his own theoretical priorities. His driving *telos* in reading *Oedipus Rex* and other canonical western texts—from Greek tragedies to romantic novels, from Shakespeare to the Bible—that tend to be structured in triangular relations is precisely *not* to follow the interplay of constantly reforming structures of relationships between self and others. Rather, it is to stabilize their structural movement by dispelling the *méconaissance* of seemingly opposed figures and recognizing that the desire of the other is already internal to the desire of the self. This is, in a nutshell, Girard's theoretical starting point.

The continuity between self and other is already implicit in the title of Girard's first book, *Mensonge romantique et vérité romanesque* (1961), which in the English translation bears the revealing subtitle: "Self and Other in Literary Structure." In Girard's interpretation, both self and other, be they fictional or real, are entangled in the same imaginary structure of mimetic relations whose interplay they do not control but controls them instead, their desires in particular. Self-knowledge, for Girard, must thus begin by dispelling this imaginary difference in order to recognize the underlying sameness at play in the mimetic desire that structurally ties the self to the other in the first place. Girard's structural model is well known and can be summarized as follows: at the origins of human desire we find nothing original, nothing proper, but mimesis instead. This also means that desire does not originate in the self but is centered in the other; not any other but an admired other, a hero, model, or mediator who directs the subject's desire toward the object the model desires—and voilà, a structure has already taken form: that is, a triangular form that frames the subject, the model, and the object, often a woman, in a relation of mimetic rivalry that leads to violence and sameness rather than play and difference. It is thus with this structure in mind that, in "Tiresias and the Critic," Girard sets out to "attract," as he says, "Oedipus's attention to the ambiguous signs from which this structure may finally reveal its outline" (1972, 17). His goal in outlining this triangular structure is to "unmask" what he calls the "false assumption of absolute autonomy" (17) characteristic of heroes of western knowledge who, like Oedipus, do not see the shadow the model casts on their egos.

This advice applies, first of all, to the mythic hero within the text that provides the Oedipal content for interpretation, but formal attention to Girard's critical language indicates that a doubling rhetorical operation is already at play, reaching outside the text as well. "Tiresias and the Critic," in fact, is also mimetic in the sense that it draws inspiration from the play the critic is commenting on, redoubling its formal address: it is parabolic in form, prophetic in tone, and, as the title suggests, exploits the metaphorical potential of the Oedipus myth to introduce implicit performative continuities between mythic characters inside the text and the critics he addresses outside the text.

Remember the context. Girard presented its first version as a paper at the 1966 Hopkins symposium, so his talk about the self was addressed to referential others listening to his talk in view of generating mirroring effects: if Tiresias is in a position of a seer who warns Oedipus of his hubris within the text, the mimetic critic might be tempted to redouble the warning for his listeners *hors-texte*. Tiresias's advice to Oedipus, whom Girard considers the "the first Western hero of Knowledge" (1972, 17) is thus Janus-faced, for it is also a prophetic advice Girard, impersonating "the critic," implicitly addresses over two millennia later, to those heroes of western knowledge present at the symposium. From a position twice removed from this mythic scene, then, we can already see that this doubling shadow in Girard's intervention crosses the line between self and other, but also fiction and reality, mythic knowledge and scientific knowledge, tragic heroes of the past and theoretical heroes of the present—a point that Girard confirms, as he sees in Tiresias nothing less than a "striking symbol of the changes that have occurred in our disciplines" (18)—changes, we should add, that are still ongoing today.

This mythic parable, then, makes us wonder: does the dramatic interplay between Oedipus and Tiresias generate effects of self-recognition among the distinguished audience present at the symposium? Put differently, does the outline in "Tiresias and the Critic" set up a mirror that might dispel the *méconnaissance* of the opposition between self and others for contemporary heroes of western knowledge, including, perhaps, Girard's own knowledge of mimesis?

There are a number of clues that point in this direction. As the choice of the case of Oedipus indicates, the emphasis on desire and imaginary *méconnaissance* suggests, and the identification of Freud as someone who "saw infinitely more in Oedipus than all Rationalists combined, beginning with Aristotle" (Girard

1972, 19) confirms, Girard is delineating a triangular structure he inherits directly form psychoanalysis, both in its classical and linguistic formulations. As I have argued in more detail elsewhere, psychoanalysis is a "science of man" Girard seeks to overturn by positing the primacy of mimesis (or identification) over desire (or object cathexis).[4] This overturning is not without theoretical purchase. It explains, for instance, why the subject's relation to the model becomes "ambivalent": if mimesis orients desire and thus the subject desires the same object that the model desires, the triangular structure *oblige*, a mimetic rivalry with the model/opponent over the contested object—which can be a person, but also a symbolic position, one of fame or prestige, including academic prestige, for instance—is likely to ensue, which does not mean that alternatives relations between self and others are not possible, as we shall see. Crucial to retain for the moment is that on the shoulders of Freud, Girard infers this structure from the classical case of Sophocles's *Oedipus Rex*. And repeatedly in his career, he confirms the supposed veracity of this structure via interpretations of other Greek tragedies, but also Shakespeare's plays, romantic novels, as well as religious rituals and myths, which turn around what Girard calls the "stationary axle [*l'axe immobile*]" (1965, 307) that stabilizes the so-called "sterilizing interplay in the constant reforming structure of relationships" (1972, 17). A stable axle, or center, is thus provided that stabilizes the destabilizing interplay of mirroring relations.

This is a condensed account of a wide-ranging theory, but it already reveals how deep the *différend* with Jacques Derrida goes. As is well known, Derrida's theoretical operation is not only opposed to Girard's; it also implicitly challenges the metaphysical foundations, or center, on which his mimetic theory rests. Writing contra structuralism in general and Lévi-Strauss in particular, Derrida, in fact, dislocates precisely such an immobile axle on which coherent structural models that traverse the entire history of western metaphysics rest—from Plato to Rousseau, Saussure to Lévi-Strauss, informing Girard's mimetic desire as well. Derrida's outline of two models of interpretation at the end of "Structure, Sign and Play" brings this theoretical difference into sharp focus. It is worth quoting in full, for it has significant implications for that critical practice par excellence, which is interpretation. As Derrida puts it:

> There are thus two interpretations of interpretation, of structure, of sign, of freeplay [*jeu*]. The one seeks to decipher, dreams of deciphering, a truth or an origin which is free from freeplay and from the order of the sign, and lives like an exile the necessity of interpretation. The other, which is no longer turned toward the origin, affirms freeplay

and tries to pass beyond man and humanism, the name man being the name of that being who, throughout the history of metaphysics or of ontotheology […] has dreamed of full presence, the reassuring foundation, the origin and the end of the game [*fin du jeu*]. (Derrida 1972, 264–265)

The driving *telos* of these agonistic interpretative activities staged at the symposium could not be more clearly opposed. On the one hand, Girard, not unlike Lévi-Strauss, focuses on structural homologies (or mimesis) and dreams as an exile of interpreting a foundational truth located at the center (or origin) of relations to stabilize the subject in a structure (or form) deprived of play. On the other hand, Derrida focuses on the heterogeneous movement of writing traced by the freeplay of signifiers on a linguistic chain that sees no end to the game and destabilizes a belief in origins, presence, and centers altogether. As Derrida anticipates in his opening paragraph, the structural method takes the form of a "*rupture*" (247). Yet, he immediately adds, playing with a mimetic trope, that it also paves the way for a "*redoubling*" (247). A mimetic rupture thus redoubles with a difference that deconstructs, or decenters, a western metaphysics characterized by logocentrism, phonocentrism, and ethnocentrism, all of which are structured around a center or a stabilizing axle—including, of course, Girard's axle.

Why, then, attempt to bridge these antagonistic methods of interpretation? Because, as the mimetic redoubling on the side of both deconstructive ruptures and structuralist axles suggests, mimesis is a protean concept that flows, like a river, in between opposed theoretical banks. And as we look down from this bridge that we are attempting to—build sounds too stable; I should rather say—*bricoler*, we might catch a glimpse of a fluttering shadow appearing and disappearing on a moving surface. This shadow is obviously not simply realistic, for a river is not a mirror and reflects no stable *imago*. Yet it generates illuminating inversions of perspectives that are not deprived of patho(-)logical moments of self-recognition. Whether they reach into the present and anticipate future reflections on homo mimeticus is what we turn to find out by considering how a *pharmakon* turned into a *pharmakos*—or perhaps the other way round.

## Mirroring Patho(-)Logies: How a *Pharmakon* Became a *Pharmakos*

Derrida's playful association between the structuralist rupture and the redoubling at play in deconstruction was, of course, not accidental. Writing, as a concept, is already inscribed in the doubling structure of mimesis, if only because from Plato to Rousseau, Saussure to Lévi-Strauss, Derrida reminds us, time and again, that western metaphysics has conceived of writing as a copy, simulacrum, or shadow of speech.

Already in *De la grammatologie*, first published in 1967, and thus already completed at the time of the 1966 symposium, Derrida shows that this logocentric bias informs Lévi-Strauss's account of the "Leçon d'écriture" among the Nambikwara he famously narrates in his founding anthropological memoir *Tristes tropiques* (1955). According to the anthropologist, this scene of origins reveals that writing and imitation are clearly intertwined in the sense that the Nambikwara of Brazil who started to trace "undulating lines" on the sheets of paper they were given, Lévi-Strauss tells us, were simply "imitating" (qtd. in Derrida 1967, 180; my trans.), or of you prefer, shadowing his own anthropological use of notebooks. As Derrida comments, the chief who senses the power of writing, in Lévi-Strauss's narrative or myth of origins, "mimes writing [*mime l'écrire*] rather than understanding its linguistic function" (178). At the "origins" of this mythic scene, then, is what Derrida calls, in a redoubling linguistic play, an "*imitation* of writing" (185). Imitation or mime has here all the negative connotations of a false, illusory, and debased copy or shadow inherited from western metaphysics we have seen at play since Plato relegated it to a dark cave in the *Republic* and degraded writing to a mere a copy of speech in *Phaedrus*. But it is not only that. In fact, in Derrida's interpretation of interpretation, this writerly imitation of yet another imitation sets in motion the destabilizing interplay of doubling and redoubling that makes the search for stabilizing mythic origins vain in the first place.

Mimesis, for Derrida, is thus both a metaphysical concept to deconstruct and, at the same time, and without contradiction, the very doubling concept without proper identity that allows him to carry out his deconstructive operation. Hence, in a section *Of Grammatology* titled "Imitation" devoted to Rousseau's "Essay sur l'origine des langues," Derrida specifies that "imitation cannot be evaluated via a simple act" (1967, 290), for it "redoubles presence, it adds to it by supplementing it [*l'imitation redouble la présence, s'y ajoute en la suppléant*]" (289). In 1967 this was a groundbreaking move that did much to set the mimetic turn in motion and would shape the practice of interpretation for decades to come, which also means that by now the move is familiar.

This improper imitation or mimesis is, of course, mirroring the doubling structure of that "dangerous supplement" that both adds to and replaces speech: namely, writing—*écriture*. Hence this time in "Plato's Pharmacy," published in 1968, which is an admirable deconstruction of Plato's relegation of writing to the secondary status of a shadow of speech in *Phaedrus*, Derrida echoes, in a reproduction of the phonocentric metaphysical view he critiques, that "writing can only mime" (1981b, 107), for it has no essence, no stable identity, no origins that are proper to itself. A view subsequently redoubled in the "The Double Session," this time via a reading of Stéphane Mallarmé's short prose poem "Mimique," in the claim that "writing *in general* is interpreted as an imitation, a duplicate of the living voice or present *logos*" (Derrida 1981a, 185),[5] and so on in a series of admirable readings. The chain of Derrida's texts establishing an explicit genealogical link that ties writing to phantoms, not only to critique logocentrism but also to affirmatively inscribe mimesis in the doubling logic of the "supplement," the "*pharmakon*," the "trace," "iteration," and related double-faced deconstructive concepts are numerous, canonical, and there is little need to insist on the destabilizing theoretical flow this chain of conceptual signifiers generated in the last decades of the past century.

What still needs to be fully bridged in the present century is the mirroring interplay Girard and Derrida implicitly generated on seemingly opposed, yet no less imitative interpretative sides. For there is a mimetic agon that both opposes and connects these two precursors of mimetic studies in productive ways that still need to be traced to further a new theory of homo mimeticus. To return to the shadow reflected in the river under the genealogical bridge I am in the process of *bricoler*, we could notice that not unlike desire for Girard, writing for Derrida has no "essence," nothing "proper" to itself, for it is always already doubled by mimesis. As Andrew McKenna perceptively argued, Girard's anthropological theory of mimetic desire is "inextricably bound up with the questions Derrida poses to philosophy in terms of what is proper and improper to language" (McKenna 1992, 4).[6] My genealogical approach agrees with McKenna's re-evaluation of Derrida and Girard as "'*frères ennemis*'" (12), an enmity I consider constitutive of the *mimetic agonism* that gives birth to new theories more generally, old and new.

Where our interpretations differ without necessarily being antagonistic is on the question of method as well as in our respective theoretical goal or *telos* that orients them. At the level of method, my aim is to provide a genealogical account of the *movement of emergence* or development of these two mirroring and competing theories in order to test both their strengths and limits, using them to supplement each other. At the level of *telos*, from the space in between that both divides and unites these competing theories of interpretation, I aim to open up a new theory of mimesis to continue giving philosophical substance to a mimetic turn. This re-*turn* is informed by both Girard and Derrida's theories, but, as the preceding chapters already made clear, is not restricted to French (post) structuralism. On the contrary, an affective, embodied, and intersubjective conception of homo mimeticus goes beyond linguistic principles by engaging with more recent developments in feminism, political theory, new materialism, film and media studies, and the neurosciences, all of which are now informing new mimetic studies.

If we turn to supplement both Girard and Derrida from a genealogical perspective attentive to the "growth, development and displacement" (Nietzsche 1996a, 8) of theories, we should specify that *both* mimetic desire *and* mimetic writing are not only tied to violence in general but also to a rivalrous violence directed against the figure of the father in particular. The patriarchal shadow of the father looms large on both theories of interpretation. We already noted how Girard's theory is structured on a mimetic confrontation between self and other, involving a rivalry between fathers and sons modeled on triangular mythic structures that harken back to *Oedipus Rex*. What we must add is that Derrida's deconstruction of logocentric metaphysical binaries is equally rooted in a familial scene. For instance, in a section of "Plato's Pharmacy," subtitled "Family Scene," Derrida writes: "the father's death opens the reign of violence. In choosing violence—and that is what it's all about from the beginning—and violence against the father, the son—or patricidal writing—cannot fail to expose himself, too" (Derrida 1981b, 146). Family triangles, rivalries, and patricidal drives: genealogical lenses are beginning to reveal important mirroring symmetries between Girard's interpretation of desire and Derrida's interpretation of writing. To be fair, we should therefore ask a symmetrical question we already asked Girard: is this theoretical claim about father and sons based on an Oedipal myth?

At first sight this seems to be the case, but the mirroring reflection is not as neat. Derrida, in fact, specifies that "the discourse we are holding here is not in a strict sense a psychoanalytical one" (1981b, 131). And in a decisive moment in his "genealogy of writing" (75) in "Plato's Pharmacy," which does not rest on the Greek myth of Oedipus as framed by Freud, but on the Egyptian myth of Thoth as dramatized by Plato in *Phaedrus*, Derrida continues: "In distinguishing himself from his opposite, Thoth also imitates it, becomes its sign and representative, obeys it and *conforms* to it, replaces it, by violence if need be" (93).

Underneath violent oppositions, then, often lurks the shadow of imitation. And yet this shadow does not simply reproduce sameness but produces differential genealogical reflections instead.

In this mythic interplay of family scenes concerned with fathers and sons, the shadow-line between self and other is blurred, and it is no longer clear *who*, exactly, is the subject of imitation. Let us thus apply the same distinction between inside and outside we started with, which, of course is not as watertight as it sounds. Inside the text this subject is a mythic figure, to be sure: Thoth for Derrida, not unlike Oedipus for Girard, stands as a hero of western knowledge of mimetic practices, be they linked to writing or desire, on which their theoretical *logos* rests. But to redouble our mirroring question *hors-texte*, and involve the pathos of philosophy in our discussion, we should also ask a second, more destabilizing and troubling question: namely, does this paradoxical movement of opposition between mythic fathers and sons such as Oedipus and Laius, Toth and Thamus, cast a formative shadow on the symposium in general and on new heroes of western knowledge such as Girard and Derrida in particular?

Let us continue to outline the moving patho-logical contours of this shadow reflected on the moving surface of the river of mimesis. In Plato's retelling of the Egyptian myth of Thoth in *Phaedrus*, who is at the origins of theories of writing, not unlike in Sophocles's dramatization of the Oedipus myth in *Oedipus Rex* at the origins of Oedipal theories, the mimetic subject (Thoth, Oedipus) needs to be violently excluded from the city in order to have pharmacological effects. Thus, in "Plato's Pharmacy," Derrida asks a question that was certainly not lost on Girard: namely, "how can this supplementary parasite be excluded by maintaining the boundary, or, let us say, the triangle?" (1981b, 102). Derrida's answer, he continues—and keep in mind that we are in 1968, that is, two years after the symposium but also four years before the appearance of *Violence and the Sacred* (1972), the book in which Girard first formulates the theory of the scapegoat—should sound familiar to mimetic theorists: via a ritual expulsion of a *pharmakos* or scapegoat. Thus, he, Derrida, writes:

> The character of the *pharmakos* has been compared to a scapegoat [*bouc émissaire*]. The *evil* and the *outside*, the expulsion of the evil, its exclusion out of the body (and out) of the city—these are the two major senses of the character and of the ritual. (1981b, 130)

Mimesis, triangles, violence between fathers and sons, and now ritual expulsions of scapegoats as well. That is, the theory he, Girard, is most known for, begins to appear, like a fluttering reflection in the genealogical mirror confronting two mimetic antagonists.

The symmetries, we can now see from our precarious bridge, have been doubling and redoubling, troubling the distinction between mythic heroes within the text and heroes of knowledge outside. So, it should be legitimate to ask: are these simple linguistic coincidences? The arbitrary product of the play of signifiers? Or, more probably, do these doubling effects bear genealogical traces of the emergence of two opposed, yet intimately entangled methods of interpretation?

Before pursuing this *bricolage* over this precarious and thus perilous bridge, a methodological warning is in order. It is certainly not my intention to deconstruct a binary opposition between two methods of reading on the basis of a pharmacology, which, as Derrida was the first to know, has never been stable—no exercise was more widespread for some time and further reproductions are not necessary for our genealogy; nor is it my ambition to establish a unilateral, patrilinear genealogy between fathers and sons, mimetic origins and differential copies—for it is precisely the unitary figure of a single, unitary origin, or father, the threefold genealogies at play aim to erase. Rather, I am gesturing toward what Derrida calls "an obscure economy," which, he says at the end of "Structure Sign and Play," momentarily "reconciles" (1972, 265) without necessarily sublating in a dialectical move what he had previously called two opposed critical activities. And I do so by taking my clue from an untimely observation Derrida made in the Q&A during the symposium: namely, that deconstruction is not synonymous with "destruction"; rather, "it is simply a question of being alert to the implications, to the historical sedimentations of the language we use" (271). And, he adds parenthetically, "(and this is a necessity of criticism in the classical sense)" (271). Another classical name in line with a figure that directly informs Derrida's interpretative method would be, of course, genealogy.

## Mimetic Genealogy: From the *Pharmakon* to the *Pharmakos*

With Derrida's genealogical reminder that the language we use bears the traces of historical sedimentations, let us return to the competing interpretations the shadow of mimesis generated during the symposium to bring it closer to our theoretical preoccupations. We have seen that Girard infers his conception of mimetic desire that blurs the boundary between self and other, generating violence and sameness in place of difference, from a classical Oedipal, and thus psychoanalytic, myth. But genealogy points to more than one origin, which, even in the case of theoretical origins, might not be deprived of a productive form of intellectual contest. This contest, as we had occasions to see, does not fit the triangular structure of mimetic rivalry and the psychic pathologies it generates; it is rather constitutive of what I call mimetic agonism and the new theory of imitation it brings to the surface. Let us thus look at the theoretically productive, differentiating, and patho-*logical*, rather than violent, undifferentiated, and pathological effects of mimetic agonism. This involves continuing to stage the dynamic interplay where sameness and difference, violence and writing, the *pharmakos* and the *pharmakon* meet, sometimes cross swords, yet productively reflect *on* each other.

On the side of violence, the theory of the scapegoat qua *pharmakos* on which, for Girard, the foundations of ritual, religion, and culture tout court rest, originates in a reproduction of a hypothetical founding murder of the primal father that can easily be traced to Freud's *Totem and Tabu* (1913) but is now tied to classics of mimetic theory like *Violence and the Sacred* (1972) and later *The Scapegoat* (1982). In these and other studies, Girard argues, with Oedipus still as a paradigmatic example but with a broader anthropological tradition to support his interpretative claims, that in different traditions, the scapegoat or *pharmakos* is both sacred and accursed insofar as it operates according to the paradoxical logic of what Girard calls a *pharmakon* (poison and remedy)—which does not mean that pharmaceutical models of interpretation were not already at play before. In a rare genealogical backward glance, Girard briefly acknowledges a precursor toward the end of *Violence and the Sacred*:

> Philosophy, like tragedy, can at certain levels serve as an attempt at expulsion, an attempt perpetually renewed because never wholly successful. This point, I think, had been brilliantly demonstrated by Jacques Derrida in his essay, "La Pharmacie de Platon." He sets out to analyze Plato's use of the term *pharmakon*. The Platonic *pharmakon* functions like [*exactement comme*] the human pharmakos and leads to similar [*analogues*] results. (Girard 1977, 296)[7]

Girard and Derrida may be opposed in theory, yet genealogical lenses reveal that they share a number of fundamental principles in practice. Girard is often antagonistic to his intellectual models, from Plato to Nietzsche, from Freud to Marcel

Mauss to Georges Bataille, erasing traces of influences that betray a still romantic "anxiety of influence" (Harold Bloom's term) that is, strictly speaking, not constitutive of *mimetic* agonism but of what I call "*romantic* agonism" instead—the romantic anxiety being directly proportional to the desire for originality that leads not so much to creative misreadings but to erasing the traces of influence altogether.[8] While this romantic agonism applies to his relation to Derrida's thought as well, rare passages like this suggest that Girard's parabolic warning to Oedipus—and at one remove, to contemporary heroes of knowledge—concerning the fragile opposition between self and other spills over beyond the text into the real world and casts a shadow on theoretical and quite referential others as well. Autonomy, as Girard is the first to know, is indeed, a myth. And this applies to theoretical autonomy as well. Hence the need of a genealogical approach that explicitly acknowledges precursors in order to open up the transdisciplinary field of mimetic studies.

The shadow under the bridge is now becoming visible, its movement of emergence perceptible. In one of those legendary footnotes that spans over numerous pages, Derrida, in "Plato's Pharmacy," convokes an anthropological tradition that goes from James Frazer to Marcel Mauss, and enlists a literary tradition that includes Sophocles and Shakespeare (1981b, 130–132, n. 56), after which, he, Derrida continues to sharpen the theory of the *pharmakos* qua scapegoat as follows:

> The city body *proper* thus reconstitutes its unity, closes around the security of its inner courts, gives back to itself the word that links it with itself within the confines of the agora, by violently excluding from its territory the representative of an external threat or aggression. That representative represents the otherness of the evil that comes to affect or infect the inside by unpredictably breaking into it [...] The ceremony of the *pharmakos* is thus played out on the boundary line [*à la limite*] between inside and outside, which has as its function ceaselessly to trace and retrace. (133)

Were it not for the last sentence, even for an experienced reader of both Derrida and Girard, it would be difficult to identify who, indeed, is the subject of such interpretations. Genealogical lenses reveal that the differential movement of the trace emerging from the dynamic of mimetic agonism in-*forms* the pathology the scapegoat is supposed to cure—and vice versa. In fact, both the movement of the *pharmakos* (scapegoat) flowing across binaries like inside/outside, poison/

remedy and the violent exclusion outside that like a *pharmakon* (poison/remedy) reconstitutes the unity of community inside, join hands to compose a Janus-faced conceptual configuration. And what we see is a transgressive conceptual feature of a deconstructive interpretation of the trace qua *pharmakon* on one side, and a mimetic reading of the scapegoat qua *pharmakos*, on the other. Which also means that Tiresias's critique of Oedipus was, in a subtle sense still in need of a redoubling interpretation, also a prophetic self-critique for the critic.

What form, then, does this shadow take? The interplay of these two opposed methods of interpretation outlines a chiasmic, mirroring reflection that is inscribed in the very doubling structure of the *pharmakon* of mimesis itself—if only because *mimēsis*, Derrida reminds us, is "akin to the *pharmakon*" (1981a, 139). And what we see from our genealogical bridge is that in the passage from the logic of writing to the one of mimesis, writing is endowed with a referential, material substance it previously lacked (via Girard), and mimesis finds a therapeutic solution to an ancient Oedipal riddle thanks to the equally ancient paradoxical structure of the *pharmakon* (via Derrida). The agonistic interplay of writing and mimesis, in other words, does not simply generate a shadow that reproduces sameness in place of difference. On the contrary, it generates a differential sameness that is inscribed in a paradoxical logic of mimetic agonism. And this logic is classical and equally shared by both Girard and Derrida, a trace that leads us to our third man—for it takes three to form a triangle.

## The Third Man: Jean-Pierre Vernant

There is, in fact, a critical figure who has remained in the shadow of our genealogy so far; yet his genealogy precedes and supplements both the copy and the model along classical pharmacological lines that should now sound quite familiar. In his contribution to the symposium titled "Greek Tragedy: Problems of Interpretation," the classicist Jean-Pierre Vernant provided a reading of Greek tragedy in general and of Sophocles's *Oedipus Rex* in particular that left important traces on both Girard's and Derrida's seminal theories of the *pharmakos* qua *pharmakon*.

Vernant's reading is historical and philological in orientation, attentive to the details of the cultural background Greek tragedies presupposed in general, and frames *Oedipus Rex* in particular against the ritual context of the Athenian Thargelia. That is, an agrarian festival of purification that culminated with a ritual expulsion qua sacrificial killing that brought out what Vernant calls the "ambiguity" of the "*pharmakos.*" As Vernant explains, during Thargelia, "at the moment when the impurities of the past season are expelled at the entrance into the new season, there is, at Athens, the expulsion of one who is called the *pharmakos*" (Vernant 1972, 277). This sacrificial figure in recent years became exemplary of the "bare life of *homo sacer*" (Agamben 2005, 125), which Giorgio Agamben traced back to transdisciplinary precursors of mimetic studies like Georges Bataille.[9]

For our purpose it suffices to say that for Vernant, "this paean [...] is characterized by its ambiguity" (1972, 276–277). And thinking of *Oedipus Rex*, he adds: "It is no accident that the tragic poet has placed this paean at the beginning of his tragedy" (277). Oedipus, for Vernant, is precisely such a *pharmakos* who occupies a double, ambivalent position, for he is both the savior of the city and the embodiment of an impurity who "must be expelled" for the benefit of the community. He equally reminds us that the Greeks could expel "as a *pharmakos* a person who has committed no crime, but who has risen too high, has too much good luck" (277), thereby pointing to jealousy, envy, or what Nietzsche would call ressentiment characteristic of the bad Eris, as the ambivalent affects already at play in this ancient ritual expulsion.

We seem, once again, to be brought back to a classical psychoanalytical scene as a *via regia* to the psychic life of the subject, including its unconscious, conflicted, and ambivalent Oedipal drives. And yet Vernant is quite firm in his opposition to psychoanalytical readings of *Oedipus Rex*. Thus, he says that "the Oedipus in the tragedy may have complexes, but he doesn't have an Oedipus complex—that is obvious" (1972, 293). He gives interpretative philological reasons to support this strong claim. For instance, commenting on the famous passage in which Jocasta says that "in dream [...] many a man has lain with his own mother" (Sophocles 1959, 52, ll. 980–983), Vernant states that this is of "no importance" for at least three reasons: first, because this claim is "not much of a censure" (1972, 293)—Jocasta tells Oedipus, "don't fear it!" (Sophocles 1959, 51, ll. 980)—and thus the text does not really dramatize a repressive hypothesis; second, because nothing in the tragedy indicates that Oedipus "had any feelings at all for Jocasta" (Vernant 1972, 293); and last, Vernant stresses that in the play, Jocasta never occupied the symbolic function of Oedipus's "mother" in the first place (293; see also 294–295). Thus, agreeing with Lévi-Strauss, Vernant adds that "what the Freudians have to say about the Oedipus myth constitutes a new myth" (293); that is, a reproductive myth that emerges from a circular process of citationality insofar as Freudian critics "cite the myth itself, but the myth has this meaning only because Freud labeled it a complex" (294)—in an endless regress that continues well into the present, despite the growing doubts concerning Oedipal theories of the unconscious.[10]

For Vernant, then, psychoanalytical and psychoanalytical-inspired readings of Sophocles's classical tragedy reveal more about modern critical and theoretical interpretations and the changes in the human sciences they reflect than about the tragic play itself—which is the genealogical hypothesis we have been pursuing from the beginning. At an additional remove, we might now supplement this anti-Oedipal insight by saying that conflicts of interpretation reveal something about the oppositions, rivalries, perhaps also jealousies at play between heroes of western knowledge themselves. This also means that mirroring reflections are not deprived of innovative inversions of perspective whose linguistic traces are still visible for genealogists of mimesis to retrace.

But more importantly, genealogy, we should not forget, is not only concerned with the critical language of the past; it also opens up new theories for the human sciences to pursue in the present and future. Let us recall that Derrida ended "Structure, Sign and Play" with a question he addresses to future generations to which, *nolens volens*, we belong. "Here there is a sort of question," he writes, "call it historical [or genealogical], of which we are only glimpsing today the conception, the formation, the gestation, the labor" (Derrida 1972, 265). This is, in a sense, still our question. And in a clear allusion to Nietzsche, Derrida specifies that he is thinking of the "business of childbearing" (265), that is, a maternal rather than a paternal business. If Derrida ends the theoretical event that was his talk with this embryonic insight, he does not say more.

A lot of water has passed under the bridge since. Perhaps, then, the time is now ripe for others to give this insight a push, so to speak. This will allow to bring our genealogy of homo mimeticus into the world out of an alternative conception of the unconscious that remained in the shadows in the past century but is increasingly difficult to ignore in the present century.

## Birth of the Subject: Out of the Mimetic Unconscious

For a long time and up to the twilight of the twentieth century, the problematic of mimesis entangled the language of criticism in rivalries with father figures that, somewhat obsessively, lead to violence and death. Pushing with and against this tradition, the passage on our genealogical bridge brings us back to maternal forms of communication that lead to life and birth vital to opening up new interpretative paths at the dawn of the twenty-first century.

As we already saw in previous chapters, the difference between these two perspectives are numerous: if patriarchal genealogies tend to privilege vertical, universal, and violent hierarchies that are located in the head of the *vita contemplativa*, maternal genealogies are sensitive to horizontal bonds of sympathy that are embodied, intersubjective, and open to the sense of a *vita mimetica*; if the former postulates ideal, abstract, and transcendental forms that serve as models or origins, the latter is inclined to start with material, immanent, and relational affects that give birth to subjectivity; if mental and theoretical anxieties of originality tend to haunt father figures (*pater semper incertus est*), bodily, fluid, and practical experiences incline maternal figures toward relational dispositions that give birth to the ego (*mater semper certa est*); if the former follows the eternal law of the *logos* with the tendency to exclude bodily pathos, the latter is attentive to both the horizontal interplay between the *logos* and the *pathos* constitutive of mimetic patho(-)logies that go beyond good and evil, for they have both patho-logical and patho-*logical* effects.

I thus let go of the thread of patriarchal rivalries that lead to violence and death and turn to re-evaluate a more maternal perspective attentive to sympathy and birth that already oriented the previous chapters. This life-affirmative perspective opens up a passage between the language of mimetic criticism and contemporary (human) sciences in an effort to give birth to a different yet still imitative conception of the subject. Having started this genealogical section with the birth of homo mimeticus at the level of the development of the species, or phylogenesis, I now narrow the focus and consider its birth at the level of the development of the child, or ontogenesis—which also means that the mimetic unconscious that gave birth to homo mimeticus is also the womb out of which each individual subject is born.

After a long period dominated by patriarchal cultures located in the ideal mind of white, male, free specimens of *Homo sapiens* that critiqued mimesis from the angle of the *vita contemplativa*, a change of perspective is in order to inaugurate a new theory of imitation on more affirmative foundations. For this delicate operation, it is wise to join forces with a minor tradition of previously marginalized voices located at the crossroads of continental philosophy, feminism, gender, and LGBTQ+ studies that have begun to reconceptualize the problematic of birth, or natality from the perspective of a *vita mimetica*.[11] This entails, among other things, reworking the patriarchal stereotype of the subordinate mother and endowing it with relational, embodied, affective and conceptual perspectives that provide a corrective to androcentric conceptualizations of the mimetic subject. The Italian feminist philosopher Adriana Cavarero occupied a privileged perspective for us not only because she posited, in genealogical continuity with Hannah Arendt, the category of "natality" at the origins of sentiments of "public happiness" vital to promoting "surging democracy" (Cavarero 2019); she also promotes an alternative, relational, and affectively inclined conception of the subject that is already located in a relational of genealogical continuity with homo mimeticus.

Cavarero and I, in fact, fundamentally agree that the subject, far from the autonomous, disembodied, and purely rational and immutable ideal erected by the dominant western tradition, is an embodied, affective, developmental, plastic, and above all relational subject that is, from birth onward, structurally inclined toward the other—the mother *in primis* but any caretaker as well—via a relational affective bond of sympathy (*sym-pathos*) between subjects we call "mimetic inclinations" (Cavarero and Lawtoo 2021). Furthering this genealogical connection in view of going beyond patriarchal inclinations that still inform poststructuralist theories of mimesis, I now return to a stereotypically patriarchal, androcentric, and at times frankly misogynist thinker who orients my genealogy of homo mimeticus. Despite his numerous flaws that we shall continue to critique, Nietzsche helps us account for mimetic inclinations that have tended to remain in the shadow but are not only already internal to his thought; they also help us explain why the subject is constitutively, consciously, but more often unconsciously inclined toward the other in the first place. There is in fact an immanent, relational, sympathetic, and I am not the first to argue, feminist perspective on the fluidity of mimetic pathos internal to Nietzsche's genealogy.[12] It supplements both Girard's and Derrida's by foregrounding maternal birth rather than patriarchal death as the genealogical horizon for mimetic studies of the future.

For Nietzsche birth was not simply a linguistic metaphor concerned with past, classical tragedies, but also a physical, immanent, and embodied reality that paved the way for a future-oriented theory of homo mimeticus.[13] It is, in fact, well known that, from *The Birth of Tragedy* (1872) onward, Nietzsche multiplies references to the language of childbearing—from wombs to pregnancy, from miscarriage to birth—to give an account of the emergence of tragic art out of mimetic principles such as visual representation and bodily impersonation rooted in classical mythic figures like Apollo and Dionysus.[14] Somewhat less known is that, starting with *Human, All Too Human* (1878), Nietzsche also paves the way for a genealogical account of the birth of a relational, communal, and porous ego that flows—from the space in between sameness and difference—out of playful maternal, nonverbal, yet still mirroring forms of mimetic communication. He does so with characteristic untimely foresight, which continues to anticipate timely developments in the human and social sciences, but also aesthetics, feminism, political theory, and the neurosciences. If we have seen in chapter 1 how this applies to his account of the birth of *Homo sapiens* at the level of the species (phylogenesis), a full genealogy of homo mimeticus needs to consider how this hypothesis concerns the development of the child as well (ontogenesis).

Like many nineteenth-century philosophical physicians, Nietzsche thought that the largest part of human mental activity remains unconscious, not in the Freudian interpretation of the unconscious based on a repressive, Oedipal hypothesis. Rather, it is unconscious in the pre-Freudian, but also post-Freudian realization that actions and reactions are triggered by involuntary habits, automatic reflexes, and mirroring repetitions of gestures that, from birth onward, bridge the gap between self and other via what we have seen him call an imitation or mimicking of gesture. The passage is now worth quoting in full:

> Older than speech is the mimicking of gestures [*Nachmachen von Gebärden*], which takes place involuntarily [*unwillkürlich*] and is even now, despite a general repression of gestural language [*Zurückdrangung der Gabärdensprache*] and a cultivated mastery of the muscles, so strong that we cannot look upon facial movements without innervation of our face (one can observe that feigned yawning evokes a natural yawning in someone who sees it). The imitated gesture led the person who was imitating back to the sensation that expressed itself in the face or body of the person being imitated. Thus people learned to understand one another; thus the child still learns to understand its mother. (Nietzsche 1995, 216:143)

Imitation, for Nietzsche, is Janus-faced in a double sense, for it is as past-oriented as it is future-oriented; it concerns the species as well as the individual. If we have seen in chapter 1 that this embodied communication is "older than language" because it allows language and consciousness to come into being, as humans tap, at the level of the species, into a social network of nonverbal communication that is not fixated on father figures, this is the moment to stress the role of maternal forms of mimetic communication in the development of the child. Derrida may have drawn on the business of childbearing metaphorically. Nietzsche does so literally, as he gives an account of the birth of the subject, out of the unconscious reflex of mimesis.

Clearly, this mimetic unconscious is not based on a triangular hypothesis that has desire as its *via regia*—for it focuses on imitation itself as the psychological, or better psycho-physiological source of bodily actions and reactions that cannot be repressed and thus go beyond the repressive hypothesis. Nor does it inscribe mimesis in the differential movement of a linguistic chain of signifiers that brackets a referential material presence—for this bodily imitation of gestures generates an immanent, intersubjective, and nonverbal communication that is rooted in the "innervation" of our "muscles," which, for Nietzsche, are at play or rather wired in an immanent body he considered the "great reason" (2005, 30). Imitation, for Nietzsche, is thus a manifold protean process that goes beyond nature/culture, self/others, mind/body dualities while being rooted in the great reason (*logos*) of bodily affect (*pathos*). This mimetic and unconscious dynamic, as I have been arguing for some time, is thus, strictly speaking, *neither* Girardian *nor* Derridean in its affective and conceptual configuration.

And yet this does not mean that our genealogical approach to mimetic studies is simply opposed to mimetic theory or deconstruction. Quite the contrary. Like a bridge, this genealogical reconstruction emerges from the space between these competing approaches: it builds starting from the opposed banks of sameness and difference, and, by doing so, pushes with and against these banks in order to cross over and go beyond them, in an exploratory mode, toward uncharted territories. On one side, Girard restricted the contagious power of mimesis to desire, rivalry, and the violence discharged on a *pharmakos* destined for a sacrificial death at the origins of culture. Nietzsche, in a balancing diagnostic move Bataille, Derrida, and later Lacoue-Labarthe, will be quick to follow, stretches to include the more general economy of mimesis itself in its life-affirmative power or *pathos* to give birth to a phantom subject. On the other side, Derrida called our attention to the supplementary properties of mimesis qua *pharmakon* that disrupt the hierarchy between model and copy, origin and shadow, truth and lies, models and simulacra.

With Nietzsche I shall now ground this destabilizing move in an immanent, physio-psychological, referential, yet equally destabilizing account of unconscious mimesis by pointing out that *feigned* yawning generates *real* yawning. The simulation of an action, in other words, generates an authentic reaction. In this playful overturning of perspectives, the aim is not to deconstruct yet again the arbitrary binary relation between truth/falsity, action/reaction, inside/outside, original/copy; nor is it to show that the copy precedes the original—though both deconstructive moves remain useful tools in the critical box. Nietzsche's point is also and above all that a simulation has the power to trigger a deeply felt bodily pathos via a mirroring reflex that opens up the subject to the other on the basis of an embodied, relational, and mimetic conception of the unconscious.

This also means that the mimetic principle we inherit from a Nietzschean tradition goes beyond sameness and difference, in the sense that it exceeds both the linguistic economy of the sign and the psychic economy of desire by zeroing in on mirroring actions and reactions that link physiology to psychology, what I see and what I feel, via a patho-logical loop that finds in an involuntary imitation, if not a grand *via regia*, at least an immanent path to the unconscious. Thus, an involuntary imitation of a gesture "led the person who was imitating back to the sensation that expressed itself in the face or body of the person being imitated" (1995, 216:143). For Nietzsche, the mimetic unconscious goes beyond the pleasure principle, for it rests on reflex principles that, like yawning, cannot be repressed by consciousness and are in this sense *un*-conscious. I involuntary mimic your facial and bodily expressions, and via a mirroring mechanism Nietzsche calls "psycho-motor induction," the expression of the other seen outside from a distance is mirrored and transformed into an inner pathos felt by an ego that is already open to alterity.

Elsewhere, with the figure of the actor or *mimos* in mind but paving the way for a future theory of imitation Nietzsche continues in a fragmentary mode:

> *compulsion to imitate*: an extreme irritability through which a given example becomes contagious—a state is divined on the basis of signs and immediately enacted—An image, rising up within, immediately turns into a movement of the limbs—a certain suspension of the will. (1968, 811:429)

Compulsion to imitate, contagious examples, mirroring movements and sensations, insights into the minds of others: these are indeed direct manifestations of the mimetic unconscious. Once well known in the pre-Freudian modernist period, this genealogy has remained in the shadows during the time the language of criticism confined mimesis to aesthetic representations and restricted the unconscious to Oedipal dramas. And yet the mimetic unconscious is currently re-*turning* to haunt the human sciences and, at an additional remove, the humanities as well.[15] If it lends empirical substance to the shadow of the symposium, it also provides steps to develop the field of new mimetic studies.

What was true at the level of phylogenesis remains true at the level of ontogenesis: our goal is to open up new perspectives to account for the psychic, aesthetic, social, and political transformations of homo mimeticus to come.

Nietzsche's untimely meditations on unconscious mimesis at the twilight of the nineteenth century provide a solid starting point, or *Stoßpunkt*, to develop a new theory of imitation at the dawn of the twenty-first century. It reveals that the humanities are at the origins of an immanent conception of affective mimesis the neurosciences are now confirming empirically and shadowing theoretically. We already alluded to the discovery of mirror neurons in the 1990s by Giacomo Rizzolatti and his team who opened up new "perspectives on imitation" for the twenty-first century.[16] This discovery is now well known and transdisciplinary connections between "mimesis and science" are now in place, though they tend to be restricted to Girard's mimetic theory.[17]

Now, while interdisciplinary dialogues between mirror neurons and Girard's theory of mimetic desire have been productive, there is a more direct genealogical connection that has remained in the shadows and now needs to be foregrounded. I concur, in fact, with Vittorio Gallese, as he notes that "these results [of mirror neuron theory] suggest that prior to any triangular mimetic relationship, the main object of infants' mimesis is the affective behavior of the 'other'" (2011, 97). Mimesis does not need to be framed in a triangle to articulate relations between self and others, if only because as we have seen, the mother in primis and then a network of social communication, not an Oedipal father, gives birth to consciousness. If Girard's Freudian genealogy leads him to compulsively posit triangular forms of desire and rivalry with father figures, the mimetic unconscious finds in intersubjective forms of mirroring communication that have what Sarah Blaffer Hrdy calls "mothers and others" as primary models an alternative starting point for a new theory of imitation for the future.

Rather than hastening to conflate a theory of mimetic desire predicated on a triangular form with a theory of mirroring reflexes that operate in self/others networks of communication, genealogical lenses encourage us to open up a less-traveled, untimely, yet for that reason future-oriented route. Here we have in fact yet another confirmation that the discovery of mirror neurons lends empirical credibility to a mirroring principle Nietzsche and other modernist figures in the humanities and social sciences described with impressive diagnostic precision a century earlier: namely, that the simple sight of gestures or facial expressions seen and felt individually or collectively triggers an unconscious reflex in the subject to reproduce such gestures/expressions and, by doing so, lead to a un-mediated understanding of the intentions that triggered them. Cooperation can emerge on such mimetic foundations. Reframing Nietzsche's physio-psychological diagnostic in more contemporary neuroscientific parlance, Rizzolatti and Sinigaglia sum up their discovery as follows:

> In humans, as in monkeys, the sight of acts performed by others produces an immediate activation of the motor areas deputed to the organization and execution of those acts, and through their activation it is possible to decipher the meaning of the 'motor events' observed, i.e., to *understand* them in *terms of goal-centered movements*. The understanding is completely devoid of any reflexive, conceptual, and/or linguistic mediation as it is based exclusively on the *vocabulary of acts* and the *motor knowledge* on which our capacity to act depends. (2008, 125)

While existence of a MNS in humans has been confirmed as a neurological fact via single-neuron measures already a decade ago (Mukamel et al. 2010), its interpretation did not fail to generate controversies—unsurprisingly so, for they call for a transformation of long-standing philosophical ideals of what *Homo sapiens* is or is supposed to be. Some claim that advocates of mirror neurons are mounting an attack on rationalist accounts of free will, intentionality, and autonomy central to a long-standing rationalizing and, let's face it, frankly patriarchal philosophical tradition that is not ready to let go of the autonomous subject of *Aufklärung* in full possessions of its rational thoughts, free deliberations, and often violent actions; others argue that mirror neurons, while not providing the only key to the riddle of consciousness, confirm ancient philosophical and aesthetic principles on the centrality of habitual forms of imitation central to learning, understanding, and collaboration by establishing nonverbal communicative bridges between self and others that open up the ego to external influences in ways already prefigured by homo mimeticus.

Either way, the specific role the MNS plays in our cultural understanding of human cognition, agency, intentionality, consciousness, beliefs, herd behavior, as well as violence and the unconscious, is currently being discussed and is far from being resolved. It is thus likely to continue triggering passionate debates between traditionally opposed cultures like the humanities and the hard sciences, which benefit from dialogic and agonistic confrontations we shall return to from related psychic-aesthetic-political perspectives constitutive of new mimetic studies.

## Genealogical Steps for New Mimetic Studies

A genealogy of mimesis with a focus on the present, then, urges new generations of theorists to go beyond the "two-cultures" binary opposition that arbitrarily divides disciplines that were not clearly opposed in the long history of this transdisciplinary concept; it also encourages us to continue bridging traditionally divided insights to set up an informed mirror for critical self-reflections in the present and future.

Such a genealogical mirror generates an inversion of perspectives that continues to be Janus-faced. On one side, it reveals that the empirical sciences should perhaps be more modest in their claims of priority; they would also benefit from engaging with the humanities so as to join forces to account for mirroring reflexes outside the confines of the lab on the basis of a long genealogy of mimesis that, as we have seen, goes back to Plato, and is aware of the power of actions to trigger unconscious reactions in both individual and social life. Important exceptions among neuroscientists already exist and inform our theory of homo mimeticus.[18] On the other side, if the humanities prove to be more open to dialogic conversations with the empirical sciences of our time, new generations of scholars might discover ways of supplementing quantitative approaches by remaining faithful to the qualitative, historical, and discerning power of interpretation constitutive of a humanistic vocation—if only because this scientific discovery, as it should be clear by now, is actually a *re*-discovery of mirroring principles that already informed the genealogy of the mimetic unconscious we have been resuscitating.

Compare, for instance, Rizzolatti and Sinigaglia's 1990s discovery to Nietzsche's 1888 claim on communication: "One never communicates thoughts: one communicates movements, mimic signs, which we can then trace back to thoughts" (Nietzsche 1968, 809:428). How does this nonverbal communication "trace back" movements into thoughts, bodily gestures into mental cognition? Nietzsche's diagnostic, as we have seen, is specific and finds in mimesis the missing link between body and gestures. Thus, he qualifies his mimetic hypothesis about the origins of communication predicated on the "imitation of gestures" as follows: "The imitated gesture led the person who was imitating back to the sensation that expressed itself in the face or body of the person being imitated" (Nietzsche 1995, 216:143). What we must add now, is that the movement of mimetic communication follows the logic of the supplement in the sense that it transgresses the line dividing self/other, inside/outside, copy/original. It also supplements it by remaining rooted in physio-psychological mirroring principles that bridge movements and sensations and can be delineated as follows: the sight of the other's external gestures or facial expressions triggers an automatic reflex within the subject (inside) to unconsciously reproduce, shadowlike, the same facial expressions (outside); this unconscious mimesis, in turn, gives birth to an inner sensation (*pathos*) that originates within the subject but is already shared (*sym-pathos*) with the other, generating a sympathetic understanding of the other as interior and exterior to the ego—both the same and different. This shared communication, or *Mitteilung*, of two subjects, imitating and being imitated, both united (*mit*) and divided (*teilung*), is the source of a dynamic interplay that gives birth to individual difference—out of mimetic sameness.

Thus reframed, mimesis is an originary experience in the sense that it engenders homo mimeticus via an unconscious communication that is already double. For Nietzsche, we have already seen that this is true at the level of the evolutionary development of the species (phylogenesis). Now he confirms this point by tying this mimetic principle to the development of the individual (ontogenesis). And as we already heard, Nietzsche joins phylogenesis with ontogenesis and adds the following genealogical supplement to his account of the origins of language: "Thus people learned to understand one another; thus the child still learns to understand its mother" (1995, 216:143–144). Much has changed since the emergence of *Homo sapiens* as a species around three hundred thousand years ago. Still, the principle that gives birth to it, for Nietzsche, remains essentially the same: every new birth re-enacts the eternal return of a mimetic experience that gives birth, each time, to a uniquely differentiated relational subject qua homo mimeticus.

In the beginning, prior to violence and writing, mimesis is thus replayed first and foremost in the smiles and countersmiles that tie a child to its mimetically inclined other or exemplary *socius*: namely, a significant other (parent, model, friend, lover, etc.).[19] This *socius*, as we have seen at the level of phylogenesis, is not necessarily one, as it includes a plurality of maternally inclined figures—from mothers to aunts, sisters to grandmothers, as Hrdy convincingly shows. But she also includes maternal fathers and uncles, brothers and grandfathers that played a key rearing role in traditional societies. As stereotypes are beginning to change in modern societies as well, new roles open up that allow males to be increasingly inclined toward newborns. At the level of ontogenesis, Nietzsche also anticipates insights into developmental psychology that show how "self-other connectedness and communication exists at birth" (Meltzoff 2011, 59). Either way, this mirroring communication generates an affective flux of becoming other based on a repetition with a *différance*, for it is inscribed in the temporal differing and deferring movement not of language alone but of an embodied, immanent, and relational consciousness.

The movement of mimetic communication, then, follows a supplementary logic in the sense that it transgresses the line between self and other, inside and outside, my affect and your affect. At the same time, it also remains rooted in physiological, mirroring reflexes, which according to Nietzsche are constitutive of the birth of subjectivity, language, and consciousness. His genealogical lenses are thus not only looking ahead to new empirical discoveries in the neurosciences that also claim that a good part of human communication is based on an unconscious neuronal simulation of gestures and expressions. With the benefit of hindsight, we notice that he also introduces a mimetic principle that goes beyond the self and other dichotomy to crack the riddle of how we understand each other's affects, beliefs, and intentions—the so-called theory of mind—on the basis of an hypothesis that is not fully confirmed yet, but that contemporary neuroscientists now consider a "fair bet."[20]

Significantly, even critics who convoke an ancient Platonic trick as they consider mirror neurons as a "myth" now agree on the truth of the ancient Aristotelian lesson that humans are the most thoroughly imitative creatures—a homo mimeticus that learns not only its lessons, but also language and culture, via "imitation." Despite the misleading title of his book, Gregory Hickok for instance, in *The Myth of Mirror Neurons* (2014) agrees that mirror neurons are not only present in monkeys but in humans as well, thereby contributing to disseminating a view of "*homo imitans*" (2014, 184–206). Yet he insists that "something else" is needed to "enable mirror neurons to support lofty human behavior such as language," namely "imitation" (189).

Mirror neurons bring us back to mimesis, then. But since Hickok does not dispute that mirror neurons are present at birth, the argument is caught in a chicken-and-egg circularity. Thus, after some twists and turns, Hickok concedes that "there is no theoretical pressure to abandon the idea that mirror neurons support imitation in a broader sense of associations between actions, as in observational learning" (199). And in a move that validates the myth he had appeared to initially expel from the order of scientific *logos*, he concludes: "mirror neurons will no doubt have a role to play in our models of the neural basis of communication and cognition" (241). The myth turns out to be constitutive of the *logos* in the end. This is, after all, an old story we have traced as far back as Plato. Mimesis, then, is an originary experience in the sense that it gives ontogenetic birth to the subject via a communication that is already doubled; it is replayed in smiles and countersmiles that do not rest on the arbitrary logic of the linguistic sign but on the intimately felt experience of a flowing *pathos*.

In the end, genealogical lenses reveal that mimesis is, paradoxically, at the origins of human understanding and communication, not of what humans are, but of who they can potentially become, individually and collectively, once caught in fluxes of mimetic communication with others. This immanent conception of mimesis, we have seen time and again, is not predicated on a mirror that sets up a unitary ideal or narcissistic *imago* that amplifies the already notable ego of *Homo sapiens*. A quote by Nietzsche we have already encountered may be worth echoing here: "The whole of life would be possible without, as it were, seeing itself in a mirror [...] however offensive this may sound to older philosophers" (1974, 354: 297). Nietzsche may be thinking of Plato's reference to a mirror to frame the movement of mimesis in visual/theoretical phantoms predicated on a static image of Being. Yet, despite his powerful overturning of perspective, Platonism is not dead. Under a more recent mask, this "ontological structure of the human world" (Lacan 1999, 2) may continue to implicitly in-*form* other contributors to the symposium—most notably Jacques Lacan who, as we shall see in chapter 5, was no stranger to mimetism.

Closer to home, in part 1, I have argued that an immanent, relational, and antimetaphysical approach suggests that an embodied intersubjective dynamic of becoming all-too-human rests on mirroring principles that, as we have seen time and again, go back to the dawn of culture, reaching back to the pre-history of *Homo sapiens*. In the process, it opens up a relational and eminently social conception of a phantom ego vulnerable to external influences, be they good or bad. Which also means that, in our genealogy, language and consciousness do not exist prior to mimesis; rather, it is the mimetic unconscious that serves as the relational matrix, or womb, out of which both language and consciousness are born.

Since imitation was arguably central to the development of a network of communication out of which an original imitative species expanded, we can perhaps go further and offer the following extravagant hypothesis: namely, that the mimetic unconscious played a key role in the "evolutionary bridge" that made the emergence of the "genius of the species" possible. Romantic phantasies aside, there is no genius born in isolation. On the contrary, it is the genial ability of humans to engage in a network of mimetic communication that made the emergence of an original, cooperative, often credulous, conformist and destructive, but also highly innovative species possible. Which also means that *Homo sapiens* perhaps needed its affective and intuitive counterpart, homo mimeticus, to reveal its full originality, in both its pathological and patho-*logical* manifestations. No wonder that Nietzsche privileged the image of the bridge to talk about humans as imitative creatures suspended between inside and outside, self and others, but also between linguistic signs and referential gestures, the human and the nonhuman, models and copies, origins and shadows, sameness and difference, past origins and future destinations.

## The Mimetic Bridge

To be sure, this is an admittedly fragile, precarious, and unstable bridge, or *passerelle*, still in progress, suspended over a river of becoming that does not mirror a unitary and stabilizing reflection, but a moving and fluttering shadow instead. Yet, as we continue to cross over this textual and referential bridge, our genealogy also offers a supplement to two sides of mimesis that have been opposed in the past but that transdisciplinary operations urge us to join in the future. What emerges from this oscillating back-and-forth movement is a reflection of/on homo mimeticus as radically indeterminate, intersubjective in origins, affectively exposed, suggestible to unconscious influences, cooperative in disposition, and dangerously at play with torrential forces that far exceed our human, all-too-human strength. It also calls attention to mimetic metamorphoses currently underway triggered by external models—be they real or fictional—that have the power to take possession of the ego, generating phantoms or shadows with real material effects still in need of genealogical diagnostics.

As we stand on the bridge we have reconstructed and look back to the shadow of the symposium on the shoulders of a genealogy that harkens back to the birth of *Homo sapiens* in view of charting possible destinations for homo mimeticus, we might still wonder: is this shadowy birth monstrous and violent, as Derrida and Girard suggested? Or innocent and life-affirmative as Nietzsche's gay science implies? Genealogical bridges do not offer unilateral answers but Janus-faced principles instead. On one side, a type of herd consciousness—triggered by the contagious power of gestures that are prior to language, reason, thought, operate massively on the mimetic unconscious, and are often triggered by what Nietzsche called "masters," or alternatively, "actors"—continues, perhaps more than ever, to be our accursed share. But on the other, life-affirmative side, Nietzsche turned to makers of shadows like artists, or, more generally, writers for theoretical inspiration. In fact, he considered these untimely figures as "heirs" of an excessive and squandering art of mimetic communication, part of a long chain that turned affective sameness into creative differences. As Nietzsche puts it in the book that provided the life-affirmative spirit to start our genealogy since the beginning, namely *The Gay Science*, and with which I end part 1:

> Those who are called artists are these heirs; so are orators, preachers, writers—all of them people who always come at the end of a long chain, "late born" [*Spätgeborene*] every one of them in the best sense of the word and, as I have said, by their nature, squanderers [*Verschwender*]. (1974, 354:298)

These untimely figures form, indeed, a "long chain." If the myth tells us that this chain originates in the Muses, we have both seen and felt that it magnetizes a number of exemplary writers of mimesis that, from antiquity into modernity, continue to inspire contemporary theorists as well. Our aspiration in tracing this genealogy is to be a worthy heir and innovator in this long philosophical and artistic tradition of squanderers. It is thus with an eye and ear to aesthetic insights and impressions emerging from an understanding of the plasticity of the subject opening up possibilities for chameleon metamorphoses that cut across the distinction between human and animal mimicry that we further new mimetic studies in part 2.

What we have seen in this part is that looking back to the role of mimesis in the emergence of homo mimeticus makes us see and feel that the shadow of protean forms of imitation continue to loom large on our present and future as well. Whether these marginal artists and writers will remain in a position to squander differential, oppositional, and life-affirmative interpretations in the indeterminate future that lies ahead, for the humanities, humans, nonhumans, and the planet more generally, remains difficult to foresee—for the river of sameness is becoming increasingly difficult to contain within opposed margins. Still, the chance to bridge critical sides and reflect on the moving shadow generated by the interplay of sameness and difference cast on the river of becoming other that carries us into the future reminds us of the power of a gay science of mimesis to face the indeterminate destination of homo mimeticus. In passing over this precarious bridge, we also saw—from the spaces between—a moving reflection of a humanities center that once served as an exemplary institutional model out which mimetic studies was born. Who knows? With some chance, a new transdisciplinary field could now be in the process of being reborn.

PART 2

# **AESTHETICS**
## CASE STUDIES

CHAPTER 4

# THE PLASTICITY OF MIMESIS

>Dad: "I don't like Plato."
>Daughter (three years old): "You *do* like Play-Doh!"

What is the link between mimesis and plasticity? Is mimesis a plastic concept? Or plasticity a mimetic concept? Or both? Either way, the duplicity of my title mirrors a destabilizing double movement that, over the past two decades, has never ceased to form, inform, and transform my understanding of what mimesis "is"—or can possibly become. In what follows, I would like to suggest that the new concept of "plasticity" is perhaps one of the most recent, most innovative, but not necessarily original conceptual manifestations of that protean shadow we have seen the Greeks call, somewhat enigmatically, *mimēsis*. Consequently, revisiting what the French philosopher and aesthetic theorist Philippe Lacoue-Labarthe called "the imitation of the moderns" (1986)—and thus of the ancients as well—furthers the alternative genealogy of *Homo sapiens* we have been pursuing so far. It also sharpens the formal contours of this emerging conceptual protagonist on the theoretical scene from the angle of aesthetics, a sensitive, embodied and affective angle at play in homo mimeticus.

To delineate this double move, let me start by dissociating the two sides of this Janus-faced title. On one side, the phrase "the plasticity of mimesis" simply indicates a certain malleability of the ancient concept of *mimēsis* itself. This point is worth recalling, for especially in the arts though not only, we are still accustomed to framing mimesis primarily within a stabilizing conception of representation characteristic of a realist aesthetics. This is, as we have had occasion to confirm, a strikingly restricted and partial definition that does not even begin doing justice to this chameleon concept. Already in the 1980s, Lacoue-Labarthe was recognized as developing "an entirely different thought of mimesis" (Derrida 1989, 8).[1] Still in the process of being fully translated into English, this thought is still waiting to be furthered from an immanent, materialist, and relational perspective constitutive of the mimetic turn, or *re*-turn, to mimesis, now animating new mimetic studies.

What, then, does Lacoue-Labarthe's different thought on mimesis reveal about the most recent manifestations of homo mimeticus? Supplementing homogeneous definitions restricted to simple representation, Lacoue-Labarthe's heterogeneous thought on what he calls a concept without "proper identity," reminds us that *mimesis* is a theoretical concept that originates in the practice of the theater. Consequently, it entails both visual representations and bodily impersonations, which, as they are enacted on a stage, generate protean affects such as psychic identification, emotional contagion, and ritual dispossession that continue to haunt what he calls the imitation of the moderns. Hence his claim in *L'Imitation des modernes* (1986) that it is philosophically urgent to *step back* to the ancients in order "to think or rethink mimesis" (Lacoue-Labarthe 1986, 282). This is, indeed, what the mimetic *re*-turn has been doing all along.

On the other, related side, stepping back remains the genealogical presupposition for leaping further ahead. From a contemporary perspective, I suggest in fact that it may be the emerging concept of "plasticity" that has mimetic (im) properties that have so far gone unnoticed. I mean this not only in the material, neuroscientific, and relatively recent sense in which the discovery of the brain's neuroplasticity is currently painting a new picture of subjectivity as flexible, impressionable, adaptable, and in this behavioral sense, mimetic. I mean this also in the specific philosophical delineation of plasticity as a "concept" in Catherine Malabou's double sense, as she provocatively asks, *What Should We Do with Our Brain?* (2008). That is, in plasticity's capacity to both *receive form* and *give form* and, in the process, generate contradictory effects such as passive adaptations and creative formations, psychic pathologies and therapeutic patho-*logies*, perhaps even revolutionary transformations as plasticity gains consciousness of itself in its dialectical development toward what Malabou calls the future—*l'avenir* (1996).

The plasticity of mimesis, then, turns around two seemingly antithetical concepts that look in two opposed directions: one back to the past origins of western poetics; the other ahead toward the future of new theoretical destinations. And yet, my wager is that Lacoue-Labarthe's account of what he calls "the plastic constitution of the subject" (1989, 178) helps us see that mimesis and plasticity are perhaps two sides of the same Janus-faced concept. Joining these two sides, I hasten to add, does not intend establish the unity of an identity. Instead, it generates a disquieting repetition with a difference in which these two concepts face each other, mirror one another, and above all, reflect *on* each other. In this reflection, I argue that mimesis gives conceptual form to the duplicity of plasticity. It also reveals that behind this new plastic mask lies an ancient actor, or mime. In the process, a genealogy of plasticity generates an inversion of perspectives that turns Lacoue-Labarthe's untimely question—"How can psychology contribute to mimetology?" (1989, 101)—into what I take to be its contemporary counterpart for new mimetic studies: namely, how can mimetology contribute to psychology, and perhaps to a patho-*logy* internal to aesthetics and neurology as well? But let us proceed in order.

## The Era of Plasticity: Malabou's Neuro Turn

While the concept of mimesis, prior to the mimetic turn, has tended to be relegated to the backstage of aesthetic and philosophical discussions, plasticity is an emerging conceptual protagonist on the theoretical scene that is currently receiving increasing attention across a number of fields. And rightly so, for it is a timely concept not deprived of empirical support. It is in fact based on recent discoveries in the neurosciences, which have shown that the human brain is far more plastic and adaptable than previously realized and remains so throughout our lives.

It is not simply the mind, or the psyche, that has the capacity to change. That we long knew. It is, rather, the structure of the brain itself, in its ability to establish new synaptic connections and modify their capacity of transmission that changes over time, depending on our activities and life experiences. Historians Nikolas Rose and Joelle Abi-Rached describe the genealogy of this discovery as follows: "By the close of the twentieth century, the brain had come to be envisaged as mutable across the whole of life, open to environmental influences, damaged by insults, and nourished and even reshaped by stimulation—in a word *plastic*" (2013, 48). Along similar lines, neuroscientist Alvaro Pascual-Leone and his team specify: "Plasticity is an intrinsic property of the human brain and represents evolution's invention to enable the nervous system to escape the restrictions of its own genome and thus adapt to environmental pressures, physiologic changes, and experiences" (2005, 377). And summarizing the main insights of neuroscientists working on different problems related to brain plasticity—from post-stroke paralysis to phantom limbs—psychologist Norman Doidge writes that "many 'circuits' and even basic reflexes that we think are hardwired are not" (2007, xv).

Somewhat paradoxically, then, the neurosciences are currently contributing to forming an image of the brain that supports a genealogy of subjectivity thinkers in the humanities have long been advocating. The brain, we are now told, can no longer be considered on the basis of an essentialist model that hard-wires our neurons in our genetic nature. On the contrary, the brain turns out to be formed and deformed by experience, culture, and education over our entire lives. Hailed as a revolutionary discovery comparable to "that of the atom or the DNA" (1997, xvii) by neuroscientists like Jean-Pierre Changeux, neuroplasticity is currently generating a collective "enthusiasm" (xiii) that is spreading contagiously across disciplinary boundaries, establishing new dialogues between the hard sciences and the social sciences—stretching to transforming the humanities as well.

"Our brain is plastic, and we do not know it" (2008, 4), writes Catherine Malabou in *What Should We Do with Our Brain*? And thanks to Malabou's popular book we now know, perhaps not what to do with our brain in practice, but at least that the brain is plastic in a theoretical sense that is at least double. Reminding us of its Greek etymology, *plassein*, to mold, Malabou writes: "the word *plasticity* has two basic senses: it means at once the capacity to *receive form* (clay is called 'plastic,' for example) and the capacity to *give form* (as in the plastic arts or in plastic surgery)" (5). This is simultaneously good and bad news, for brain plasticity makes us open to both good and bad impressions: plasticity can, in fact, be the source of therapeutic *cures* (reparative plasticity or brain regeneration), but it can also make us vulnerable to brain *pathologies* (traumatic wounds and neurodegenerative disorders).

We have encountered this duplicity before. There is, in fact, a patho(-)logy of plasticity that strangely mirrors the patho(-)logies internal to our genealogy of homo mimeticus. Moreover, plasticity can be passively *subjected* to typical formations that fit humans into restricted social molds or types, but it can also turn humans into the active *subjects* of creative transformations that disrupt such molds and stereotypes. Building on this paradoxical double structure, Malabou exploits a third etymological development of plasticity, as in plastic explosive or "*plastiquage*" (5) to argue that plasticity has the revolutionary potential to "resist," "negate," and ultimately "explode" the rigid capitalist structures that generate "docile" and submissive subjects complicit with neoliberal capitalism's increasing demand for "flexibility" (12)—thereby opening up new transformative possibilities for the future. Hence Malabou's delineation of a dialectical concept that is encapsulated in what she calls the "threefold movement of reception, donation, and annihilation of form" (2012, xiv).

And yet, if neuroplasticity is a relatively recent scientific discovery, originating in the 1940s with neurologist Donald Hebb's realization that neurons that fire together wire together, the conceptual *form* of plasticity—which is my main concern in this chapter—has a much longer and complicated genealogy. And Malabou knows it. Thus, she introduces an important distinction between the notion of "flexibility" and the concept of "plasticity," as she specifies:

> Flexibility is a vague notion, without tradition, *without history*, while plasticity is a *concept*, which is to say: a form of quite precise meanings that bring together and structure particular cases. This concept has a long philosophical past, which has itself remained too long in the shadows. (2008, 13)

Neuroplasticity, then, may be a recent scientific discovery, but plasticity is a philosophical concept with a specific form in line with a past tradition of thought that has remained too long in the shadows, and that Malabou brings back to light. Building on her thesis *L'Avenir de Hegel* (1996), the French philosopher identifies the origins of this tradition as she writes: Hegel "is the first philosopher to have made the word *plasticity* into a concept" (1996, 80), and she specifies that "the concept of plasticity" was "discovered for the first time in the preface to Hegel's *Phenomenology of Spirit*" (2010, 8).[2]

Time and again, Malabou argues that in Hegel's speculative thought we find, for the first time, plasticity as a concept that is not only aesthetic and linked to the plastic *arts* but also philosophical and linked to the formation of a plastic *subject*. As she puts it in her introduction to an edited collection titled *Plasticité* (2000): "For the first time with Hegel, plasticity reaches the essential. The philosopher snatches plasticity from its strictly aesthetic anchorage in order to attach it to a problematic space which, so far, had not been its own: *subjectivity*" (Malabou 2000, 8–9; my trans.). This genealogy, then, establishes an important genealogical link between the ancient aesthetic origins of plasticity and the modern question of the subject. It also opens up a space for innovative dialogues between the humanities and the neurosciences along lines that are neither reductionist nor confined to cognitive methods, and Malabou's work testifies to the productivity of this connection. Her thought is in line with the exploratory, transdisciplinary perspectivism at play in homo mimeticus and helps us go beyond dualisms that were dominant in the past yet need to be challenged in the present and future.

That said, with respect to the past, when it comes to the *genealogy* of plasticity, I cannot help but to register a suspicion. For a French philosopher inscribed in a tradition of thought that has taught her—via the filter of Nietzsche, most notably—to be skeptical of genealogies that can be traced back to single, unitary, and stable origins, Malabou seems surprisingly certain about the so-called first discovery of plasticity. This certainty is all the more striking, since Hegel—and Malabou is the first to know it—in the *Aesthetics* makes clear that his source of inspiration for linking plasticity to subjectivity is not modern but ancient, goes back to the dawn of western thought, and is rooted in what he calls "exemplary [*exemplarische*]" figures such as Socrates, Sophocles, and, of course, Plato. That is, "plastic individuals," who, Hegel writes, "possessed to the highest degree this perfect plastic sense in their conception of the divine and of the human" (qtd. in Malabou 1996, 22; my trans.). Given the broader genealogy informing Hegel at the twilight of philosophy at a moment when aesthetics is beginning to develop into an autonomous area of inquiry that remains nolens volens rooted in classical models, we may thus wonder: why this insistence on the *Phenomenology of the Spirt* as a stable point of origin when Hegel admittedly stands at the dusk of a long tradition?

We can only speculate, but let me venture a mimetic hypothesis. This certainty concerning the origins of plasticity might well be directly proportional to the broader ontological move Malabou is attempting. Namely, to displace, dislocate, or disrupt—with plasticity as a lever and Hegel as a fulcrum—the ontology of writing she inherited from her mentor, Jacques Derrida, to promote what she calls, in *Plasticity at the Dusk of Writing* (2010), nothing less than "the style of an era" (Malabou 2010, 1). This era, Malabou argues, traces the contours of what the ontology of writing erased: namely, a concern with form. Grounding her dislocating move in the claim that *écriture* is "formless" whereas "form is plastic," Malabou writes: "I realized that writing was no longer the right image and that plasticity now presented itself as the best-suited and most eloquent motor scheme for our time" (15). This era, then, marks the dusk of writing and the dawn of plasticity.

At the twilight of the idols a new start is born. Thus, Malabou announces what she calls, in a confessional mood, the birth of "a still uncertain, tremulous star, [which] begins to appear at the dusk of *written form*" (15). Clearly, when the theoretical stakes are so high, the model so close, the linguistic traces so intimately intertwined, the *logos* so imbued with *pathos*, and—why not say it?—the mimetic agon so openly visible in plasticity's "refusal to submit to a model" (Malabou 2008, 6) and thus also to "imitate or to copy" (Malabou and Noëlle

2008, 2), it is understandable that a clear-cut "rupture" with one's intellectual "origins" might appear necessary so as to dissipate old phantoms—and the impressions they have left behind.

In light of our genealogy informed by the paradoxical logic of mimetic agonism, the anti-mimetic scene is classical. What Derrida says in his groundbreaking critique of Lévi-Strauss at the symposium equally applies, at some removes, to my genealogical evaluation of Malabou: "the appearance of a new structure, of an original system, always comes about—and this is the very condition of its structural specificity—by a rupture with its past, its origin, and its cause" (Derrida 1972, 263). This rupture is nothing less and nothing more than the distancing internal to a mimetic agon whose pathos has already taken possession of the ego, generating a phantom driven, as we saw in chapter 3, by the interplay of sameness and difference—which does not mean that the phantom is deprived of original insights we can now put to use for new mimetic studies.

Phantoms, just like shadows, models, and forms, are mimetic tropes. And Malabou knows it. This is why she acknowledges, this time in a more Freudian mood, that "because plasticity never presents itself without form, plastic is always thought as a factor of identification" (2010, 74). There are thus important genealogical links between plasticity and identification—and Malabou's most recent work testifies to her commitment to critically revisiting a psychoanalytical tradition, which, as Girard, Lacoue-Labarthe, and Borch-Jacobsen, among others, have shown, cannot easily be disentangled from the problematic of the "mimetic subject."[3] And yet, given Malabou's theoretical emphasis on the paradoxical conceptual delineation of "plasticity" as something that can simultaneously give form and receive form on the basis of what she calls "models" whose paradigmatic examples are already at play in the "plastic arts" as well as in "education" (2008, 21), Malabou has so far been strangely silent on the concept of *mimesis* itself. This is surprising since mimesis is arguably *the* paradigmatic concept in formative matters, both in terms of onto-aesthetic *forms* and of plastic *subject* formations.

And here is where Lacoue-Labarthe re-enters the theoretical scene. In his company, we ask plasticity a question in light of an alternative, more ancient, less known, but not less destabilizing genealogy of plasticity, which, this time, has remained too long in the shadows, indeed.

## Shadowing Plasticity: Lacoue-Labarthe's Mimetic Re-*Turn*

Philippe Lacoue-Labarthe was always the last to claim any originality for his thought and always the first to trace genealogies that offer new perspectives for future thought. Had he witnessed the return of interest in plastic subject matters, he may have reminded future-oriented theorists that Roland Barthes was not the only thinker who spoke of the malleability of "plastic" in the twentieth century. It is true that in *Mythologies* (1957) Barthes defines plastic as a substance characterized by its power of "infinite transformation" that generates the "trace of a movement" (1972a, 97). He also implicitly establishes a link between plasticity and mimesis as he defines plastic as an "'imitation material' [*simili*]" that no longer belongs to "the world of appearances" but to a "household material" instead (98), thereby inverting a Platonic idealist ontology that is not deprived of attention to the materiality of plastic lives, as we shall see. But it is equally true that before Barthes, Georges Bataille spoke of plasticity too, and in relation to subjectivity, namely his own. Thus, in *Inner Experience* (1943), Bataille speaks of his ego in terms of what he calls "a disarming plasticity [*plasticité désarmante*]" (1988, 147). And in a genealogical move directly aligned with Nietzsche's chain of squanderers, Bataille turns restricted mimesis linked to "slavery" into general mimesis characteristic of "sovereignty." Or, perhaps, Lacoue-Labarthe would have started with a reminder that plasticity is already at play in *On the Genealogy of Morals* (1887) insofar as Nietzsche understands will to power in terms of "shaping forces" (1996a, 58) that "impress form [*Formen aufdrücken*]" on a malleable psychic material he calls "crowd [*Masse*]" or "unshaped population [*ungestaltete Bevölkerung*]" (66). Or maybe he would have started with the Romantics, or maybe with psychoanalysis, or perhaps music—who knows? Plastic subjects circulate endlessly through the channels of his mimetic thought, and it is unwise to speculate.

What is possible to say is that for Lacoue-Labarthe mimesis and plasticity cannot be easily dissociated. Though plasticity is the hidden face of mimesis, they constitute two sides of the same aesthetic-psychic concept, a Janus-faced concept he inscribes in a tradition of thought that brings him—via Hegel and Freud, for sure, but also Heidegger and Diderot, Bataille and Nietzsche, and many others—back to the very beginning of philosophy, in Plato's thought where the philosophical genealogy of homo mimeticus started in the first place.

What we must now add is that this is where the joint philosophical adventure of the plasticity of mimesis also begins. Lacoue-Labarthe makes this point in "Typography." This is a foundational essay in the revival of interest in a different conception of mimesis started in the wake of structuralist controversies, which prefigured the mimetic turn and we considered in chapter 3. It was first published in *Mimesis: Des articulations* (1975) along with essays by Sylviane Agacinski, Sara Kofman, Jacques Derrida, and Jean-Luc Nancy, among others;[4] it was subsequently translated and reprinted in *Typography* (1989) as an agonistic alternative to Girard's mimetic theory. This long and complex essay inaugurates what Jean-Luc Nancy calls, not without admiration, the "great construction site of 'onto-typology' [*le grand chantier de 'l'onto-typologie'*]" (2008, 109; my trans.). It is a construction site on whose foundations I provisionally reconstruct my genealogy of plasticity before taking it into uncharted territories.

A lengthy commentary to position Lacoue-Labarthe's engagement with the onto-typographic qualities of mimesis in relation to Nietzsche, Girard, and Heidegger (his three main interlocutors) would be necessary in principle.[5] Given the specific perspective on homo mimeticus that drives us, I will spare you the philological niceties and go directly to the subject matter in order to delineate the general contours of the seal of mimesis as it in-*forms* (gives form to) the concept of plasticity.

The question of form or formation should not generate false ontological impressions. Lacoue-Labarthe, in fact, zooms in on books 2 and 3 of the *Republic*, that is, the books in which Plato inaugurates the problematic of mimesis *not* on the basis of an ontological critique of representation at three removes from the ideal Forms. We will have to wait book 10 for this stabilization of mimesis via the trope of the "mirror" and the "phantom [*phantasma*]" of reality it generates (Plato 1963c, 601c), though this metaphysical addendum continues to cast a long shadow on western aesthetics. Rather, Plato—or better, Socrates—starts by discussing mimesis in the context of an aesthetic theory first and foremost preoccupied with the psychic effects of theatrical impersonations on the formation of the subject, or ego—preoccupations we have seen as central in the animated shadows at play in the "Allegory of the Cave" with the power of generating phantom egos in chains.

We can now continue to give aesthetic specificity to this Platonic concern from the angle of the plasticity of the mimetic subject. It is, in fact, in the context of a discussion of the educative function of myths in general and poetry in particular as it is dramatically re-enacted by actors on the stage who impersonate fictional models, exempla, or as Plato says, "types" that have the power to form the guardians, and by extension subjectivity tout court, that the question of mimesis is first introduced in the *Republic* and by extension in western aesthetics, culture, and subject formation. As Lacoue-Labarthe succinctly puts it, the "problematic of mimetism" in these first books "is not, as is repeated endlessly, principally a problematic of the lie, but instead a problematic of the *subject*" (1989, 125), which does not mean that this subject is not impressed by aesthetic forms.

*Mimesis*, as we already noted, comes from *mimos* (actor or performance), and Lacoue-Labarthe is distinctive among philosophers in insisting on the theatrical origins of mimesis in order to emphasize its formative psychic power. He even goes as far as speaking of Plato's "'psychology'" (1989, 100) in this context, thereby implicitly agreeing with classicists like Eric Havelock who foreground the spectators' "emotional identification" (Havelock 1963, 44; see also 20–35) as central to the Platonic critique of mimesis. In light of what we have seen so far, we are thus in very familiar territory. What is new in our genealogy of homo mimeticus is that at the center of this theatrical scene, Lacoue-Labarthe operates a second, less visible but not less fundamental theoretical move that binds the psychology of dramatic mimesis to the plasticity of the subject. The following passage outlines the essential contours of the plasticity of mimesis in its double-faced articulation that already seals its theoretical destination:

> Things begin, then—and this is what "imitation" is all about—with the "plastic" [*la 'plastique'*] (fashioning, modeling, fictioning), with the impression of the *type* and the impression of the *sign*, with the mark that language, "mythic" discourses (whether they are true or not matters little […]), originally inscribe in the malleable—plastic—material of the infant soul. (Lacoue-Labarthe 1989, 126–127)

This is as a scene of beginnings, yet no singular concept originates here. On the contrary, there are many "things" that are simultaneously taking form in this scene, both with and against each other: philosophy and literature, aesthetics and ethics, models and copies, subjects and objects, fictional forms and political realities, and yes, mimesis and plasticity as well.

The importance of this beginning cannot be underestimated. It gives birth to the fundamental "mimetology" that traverses Lacoue-Labarthe's entire thought and in-*forms* his account of typography, the subject, the figure, fiction, myth, and the fascist horrors that ensue as mythic fictions are put into political practice—all perspectives we will further from the angle of new mimetic studies now entangled with the problematic of plasticity as well. This is why Lacoue-Labarthe speaks of a *"necessary reversibility of the motifs of engenderment and of the figure, of conception, and of the plastic"* (1989, 128).

This reversibility cuts both ways. On the one hand, Lacoue-Labarthe stresses that mimesis is a plastic concept in search of an identity that assumes different dramatic forms. Thus, he defines it as a concept whose essence is to "lack a stable essence," whose proper being is, paradoxically, a "lack of being-proper" (1989, 115)—in short, an unstable, malleable, and thus plastic concept that, like the protean *mimos* it designates, constantly changes form, fashioning, modeling, fictioning different conceptual protagonists on the theatrical/theoretical scene. Hence the difficulty—Bataille would say the impossibility—of fixing, once and for all, the plastic contours of mimesis itself in a unitary figure, form, or configuration. On the other hand, the fact that mimesis cannot be stabilized in a theoretical form does not mean that typical psychic formations are not already at play in theatrical practice. This leads us to a second, related, but for our purpose, more fundamental sense in which mimesis is plastic in the sense that it *gives aesthetic form*—via mythic types, models, or figures that, as we have seen and heard, are embodied on a stage—to the material plasticity of what Plato calls "soul" and Lacoue-Labarthe calls "subject." As Lacoue-Labarthe and Nancy put it elsewhere:

> Myth is a fiction, in the strong, active sense of "fashioning," or, as Plato says, of "plastic art" [*la 'plastique'*] it is, therefore, a *fictioning*, whose role is to propose, if not to impose, models or types [...] types in imitation of which an individual, or a city, or an entire people, can grasp themselves and identify themselves. (Lacoue-Labarthe and Nancy 1990, 297)

The political power of such fictional types on real subjects was clear to the ancients, generated phantoms responsible for what Lacoue-Labarthe calls "the horror of the West" (2012) for the moderns, and, we shall see in subsequent chapters, under different theatrical and digital masks, continues to haunt the increasingly precarious condition of the contemporaries as well.

There is thus a fundamental genealogical link between Plato and plasticity that has so far received little attention. It needs to be foregrounded to supplement accounts of *Homo sapiens* that recognize the role fiction played in the history of civilization[6] but left its formative and plastic properties for others to explore. This is where a chain of thinkers internal to *Homo Mimeticus* can make a difference. Lacoue-Labarthe, for one, who, in addition to his well-known debt to Derrida, shares a philological ear with Nietzsche, even reminds us of a tradition reported by Diogenes Laertes that links the name Plato (*Platon*) to "the verb *plassein* (in Attic, *plattein*): 'to model,' 'to fashion'—and also 'to imagine,' 'to feign,' 'to simulate,' and so on (compare French *plastique*)" (Lacoue-Labarthe 1989, 96), a plasticity inscribed in the saying, "Plato fashioned plastic words [*Os aneplasse Platon [o] peplasmena thaumata eidus*]" (96). We are now in a position to both see and hear that "Plato" was not only an exemplary plastic individual in Hegel's sense; with his "plastic words" (96); he also played with the malleability of mimetic figures that resemble the plasticity of "wax."

Wax is a plastic subject matter, but it is not the only one. Supplementing this classical analogy, let me exploit the resonances of a contemporary subject matter familiar to those mimetic subjects par excellence who are children. To bring our genealogy into the present, we could also speak of the plasticity of "Play-Doh." Play-Doh is indeed a plastic material object that speaks directly, or rather echoes, the problematic of the plasticity of the subject. Rather than offering an erudite philological interpretation of this subject matter, a personal anecdote directly drawn from life experience might perhaps best illustrate a linguistic-philosophical point on a more informal, material, yet not less imitative basis.

I owe a contemporary version of this confusion between Plato and plasticity to my daughter. A few days before I presented the first version of this chapter at a Johns Hopkins conference I had organized on Lacoue-Labarthe titled Poetics and Politics,[7] my daughter (then three years old) interrupted a theoretical conversation I was having with my partner over breakfast—in a dramatic way. Picture the scene: early morning, two adults talking seriously, children quietly eating, but secretly listening. To express my discontent with a transcendental western metaphysics spellbound by ideal Forms you have heard me critique in chapter 2, I made a rash and rather unforgivable statement. I said, in the spur of the moment: "I don't like Plato." Before I had realized that this statement was only partially true, and at best incomplete, my daughter instinctively turned toward me with a personally offended look in her blue, ferocious eyes. She stared at me in disbelief with the ethical indignation of someone who just caught a big liar in the act, and then cried out, pointing her finger toward me: "You *do* like Play-Doh!!" I could not deny it. This mime of a daughter had, indeed, caught me in a theoretical double bind that delineates the general contours of my argument. To regain my daughter's respect, I should thus minimally specify my rash claim as follows: "I don't like Plato for metaphysical reasons, but I do like Play-Doh. Ergo, I like Plato for materialist and quite playful reasons!"

This Socratic irony on the plasticity of Plato/Play-Doh is as linguistically playful in theory as it is materially true in practice. Children, as Socrates was the first to know, are imitative creatures in both theory and practice. Here is what

"Plato" says, as he gives voice, in mimetic speech, to his psychological concern with the pedagogical effects of mimesis on those plastic subjects:

> Do you not know, then, that the begging in every task is the chief thing, especially for any creature that is young and tender? For it is then that it is best molded [*plattetai*] and takes the impression [*tupos*] that one wishes to stamp upon it? (Plato 1963c, 377ab)

So, this is the moment to echo the question with which we started: did we know that plasticity is central to subject formation? Yes, we did. This is, in fact, an ancient typographic inscription that, I do not want to say for the first time, but certainly before Hegel, snatches plasticity from its aesthetic anchorage to inscribe it in the psychic language of subject formation.

Plato's concern in these early books is not with metaphysical forms but, rather, with the psychological and pedagogical role aesthetics in general and dramatic mimesis in particular plays in the psychic formation of plastic subjects. Fiction is not only mimetic in the idealist sense that it shadows the world; it is also and above all mimetic in the materialist sense that it forms and transforms subjects. Far from having only a spiritual, disembodied, and transcendental side, the soul—even for Plato, or better, especially for Plato—has a plastic, material, and thus immanent side, which is best molded by the formative power of fictional impressions generated by mythic and exemplary models. These impressions are especially strong in childhood, but Plato makes clear later in the *Republic* that they continue to shape the subject in adulthood as well, especially as it is part of what he calls "the mob assembled in the theater" (1963c, 10.604e). It is thus because plasticity is constitutive of the formation of the subject, of the *polis*, and thus of our political life in common that Lacoue-Labarthe will later say that "the political (the City) pertains to plasticity [*relève d'une plasticité*], formation and information, fiction in the strict sense" (1987, 102; my trans.). Similarly, it is on the basis of Plato's diagnostic of mimesis that Lacoue-Labarthe speaks of *subjectivity* in terms of a "pure and disquieting *plasticity* [...] which doubtless requires a subjective 'base'—a 'wax'" (1898, 115). A plastic view of the subject understood in its classical philosophical sense of *subjectum* (what is underlying or subjacent) is, indeed, internal to a most classical literary and philosophical definition of mimesis. And Lacoue-Labarthe knew it. The human soul or character (from *kharassein*, to stamp or engrave) has been defined from the beginning of philosophy in terms of a waxlike plastic matter that is formed by exemplary models. And Lacoue-Labarthe equally knew it.

But there is more. Lacoue-Labarthe not only allows us to establish a genealogical continuity between mimesis and plasticity that converges on the problematic of subject formation, or homo mimeticus; he also delineates the paradoxical conceptual form that serves as *the* exemplary model for the double structure of plasticity to emerge on the philosophical scene. As we retrace Lacoue-Labarthe's characterization of plasticity in its complete form, let us pay careful attention to the shift from two seemingly opposed sides of mimesis: one side conceived as passive reception of form, the other as active capacity to give form. Speaking of the poet Plato wants to expel from the ideal *Republic*, Lacoue-Labarthe writes that this subject is an incarnation of what he calls

> *mimetism* itself, that pure and disquieting *plasticity* [*pure inquiétante* plasticité] which potentially authorizes the varying appropriation of all characters and all functions (all roles), that kind of "typical virtuosity" which doubtless requires a "subjective" base—a "wax" [*une 'cire'*]—but without any other property than an infinite malleability: *instability* "itself." (1989, 115)

A duplicity is at play here: what is plastic now is not only the concept of mimesis but also the mimetic subject itself, its subjective base, sub-stance, or *subjectum* on which mythic types are impressed generating stereotypes, which, as we have seen, reach into the present. The movement of this process of subject formation is not singular but double, and this double movement begins to generate a paradoxical logic that will keep Lacoue-Labarthe's destabilizing thought on the move—reaching a genealogy of plasticity that brings it into the present.

We can delineate this double movement now animating the two drawing hands of homo mimeticus as follows. On the one hand, it inaugurates the ontotypology Lacoue-Labarthe tirelessly denounces as a source of plastic vulnerability to totalitarian figures whose will to power, as Nietzsche also warned, can be violently impressed on what he called *Masse*, or "unformed populations" (1996a, 66). This passive mimesis entails a plasticity that is disquieting for political reasons, for it is based on an aestheticization of politics that renders subjects—especially in a mass but not only—docile, and easily subjected to fascist leaders (old and new) who erect themselves as figures of authority along typographic lines Lacoue-Labarthe, echoing Bataille, will later qualify in terms of "restricted mimesis."[8] In our language, there is thus a pathological politics of mimesis we shall return to in part 3. On the other hand, this passage already entails—in embryo—an active, creative, productive, or better re-*productive* supplement, which Lacoue-Labarthe endorses for poetic or aesthetic reasons. This "general mimesis," as he calls it, in-*forms* a typical virtuosity of a plastic subject who is not one, for it is deprived of proper individual qualities; yet, paradoxically, it has the power to put this plasticity to productive use by playing all characters, roles, and aesthetic figurations whose formal properties he defines, once again, in terms of "an absence of proper qualities—or if you will, as a plasticity" (Lacoue-Labarthe 1989, 124).[9]

So, Plato is playing with Play-Doh, after all. And in the process, a paradoxical figure is taking shape. Reception of form and creation of form, passivity and activity, docile malleability and plastic virtuosity: the structural similarities between mimesis and plasticity are now becoming visible, the contours of this Janus-faced concept marked. Mimesis, just like plasticity, is the property of a subject without property, a homo mimeticus whose defining characteristics are, indeed, to receive form and give form. A mimetic, yet not simply realistic aesthetics is thus already inscribed in the formation of the subject in a way that is double: it is both the subject of a passive *reception of form* (the subjective base, or "wax") and the subject of a typical virtuosity to *give form* (the plastic subject who assumes different "roles"). As Lacoue-Labarthe puts it, furthering a deconstructive genealogy on the way to gaining a semblance of material substance: "the true distinction passes instead through the difference between *activity* and *passivity*, which embraces the difference between, on the one hand, matter/receptacle/matrix/malleable wax, and, on the other, seal/imprint/stamp/stylet" (1989, 126, n.126), which is exactly what the passage from restricted to general mimesis, reception of form and creation of forms, formalizes. In short, the duplicity of plasticity shadows the duplicity of mimesis, generating a spiraling, paradoxical double movement that blurs the line between active and passive, copy and original, subject and object, inside and outside, and triggers a mirroring interplay that turns stable oppositions into destabilizing equivalences.

Does Malabou know this? If she does, she doesn't say it. Her only reference to Lacoue-Labarthe I could find is critical. In a characteristic agonistic move, it marks a clear-cut demarcation from mimetic models, which is not deprived of patho-*logical* value and which I qualify as romantic agonism, for it is intent on erasing the traces of models in view of promoting an original view. Thus, in *Plasticity at the Dusk of Writing*, Malabou splits Lacoue-Labarthe's Janus-faced account of the plasticity of mimesis in two, and reveals only the passive, restricted, and politically problematic side. As she puts it, her own conception of "formality and figurality—does not [...] open the ideologically questionable space of 'ontotypology' as defined by Philippe Lacoue-Labarthe" in whose interpretation, Malabou continues, "form is the most suspect of all metaphysical concepts" (2010, 54). True, Lacoue-Labarthe is extremely suspicious of mimetic figures for the ontotypology they presuppose and the totalitarian politics they lead to. And this Nietzschean suspicion turns into a virulent critique as fictional figures that erect themselves as authoritarian political leaders who rely on the power of "mythic identification" (Lacoue-Labarthe and Nancy 1990, 296) to generate horrors on a massive scale. This is a lesson that, as we shall confirm in part 3, remains constitutive of the banality of evil with respect to both historical fascism and what I call, (new) fascism.

But politics is clearly only half the story. The other half concerns poetics. That is, an active, productive, and creative mimesis qua "formative force [*force formatrice*]" that is central to Lacoue-Labarthe's mimetology, if only because there would be no "virtuosity" of mimesis were actors—and the plastic subject they embody—not given any aesthetic forms to play with in the first place.

## Plastic Plays: From Restricted to General Mimesis

While playing with Plato, Lacoue-Labarthe can help us, if not to fully answer, at least to address a fundamental question that Malabou's dialectics of plasticity does not clarify: namely, how does restricted plasticity as passive reception of form turn into a general plasticity that has the power to give form? At first sight, the paradoxical logic of this trans-*formation* based on what Lacoue-Labarthe calls an "identity of contraries" (1989, 252) does not seem deprived of dialectical power to turn negative into positive, passivity into activity, perhaps even leading to an explosive future. And yet Lacoue-Labarthe insists that this logic is not dialectical: "Nothing can hold it," he says, "and in particular no dialectical operation, despite its strange proximity to speculative logic" (253). This mimetic logic, then, does not progress from negation to recognition to a sublation of contrasting difference into the sameness of the Self qua self-consciousness. On the contrary, it is based on a "hyperbologic" that constantly unsteadies the opposition between active and passive, wax and seal, giving and receiving form, generating an endless circulation "without resolution" which, for Lacoue-Labarthe, "is nothing other than the very logic of mimesis" (260). In our language, this mimetic logic, or patho-*logy*, requires some material, digital, and transdisciplinary supplements this book aims to provide, but, in substance, continues to inform and transform homo mimeticus in the twenty-first century.

Lacoue-Labarthe delineates the formal contours of his hyperbologic in the sequel to "Typography," *L'Imitation des modernes* (*Typographies II*) (1986), specifically in what he calls "the 'matrix' text [*texte 'matriciel'*] of the modern re-elaboration of the question of *mimesis*" (Lacoue-Labarthe 1986, 10) that informs the whole book: a chapter titled, "Le Paradoxe et la mimésis."[10] We are thus back to the problematic of the actor as a paradigmatic embodiment of the plasticity of the mimetic subject. But the theoretical perspective on the theatrical scene has changed. This time, the focus is not on the effect of the actor on the plastic mass of spectators who are passively subjected to a model they identify with (restricted mimesis). Rather, the focus is on the plastic actor as a virtuoso mimetician who generates artistic characters not deprived of formal qualities (general mimesis). We have thus moved from a passive mimesis receptive to forms to an active mimesis generative of forms via a paradoxical (hyperbological) movement that turns an absence of proper qualities into its very opposite: namely, a potential excess of protean transformations.

What the great actor imitates, if I schematize the paradox to the extreme, is not nature, let alone natural models. Rather, the actor imitates nature's creative force itself and, by doing so, Lacoue-Labarthe says, "*supplements* a certain deficiency in nature [supplée *à un certain défaut de la nature*], its incapacity to do everything, organize everything, make everything its work—*produce everything*" (1989, 255). The foundations of this mimetology are different, for they rest on an Aristotelian rather than Platonic account of mimesis. It is in fact well known that Aristotle, contra Plato, famously redefines mimesis in the *Poetics* as "a representation of an action [*mimesis praxeôs*] which is serious, complete and of a certain magnitude [...] in the mode of dramatic enactment, not narrative" (Aristotle 1987, 37). In a mimetic agon with Plato, who, as we saw, critiqued mimesis for the irrational and contagious *pathos* it generates, Aristotle is indeed intent on defending poetry by stressing both its philosophical value on the side of logos and its cathartic properties on the side of pathos.[11]

So far, so good. Less known is that Aristotle returns to mimesis in *Physics* with the following supplement, as he writes in book 2: "generally art in some cases completes what nature cannot bring to a finish, and in others imitates nature" (8.199a, 340). For Lacoue-Labarthe this second definition whereby imitation does not simply copy or represent nature but, rather, finishes its process of creation, provides what he calls the "generative matrix-scheme" (Lacoue-Labarthe 1986, 23) of what he calls, oxymoronically, the imitation of the moderns. Far from being simply opposed to the imitation of the ancients, as a simplistic framing of the *querelle* between *les anciens et les modernes* tends to suggest, "one can be Modern with the Ancients, thanks to the Ancients, just as one can be against them," as Marc Fumaroli notes (2001, 37; my trans.). Lacoue-Labarthe would concur. In his genealogical reconstruction, he also specifies that the moderns, with and against the ancients, are driven by a different, more affirmative, and creative imitation. This modern imitation is not a passive reproduction or representation of any object but, rather, is at play in an active production or dramatization of a subject who imitates not nature itself but its power of creation.

The overturning of perspectives is significant; it also reloads an ancient quarrel between the ancients for the moderns from an original perspective that finds in theatrical mimesis its starting point and now informs new mimetic studies as well. We have in fact moved from a critique of passive mimesis and the pathological impressions it generates (Plato) to the creative power of mimesis to supplement nature itself (Aristotle). And yet, the agon is not as clear cut as it appears to be for a reason that is, once again, double. First, recall that Aristotle and Plato disagree in their evaluation of mimesis as representation but fundamentally agree that humans are imitative creatures who imitate with their bodies as in ritual dance or dramatic actions—hence their shared insistence on "dramatic mimesis." And second, the form of the mimetic paradox Lacoue-Labarthe infers from the founders of philosophy is essentially the same. At the heart of this mimetic "supplement," we find the same lack of proper qualities Lacoue-Labarthe, on the shoulders of Derrida, described via Plato in "Typography": this subject has no essential, proper, and thus natural properties; the subject is pure and unstable plasticity; a mime without qualities.[12] Yet, precisely because of this lack of essence, or property, this subject is simultaneously endowed with a formative, plastic, and re-*productive* gift to assume all kinds of forms. On the shoulders of a long genealogy of thinkers, Lacoue-Labarthe calls this supplementary gift by different names: the "*gift of impropriety*," the "*gift of nothing*" the "*gift of nature*," or the "*gift of mimesis*" (Lacoue-Labarthe 1989, 259)—which, as we now know, is also the *gift of plasticity* in both its capacity to give form and receive form.[13]

Who, then, is the subject of plasticity? Are we authorized to say that this energy that supplements nature, reproduces nature's creative force, and stems from a plastic/mimetic subject that is ultimately rooted in a human, all-too-human nature? And, by extension, that what used to be called the plasticity of the soul can now be called—to use a more immanent, contemporary term—the plasticity of the brain? These questions take us to the limit of Lacoue-Labarthe's mimetology and deconstruction more generally—and encourage us to go beyond them on the basis of the genealogy of homo mimeticus we have been tracing to chart future directions of investigation.

## Plastic Power, Material Impressions

When it comes to *phusis*'s plastic force, or power, the French philosopher usually deals with the concepts of "soul," "psyche," or "character," rather than with the brain itself. As Jane Bennett points out, Lacoue-Labarthe's "poststructuralist" ontology restricts the reach of his materialism of the soul to human mimesis and does not fully tap into *phusis*'s "non-human" creative possibilities (Bennett 2007, 1198).[14] This critical observation is faithful to the driving *telos* of Lacoue-Labarthe's account of general mimesis, which always posits a *poiesis* already at play in a mimetic supplement to *phusis*. Deconstruction is not quite a materialism and should not be confused with it. On the contrary, it needs a materialist supplement our theory of imitation sets out to provide.

And yet this does not mean that the two deconstructive and materialist perspectives cannot or should not be joined in order to push reflections on the materiality of mimesis further, toward the theory of homo mimeticus we are proposing. The influences, as we shall see in chapters 7 and 8, can go both ways and productively so. For the moment, it suffices to say that there is an unusual passage in "Paradox and Mimesis" where Lacoue-Labarthe roots the plastic force of the actor in the materiality of the "brain." There, he recognizes that what is at play in Diderot's account of the great actor is not a state of (Platonic/Romantic) inspiration characteristic of the man of "sensibility" who is dispossessed of its soul via a form of "enthusiasm" first denounced by Plato in *Ion*, as we noted in chapter 2. On the contrary, Diderot promotes the value of "judgment [*entendement*]" over "sensibility [*sensation*]" (1992, 365) or, to put it in our language, critical *distance* over bodily *pathos*. Interestingly, Lacoue-Labarthe considers this patho-*logical* perspective in terms of what he calls "the affirmed superiority (in the physiological register) of *the brain* over the diaphragm" (Lacoue-Labarthe 1989, 258; emphasis added) necessary for the actor to assume different phantasmal forms.[15] From mimesis as a phantom of reality to mimesis as a phantom of the ego, the perspective is overturned from transcendence to immanence, metaphysics to physiology, yet an ancient, modern, and still contemporary homo mimeticus continues to be at play.

Now, the "physiological register" Lacoue-Labarthe convokes in order to root the actor's plastic power in the "brain" is in line with Diderot's materialism but also finds a supplement in another thinker of mimesis who casts a long shadow on *L'Imitation des modernes* and continues to give genealogical substance to our theory of homo mimeticus as well. Nietzsche is, in fact, a self-proclaimed "physician of culture" whose diagnostic of plasticity as "energy," "power," or "*dunamis*" (Lacoue-Labarthe 1986, 97) directly in-*forms* Lacoue-Labarthe's account of the plasticity of the moderns. Already in the second of the *Untimely Meditation* (1874), Nietzsche in fact speaks of the importance "to know exactly how great the plastic power of man [*sic*], a people, a culture is (2007, 62). He defines "plastic power" as follows:

> I mean by plastic power [*plastische Kraft*] the capacity to develop out of oneself in one's own way, to transform and incorporate into oneself what is past and foreign, to heal wounds, to replace what has been lost, to recreate broken moulds. (62)[16]

Plasticity, then, not only renders the subject, especially if part of a mass but not only, malleable, passive, and pathologically suggestible to authoritarian types (restricted or pathological mimesis); it also has a formative, active, and therapeutic power that recreates molds and heals wounds (general or patho-*logical* mimesis). Plasticity deforms, then, but also forms, and transforms what in the sphere of the physiological register goes under the rubric of the "brain," generating creative possibilities that turn what is foreign and exterior into what is intimate and interior, the wounds and weakness of the past into the health and strength of the future. This therapeutic power, in short, is plastic, metamorphic power insofar as it is creative, vitalist, and affirmative brainpower.

Can we go as far as to say that this natural gift located in the actor's plastic "brain" is ultimately a neuronal gift? Again, Lacoue-Labarthe does not say this. Far from it. Yet he paradoxically comes close to saying it nonetheless. After all, on the shoulders of Aristotle, he constantly reminds us that "mimesis is the most primitive determination of the human animal" (Lacoue-Labarthe 1986, 50) and sets out to root this faculty in "an imitation of *phusis* as a productive force" that also animates "*poiesis*" (1989, 256); and on the shoulders of Plato, he roots the instability of mimesis in a *poetics* that, as we have seen, is founded on the material "plasticity" of the subject qua homo mimeticus. True, this subject without proper qualities is endowed with a disquieting plasticity that is both receptive to forms and creative of forms, is mediated by aesthetics, and is rooted in what Lacoue-Labarthe generally calls "nature," and only once "brain." I thus take the risk—and thus responsibility—to add a materialist supplement of my own to broaden the reach of new mimetic studies; namely, that at the formal and conceptual level, this mimetic paradox also captures the double movement of what now goes under the rubric of synaptic plasticity. That is, a supplementary gift of nature at play in the brain, which leads neurons not to have any proper function, or essential role; and precisely for this plastic reason, we can now suggest, they can paradoxically assume a multiplicity of roles.

Neurons, we are in fact told, do not have essential properties that are fixed in our genetic nature, but are plastic, open to transformation, and endowed with the capacity to "rewire." Neuroscientist Paul Bach-y-Rita, for instance, argues that due to synaptic plasticity "any part of the cortex should be able to process whatever electrical signals were sent to it" (qtd. in Doidge 2007, 18). Alvaro Pascual-Leone, another specialist of neuroplasticity, is more moderate in his diagnostic, as he argues that "formation of new pathways is possible only following initial [cultural] reinforcement of preexistent [genetic] connections" (Pascual-Leone et al. 2005, 379). And yet, he agrees that "ultimately, plasticity is a most efficient way to utilize the brain's limited resources" (396). Neuroplasticity is a burgeoning area of scientific inquiry, and these statements will certainly not be the last words on the matter. What is certain is that the culture/nature binary is indeed deconstructed by the problematic of neuroplasticity, which should play an important role in metamorphoses of the future.

Now, I am not suggesting that what Lacoue-Labarthe calls plastic subject can be reduced to a plastic brain, for it is the dynamic interplay between the brain and the soul that interests philosophical physicians; nor that plasticity opens possibilities for endless transformations that allow us to "become everyone," as enthusiasm for deconstructive possibilities led Lacoue-Labarthe to perhaps too hastily suggest in theory—and luckily so, for this subject would amount to being "no one" in practice. As patients failing to recover from brain damage remind us, there are material limits to brain plasticity that need to be recognized and that no hyperbologic can possibly supplement. Humans are plastic creatures to be sure, yet as any parent has experienced, there are innate predispositions as well that, already at an early age, are resistant to change; and if you try to learn a new language in your thirties and forties, you may notice that not unlike Play-Doh this plasticity tends to diminish over time—which does not mean that, with some nomadic training, it cannot be kept at play. What is certain is that the neurosciences are beginning to catch up with (and lend empirical support to) the ancient paradox concerning the plasticity of the mimetic subject and the physiological laws of impropriety it entails. And what genealogical lenses supplement, in the sphere of theory, is the following insight: the paradox of mimesis served as a model for the paradox of plasticity to take form in the first place.

Lacoue-Labarthe, for his part, will continue to speak of this natural or plastic gift in terms of *poesis* or auto-poesis. Thus, he understands "plastic force" as "the faculty of 'self-growth' and self-accomplishment [*s'accomplir par soi-même*]" (Lacoue-Labarthe 1986, 98; my trans.). This individual conception of artistic creation as a natural force is, once again, not entirely original, nor is it meant to be. It is based on a romantic account of *poesis* that not only reproduces nature but rather re-*produces* the creative force of Being itself, thereby supplementing nature's creative abilities. Or, to put it in Spinozist language, it is based on an imitation of *natura naturans* rather than *natura naturata*. This creative interplay between *phusis* and *poesis* whereby the subject reproduces the creative power of nature is mysterious, masked, and perhaps still of romantic inspiration in its creative appropriation of Aristotle's aesthetic categories.

Yet Lacoue-Labarthe also adds a modernist touch, for the language he mobilizes belongs to the experiential and perhaps transgressive register of erotism. Thus, he speaks of "A pure gift in which nature gives itself up and offers itself in the most secret essence and intimacy, in the very source of its energy," a "pure gift," he specifies thinking of Bataille, "of no economy or no exchange" (Lacoue-Labarthe 1989, 260). The paradigmatic model of this squandering natural gift, the general gift of a heterogeneous mimesis that is not restricted to a homogenous exchange, for it plunges in the secret intimacy of Being, squanders its energy in the matrix of a secret essence in general via a sacred being in particular is, for Bataille, the lover—but that is another story.[17] In Lacoue-Labarthe's portrait of the moderns, he insists that we are confronted with the figure without a proper being he calls, echoing Diderot, a "'genius'" (259).

And this time, Malabou equally knows it.

## *Homo Plasticus*: Patho(-)logies of a Mimetic Brain

Our genealogy gave us sufficient distance to step back and see how deep the continuities between plasticity and mimesis actually go in the history of western philosophy in general and of aesthetics in particular. Homo mimeticus, as it turns out, is also a *homo plasticus*. These mirroring continuities hinge on a paradox based on a logic of the supplement that turns a passive form into active formation and that has remained in the shadows so far. A genealogy of mimesis attentive to the interplay of sameness and difference help us foreground this patho(-)logical paradox in order to go further.

Let us now listen to Malabou's distinction between flexibility and plasticity with this broader genealogy of *homo plasticus* qua homo mimeticus in mind. As she puts it: "To be flexible is to receive a form or impression," but "what flexibility lacks is the resource of giving form, the power to create, to invent or even erase an impression, the power to style" (Malabou 2008, 12). And with a nod to this romantic source of "creation," which was indeed erased, she adds: "Flexibility is plasticity minus its genius" (12). Plasticity, in its double power to give form and receive form, has genius; and a plastic reading should be attentive to plasticity as a source of cures and therapies, good and bad impressions. Thus, Malabou urges us to retrace what deconstruction supposedly erased, that is, what she calls the "impression," "form," but also the "figure," "contour," and "rhythm" of plasticity (2010, 49).

Impression and form; figure and rhythm. The traces may no longer be visible, but the echoes are still audible, if only because Lacoue-Labarthe has insisted on delineating the conceptual contours of mimesis in those very same terms.[18] The echoes are accentuated, as Malabou conjures one of Lacoue-Labarthe's privileged poetic trope—the "caesura"—to identify not the gap between poetic phrases of romantic inspiration but between neural "synapses" of material origins instead. Still, to genealogists, echoes reverberate across linguistic and materialist binaries, as Malabou writes, for instance: "Between two neurons there is thus a caesura, and the synapse itself is 'gapped'" (2008, 36). To be sure, any impressions left by genial models must have been erased for plasticity to come to consciousness, yet some unconscious echoes of the mimetic tradition that gave birth to a dialectical consciousness remain to be heard between the spaces created by writing.

These echoes signal the return of a haunting repetition of mimesis that shadows plasticity, but important differences remain to be signaled—and in this *différend* lies, perhaps, an original supplement to plasticity. For Malabou, in fact, this caesura between neurons is based on a logic of "negation" or "resistance" that is clearly Hegelian in nature and leads to a progressive dialectical development of self-consciousness oriented toward a potentially revolutionary and anarchic future. The philosophical task she sets herself is thus to endow the concept of plasticity with consciousness so that its explosive potential can erupt in the future. The idea is noble in theory and is not deprived of political potential in practice, especially in times of crises under the shadow of tyrannical leaders that call for revolutionary resistance on multiple fronts.

At the same time, dialectical progress is not the only possible future for plasticity. Lacoue-Labarthe, in fact, in a mirroring countermovement, had outlined what he called a "caesura of the speculative [*césure du spéculatif*]" (1989,

208–235) that supplements the logic of dialectics with a paradoxical mimetic logic, or hyperbologic, that does not lead to any progress of consciousness—let alone self-consciousness. Rather, it leads to a radical instability of a plastic homo mimeticus that is unconsciously open to *both* revolutionary movements *and* fascist impressions. As Plato had already indicated in his founding myth of the cave that Lacoue-Labarthe echoes, once we are subjected to types, be they good or evil, "the stakes are moral" (264). But since a conception of "sovereignty" (264) is already at play in the *vita mimetica*, he adds that "there is also a politics involved" (265), which unsurprisingly will turn out to be a hypermimetic politics, as we shall see in part 3.

A genealogy of mimesis, then, leads from aesthetics to politics without necessarily passing via an ascending dialectical metaphysics. As the genealogical trajectory of this book indicates, this immanent development is still very much our *telos*. Significantly, Lacoue-Labarthe ends his diagnostic of the plasticity of mimesis by reminding us that when actors are at play on theatrical stages that appeal to plastic subjects assembled in a mass and chained to magnetizing figures, a danger always lurks behind the scene: namely, the danger of "mimetic epidemic or contagion, that is to say, the panic movement that is the dissolution of the social bond" (Lacoue-Labarthe 1989, 265). We have seen in recent years that epidemics have contagious effects we thought we had long left behind, yet return to haunt the body politic, threating to dissolve the social bond in pathological ways we shall return to in chapter 9.

It is perhaps no accident that this philosophical physician ends his account of "general mimesis" defined by a healthy, active, and creative process of giving form to the plastic subject, with a general reminder that this formation can quickly morph into its other formless, contagious, and pathological side: namely, a "restricted mimesis" whereby the plastic subject is passively formed by fascist figures who impress types on *homo plasticus*. This is indeed the risk of a life-negating pathological *pathos* that dissolves the *sym*-pathos on which the social bond rests, exploding in the process the creative potential of ethical, political, and fictional formations.

To be sure, this is a "different thought of mimesis" (Derrida 1989, 2) whose echoes are only now beginning to fully resonate in new mimetic studies. And like all echoes, this voice is already shared. Lacoue-Labarthe, in fact, gives voice to an ancient Platonic lesson central to that other formidable reader of Plato and model par excellence who in-*forms* both Lacoue-Labarthe's diagnostic of mimesis and Malabou's accounts of plasticity as "something that allows play within the structure" (Malabou 2015a, 244). We have already encountered this precursor who, for many of his generation, seemed to embody the romantic (im)properties of a genius who can now be supplemented as well.

Here is how Jacques Derrida diagnoses this structural play as the plasticity of mimetic types takes form in "Plato's Pharmacy": "The imprints (*tupoi*) of writing," for Plato, writes Derrida, have the power to "inscribe themselves [...] in the wax of the soul *in intaglio*, thus corresponding to the spontaneous, autochthonous motions of psychic life" (1981b, 104). A genealogical model had already outlined the plastic form that for Plato always makes an intaglio in the waxlike plasticity of homo mimeticus. Mimetic, written, and plastic forms are, indeed, intimately tied and cannot be easily disentangled, if only because it is the *pharmakon* of mimesis—and the "malleable unity of this concept" it entails (71)—that gives conceptual form to a paradoxical play of plasticity that reaches into the present, which does not mean that this genealogical interplay between nature and culture, souls and brains need to be restricted to a linguistic economy, as our longer genealogy of homo mimeticus already outlined.

As we have seen, mimesis traces the contours of a disquieting plastic concept whose undecidable double face looks both ways as it is both the locus of origins and copies, presence and absence, passive formation and creative transformation, *pathos* and *logos*, political pathologies and diagnostic patho-*logies*. Or if you prefer Plato's terminology, plasticity, like mimesis, has the (im)properties of what Lacoue-Labarthe, echoing Derrida, echoing Plato, calls "a *pharmakon* that must be handled delicately," for, says Socrates in book 3 of *Republic*, "'it is obvious that such a *pharmakon* must be reserved for physicians'" (qtd. in Lacoue-Labarthe 1989, 132).

Like Derrida before him, but with a distinctly theatrical focus, Lacoue-Labarthe tended to restrict the general economy of mimesis to a household of language. And yet, as modernist physicians of the soul like Nietzsche made strikingly clear, the "whole economy of [his] soul" (1974, 338) is traversed by an immanent bodily pathos that operates on the nervous system of homo mimeticus generating forms of preverbal communication that go beyond good and evil. Interestingly, contemporary physicians of the soul have been following precisely this genealogical trajectory. Alvaro Pascual-Leone and his team, for instance, echo a patho(-)logical diagnostic, as he writes: "Plasticity is the mechanism for development and learning, as well as the cause of pathology" (Pascual-Leone et al. 2005, 396). Nietzsche, but also Plato, would not have disagreed. On the contrary, they develop a Janus-faced aesthetics on the basis of this pharmacological lesson. Closer to *homo plasticus*, Jean-Pierre Changeux, a major influence on Malabou, as he retraces the discovery of synaptic plasticity in *Neuronal Man*

(1983), joins past and present diagnostics, as he writes: this new science "was to take shape only with the arrival on the scene of a very old discipline concerned with poisons, drugs, and medicines: pharmacology" (Changeux 1997, 33).[19]

In the liminal twilight of philosophy, there might not be an essential difference between the dusk of writing and the dawn of plasticity, after all. They both shine through with a mimetic light projecting different facets of homo mimeticus now attentive to the patho(-)logies of *homo plasticus* as well. In the end, then, pharmacology and neurology might not be as simply opposed as they appear to be at first sight. And who knows? If these often-opposed *logoi* on the plastic power of mimetic *pathos* turn to face each other, they might not simply passively mirror each other; they can now also actively reflect on one another in productive patho-*logical* ways.

On one side of this Janus-faced logos, Malabou convincingly shows how contemporary neurology can indeed help scholars in the humanities give material substance to the concept of writing by inscribing linguistic traces in the materiality of the brain. This perspective opens up transformative possibilities for the human sciences, if not to completely explode, at least to offer some "resistance" (Malabou 2008, 68) to passive subjections to dominant pathologies now proliferating in an increasingly precarious, interconnected, and damaged planet. Political resistance is, indeed, more needed than ever in a neoliberal world that demands increasing docile adaptation to (new) fascist and authoritarian leaders endowed with a will to power that not only risks turning the ego into a phantom via the use of new algorithm media; they also threaten escalating violence to the extreme by resuscitating the phantom of nuclear catastrophes. Malabou's plastic work on mimetic subjects par excellence such as trauma, epigenetics, crowd behavior, and the unconscious, offers timely contributions to the mimetic turn. The *re*-turn to mimesis is already at play in Malabou's realization that "every act of shaping, repairing, remodeling" at play in plasticity "illustrate[s] the return of repetition" (2015b, 71). And in a mirroring move, she adds: "repetition has become the question, what questions us" (71). Mimesis, I have argued, is not only the subject that questions; it is also the subject *of* this question—and this questioning subject leads us through the other side of the looking glass.

On the other side, we have been pushing against the shoulders of an ancient genealogy of philosophical physicians that considered plasticity and imitation two sides of homo mimeticus. Lacoue-Labarthe's untimely question makes us wonder if plasticity is, perhaps, nothing less than a contemporary repetition of an ancient pharmakon. That is, a more embodied, affective, and material pharmakon whose logical and pathological effects always escape grand dialectical narratives of progress or coming to consciousness—including political progress and enlightened consciousness. If the double diagnostic of plasticity echoes an ancient pharmacology of mimesis that blurs the line between activity and passivity, giving form and receiving form, theatrical figures and fascist figures, *logos* and *pathos*, therapy and sickness, this repetition with a difference continues to be in urgent need of diagnostics—if only because the dark reality of political pathologies that render the plastic masses prey to the mimetic unconscious risks exploding the fictional logic of plasticity coming to consciousness.

Lacoue-Labarthe's mirroring reflections never claimed to be fully original. As he puts it, in a confessional, theatrical, but also hermeneutical phrase: "I'm only a messenger, a spokesman. Let's say, a '*passeur*'" (Lacoue-Labarthe 2000, 102). The message has been well received; the role of the *passeur* is now replayed. Hence the echoes can be heard in the *re-*turn to homo mimeticus. From the space between passing phrases, aesthetic impressions, and protean subjects our genealogical gesture took the apparently simple form of play. While playing with Play-Doh, daughter and dad, overturned in passing the new form of plasticity. And what we found underneath Plato is the formative imprint of a complex Janus-faced figure: an old *pharmakon* that captures the two sides of what we called, for lack of a better phrase, the plasticity of mimesis.

CHAPTER 5

# ON ANIMAL AND HUMAN MIMICRY

*La fin semble bien être l'assimilation au milieu.*

—Roger Caillois

To this day, the French transdisciplinary thinker Roger Caillois remains a marginalized figure in critical theory. An untimely and unclassifiable writer fascinated by sacred rituals and political rituals, play and games, Dionysian possessions and nonhuman dispossession, animal mimicry and stone writing, he developed what he called a "diagonal science" that cuts across disciplinary discourses and never conformed to the dominant schools that—from surrealism to psychoanalysis, structuralism to poststructuralism—dominated the French intellectual scene over the past century, casting a long shadow on different strands of critical theory across the world that continue to relegate Caillois to the margins of academic discourses. At best, he is considered as the negative double of his now influential counterpart Georges Bataille. Equally unread in his lifetime, Bataille was resuscitated posthumously in the 1960s by figures like Michel Foucault, Roland Barthes, Jacques Derrida, Jean-Luc Nancy, and other thinkers at the margins of philosophy who considered him as a heterogeneous source of inspiration for the linguistic turn and, more recently, for the mimetic turn as well.[1]

After a century of benign neglect, it is now time to fully recognize that Caillois's diagonal theory of mimetism (*mimétisme*), which straddles discourses or *logoi* as diverse as aesthetics, anthropology, philosophy, psychoanalysis, and biology, played not only a major role in the development of imaginary theories of the ego in the past century; an unacknowledged precursor, he helps us account for the dynamic interplay between human mimetism and animal mimicry that cuts across the nature/culture binary of the past and goes beyond object-oriented and subject-oriented ontologcal binaries in the present as well.[2]

To gauge Caillois's untimely contribution to new mimetic studies, let us introduce him as a thinker who did not develop his theory of mimetism in a position of epistemic isolation but in a relation of communication with other theorists of imitation he encountered.

## Mimetic Encounters: Lacan, Bataille, Caillois

Caillois's name tends to be entangled with Bataille due to their shared intellectual efforts to re-evaluate the power of the sacred in modern societies in the wake of surrealism in the late 1930s, a period haunted by the looming shadow of war. It might thus appear just an anecdotal coincidence that it was actually an even more influential figure associated with surrealist projects who introduced Caillois to Bataille back in 1934: namely, Jacques Lacan. As Caillois recalls in an interview: "I first met Bataille at Jacques Lacan's home. After that we met fairly often, and together with Michel Leiris we had the idea of founding a study group, which then became the College of Sociology" (qtd. in Frank and Naish 2003, 143). Without being conscious of doing so, and thus, in our specific sense, *un*-consciously, Lacan sparked a collaboration between Caillois, Bataille, and Michel Leiris that would witness a break with surrealism via the famous jumping beans episode.

This mythic episode is worth recalling. As the story goes, Breton, Caillois, and Lacan met at a market and came across a stand with mysterious Mexican beans called "jumping beans." To give away the secret at the outset—spoiler alert—they are inhabited by a larva that makes the seeds jump. Caillois, suspecting the presence of the larva, wanted to slice the beans open to understand the source of the movement; Breton objected that such a positivist biological understanding would destroy the mystery. To which Caillois replied: "The irrational: granted. But first and foremost it must be coherent" (qtd. in Frank 2003, 85). To know or not to know, that seems to have been the question. This escalating agon eventually led to Caillois's break with Breton and surrealism. Lacan is said to have walked away, but not without taking Caillois's insight into mimetism in his pocket, or rather, theory, as we shall see.

Caillois's break with surrealism didn't prevent the formation of other transdisciplinary groups. Joined by Michel Leiris, and under the leadership of Bataille, Caillois became part of an elective community of heterogeneous thinkers who assembled in 1937 under the rubric of the *Collège de sociologie (1937–1939)* (Hollier 1998). An alternative to surrealist groups, the aim of the Collège was to account for strange, perhaps magical, but not less real phenomena of dispossession that were casting a shadow on a Europe on the brink of war at the time; under new masks, such phenomena now threaten present times haunted by the horror of war as well. Hence the urgency to look back to the Collège in the company of Caillois to prepare for new mimetic phenomena to come.

Funded on the eve of World War II by Bataille, Caillois, and Leiris, the Collège assembled heterogeneous thinkers whose interests were not restricted by disciplinary academic affiliations. Instead, they shared a concern with the value of the humanities to understand the present, paving the way for reflections on the future as well. It included figures like Walter Benjamin, Jean Wahl, Pierre Klossowski, Denis de Rougemont, Alexandre Kojève, among other participants whose shared goal was to account for disconcerting phenomena that anthropologists in the wake of Émile Durkheim and Marcel Mauss traditionally grouped under the rubric of the "sacred" central to so-called "primitive" societies.

Somewhat uphill, these untimely figures argued that sacred states of dispossession at play in shamanism, magic, myth, tragedy, festivity, sex, political power, among other heterogeneous phenomena that tended to be relegated to the margins of academia were resurfacing at the very heart of "modern" and supposedly "civilized" western societies as well. In the process, they put Durkheim's and Mauss's anthropological insights into the "sacred" and the "effervescence" it generates to contemporary critical use by uncovering affective, contagious, and in this sense, imitative principles that transgressed the individualistic problematic of the formation of an autonomous, solipsistic, and narcissistic human ego.

They also took mimesis beyond the pleasure principle by confronting reality principles like the army, war, and totalitarian leaders, most notably Hitler and Mussolini, who cast a political shadow on European democracies in the late 1930s. Despite the plurality of perspectives involved at the Collège, then, the driving undercurrent consisted in accounting for social, anthropological, aesthetic, and political phenomena of mass contagion that, most notably via fascism and Nazism, were generating intoxicating forms of hypnotic depersonalization on an unprecedented collective scale. Well before structuralism, let alone poststructuralism, these untimely thinkers were thus clearly decentering the myth of an autonomous, rational, and self-contained subject, or *Homo sapiens*, while paving the way for the *re*-turn of attention to a relational, porous, and embodied subject open to human and environmental forces that we call homo mimeticus.

The disagreements at the heart of the Collège eventually led to a break between Caillois and Bataille as well; yet a shared consensus remained in place: participants tended to agree that modern humans are eminently vulnerable to contagious flows of intoxicating effervescences that could not simply be projected outside of "civilization" via a form of mimetic racism characteristic of ethnocentric colonial principles dominant in the modernist period. The heart of darkness, they implicitly agreed with Conrad, was not at the heart of Africa but at the heart of Europe instead. In the process, they registered that this palpitating heart tends to generate a double movement of attraction and repulsion that, Bataille and Caillois agreed, is constitutive of sacred forms of mimetic communication with spellbinding powers. If the subject of *Aufklärung* had relegated these double binds to the bottom of mythic caves in the philosophical past, Bataille and Caillois would have agreed that they animate the *vita mimetica* of their contemporary body politic nonetheless.

## A Precursor of Mimetic Studies

Almost a century later, we are now well positioned to re-evaluate the validity of these heterogeneous subject matters. A lot of water has flowed under the bridge and many changes were made for the better, rendering if not the world in general, at least the West, a safer place overall in the postwar period. And yet, when it comes to the contagious flows of mimetic affects and the violent escalations that ensue as the body politic falls under the spell of (new) fascist and totalitarian leaders, we are far from having made the progress many hoped.[3] Thanks to the recent return of interest in the theoretical relevance of the Collège in a period that does not transparently mirror the late 1930s but echoes nonetheless similar preoccupations with issues of mass contagion, neofascist charisma, hypnotic spells, magical influences, authoritarian lies, imperial wars, and violent escalations triggered by autocratic phantoms, both Bataille's and Caillois's accounts of fascist psychology and the workings of a communicative *sym-pathos* that flows like a river, for better and worse, through the pores of homo mimeticus turn out to be (un)timely contributions to face challenges of the present and future.

With few exceptions, Caillois has tended to remain in the shadow of his former friend and collaborator in the past century.[4] Yet, as we enter deeper in the epoch of the Anthropocene characterized by an increasing realization that the powers of mimesis entangle human and nonhuman animals in planetary forces that do not fit into structuralist binaries that neatly divide nature and culture, human and nonhuman agency, it is perhaps Caillois who can best help us confront and overcome the fallacy of anthropocentrism internal to mimetic theories of the past that can no longer contain the protean manifestations of homo mimeticus in the present and future.[5]

We have already seen that the mimetic faculty is rooted in mirroring, chameleonlike mechanisms of mimicry that are shared with nonhuman animals. Rooted in primordial times driven by the attempt to "elude one's pursuers" (Nietzsche 1982, 26:20), Nietzsche was quick to sense that "mimicry" is embedded in the evolutionary history of *Homo sapiens* informing moral prejudices, herd behavior, and a tendency among philosophers to "hide in the general concept of 'man'" (20). This drive to merge against social, political, moral, intellectual, as well as natural and environmental backgrounds generates a permeability to human and nonhuman influences that trouble the ontological foundations of the ego, generating what we call, echoing Nietzsche, phantom egos instead.

Given this background that informs our genealogy of homo mimeticus, a re-evaluation of mimesis beyond anthropocentrism is thus urgently in order to bring new mimetic studies up to date with contemporary developments. For a long time, in fact, philosophers have defined the genus *homo* as *the* most imitative animals par excellence. As Aristotle famously puts in the *Poetics*: "this distinguishes man [sic] from other creatures, that he is thoroughly mimetic and through mimesis takes his first steps in understanding" (1987, 34). This statement has not lost its interest, as we set out to re-evaluate both the logical and pathological manifestations of the all-too-human drive for imitation for the present century. And yet, this does not mean that nonhuman animals are deprived of the "natural propensity" for "mimetic activity" (34). Quite the contrary. Well before the nonhuman turn, Caillois's nonanthropocentric account of both animal and human mimicry pursues the Nietzschean project of reinscribing humans in general and their mimetic drives in particular, back in nature. He does so by putting humans back in touch with an animal mimicry that, for better and worse, remains constitutive of human nature as well. If Caillois's attention to the continuities between human and nonhuman mimicry has often been derided as vaguely surrealist, he was never under the spell of surrealist fascination with magical mysteries. On the contrary, as the jumping beans episode made clear, he wanted to understand the mysteries in nature to better understand a human fascination for magical forces he considered rooted in biological and environmental forces—immanent, material forces that, for the moment, still sustain us, but with our help, also threaten to dissolve us.

It is only recently that, in the wake of new materialist turns to the nonhuman, Caillois's thought has gained greater traction in visible strands of critical theory. If the power of mimesis to open up the ego to a (non)human "process of influence that operates below consciousness" (Bennett 2020, xvii) has long been marginalized, Jane Bennett, who is well known for her groundbreaking work on the nonhuman turn and the vibrant matters it entails, is currently contributing to the mimetic *re*-turn as well.[6] In a productive dialogue animated by reciprocal influences, Bennett recently recognized, for instance, that Caillois's concern with an "automatic biomimesis working to destroy individuation" (xvii) is constitutive to her "return to the question of the I" (xii) that is prone to "altered states of mind," "influence" and "*sympathy*" (xv, xi), among other affective powers animating phantom egos.

Thanks to collective efforts to promote a re-*turn* to a different, immanent, and relational conception of unconscious imitation, the mimetic unconscious, once neglected in the Freudian century, is now taken seriously in different strands of critical theory in the present century. Caillois occupies a key and so far largely unacknowledged role as a mediator or *passeur* between the nonhuman turn and the mimetic turn. In fact, his comparative, transdisciplinary, or as he called it, "diagonal" account of *mimétisme* relied on a materialist ontology that goes beyond human/nonhuman binaries, subject-oriented and object-oriented ontologies; it was long marginalized in an epoch dominated by structuralist oppositions between nature and culture and should be revitalized today for reasons that are entangled in the genealogy we are tracing in this book in particular and will continue to drive new mimetic studies in general. To pave the way, I take two steps in that direction.

First, it is important to recall that it was not only Lacan that did Caillois a favor by introducing him to Bataille early in his career; in a mirroring gesture, Caillois reciprocated the favor by providing Lacan with theoretical insights into mirroring processes of psychic formation and dissolution that served as a theoretical blueprint for the latter's celebrated account of "The Mirror Stage" (Lacan 1977 [1949]). If this often-anthologized text cast such a spell on the structuralist and, later, poststructuralist generation, it has not been sufficiently stressed that Lacan's dialectics of the "relation between the organism and its reality—or as they say, between the *Innenwelt* and the *Umwelt*"

(4)—rests on imitative principles central to the Collège in general and outlined by Caillois in particular. He did so in his often mentioned but little studied essay, titled "Mimicry [*Mimétisme*] and Legendary Psychasthenia" (Caillois 1938),[7] where Caillois set materialist foundations for homo mimeticus that went beyond human and nonhuman binaries, animal mimicry and human mimetism, but also psychic *Innenwelt* and environmental *Umwelt*.

With few exceptions, the mirroring continuities between Lacan and Caillois on mimetic subject matters have tended to go unnoticed or downplayed within psychoanalytic circles, more concerned with Lacan's original reframing of Freudian or linguistic principles. But as Matthew Potolsky recognized, "Caillois' discussion of insect mimicry [...] was a decisive influence on Lacan's theory of the mirror stage" (2006, 140).[8] The Freudian and linguistic turn now behind us and the nonhuman and environmental turn ahead of us, this is indeed the moment to retrieve Caillois from the theoretical background where he has long been relegated. This also means that his influence on once dominant theories of homo mimeticus needs to be re-evaluated from a less anthropocentric perspective. If we look past the imaginary image of a narcissistic ego whose unity is reflected on the specular surface of a mirror, genealogical lenses reveal how profound Caillois's formative impression on Lacan actually were. As we shall see, Lacan was indeed writing in the shadow of Caillois's materialism in his mirroring, and thus reversed, account of the birth of the ego—out of an ideal image or *imago*.

Second, and perhaps more important, Caillois's account of mimetism straddles disciplines as diverse as psychology, anthropology, aesthetics, and biology among other *logoi* to explore diagonal connections between human pathologies and nonhuman forces. In the process, he calls attention to the interplay between animal mimicry and human mimetism in ways that have been dismissed as "anthropomorphic" in the past, or have simply been ignored. Yet, among mimetic theorists of the twentieth century, it is arguably Caillois who went furthest in developing both a science and a poetics of mimesis that goes beyond what is arguably one of the greatest fallacies of the present century: namely, "anthropocentrism" and the blindness to the agentic power of nonhuman influences it entails.

Anticipating and countering the accusation of anthropomorphism redoubled by an agonistic move characteristic of untimely thinkers, Caillois offers a critique of anthropocentrism that has fallen on deaf ears in the past but that should resonate in the present: "Human are animals like others, their biology is the one of other living beings as well" (Caillois 2008, 484; my trans.). And in an arrow directed to the future, he adds: "It seems to me that if this is not anthropomorphism, it is anthropocentrism to exclude the human from the universe and to subtract him [sic] from a common legislation" (484). This agonistic mirroring inversion of perspectives turning the critique of anthropo*morphism* into a countercritique of anthropo*centrism* is only beginning to be taken seriously today. We are in fact entering a new epoch that reframes *Homo sapiens* in a genealogy that is not only part of nature but contributes to changing the very geology on which nature lives and dies—including human nature.

As the entry into the epoch of the Anthropocene made clear, since the Great Acceleration of 1950s, whose foundations go back at least since the industrial revolution of 1750s (Crutzen and Stoermer 2000), humans are exceptional not in the usual anthropocentric sense that they are separate from nature and thus above it. Rather, we are exceptional in the sense that we are and "will remain a major geological force for many millennia, maybe millions of years to come" (41). This also means that humans cannot be subtracted from the nonhuman influences they set in motion, and now, via spiraling feedback loops we have been drawing from the beginning, reveal a drawing hand to be a nonhuman hand, retracting on the formation and transformation of human life—with a vengeance. As William Connolly puts it, this materialist inversion of perspectives should "render us more sensitive to a variety of nonhuman force fields" (2013, 9) that are already rapidly erasing all-too-human boundaries artificially set up to distinguish human animals from the environments on which we radically depend. As human history is being reframed against the longer, deep history of life on earth, it is sobering to recall that the history of *Homo sapiens* as a species is relatively short (ca. 300,000 years). We are in fact part of an ancient genealogy of hominini that makes *Homo sapiens* "the last surviving twig on a vast and intricately branching bush" (Tattersall 2022). If we consider the even shorter history of human civilization via the development of agriculture (ca. 12,000 years) that led to organized city-states, and place it against the very recent anthropogenic assaults on the biosphere over the past fifty years, speaking of "many millennia or millions of years" to come for *Homo sapiens* smacks of unrealistic scientific optimism, to say the least. Unless we urgently change course and use the metamorphic powers of mimesis for the better, genealogists don't see a long future ahead of us.

While the new climate sciences are providing reliable empirical information that is currently transforming the human sciences and the humanities, the collaboration would prove mutually beneficial. In fact, there could well be a chiastic relation between magic and science in the sense that science is also sometimes driven by magical beliefs in progress—and magic is, at times, not deprived of scientific insights. What Connolly says of the human sciences also applies to the sciences more generally: there is indeed a "need […] to dwell creatively from time to time in literary and artistic practices" in order to come to terms with the "fragility of things" (2013, 16). As an untimely precursor working across the science/human sciences/literature divides, Caillois is a good ally in this respect. As we sail deeper in the epoch of the Anthropocene, it seems that never have Caillois's premonitions about end times sounded as closer to the reality principle: "Indeed, the end would appear to be *assimilation to the environment* [milieu]" (Caillois 1938, 108; my trans.).

But before we reach the end, let us start in the proximity of the beginning. This entails framing Caillois's diagonal theory of mimetism as a precursor of a mimetic turn that, it should be clear by now, goes beyond human and nonhuman binaries and the anthropocentric fallacy they entail.

## Toward a Diagonal Science of Mimesis

Well before the affective turn and the cognitive turn, the new materialist turn and the environmental turn, Caillois supplemented anthropocentric accounts of mimesis restricted to human techniques of representation from the more general perspective of animal mimicry based on continuities between human and nonhuman animals that go all the way to inorganic matter. He thus paved the way for a nonhuman turn that re-emerged only in recent years. In the process, he also zeroed in on mimesis as a diagonal concept that cuts across subject-oriented and object-oriented ontologies to articulate the entangled continuities between the two now central to new mimetic studies as well. He did so from the margins of academia on the critical side but also from "the edge of surrealism" (Frank 2003) on the aesthetic side, thereby opening up diagonal conversations between the objective rigor of science and the subjective intuition of arts—without setting up a binary between the two.

One of Caillois's sharpest scientific/aesthetic wedges was, indeed, behavioral mimesis, or as he called it, "mimetism" (*mimétisme*). In fact, he foregrounded the biological fact that the human "mimetic faculty," as Walter Benjamin called in his famous 1933 essay, should not be considered from the point of view of visual representation alone, nor was it completely overshadowed by the birth of language. On the contrary, it continues to animate, in imperceptible, often magical, yet not less immanent, material, and experiential ways heterogeneous continuities between human/animal mimicry and the natural world. As Caillois succinctly puts it: "I will never tire of saying this: both [humans and nonhuman animals] belong to the same world" (2003a, 343).[9] This repetition was left unheard in the past century but as anthropogenic climate change keeps devastating both human and nonhuman life on earth, there are better chances to hear it in the present century.

A metamorphosis is, indeed, urgently in order. This also means that the cultural "transformation" of the mimetic faculty we have been tracing back to prehistoric time rests on broader nonhuman foundations homo mimeticus should draw on. Recall in fact that Benjamin compared "the powerful compulsion in former times to become and behave like something else" (2007, 334), which is still at play today in children imitating living and nonliving entities—"the child plays at being not only a shopkeeper or a teacher but also a windmill and a train" (333)—to the more abstract or "nonsensous" similarity of language still audible in onomatopoeic words. What Caillois adds is that there is an underlying biological mimetic drive, or power, that cuts across not only different periods in human history but also the metaphysical divide between the human and the nonhuman. This is a decisive supplement to a genealogy of homo mimeticus for the epoch of the Anthropocene.

The recent turn to the agentic materiality of things and to processes of becoming (other) that are as human as they are nonhuman is currently contributing to a return of interest in Caillois's pioneering efforts to move the human sciences and aesthetic theory beyond the fallacy of anthropocentrism. Jane Bennett's already mentioned reliance on Caillois to further her new materialist approach to the mimetic vibrations that entangle matter and a porous relational self genealogically in line with homo mimeticus is a case in point that testifies to his growing influence in the anglophone world, as we shall see in more detail in chapter 8. For the moment it suffices to say that Caillois was, indeed, an untimely thinker in the Nietzschean sense that he was ahead of his time. He foresaw the delusion of positing *Homo sapiens* as divided from nature, thereby adding a fourth narcissistic blow to all-too-human delusions that usually start with Copernicus and Darwin and stop at the name of Sigmund Freud. The retrospective genealogy is flattering for the latter but needs to be furthered beyond anthropocentric principles in the present century. Caillois did so via what he called a "diagonal science" that paid particular attention to "latent complicities" and "neglected correlations" (Caillois 2003a, 347) between, among other things, animal and human mimetism and whose "underground correspondence" (Caillois 2008, 483) required a transdisciplinary perspective in order to be perceived in the first place.

Caillois's first theoretical articulation of "Diagonal Science" develops methodological principles that we took seriously for the development of our theory of imitation and speak to epistemic concerns central to new mimetic studies more generally. As he puts it in *Méduse et Cie* (1960):

> Erudite scholars who know a lot in a restricted domain rarely find themselves in a position to perceive a type of relation that only a polyvalent knowledge is apt to establish [...] It is probable that a small number of researchers spontaneously attached to the study of phenomena that cross-over [*enjambent*] traditional boundaries in different sciences, find themselves best placed to identify neglected correlations, and able to complete the network of established relations. (Caillois 2008, 483–484)

The poetic trope of *enjambement* is well taken, for it walks across poetic and scientific lines. Just as poetic phrases can be connected across different lines, so scientific discourses can be connected across different disciplinary lines—if only because they are both part of a continuous scientific-poetic delineation of the correlated patho-*logies* of homo mimeticus. One of the underlying assumptions of the present book is, in fact, that mimesis is precisely such a diagonal bio-psycho-anthropo-politico-aesthetic phenomenon that steps over, or *enjambe*, disciplinary boundaries.

Caillois's diagonal observations are particularly apt to cut across the different manifestations of mimesis we have been tracking. He also stresses the importance of overlapping perspectives on protean phenomena that may appear aberrant in isolation but reveal interconnected patho-*logies* that once were in diagonal communication. As he puts it:

> transversal cuts [across disciplines] play an indispensable role in illuminating phenomena that isolated may sometimes seem aberrant, but whose meaning would be better perceived if we dared aligning these exceptions and if we attempted to superpose their related mechanisms. (Caillois 2008, 482)

From animal mimicry to human mimetism, visual representations to bodily impersonations, phylogenic to ontogenic imitation, contagious affects to mirroring effects and plastic transformations, among other manifestations of mimesis, these phenomena may have seemed "aberrant" in the past century, for they transgress dominant accounts of realism or representation, revealing porous continuities between self and others, inside and outside, consciousness and the unconscious, the human and the nonhuman. And yet, Caillois' pledge for a diagonal science of mimesis reveals overlapping continuities indispensable to cast light on that protean natural-cultural creature that is homo mimeticus in the present century. As he succinctly puts it, in an invitational gesture we relay and echo for present generations: "It is time to try the chance of *diagonal sciences*" (2008, 484).

With few exceptions, this call was not heard by Caillois's contemporaries. As Maurice Blanchot pointed out, many considered that Caillois "was interested in too many things" and therefore "did not figure in the number of those who held some form of recognized knowledge" (qtd. in Frank 2003, 1), by which Blanchot means academic, disciplinary, and thus specialized knowledge. Still, Caillois's surrealist bio-psycho-anthropo-aesthetic lenses on mimetism allowed him, well before the affective turn, to "envisage the social in affective and religious terms" (Hollier 1993, 56). Recent accounts of the centrality of affective, religious, and fictional forces in the history of *Homo sapiens* would not have surprised Caillois and the members of the College. On the contrary, he was already revealing a human and nonhuman vulnerability not only to mythic fictions but also to the enveloping materiality of the environment, both of which resonate with a number of transdisciplinary turns to materiality and affect today.

For instance, Caillois is attentive to what Teresa Brennan calls a "transmission of affect" that operates below conscious awareness and troubles the boundaries of a stable ego while also "undermining the dichotomy between the individual and the environment and the related opposition between the biological and the social" (Brennan 2004, 7). Brennan does not mention pioneering figures like Nietzsche, Tarde, Bataille, let alone Caillois, who went a long way in challenging the ideal of the "emotionally contained subject" (2) the affective turn is now also up against; she might also be too critical of theories of crowd psychology that, as we shall see, paved the way for mechanisms of affective communication internal to the mimetic unconscious via mirroring principles that turned out to have empirical foundations. Still, her insights into a transmission of affect not limited to desire alone but involving the sphere of pathos more generally and sensible to the patho-*logical* realization that "there is no secure distinction between the 'individual' and the 'environment'" (6) is perfectly consistent with our theory of homo mimeticus in general and Caillois's diagonal take on mimetism in particular.[10] Given the recent turn of attention to a type of affective contagion central to the affective turn and the nonhuman turn untimely figures like Caillois anticipated in the first place, a new generation of diagonal thinkers are in a position to overturn perspectives to push mimetic studies further. This entails, among other things, considering that the environment is radically vulnerable to anthropocentric activities as well, entangling human and nonhuman animals in a spiraling vortex of mimetic transmissions in which we are, nolens volens, already caught.

Caillois's diagonal perspective may have been marginalized by dominant academic institutions that did not grant him the position he deserved.[11] Still, he was recognized by influential intellectuals nonetheless. Apparently, his former teacher Georges Dumézil did not hesitate to call Caillois "'the genius of our time'" (qtd. in Frank 2003, 9). We should, however, specify that this "genius" was not harkening back to individualistic times driven by romantic anxieties of influence. He was thus not opposed to practices of imitation but, rather, put mimesis to re-*productive* theoretical use. Caillois's agonistic attitude toward older contemporaries like André Breton and Georges Bataille is often noted, but the logic animating this agon often escapes critical attention. In her informed introduction to Caillois for the anglophone world, for instance, Claudine Frank rightly notes that his "writing is generally grappling with another body of thought" via a principle she calls "dialogical or self-reflexive" (2003, 6) that generates the following double movement: "While fending off others, though, Caillois also tends to build on, or rework, his own previous ideas" (6). This principle can be sharpened by the dia-logic of mimetic agonism in which the thoughts of an older model are incorporated to develop a thought with and against him. As Bataille, the older model in question, was quick to recognize in a letter to Caillois: "essential matters derive from the god *Polemos*" (qtd. in Frank 365 n. 32). And who is Polemos if not an agonistic god who is also the principle of all things according to a genealogy of philosophers of becoming that harkens back to Heraclitus?

Caillois's mimetic agonism led to the emergence of an original and untimely thought that may have been polemic as it increased his academic marginalization in practice but allowed him to see further than most in diagonal theory. Caillois warned, for instance, that the ideal scholar risks turning into what he called, not without irony, an "efficient and myopic mole" (2003a, 344). The animal metaphor is not innocent. Caillois resorts to a nonhuman analogy, or homology, to reframe what is traditionally conceived as the culmination of human differentiation in the sky of ideas (the scholar) back to the immanence of an industrious animal laboring alone under the earth (the mole). In the process, the solipsistic animal efficacy in digging holes is revealed as lacking in sight, let alone insight and foresight (myopic). The methodological paradox Caillois is outlining is clear: the more specialized and individualist the research, the more limited the insights.

Contra this still dominant bias in favor of hyperspecialization, Caillois's diagonal methodological hypothesis consisted in a different, perhaps more modest and imitative, but not less insightful conception of genius. Far from being possessed by a form of divine inspiration whose genealogy, as we have seen, goes back to Plato's mimetic agonism with Homer, Caillois considers that "genius almost always involves borrowing a proven method or fruitful hypothesis and using it in a field where no one had previously imagined that it could be applied" (2003a, 343). Thus reframed, what a romantic tradition called "genius" does not stem from individual (from Latin, *individuum*, indivisible) originality. On the contrary, it emerges from a dialogic relation of "borrowing" from other fields, predicated on the contagious hypothesis that an invisible underlying homology often exists between phenomena that academic lenses tend to perceive as heterogeneous in nature. Thus, Caillois later speaks of his diagonal meditations as belonging to what he calls, "answers to the contagious interrogation [*interrogation contagieuse*] displacing from subject to subject a sensibility that is more faithful than realized to the same communicating enigmas" (2008a, 560). In this mirroring reflection, the underlying methodological assumption is that biology casts light on human psychology, just as much as psychology and related human sciences, most notably anthropology, cast new light on biology—including the biology of an eminently imitative species prone to contagious forms of communication.

The heterogeneous phenomena we have grouped in this book under the diagonal rubric of "mimesis" are thus a perfect example to put Caillois's polyvalent diagonal science to the test. As Edgar Morin will later confirm, mimesis is a bio-psycho-socio-anthropological phenomenon that, by definition, calls for transdisciplinary perspectives in order to be properly theorized. Nietzsche called this shift of perspectives, which is not relativism for it illuminates different facets of a complex phenomenon, *perspectivism*. While dominant academic tendencies, especially in analytic philosophy but not only, have tended to introduce clear-cut distinctions between different manifestations of what the Greeks grouped under the rubric of *mimēsis* (imitation, emulation, simulation, mimicry, mimetism, etc.) in order to stress *discontinuities* between the spectrum of what is traditionally conceived as an essentially human phenomenon, Caillois opted for the opposed methodological strategy: namely, he started his re-evaluation of the mimetic faculty where Benjamin had left it.

In his essay "On the Mimetic Faculty" Benjamin started with the realization that "nature creates similarities. One need only think of mimicry" (2007, 331). However, if Benjamin, echoing Aristotle, claimed that "the highest capacity for producing similarities [...] is man's" (333), Caillois set up no binary or hierarchy. Thus, instead of considering that in its "historical development" the mimetic faculty was absorbed by the "nonsensous similarity" at play in language and "liquidated [...] magic" (334, 336), Caillois took the mimetic faculty on a different, more diagonal rather than evolutionary path. In fact, he zeroed in on the sensuous continuities internal to heterogeneous phenomena of depersonalization characteristic of both human and nonhuman animals. And he did so by taking the diagonal inquiries at play at the Collège to develop his diagonal perspectivism that entangled biological, psychological, anthropological, political, and ontological discourses on the human and nonhuman patho(-)logies that go from mimicry to mimetism.

## From Mimicry to Mimetism[12]

It is true that Caillois does not often refer to the concept of "mimesis" itself, preferring the one of "mimetism" (*mimétisme*). And yet, this distinction is not watertight. In fact, influential critical theorists echoed Caillois's account of mimetism, as they paved the way for interdisciplinary approaches to come by also straddling disciplines as diverse as aesthetic theory, anthropology, and philosophy among others. For genealogists, it is in fact no accident that thinkers of mimesis in the second half of the twentieth century—from Theodor Adorno to René Girard and Philippe Lacoue-Labarthe—all came to rely on the concept of "mimetism" to reinscribe, from different perspectives, the aesthetic concept of mimesis traditionally confined to realism back in human and sometimes nonhuman behavior constitutive of the mimetic re-*turn*. On the shoulders of this genealogy that finds in Caillois an often-unacknowledged precursor, we now need to go further. And going further, as we indicated time and again, for us consists in stepping back to Caillois's genial/mimetic insights into the subterraneous continuities and correspondences between animal and human mimicry in the past century to leap ahead to nonanthropocentric accounts of mimesis that are currently reloaded in the present century.

Caillois in fact opens up less subject-oriented and more environmental-oriented perspectives by calling attention to the affective powers of the environment traditional left in the background of anthropocentric approaches to dissolve the all-too-human subject, or *anthropos*, narcissistically placed in the foreground. In a chapter titled "Mimétisme et psychasthénie légéndaire," collected in *Le Mythe et l'homme* (1938),[13] Caillois broke with what may have appeared as a taboo for scholars formed in the wake of structuralist distinctions opposing nature to culture. Still, he is in line with theories of magic that induce participatory and sympathetic continuities between humans, animals, and natural forces more generally.[14] Furthering this anthropological tradition while focusing specifically on phenomena of physical camouflage and mimicry in the animal world of insects, Caillois set out to cast new light on phenomena of psychic depersonalization in the human world as well—and vice versa. While this essay is often aligned with a protosurrealist aesthetics presumably indebted to Breton, as the episode of the jumping beans already suggested, Caillois was up against surrealist mysteries given his reliance on empirical sciences, which does not mean he was less attentive to the aesthetic luxury of mimetism.

It is important to recall that Caillois wrote this essay when he was still collaborating with Bataille and Leiris in the antifascist activities of the Collège de Sociologie where we started. Like Leiris, and especially Bataille, Caillois was intimately aware that human behavior cannot be reduced to the rationality and utility characteristic of profane "homogeneous" activities. On the contrary, it is driven by excess, luxury, and squandering forces characteristic of sacred, transgressive, or as Bataille called them, "heterogeneous" activities predicated on the model of useless expenditure. Caillois had in fact read early Bataille's essay, "The Notion of Expenditure" (1933), which "struck [him] as very revealing" (Caillois 2003b, 142) to account for contagious phenomena central to the Collège more generally.[15]

The members of the group approached the contagious and, in this sense, mimetic forces of the sacred from heterogeneous perspectives. Still, they agreed that "sacred sociology," as they practiced it, was not only antifascist but also aimed to "establish points of coincidence between the obsessive fundamental tendencies of individual psychology and the directing structures that preside social organizations and command its revolutions" (Hollier ed. 1995, 27; my trans.), as Bataille, Caillois, Klossowski, and other founding members put it in their founding declaration. In substance, Caillois agreed with Bataille on the limits of utilitarian or functionalist approaches. For both, social cohesion is based not on utility but on useless forms of luxurious, squandering, and highly contagious expenditure of Dionysian energy at the core of sacred rituals and myths. Yet he disagreed with Bataille by extending this luxury to the animal world as well. As Denis Hollier puts it, Caillois's "monism" tends to be opposed to Bataille's "dualism" and informs "the oblique, diagonal monism whereby the rest of his oeuvre will serve as its most minute confirmation" (85). Caillois's diagnostic of human and animal mimicry must thus be seen as part of his generalized insistence that in both worlds "mimetism exists incontestably and exists as an autonomous mechanism" (Caillois 2008, 522).

Be it under the rubric of animal societies or spiritual power, Dionysus or shamanism, hypnotic spells or totalitarian prestige, or to use Caillois's own Nietzschean categories, "will to know [*connaissance*]" or "will to power [*puissance*]" (qtd. in Hollier ed. 1995, 301), for Caillois the line dividing animal mimicry from human mimetism was always thin and porous at best. His materialist monism, in fact, postulates physio-psychological continuities between human and animal mimicry he considers constitutive of both human and animal behavior. The overt Nietzschean overtones of Caillois's language are often noted given his attention to what he will call, in one of his lectures at the Collège, "Dionysian Virtues." Less noted is that the continuities with Nietzsche concern the phenomenon of human and animal mimicry as well. In a section of *Daybreak* titled "Animals and Morality," Nietzsche had in fact rooted human mimetism in animal mimicry in nonanthropocentric terms Caillois will pursue as well:

> one wishes to elude one's pursuers and be favoured in the pursuit of one's prey. For this reason the animals learn to master themselves and alter their form, so that many, for example, adapt their colouring to the colouring of their surroundings (by virtue of the so-called "chromatic function"), pretend to be dead or assume the forms and colours of another animal or of sand, leaves, lichen, fungus (what English researchers designate "mimicry"). Thus the individual hides himself in the general concept "man", or in society, or adapts himself to princes, classes, parties, opinions of his time and place: and all the subtle ways we have of appearing fortunate, grateful, powerful, enamoured have their easily discoverable parallels in the animal world. (Nietzsche 1982, 26:20–21)

Caillois fundamentally agrees with Nietzsche that animal and human mimicry should be considered as part of a monistic continuum. There is thus much to learn from seeing correspondences between what are traditionally considered as two distinct mimetic phenomena: one moral and human, the other animal and biological. We shall see in the next chapter that Nietzsche and Caillois are here prefiguring forms of depersonalization that will render the most radical form of evil "banal." And yet, if Nietzsche follows evolutionary principles that consider, *with*

English researchers, that mimicry is a strategy of survival, for animals and humans alike, Caillois posits, *with* Bataille, *contra* evolution, a squandering, luxurious principle at the origins of mimetism that counters useful evolutionary principles. For him, in fact, "mimetism is useless, even harmful" (Caillois 2008, 531)—which does not mean that this phenomenon is deprived of a patho-*logy* of its own.

Taking as his starting point certain "lower animals," such as spiders and lizards but also insects and birds, Caillois observes that they are mimetic, not in the dominant anthropocentric sense that they represent or copy the external world. Rather, they are mimetic in the physical, biological sense of mimicry that allows them to visually disappear—chameleonlike—in order to blend with the homogenous background against which they are situated.

Caillois notices that in such a state, the mimetic animal in the foreground is, quite literally, indistinguishable from the background. With an aesthetic eye ready to suspend habits of perception, he wonders about the origin of this disquieting phenomenon that tends to be taken for granted. The classical biological answer is that animal mimicry is a defense mechanism perfected through evolution meant to guarantee the survival of the species. This is certainly a realistic, positivist, and evolutionary hypothesis in line with scientific and philosophical principles Caillois was well familiar with.

But Caillois has a different, more diagonal, and intuitive hypothesis in mind. His main objection to the evolutionary hypothesis is that some of these insects are actually inedible; or, alternatively and even more problematic, disappearing against a given background (such as edible plants) may actually diminish rather than increase their chances of survival—in the sense that the mimetic creature might inadvertently be swallowed by herbivorous animals. Mimicry, in numerous cases of defensive mimetism (*mimétisme défensif*), seems indeed a dangerous activity of dissimulation. Perhaps it is even a luxury on the side of nature that can afford to squander its excessive energy via what Caillois will later call, in characteristic Batillean language, a "luxury of precaution" or "excess of simulacrum" (Caillois 2008, 531).

There is thus a dangerous excess at the heart of mimetism that does not fit narrow utilitarian purposes internal to evolutionary hypotheses. Caillois also calls it a "dangerous luxury [*luxe dangereux*]" (1938, 106) that calls for a different, perhaps more aesthetic-oriented, but not necessarily representational hypothesis. In his view, in fact, what is essential about mimicry is that the blending between living organism and environmental background is not only a visual but also physiological phenomenon. As he puts it: "The important point is not the exterior appearance but immobility" (2008, 531). It is thus from the inside out

**Figures 1–2:** Caillois's examples of animal mimicry from "Mimicry and Legendary Psychasthenia"

rather than from the outside in that he approaches the riddle of mimetism. For Caillois, this immobility points to what he calls a form of biological regress or "return to an inorganic state" (1938, 116). In fact, he notices that the immobile animal nested against inorganic matter is not simply invisible to the observer's eye—a question of exterior representation. Rather, it enters in what he calls a state of "catalepsy" whereby "life," as he says, "steps back a degree [*recule d'un degré*]" as in a sort of "trance" (113, 94)—a question of inner experience.

Caillois's hypothesis is the following: rather than an evolutionary strategy for survival, this mimetic principle is associated with a drive that pulls the animate, organic, and living being toward inanimate, inorganic, and dead matter. Coming close to the Freudian conception of *Thanatos* but echoing philosophical principles that go back, via Bataille, to Nietzsche, Schopenhauer, and Spinoza, Caillois infers from these phenomena a death drive that induces a dissolution of the boundaries of individuation. As he puts it: "the being's will to persevere in *its* being [*la volonté de l'être de persévérer dans son être*] consumes itself to excess and secretly attracts it toward the uniformity that scandalizes its imperfect autonomy" (Caillois 1938, 122). It is thus nothing less than the "autonomy" of the living organism that is scandalized by the transgressive power of animal mimicry.

There is an interesting and rarely noticed inversion of perspectives at play in Caillois's untimely observation that goes beyond anthropocentrism or even biocentrism and is worth underlining. On the one hand, the *exterior* "scientific" observer only sees—or, if mimicry is successful, fails to see—a continuity between a living organism and the environment that is interpreted in terms of an evolutionary strategy for survival. On the other hand, Caillois overturns perspectives to consider the mimetic phenomenon from the *inside* of a nonhuman organism in a cataleptic state akin to trance instead. And what he *senses*, rather than *sees*, via his surrealist-diagonal antennae that blur the human/nonhuman divide, is that in this state of trance, it is the self-sufficient "autonomy" of the biological organism that is radically threatened by the inner experience of animal mimicry. In sum, for Caillois, this disquieting form of mimesis whereby a figure disappears against the environmental background that surrounds it is not simply a *visual* exterior phenomenon. It is rather an *affective*, interior, or as Bataille would say, "inner experience" that pulls a living being on the side of death, while leaving it on the side of life, or better, on the shadow-line that both connects and divides organism and environment, foreground and background, life and death. This inner experience, he adds, is not only constitutive of animal mimicry; it equally animates homo mimeticus—if only because, for Caillois, "humans and insects belong to the same nature" (1938, 70).

What then, are the human, all-too-animal implications of a squandering principle that, via an inner trance, leads the subject to blend against its surroundings, be they human or not? What does animal mimicry tell us about human mimetism and the pathologies that animate it? To answer such questions, we need to look in the mirror first. Rather than stopping at imaginary and rather anthropocentric human *imagos* in the foreground, let us go through the looking glass, beyond the mirror stage, to sense the nonhuman environment in the background.

## Mimetic Trouble for the Ideal Mirror

Caillois's diagonal account of mimicry changes perspectives that go from animal mimetism to primitive magic to modern politics; still, the mimetic will to power he diagnoses is essentially the same. In the process, he also supplements new disciplinary perspectives for mimetic studies in order to account for a type of depersonalization that crosses the human/animal boundary. In particular, he relies on the long-neglected French philosopher and psychologist Pierre Janet

(1859–1947), whose contribution to the history of psychology is more significant than is often acknowledged still today.

Janet, it should be recalled, invented the term "subconscious" to account for phenomena of automatism, hypnotic dissociation, trauma, and double personality, among other mimetic pathologies. Professor of experimental and comparative psychology at the Collège de France, where he was appointed with the support of Henry Bergson, Janet was a major source of inspiration for the surrealist generation in general and for members of the Collège de Sociologie like Bataille and Caillois in particular.[16] Above all, Janet paved the way for a Freudian discovery of the unconscious, which contrary to received knowledge was not a Freudian individual discovery, after all. In *The Discovery of the Unconscious* (1970), the historian of psychology Henri Ellenberger convincingly shows how Janet's psychological analysis of subconscious states, dissociation of personality, fixed ideas, trauma, cathartic cures of neuroses where unduly appropriated by his "great rival, Sigmund Freud" (1970, 409), including the very concept of *Psychoanalyse* itself, which is but Freud's translated inversion of Janet's *analyse psychologique*.[17] Caillois had thus an original psychologist to draw from directly to further his patho-*logy* of depersonalization.

As the title of his essay makes clear, in "Mimetism and Legendary Psychasthenia," Caillois establishes a connection between animal mimicry and human mimicry via a psychic pathology of depersonalization central to Janet's psychological analysis. In a book titled *Les Obsessions et la psychasthénie* (1903), Janet had in fact devoted a lengthy study to a mysterious psychic pathology or "*psycho-névrose*" called "psychasthenia." He defined it as a personality disorder (*trouble de la personnalité*) that affects people's relation to their environment, generates a lowering of psychic energy or tension, a loss of identity, "depersonalization" (Janet 1903, vii; my trans.), all of which blur the boundaries between self and other, and generally induce a "weakening of their psychological functions" (vii).[18] Building on Janet's case studies, Caillois adds a patho-*logical* supplement of his own. In particular, he explains:

> for these dispossessed spirits, space seems to be endowed with a devouring capacity […] The body, then, dissociates itself from thought so that the individual crosses the frontier of its skin and lives on the other side of its senses. (Caillois 1938, 111; my trans.)

The psychic boundaries of the subject, for Caillois, are indeed porous, open to the outside, and prone to suggestive influences that cross the thin skin of individuation, generating shadows or phantoms of egos instead. This personality trouble is thus a mimetic trouble in the sense that it is the experience of mimetism human animals partially share with nonhuman animals that is responsible for this affect of depersonalization.

Well before poststructuralism and posthumanism, the affective turn and the nonhuman turn, Caillois was already troubling the stability of the metaphysical category of the subject as unitary, autonomous, and self-contained. Instead, he painted a blurry picture of homo mimeticus as traversed by heterogeneous continuities that blur the line between the inside and outside, the human ego and the nonhuman space, generating processes of becoming lost in space. This is why he concludes: "The subject itself feels that it is becoming space, *black space*" (Caillois 1938, 111). Once again, what applies to animal mimicry equally applies to human mimetism: Caillois is not simply describing individuals who are physically invisible in the darkness from the outside. Rather, he is accounting for a mimetic drive that is much more disquieting and fundamental, for it operates from the inside. Mimetism, in other words, is not only something seen, or a mimetic representation; it is above all something felt, or a mimetic pathos.

Based on a Dionysian affect more than on Apollonian vision, mimetism points to an animal, all-too-human permeability to space in general and darkness in particular that blurs the boundaries of individuation. Hence, following the phenomenological and psychological work of Eugène Minkowski, Caillois explains that "'the ego is *permeable* to obscurity whereas it is not so to light'" (1938, 112). Does this inner/outer experience sound too surreal? Let us try a little subjective experiment: go back in time and think of that all-too-real fear of the dark you experienced as a child at night. Why were you afraid? After all, as we now say in our role as parents, there is nothing to be afraid of. But the child in us might still reply: it is precisely this nothing that is so frightening!

This is, in a sense, also Caillois's reply. For him, children fear the dark because their egos are still permeable to the outside, for they are not yet fully formed inside. He specifies that they do not fear darkness as such. Rather, what they fear is a loss of selfhood generated by the dissolution of boundaries between the figure and the background, the human organism and the nonhuman environment: "The magical hold [...] of night and obscurity, *the fear of the dark [la peur dans le noir*], has unquestionably its roots in the threat it generates with respect to the opposition between the organism and the environment" (Caillois 1938, 112). If a visual, rational, and Apollonian mimesis represents reassuring forms that are visible at daylight from a distance, Caillois is still in touch with the magical hold of an embodied, affective, or Dionysian mimesis haunting the *vita mimetica* and generating a fear of the dark that reaches into the present.

This fear is indeed familiar since childhood. If its source might not be visible, it can be intimately felt nonetheless. If you can't see this fear clearly represented, you can hear it—even on popular culture since the 1990s you can hear echoes on the radio: As homo mimeticus walks alone...

> When the light begins to change
> I sometimes feel a little strange
> A little anxious when it's dark
> Fear of the dark
> Fear of the dark [...] (Harris 1992)

Caillois could not have put it more lyrically. The *patho*-logical lesson of Iron Maiden's "Fear of the Dark" (1992) is clear and in line with Caillois's diagonal diagnostic: not only patients suffering from psychasthenia, but all humans have, to different degrees, experienced this fear of the dark. No wonder the phrase speaks to new generations as well.

In light of this detour via the enveloping power of dark space, this is the moment to recognize that Caillois was not alone in suggesting this mimetic hypothesis at the foundation of psychic development. That other theoretical chameleon of surrealist inspiration par excellence we already mentioned, Jacques Lacan, will also claim that children fear darkness for its affective power to dissolve the boundaries of the ego. Conversely, they jubilate to see their own mirror image for its power to delineate and give form to the ego—via a mimetic experience we can now revisit from the angle of our genealogy of mimetism.

Lacan, just like Freud, has received much critical attention in the past century, whereas other figures like Janet and Caillois have not. It has thus often gone unnoticed that Caillois's Janetian psychological analysis of mimetism and psychasthenia, quite literally in-*forms* (gives form to) Lacan's celebrated "mirror stage." At a first reading, Caillois's opening claim that the "ultimate problem" of mimetism consists in the "distinction between the real and the imaginary" (1938, 86) may appear coincidental, for "the Real" and "the imaginary" are also concepts central to Lacan's structuralist theory. Still, at a second, more attentive reading, there is a specific genealogical sense in which Caillois provides Lacan with a model, or form, for his influential account of ego formation. Janet's influence on Lacan's "analysis of the ego" has been characteristically erased, but the theoretical shadow Caillois casts is still clearly visible if we take a look at "The Mirror Stage" essay itself.

The myth of origin is now familiar: it tells the experience of the pre-Oedipal child who, by the age of six months, still wobbly on its feet, with the help of a support, or *trotte-bébé*, erects itself to face this double in the mirror and falls under the spell of an "illuminative mimicry of the *Aha-Erlebnis*" (Lacan 1977, 1). The child, the story continues, recognizes the reflected image, and via an imaginary "identification" misrecognizes the "ideal unity" (*unité idéale*) of that static image with its own ego. This phantom ego is thus not simply represented in a static mirror but is given form in a turbulent body. In Lacan's formulation, the subject is transformed by this impressive *imago* aspiring to the status of "an ontological structure of the human world" (2). The philosophical foundations of Lacan's theory of identification have long been recognized—precisely by philosophers like Lacoue-Labarthe, Nancy, and Borch-Jacobsen informed by the role the mirror has played in erecting western speculative ontologies that, at least since Plato, privilege visual distance over bodily pathos and divide ideal forms from the turbulence of the sensible.[19]

Furthering this genealogy from the angle of a diagonal science of mimesis, it is important to note that, after erecting a binary between baby *Homo sapiens* and the monkey that, in Lacan's anthropocentric account, considers the reflection "empty,"[20] he nonetheless reveals that this narcissistic all-too-human identification has deeper mimetic origins, as he writes: "But the facts of mimicry [*mimétisme*] are no less instructive when conceived as cases of heteromorphic identification, in as much as they raise the problem of the significance of space for the living organism" (Lacan 1977, 3). The language of "living organism," you will have recognized, is less vertical than before, and the "facts of mimetism" reveal the figure in the background who is calling Lacan's attention to nonhuman mimicry as well. In fact, Lacan specifies:

> We have only to recall how Roger Caillois (still young, his thought still fresh from his break with the sociological school in which he was trained) illuminated the subject by using the term "*legendary psychasthenia*" to classify morphological mimicry [*mimétisme morphologique*] as an obsession with space in its derealizing effects. (3)[21]

This is a revealing genealogical connection to rediscover in the twenty-first century. If you put on Caillois's diagonal lenses that call attention to the relation between form and background, organism and environment, *Innenwelt* and *Umwelt*, we should be in a position to see what has remained mimetically dissimulated so far: namely, that the mythical "mirror stage," with its celebrated account of the birth of the ego out of the subject's identification with a bright, imaginary, and ideal form (or *Gestalt*), entails nothing less and nothing more than a *mirroring inversion* of what Caillois, following Janet, called "legendary psychasthenia."

For Caillois, and Janet before him, in fact, the inner experience of mimetism threatens to dissolve the unity of the ego against the material background, generating a feeling of depersonalization. Conversely, for Lacan, an identification with an ideal image in the foreground gives form and unity to a formless ego. The *telos* of Caillois's diagnostic of mimetism goes from the discontinuity of the human ego to a continuity with the nonhuman background; Lacan's mirroring *telos* is the mirroring opposite: it goes from a state of formless undifferentiation to the unitary formation of the ego. Mimetism *is* the inner/outer experience that mediates between these two states. The Lacanian ego, in other words, is the positive imprint of Caillois's negative mimetic configuration. The exterior and ideal form of the ego is what appears in the foreground once the bodily experience of formless dissolution is left in the background. Given the primacy of ideal images and forms in western thought based on the *vita contemplativa*, this is perhaps part of the reason the mirror stage became a legend, while psychasthenia and the mimetism that animates a *vita mimetica* was theoretically dissolved.

Still, a genealogical lesson remains visible nonetheless: seemingly "original" theories, we should not be surprised by now, have "mimetic" origins, which does not mean that the pathology can easily be cured. Caillois is, in fact, careful not to dismiss this personality trouble as an anomalous, mimetic pathology that affects only children or neurotic cases. Rather, as we have seen, he considers both the animal (physical) mimicry and the human (psychic) pathology as revealing of a more generalized (metaphysical) anxiety of dissolution of the boundaries of individuation in "black space" that affects humanity in general. Moreover, his hypothesis has nothing to do with a fully visible, mirrorlike representation of the self. Instead, it designates an intimately felt, yet truly invisible psychic dissolution of the boundaries of selfhood in spatial darkness, a dissolution that is most intimately and obscurely connected to the horror of death.

In sum, there are numerous mirroring similarities between Lacan's (Freudian) mirror stage and Caillois (Janetian) mimetism that reveal the imitative foundations of what I call, following Nietzsche, a phantom ego. Still, unlike Lacan and closer to Nietzsche, Caillois stresses the importance of affect over vision, turbulent bodily senses over unitary images, material dissolution over ideal formation, becoming space rather than being an ideal *imago*. The focus on an imaginary ideal image at the source of misrecognitions is not innocent. This is perhaps the reason psychoanalytic theorists with a philosophical background have recognized in Lacan's theory of the mirror stage a "twentieth-century Platonism" (Borch-Jacobsen 1991, 64). What we can add is that an idealist theory of narcissistic subject formation in the foreground reveals a materialist theory of nonanthropocentric dissolution in the background. And if the former spoke to the structuralist generation under the spell of the linguistic sign, the latter addresses future generations increasingly under the spell of mimetic drives that threaten the boundaries of individuation, both individually and collectively.

In this overturning of perspectives constitutive of his diagonal account of mimetism, lies, perhaps, Caillois's original contribution to new mimetic studies.

## Through the Looking Glass: Mimetism Now and Then

As an anthropologist with protosurrealist inclinations, Caillois draws inspiration from the animal world but remains fundamentally interested in reframing dominant conceptions of what the human is—or can potentially become. If he focuses on the natural phenomenon of animal mimicry, it is because, in his view, this disconcerting *biological* mechanism reveals a fundamental *psychic* principle at the heart of humans as well. Let us thus not forget the point with which we started: Caillois's diagnostic of mimetism and psychic depersonalization coincides with his rising preoccupations with fascist psychology in the later 1930s and the massive forms of contagious trance it generated in heterogenous crowds—a phenomenon that almost a century later we are far from having overcome. Quite the contrary; it is still at the palpitating heart of (new) fascist movements that—via new media—generate massive phenomena of uniformization constitutive of what I call, echoing both Caillois and Bataille, "mimetic contagion" (Lawtoo 2019b).

If we adopt Caillois's diagonal lenses that do not simply take phenomena of mass contagion and the hypnotic trance that characterizes them for granted, we should wonder: what is the mysterious force that troubles the boundaries of individuation, introducing affective continuities in place of discontinuities that reached massive proportions in the 1930s but continue to resurface in the present as well? And what is the psychology that drives human forms of mimicry and the loss of "distinction" (Caillois 1938, 86) it entails?[22] Caillois's hypothesis

**Figure 3:** Italian fascist crowd, Italy

**Figure 4:** (New) Fascist insurrection, January 6, 2021

rests on the "psychological analysis" of Janet, but despite his reference to Freud's death drive and anticipation of Lacan's imaginary identification, we should not hasten to align him with psychoanalysis. If only because Caillois tends to be critical of Sigmund Freud whose "error," as he puts it, consists in reducing all phenomena to his "schema" (84). Rather, as he relies on Janet, one of the main advocates of hypnosis and suggestion, Caillois is attentive to a pre-Freudian tradition of the unconscious I call mimetic because it finds in hypnotic spells, possession trances, and massive forms of affective contagion its most manifest symptoms.

The states of "trance" Caillois identified in animal mimicry will continue to remain internal to his diagnostic of human mimicry, in both traditional, modern, and contemporary societies. Thus, furthering Huizinga's account of *homo ludens* from the angle of homo mimeticus, Caillois's account of the spells of games is very much an offshoot of his diagnostic of animal mimicry.[23] As he puts it, in *Man, Play and Games* (1958): "it seems legitimate to me at this point to take account of mimetic phenomena of which insects provide most perplexing examples" (Caillois 1961, 20). And Caillois specifies:

> The inexplicable mimetism of insects immediately affords an extraordinary parallel to man's [*sic*] penchant for disguising himself, wearing a mask, or *playing a part* [...] Among vertebrates, the tendency to imitate first appears as an entirely physical, quasi-irresistible contagion, analogous to the contagion of yawning, running limping, smiling, or almost any movement. (20)

In line with the tradition of the mimetic unconscious, then, Caillois relies on a motor hypothesis to account for mirroring physio-psychological reflexes that are not under the control of consciousness and are thus *un*-conscious. From yawning to smiling, wearing a mask to playing a role, homo mimeticus is a relational, embodied, and social creature that finds in unconscious mirroring reflexes the physiological drive not only to feel the pathos of the other but also to become other via theatrical practices that find in mime and performance paradigmatic aesthetic starting points.

We can thus add Caillois's name to a genealogy of modernist philosophical physicians who—from Nietzsche to Tarde, Janet to Bataille—paved the way for the discovery of mirroring mechanisms whose existence is now confirmed empirically. Non unlike Nietzsche's hypothesis on the origins of consciousness, Caillois's hypothesis may have sounded extravagantly surrealist to the dominant sciences of his time, yet it points to an all-too-real phenomenon. Without the mediation of a mirror stage, unconscious mimetism lends empirical credibility to the diagonal hypothesis that, from birth onward, a movement seen triggers an affect felt, opening the channels of communication for a thoroughly relational species.

At the same time, as the examples internal to Caillois's diagonal patho-*logies* of mimesis already suggest, he expands the implication of physiological mirroring reflexes to the broader sphere of aesthetics, culture, religion, and politics along diagonal lines constitutive of new mimetic studies as well. Thus, elaborating on the entrancing effect of masks as an "instrument of metamorphosis" in primitive societies, Caillois notices that via such "phantoms" the individual "mimics, and identifies with these frightening powers and soon, maddened and delirious, really believes that he is the god" (1961, 88) that casts a spell on the ritual participants. Thus, he adds:

> They conform because they are required to by society and, as do the performers themselves, because they believe that the actors have become transformed, possessed, and prey to the powers animating them [...] Suggestion and simulation increases one's susceptibility and stimulate the trance. The loss of consciousness, exaltation, and oblivion that they cause are favorable to the true trance, i.e., possession by the god. (88, 94)

Conformity is not only a physiological reflex; it is also supplemented by cultural expectations that have a suggestive power over participants and performers alike. Borrowing the psychological concept of "suggestion" from Hippolyte Bernheim and coupling it with the aesthetic and playful notions of "simulation," Caillois's diagonal science of mimesis accounts for a type of "trance" that is traditionally restricted to religious phenomena of dispossession in archaic societies, but he considers at play in modern societies as well, for both good and ill.

It is thus no accident that the language of play and games finds a pathological counterpart in the language of power and politics. Thus, taking a paradigmatic example that casts a long shadow on the history of western civilization, Caillois, in an essay titled "Le pouvoir charismatique: Adolf Hitler comme idole" (1951), refers to the same language of trance, magic, and mimicry in order to account for the magnetic will to power the *Führer* used to magnetize the spellbound masses. Quoting Alfred Rosenberg's claim that "'the people [*peuple*] is to the leader [*chef*] what lack of conscience [*inconscience*] is to conscience'" (in Caillois 2008, 324; my trans.), he adds in his proper voice: "the charismatic leader is not opposed to the crowd. It is precisely because he shares [*partage*] in its passions and feels them with a contagious intensity that the crowd makes him its leader" (323). We have seen the efficacy of these passions in the past; we have felt them in the present, which does not mean that this sharing or *partage* of pathos cannot set up a distance from affective contagion and the communal fusion it entails.

How does this partage of *pathos* operate? Convoking motifs that are central to Nietzsche, but as we know, are as old as Plato, Caillois relies on the trope of the Dionysian "drum" and the "magnetic stone" to account for the "magical" power of the "inspired *meneur*" to generate a state of trance in the crowd. He notices, for instance, that Hitler shifted his speeches late in the evening so as to facilitate the crowd's capitulation to the "dominating force of a most powerful will" (325), or that he staged a spectacle in which drums accompany the illumination of the leader alone in view of generating "hypnosis" (325). Both vision and hearing are once again central to this spell-*binding* operation. And Caillois adds: "soon the contact is established between him and the room of which he captures the excitation. Now he hammers long and violent phrases, pronounced as if in a trance" (326), generating a "mystical union" in which subjects admit being "'entirely lost in the *Führer*'" (328). And drawing on the tradition of crowd psychology we shall encounter in later chapters, Caillois specifies that Hitler's will to power stems from an "inspired *meneur*" whose "somnambulistic certainty" (319) is in tune with the crowd. There is thus a spiraling mimetic loop at play here with amplifying properties in which the leader and the mass work hand in hand, so to speak, to amplify fascist mass contagion. For Caillois, then, as for the tradition of crowd psychology before him, fascist will to power is mimetic willpower insofar, as it is based on a contagious, hypnotic, and depersonalizing form of sovereign communication that troubles the boundaries of individuation and turns the egos of homo mimeticus into phantom egos.

In guise of conclusion, let me flesh out some perspectives internal to Caillois's account of diagonal mimicry that go beyond anthropocentrism to address anthropogenic challenges new mimetic studies will have to face in the epoch of the Anthropocene.

## Diagonal Mimicry: Perspectives for the Anthropocene

In light of this genealogy of Caillois's diagnostic of animal and human mimicry that paved the way for what is arguably one of the most influential theories of the subject in the twentieth century, we might still wonder: what, then, is the theoretical and artistic purchase of revisiting Caillois's take on mimicry in the twenty-first century? I schematically outline four entangled perspectives that were untimely when Caillois first developed his diagonal account of mimicry qua mimetism but are now timely and urgent to pursue in the age of environmental transformation constitutive of the Anthropocene.

First, "diagonal science," as Caillois theorized and practiced it, was not based on a nature/culture binary opposition that, under the aegis of structuralism, dominated good part of the past century. On the contrary, he went beyond "two-cultures" oppositions to account for a transdisciplinary, (non)human phenomenon like mimicry that has biological, psychological, social, philosophical, and aesthetic manifestations, all of which escape the "increasing specialization" (Caillois 2003a, 343) of academic knowledge. As he puts it: "What we need are relay stations at every level: anastomosis and coordination points, not only for assembling the spoils but above all for comparing different processes" (344). *Homo Mimeticus* aims to further this diagonal, comparative, and transdisciplinary approach. And he concludes: "A network of shortcuts seems ever more indispensable today among the many, isolated outposts spread out along the periphery, without internal lines of communication—which is the site of fruitful research" (347). The human and nonhuman tendency to imitate at different levels of behavior—biological, psychic, aesthetic, social, political, etc.— is a case in point. Caillois's plea for a diagonal science of mimesis provides important transdisciplinary steps the mimetic turn intends to fruitfully explore via networks of collaboration.

Second, Caillois's attention to animal mimicry challenged anthropocentric tendencies that go back to the dawn of philosophy and traverse western humanistic thought and aesthetic practices, which consider humans as the most imitative animals. If humans remain indeed thoroughly imitative, other animals are not foreign to mimicry. Quite the contrary, the human mimetic faculty is an extension of animal mimicry, which allows for fruitful communications between the two. As he puts it, addressing the specifically human sphere of aesthetics: "Aesthetics studies the harmony of lines and colors. Could it not conceivably compare paintings with butterfly wings?" (Caillois 2003a, 345) And Caillois continues, anticipating the objection that was routinely addressed to him in the past century but might no longer work today: "'Anthropomorphism!' people will say, but it is exactly the opposite" (345). As his account of mimicry makes strikingly clear:

> the point is not to explain certain puzzling facts observed in nature in terms of man [sic]. On the contrary, the goal is to explain man (governed by the laws of this same nature to which he belongs in almost every respect) in terms of the more general behavioral forms found widespread in nature throughout most species (345–346).

While the human animal remains thoroughly mimetic in its ability to represent the world, Caillois rooted the foundations of mimetism in an animal, all-too-animal tendency to merge against dominant backgrounds, be they natural (mimicry) or cultural (mimetism)—a tendency that is now radically amplified by new media and the enveloping technological environment in which homo mimeticus is immersed and that urgently deserves new studies of what I call, "hypermimesis."

Third, Caillois's diagnostic of the power of the natural environment to form, transform, and dissolve the autonomy of human and nonhuman animals entails an overturing of perspectives that we should take to heart in the age of rapid climate change characteristic of the Anthropocene. Caillois was ahead of his time in stressing that (non)human animals are not the "autonomous" creatures they appear to be and are radically open, entangled, and vulnerable to the "enveloping" powers of the environment. What we must add is that humans are now caught in a spiraling vortex in which their influence on the environment generates complex feedback loops that retroact on human and animal behavior alike, entangling humans in what is already recognized as a sixth extinction. Well before the environmental turn, Caillois teaches us that the environment is never simply background; it is the very ground from which human and nonhuman life emerges and to which it is bound return. As he puts it in a phrase that served as the epigraph for this essay: "Indeed, the end would appear to be *assimilation to the environment*" (Caillois 1938, 108).

Last but not least, Caillois's diagnostic of mimicry/mimetism as a "dangerous luxury" locates a squandering excess, or expenditure, at the heart of human and nonhuman life, which figures like Nietzsche and Bataille already placed at the heart of aesthetic experience. If, since its dawn in romanticism, aesthetics was traditionally considered without instrumental purpose, or use—Bataille would later say, *sans emploi*—surrealist writers like Caillois insisted that it remains the palpitating heart of inner experiences that do not simply aim to realistically represent the world. Rather than being without purpose as an aesthetic tradition that goes from Kant to Bataille suggests, Caillois reminds us that the aesthetic drive is rooted in purposive yet not necessarily utilitarian drives that are rooted within a human, and thus animal body (from *aisthetikos*, "sensitive, pertaining to sense perception," derived from *aisthanomai*, "I perceive, feel, sensation"). It entails, among other things, the ability to step into others' shoes via a form of empathy, or better, *Einfühlung*, that entails the "feeling into" the inner affects others. Caillois took this aesthetic principle by stepping beyond anthropocentric shoes so as to consider the mimetic drive from the perspective of nonhuman animals who, like homo mimeticus, are part of nature. As he puts it: "nature (which is no miser) pursues pleasure, luxury, exuberance, and vertigo just as much as survival" (Caillois 2003a, 346).

The pleasure, luxury, and exuberance of mimicry is constitutive of this vertigo. If humans had their share—a "share [*part*]" Bataille would call "accursed [*maudite*]"—driven by excessive consumption and pollution in the last century, it is perhaps time to put the mimetic faculty to aesthetic, cognitive, and ethical use to affirm metamorphoses of the spirit necessary for survival in this century as well—for humans and nonhumans. In the midst of an environmental catastrophe that is currently causing a sixth extinction, this mimetic tendency might have a purpose after all, albeit this purpose will not be singular for its manifestations will have to be plural. One of them could entail a (will to) power to animate and perhaps reanimate life on earth via nonanthropocentric principles that trace the dynamic interplay between (non)human life and the environment that envelops us and—for the moment, but for how long?—still sustains us.

New generations of artists are already going beyond mimesis restricted to anthropocentric forms of realistic representation. The fragility of the earth should not only be seen from the outside; it should also be felt from the inside. If the environment continues to envelop us, we should not forget that we are also enveloping the earth, generating geological changes in the *Umwelt* that will

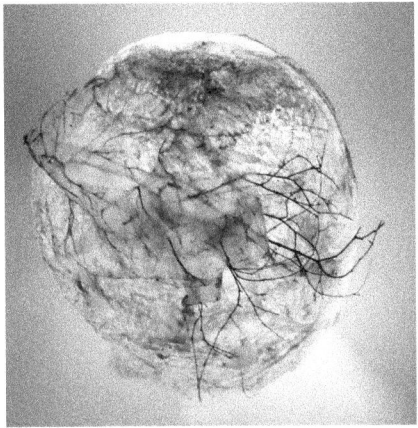 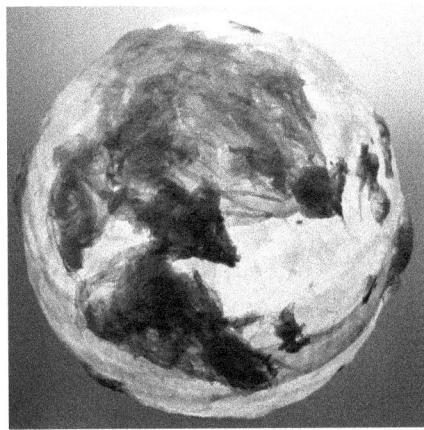

**Figure 5:** *Holocene* (©Michaela Lawtoo, 2020)

**Figure 6:** *Anthropocene* (©Michaela Lawtoo, 2020)

radically affect the *Innenwelt* as well. Hence the urgency of giving new aesthetic expressions to chameleonlike metamorphoses that operated for the worse in the past century, yet are vital to the survival of (non)human animals in the epoch of the Anthropocene that cast a shadow on the present and future centuries.

CHAPTER 6

# THE HUMAN CHAMELEON

> EUDORA: Who are you?
> ZELIG: What do you mean who am I? These are tough questions.
>
> —Woody Allen, *Zelig*

So far, we have seen that the ancient lesson that humans are mimetic and plastic creatures is currently returning to the forefront of aesthetic theory, but it is only recently that the non-anthropocentric insight that mimesis cuts across the human/nonhuman binary is returning to inform contemporary debates across the humanities. Recent developments in affect theory, film studies, literary theory, continental philosophy, but also sociology, anthropology, and political theory, stretching—with the discovery of mirror neurons—to include the neurosciences and the cognitive sciences, have been reconsidering the power of mirroring reflexes that, in human and nonhuman animals, individually and collectively, consciously and, more often, unconsciously, generate underlying continuities between self and others, subjects and models, citizens and leaders, including political leaders that verge on (new) fascist and authoritarian politics.

As the harrowing reality of war, doubled by the phantom of nuclear war, rages once again in Europe after over fifty years of relative peace, it is urgent to account for the will to power of tyrannical leaders that cast a shadow on the world as a whole. Different voices in the heterogeneous field of new mimetic studies agree that these leaders do so, among other means, by reloading the rhetoric of fascism and Nazi politics via new media that cast a spell on the digital age. In the process, they also trigger intersubjective fluxes of affective sameness that trouble the boundaries dividing individual differences. The number of recent books that stress the centrality of affective contagion, involuntary mimicry, psychic influences, mirroring reflexes, the mimetic unconscious, and other contemporary manifestations of homo mimeticus we have encountered so far testifies to the liveliness, timeliness, and relevance of emerging transdisciplinary "perspectives on imitation" that took some time to be "assimilated" (Hurley and Chater 2005, 1) in the humanities but now animate the *re*-turn of mimesis we are promoting in this book.

Furthering this recent return of attention to the power of unconscious forms of imitation that lead the ego to mimic others via mirroring mechanisms first found in macaque monkeys in the 1990s and anticipated by Caillois's Nietzschean realization that human and nonhuman mimicry are part of a continuum, I would like to revisit the case of the "human chameleon" dramatized by Woody Allen's 1982 mockumentary *Zelig*. This film reflects an all-too-human drive for mimicry that allows us to reflect on the dangers of dispossessions of identity that reached massive proportions in the past century and, via new social media, continue to cast a shadow on the present century. Drawing on Nietzsche's diagnostic of the actor in *The Gay Science* (1882), where he supplements his genealogy of the origins of consciousness (chapter 1) from a modern psychological perspective, I now argue that the cinematic case of *Zelig* remains our contemporary for a reason that is at least double, for it concerns individual psychological metamorphoses and collective political transformations still ongoing today.

On the psychological side, *Zelig* dramatizes unconscious mirroring tendencies to adapt, conform, and mirror others in terms that might be amplified by racist oppression, class disadvantage, and social discrimination, yet despite the film's cultural specificity, cannot be restricted to Jews and other US minorities in the melting pot of the 1920s alone—if only because Zelig's reflex to mirror other people found, like the other diagnostics we have encountered, an empirical confirmation in the discovery of "mirror neurons" in the 1990s. On the aesthetic side, the film *Zelig* provides a cinematic surface that reflects a larger moving picture of a human chameleon that may not be narrowly realistic yet provides an illuminating case study to reflect *on* the psychic, historical, political, and, ultimately, philosophical implications of hypnotic dispossessions of identity that deprive subjects of the ability to think in terms characteristic of what Hannah Arendt influentially called in *Eichmann in Jerusalem* (1963), the "banality of evil."

Although the connection between the case of Zelig and the case of Eichmann, a comic fictional case and a horrifying historical case, might initially surprise, we shall see in this and in the following chapter that these two cases are not deprived of troubling mirroring effects that reach into the present. If Arendt controversially claimed that "Eichmann constitutes a veritable gold mine for a psychologist—provided he [*sic*] is wise enough to understand that the horrible can be not only ludicrous but outright funny" (48), I argue that the reverse is equally true: namely, that *Zelig* constitutes a gold mine for psychologists, provided they consider that what is outright funny can help us seriously reflect on transformations of personality that can be truly horrifying.

Thus reframed, the case of *Zelig* sets up a mirroring interplay between aesthetics and politics that turns out to be more forward oriented than previously realized. It urges us to look back to mimetic drives to conform to totalitarian leaders that were becoming visible in the 1920s, generated massive dispossessions of identity that already preoccupied Caillois, and culminated in Nazi horrors in the 1930s and '40s. My wager is that *Zelig* calls attention to the contemporary danger of unconsciously conforming to (new) fascist and authoritarian leaders at the dawn of the twenty-first century, endowed with the will power to cast a hypnotic spell that is not only constitutive of the mimetic turn in theory but also induces a "collective trance" (Snyder 2017, 61) on disenfranchised subjects in practice. While the psychological case of Zelig reveals an excess of mimesis that is considered comically pathological, the film *Zelig* shows that this mimetic pathology is not only fictional but also historical, not simply individual but collective, not only past-oriented but present and, possibly, future-oriented. In the process, it also provides a patho-*logical* diagnostic that can be put to work contra the rise of (new) fascist and tyrannical phantoms that, via new and increasingly invasive social media, are currently casting a shadow on the present century.

## The Case of *Zelig*: Reframing the Human Chameleon

Woody Allen's *Zelig* (1983) is a film that dramatizes, perhaps most clearly than any other film or narrative, the ultimate manifestation of that protean creature we have been calling homo mimeticus and the film calls "human chameleon." Located at the juncture between fiction and history, aesthetics and politics, comedy and tragedy, personal mimetic pathologies and collective social pathologies, the different faces of this mimetic animal not only face and mirror each other but also reflect on one another. A mockumentary that relies on archival footage from the 1920s and 1930s in order to dramatize a fictional Jewish character without proper identity who suffers from a pathological tendency to "metamorphose," chameleonlike, into any type of person he is facing, *Zelig* blurs the boundaries between past and present, fiction and reality, comedy and drama, historical truth and fictional lies, being oneself and appearing as someone else, along imitative lines that in-*form* (give aesthetic form to)—beginning, middle, and end—both the medium and the message of the film.

At the level of the medium, *Zelig* opens with a series of mock interviews that frame the film from the perspective of the 1980s in which prominent Jewish public intellectuals representing fields as diverse as philosophy/cultural studies (Susan Sontag), literary criticism (Irving Howe), creative writing (Saul Bellow), and psychology (Bruno Bettelheim) impersonate themselves—that is, play or enact their professional roles—in order to reflect on the fictional case of Zelig in an academic language that is intended to sound realistic. Obviously meant to lend historical credibility to the "bizarre" fictional story of Leonard Zelig, these framing interviews aim to reinforce viewers' suspension of disbelief already successfully induced by the mockumentary genre.[1] Less obvious is that the mocking side of this genre introduces a more subtle, not simply realistic, but no less mimetic principle: namely, that by playing their "real" professional roles (cultural critic, writer, historian, psychologist, etc.) to introduce a "fictional" character, these public intellectuals implicitly call attention to the performative dimension of public personalities (from Latin, *persona*, mask worn in the theater), not only on the side of fiction but also on the side of reality. Hence, the framing interviews foreground the interplay between fiction and reality, playing a role and being a role that is constitutive of the pathological case they so effectively frame. Their cinematic performance, in other words, implicitly anticipates that the case of *Zelig* might not be realistic in its representation of a real historical character, yet it reflects mimetic principles that are actually at play in real life, perhaps even stretching beyond the screen, to affect viewers as well.

This second mimetic lesson is confirmed within the diegesis, as we are first introduced to the case of Zelig "himself," played by Woody Allen. This nondescript figure is framed against the background of documentary footage that reflects an entire decade of US culture, mostly condensed in New York City but heterogeneous enough to include iconic historical events (Lindenberg's first transatlantic flight), creative writers who influentially narrated the 1920s in exemplary fictions (F. Scott Fitzgerald), emerging and catchy fashions in the arts, from music (jazz) to dance (Charleston), not to speak of the growing power of mass media to shape public opinion, from traditional (print) to "new" media (radio, cinema). There is thus a larger background that shapes the case of the human chameleon in the foreground.

Furthermore, this cultural and historical background, in turn, reflects wider ideological and political battles at play both in the US and in Europe that pit capitalism contra communism, egalitarianism contra racism, stretching to include ominous references to the Ku Klux Klan in the US and, above all, fascism and Nazism in Europe. *Zelig*, then, documents a historical reality in a mocking cinematic genre that is funny and makes us laugh; and yet, the comic mimetic figure in the (fictional) foreground also encourages viewers to reflect critically on the tragic political events in the (historical) background that both form and transform him. In the process, the film reveals a human tendency to unconsciously mimic others which, as the designation of "human chameleon" suggests, finds in animal mimicry or, as Caillois called it, *mimétisme*, its clearest manifestations. To be sure, this mimetic drive is pushed to pathological extremes in the case of Zelig for comedic reasons; yet it is also shown at play in the culture at large for critical reasons. In short, the frame already makes us see that the case study in the foreground may be fictional, personal, and comic; still, the imitative powers he dramatizes cannot be easily disconnected from the historical footage in the background, which is real, collective, and goes beyond comic principles— stretching to affect real, historical, and potentially tragic principles.

This Janus-faced point internal to the medium is subsequently reflected and redoubled at the level of the film's message. Despite the different disciplines at play in the framing interviews, the public intellectuals tend to agree that viewers should not consider Zelig simply as an individual case—though the newspapers later claim he suffers from a "unique mental disorder"; nor is it solely a story rooted in Jewish drives toward assimilation predominant in the US melting pot of the 1920s—though Zelig certainly "reflected a lot of the Jewish experience in America." While representing a specific psychological/cultural/ethnic case, we are also told that his story is broader in scope. Thus, he is initially introduced as "*the* phenomenon of the 1920s" (Sontag) and as a chameleon phenomenon that "reflected the nature of our civilization," as well as the "character of our time" (Howe). These grand, totalizing claims about the *Zeitgeist* are, of course, ironic; they are constitutive of the genre of the *mock*umentary and, thus, should not be taken seriously.

And yet, the irony is not deprived of real documentary insights that mirror tendencies at play in the 1920s and '30s. In fact, what is "reflected" in the case of Zelig is a general mimetic drive to "conform" in the most literal sense of the term (*con*-form, form together) that was particularly intense at the dawn of the past century but continues to remain central to the formation of "character" and "civilization" in the present century as well. Defined by Bettelheim as "the ultimate conformist," the case of Zelig is a psychological case that urges viewers to reflect on larger social, cultural, and political tendencies to conform, thereby "touch[ing] a nerve in people, perhaps in a way in which they preferred not to be touched" (Bellow). As we shall see, this mirroring nerve continues to touch people, if not consciously at least unconsciously so. But let us take a closer look beyond the framing interviews by having a first look at the case of Zelig "himself."

From the beginning it is clear that the stakes of *Zelig* cannot be dissociated from the politics foregrounded at the end. Initially noticed at a party held by socialites in Long Island, Zelig catches the attention of F. Scott Fitzgerald who, from within the diegesis, doubles the initial cinematic frame via a narrative supplement by specifically tying Zelig's mimetic tendency to both class and politics. Fitzgerald, in fact, notes in his diary that he first hears Zelig speak "adoringly of Coolidge and of the Republican party with an upper-class Boston accent," and then the voice-over continues, in an ominous tone: "An hour later, I was stunned to see the same man speaking with the kitchen help. Now he claimed to be a Democrat and his accent seemed coarse, as if he were one of the crowd."

If we stop to reflect on this opening scene, this "first small notice" of Zelig already encapsulates essential questions for framing our case: for instance, does this initial transformation indicate that this strange case represents, first and foremost, a mimetic phenomenon that is triggered by class disadvantage—as Zelig's "poor" origins and "lowbrow" tastes later suggest? Or does it rather say that everyday manifestations of imitation can first be identified in *all* people's accents, cultural registers, social tastes, and political affiliations—as the "typical party" in which "socialites" representative of a dominant class and culture "rub elbows" indicates? Alternatively, does Zelig's chameleon tendency to assimilate and conform to dominant political opinions indicate that minorities, due to their cultural disadvantage, are particularly vulnerable to ideological manipulation—as Zelig's "immersion in the mass" of Hitler's supporters indicates at the end of the film? Or does his ability to radically switch ideological positions to adapt to his interlocutors imply that political distinctions between Right and Left can easily be destabilized by mimetic figures who can address opposed constituencies—as the case of Hitler swaying fascist crowds across class/ethnic/religious divides later suggests? Or perhaps a mixture of all of the above? Fitzgerald does not specify it in his notes, and the voice-over has nothing to report on the matter. Still, *Zelig* begins to attune viewers' nerves to these multiple interpretative possibilities at play in the film's opening—a multilayered, pluralist opening if there ever was one that serves as a paradigmatic illustration of the entangled aesthetic, psychic, cultural, historical, and political ramification of mimesis.

**Figure 7**: Zelig becoming Chinese (*Zelig*, USA Warner Bros, 1983)

What is clear at this stage is that to adequately diagnose this homo mimeticus that is not one, politics must first be framed within questions of *identity* politics whereby class/social disadvantage is doubled by ethnic/racial disadvantage. The protagonist is, in fact, endowed with the disconcerting capacity to cut across differences that are not only cultural or ethnic but have racial and physiological overtones. Zelig's defining characteristic is that he becomes other in the sense that he can literally assume the phenotypical features of African Americans, Native Americans, but also Irish, Mexican, and Asian Americans he encounters.

As the framing interviews had anticipated, Zelig manifests a mimetic drive toward assimilation characteristic of the 1920s—a view echoed, at one remove, by numerous critics of the film as well.[2] Such cultural perspectives rightly stress that Zelig's protean transformations are "metaphorical" of the pressure for ethnic minorities to assimilate during this period. They also underscore the performative, and thus constructivist, dimension of identity formation that is reflected in the play of "citationality," "intertextuality," and "iteration" (Johnston 2007, 300) that deconstruct binary oppositions (copy/origin, appearance/being, truth/lies) in terms characteristic of a "poststructuralist mimesis" (Nas 1992, 95) that lends cultural specificity to the metamorphoses *Zelig* represents. There is thus a sense in which the case of the human chameleon not only reflects concerns with identity politics that were center stage in the 1980s; at one remove, it also provides a mirror for theoretical reflections that culminated in this period. This is a subtle indication

**Figure 8:** Zelig's protean metamorphoses (*Zelig*, USA Warner Bros, 1983)

and warning that film criticism, and by extension all interpretative activities, might not be completely immune to the mimetic phenomenon they reflect on—a self-reflective epistemic point homo mimeticus should not lose sight of.

No matter how important these reflections were in the past century, contemporary viewers cannot fail to notice that mimesis in *Zelig* operates quite literally as a chameleon phenomenon that does not remain confined to the sphere of cultural representation; nor is he solely "metaphorical" of ethnic assimilation—though it is both. *Zelig* also, and above all, dramatizes a literal, embodied, material, perhaps protosurreal if we recall Caillois, but as we shall confirm, also real, all-too-real mimetic drive that operates on a multiplicity of different yet related planes. I summarize them as follows: first, the film stages a professional actor (Allen) who plays the role of "the son of a Yiddish actor" and dramatizes mirroring mechanisms that may have interior, psychological explanations, but above all display external, physiological manifestations; second, this mimetic drive concerns the protagonist in the foreground, but also casts light on the masses that are often in the background; third, Zelig is representative of what appears to be a positive US cultural phenomenon (assimilation), but he also moves back and forth between the US and Europe, thereby revealing that this homo mimeticus is entangled in disquieting transatlantic political phenomena (KKK, Nazism); and fourth, the case of *Zelig* roots the protean metamorphoses—in terms of race, ethnicity, class, profession, appearance, nationality, and politics—in a mirroring physiological drive that concerns simultaneously all of these different yet related levels.

Despite the cultural differences at play in Zelig's comic metamorphoses, then, what they have in common is that they ultimately find in the figure of the actor or mime their common denominator. This protean aesthetic (*aisthetikos*, remember, comes from *aisthēsis*, "sensation") figure, then, is extremely sensitive to others. It is this disconcerting mirroring sensation that makes these transformations possible in the first place. Hence the need to come to a better understanding of the specifically *dramatic* origins of Zelig's pathological chameleon drive in the first place. If we have seen that this will to mime is inscribed in the phylogenetic history of *Homo sapiens*, is constitutive of a *vita mimetica* at the margins of philosophy but at the center of the polis, and originates in animal mimicry, this is the moment to stress that this mimetic drive is most manifest in the case of the actor and is ultimately human, or as Nietzsche would put it, all too human.

## The Case of the Actor: Nietzsche with/contra *Zelig*

Given the cultural frame internal to the film, the choice to reframe the case of *Zelig* via Friedrich Nietzsche might initially surprise. Not only is Nietzsche a nineteenth-century German philosopher with a tragic sensibility and Allen a twentieth-century Jewish filmmaker qua comic actor, but in popular culture, the name of Nietzsche is still tied to fascist and Nazi stereotypes *Zelig* ironically denounces. If we then recall that Nietzsche's conceptual categories privilege a set of dichotomies that posit "masters" contra "slaves," "activity" contra "passivity," the original "individual" contra the mimetic "herd," then we have ample reasons for staging an argument in which the case of Zelig could be read *contra* Nietzsche—a tendency reinforced by Nietzsche's own preferences for antagonistic titles.

And yet, at a closer genealogical look, the binary dividing the philosopher and the actor might not be as stable as it appears to be, and for at least two reasons. First, as Nietzsche scholars have long noted, the German philosopher should not be quickly conflated with the anti-Semitism and German nationalism he repeatedly condemns in his writing as pathological, contra his anti-Semitic sister.[3] Interestingly, writing contra another figure he considers an "actor," namely Richard Wagner, late in his career, Nietzsche goes as far as comparing this actor's will to power to an authoritarian "leader [*Führer*]" who casts a hypnotic spell over the "masses [*Massen*]"[4] in terms we will see dramatically re-enacted in *Zelig* as well. Second, and for the overarching goal of this book more important, Nietzsche establishes a specific genealogical connection between the figure of the "actor" and the mimetic "instinct" he sees at play in working-class and Jewish subjects in terms that are not simply pathological but, as we have been calling them, patho-*logical* in the sense that he provides an account (*logos*) on mimetic affect (*pathos*) that can productively be aligned *with* Zelig. Either way, Nietzsche's reflections on the actor in general, and Jewish identity in particular, lend philosophical substance to the case at hand in a way that foregrounds both pathological and patho-*logical* accounts of mimesis that cut both with and contra *Zelig*. Let us consider both sides of the patho(-)logies in more detail.

In an (in)famous section of *The Gay Science* (1882) titled "On the Problem of the Actor" that follows Nietzsche's genealogy of the birth of homo mimeticus out of nonlinguistic communication with which we started, he offers an account of mimicry that resonates strikingly with *Zelig*. In the process, anticipating Caillois, Nietzsche also opens up new patho-*logical* lines of inquiry on a mimetic power or *pathos* that goes beyond the logic of visual representation. Nietzsche's diagnostic is predicated on a genealogical connection that, as we have seen in chapter 1, runs deep in the phylogenesis of the species. What is different is that he now ties the culturally specific case of the actor to an imitative drive shared among the lower classes, women, and Jews—chameleon figures who, in Nietzsche's view, reveal a human penchant for "all kinds of adaptations," which, he adds, "in the case of animals is called mimicry" (1974, 361:316).

Derogatory in tone and critical of these figures' lack of an original individuality, Nietzsche writes that the lower classes "turn their coat with *every* wind and thus virtually [...] *become* a coat" (316). Characteristic of his critique of mimesis, Nietzsche is here indicating a widespread tendency to let external roles (the coat being metonymic of a professional, social, or public identity) shape inner character. Similarly, and even more problematic, in the same aphorism, Nietzsche speaks of "*Jews*, [as] the people who possess the art of adaptability [*Anpassungkunst*] par excellence," which, in his view, hinges on what he calls "histrionic gifts" (316). Hence, Nietzsche ironically asks: "what good actor today is *not*—a Jew?" And leaving women last, Nietzsche wonders whether they are not "above all else, actresses?" The ironic, misogynistic, and rather condescending patriarchal diagnostic immediately follows: "Listen to physicians who hypnotized women" (317).

These are, to be sure, embarrassing moments in the philosopher's corpus and for a number of obvious reasons: first, this evaluation is part of widespread ethnocentric and phallocentric tendencies dominant in fin de siècle Europe to project mimetic behavior on the side of racial and gendered minorities in terms I condemned elsewhere under the rubric of "mimetic racism" and "mimetic sexism" (ethical reasons); second, the language of "instinct" coupled with the reference to "animal mimicry" to talk about human behavior indicates an essentialist bias that appears to be derivative of social Darwinism and the blatant racism that informs later nineteenth-century narratives of progress (ideological reasons); last but not least, the aggressive tonality directed contra the figure of the actor in a philosopher who consistently sides with dramatic principles at play in what he calls Dionysian "imitation" reveals not only a fundamental aporia in Nietzsche's thought—it is also part of a confessional tendency in which the "mimetic pathologies" that are excoriated on the outside, are actually constitutive of the case of Nietzsche "himself" (philosophical reasons).[5]

This pathological evaluation of mimesis is real, by now well attested, and should be taken seriously. At the same time, and without contradiction, it should not mask a less visible, more discerning, and insightful patho-*logical* perspective on mimetic behavior, which can help us cast new light on chameleon tendencies that may affect minorities more directly, but ultimately are at play in all humans. If we situate Nietzsche's diagnostic of mimicry in its proper philosophical context, it is clear that he is not only denouncing the working class, Jews, and women for their mimetic tendencies to adapt to their surroundings as pathological—though he does that; he also develops a complex patho-*logical* argument that frames his diagnostic within a larger theatrical, and thus aesthetic, problematic that troubled Nietzsche for a long time.

Originating in *The Birth of Tragedy* (1872), this aesthetic problem concerns the relation between identity formation, acting, and mimesis and traverses his entire corpus. In many ways, this obsessive leitmotif finds a condensed expression in the aphorism "On the Problem of the Actor" under consideration. As the title already suggests, it is, in fact, from the dramatic point of view of the *actor* (or *mimos*), more than from the biological one of *instinct*, that Nietzsche approaches the joint problematic of the mimetic instinct. As he puts it in his opening statement: "The problem of the actor has troubled me for the longest time," and not only for aesthetic reasons at play on theatrical stages, as Nietzsche had made clear in *The Birth of Tragedy*, but also, and above all, because the actor manifests "an excess of the capacity for all kinds of adaptations" (Nietzsche 1974, 361:316), which are at play in social life, as he makes clear in *The Gay*

*Science*. Hence, as he returns to consider the figure of the actor toward the end of his career, he does so in order to evaluate "the inner craving for a role and mask" (316) he sees at play in class, ethnic, and gender minorities in order to unmask the fundamental reason (*logos*) that triggers this craving for mimetic affect (*pathos*) in social life tout court.

Thus reframed, Nietzsche's mimetic patho-*logy* is more subtle than it first appears to be. For him, in fact, it is not a primary biological "instinct [*Instinkt*]" for adaptation essentially tied to the working class, the Jews, and women that drives their will to mime, as the term "instinct" misleadingly suggests. It is rather social disadvantage, cultural oppression, and material dependency characteristic of social groups, which, as Nietzsche specifies, "had to survive under changing pressures and coercions" (1974, 361:316) that forces these (and by extension other) minorities to adapt, chameleonlike, to the dominant culture they radically depend on for their survival. This also means that Nietzsche unmasks the mimetic instinct he sees at play in minorities as an *effect* rather than as a *cause* of cultural adaptation. The overturning of perspective is key to our diagnostic: it turns an apparently essentialist argument grounded in nature or biology into a constructivist diagnostic grounded in second nature or culture. What appears to be a past-oriented evolutionary theory turns out to be future-oriented: it goes beyond nature and culture oppositions that were still dominant in the past century yet no longer hold in the present century.

Nietzsche furthers the genealogy the "genius of the species" that gives birth to *Homo sapiens* out of the instinct for communication constitutive of homo mimeticus. The specific case of the working class, which frames the other cases he discusses (Jews, women, actors), sheds light on our case study (Zelig) as well. The passage is worth quoting at length:

> Such an instinct will have developed most easily in families of the lower classes who had to survive under changing pressures and coercions [*Druck und Zwang*], in deep dependency, who had to cut their coat according to the cloth, always adapting themselves again to new circumstances, who always had to change their mien and posture, until they learned gradually to turn their coat [*Mantel*] with *every* wind and thus virtually to *become* a coat—and masters of the incorporated and inveterate [*eingefleischten*] art of eternally playing hide-and-seek, which in the case of animals is called mimicry—until eventually this capacity, accumulated from generation to generation, becomes domineering, unreasonable, and intractable. (1974, 361:316)

Nietzsche's patho-*logical* diagnostic of the powers of mimesis has remained in the shadow of his most visibly pathological affirmations directed contra marginalized mimetic subjects. It now deserves to be foregrounded for it unmasks a psycho-social-biological dynamic responsible for a human drive to adapt that develops "most easily" among minorities, but not only—far from it. As Roberto Esposito also recognized, for Nietzsche, "the human species is not given once and for all but is susceptible, for good and evil, to be molded [*plasmata*] in forms of which we do not yet have the exact notion but that constitute for us both an absolute risk and an unavoidable challenge (2004, 85; my trans.). What we add is that the plasticity of homo mimeticus is not only the subject matter that can be molded by biopower; it is also responsible for the paradox of patho(-)logical practices of contagion/immunization constitutive of our chameleonlike metamorphoses.

This mimetic drive is constitutive of his reevaluation of the modern ego qua phantom ego; minorities only reveal this generalized principle constitutive of homo mimeticus. For Nietzsche, in fact, "changing pressures," "coercions," and "dependency" among constituencies deprived of power trigger a socially induced tendency to *con*-form, chameleonlike, to dominant backgrounds, which in turn, *in*-form subjectivity from the outside in terms that are not only psychological but are constitutive of what he calls "physio-psychology" (1990, 23:53). Thus, an exterior and contingent form that is initially meant to project a social identity to the outside (a coat) has the power to retroact on the subject, press in from the outside into the soul, body, and flesh, and take possession of an identity from the inside—a subject becoming a coat.

Nietzsche, then, not only agrees with *Zelig* that minorities such as the working class and the Jews—and, by extension, all oppressed subjects deprived of power and exposed to biopower—are subjected to pressures to conform to dominant others so profound and fundamental as to become other; he also urges us to consider Zelig's chameleon tendencies literally by rooting them in animal mimicry in ways that prefigure not only Caillois's diagnostic of mimetism but also recent empirical discoveries of mirroring reflexes that cast a new light on the contagious dynamic of the pathos of will to power, or biopower. From a Nietzschean perspective, in fact, Zelig's chameleon metamorphoses are not simply metaphorical of a psychic or cultural tendency to conform—though they are certainly that too; they also reveal a deeper, bio-physio-psycho-socio-*logical* drive that goes beyond the nature/culture opposition in view of articulating a dynamic interplay between the physio-logical and psycho-logical manifestations of both human mimetism and animal mimicry.

That Nietzsche considers the phenomenon of animal mimicry as a relevant background to account for humans' chameleonlike penchant for the cultural adaptations *Zelig* foregrounds is confirmed in a related aphorism in *Daybreak* (1881) titled "Animals and Morality" (1982, 26:20–21) that we have already encountered in chapters 1 and 5. It suffices to recall that foregrounding a genealogy of mimesis that is rooted in human "instincts" (nature) but *trans*-forms—or forms via states of trance we shall soon consider—moral norms (culture) as well, he reevaluates morality in terms that require "self-adaptation, self-deprecation, submission to orders of rank," stressing that basic traces of such tendencies can be found "everywhere, even in the depths of the animal world" (20).

The case of the actor diagnosed by Nietzsche, then, brings us back to the case of Zelig dramatized by Allen. But Nietzsche also adds a patho-*logical* supplement that renders manifest a *moral* problem that is left in the background of the film, has tended to elude commentators, yet fundamentally informs the chameleon transformations in the foreground. Nietzsche, in fact, makes us see that this cinematic case might be representing a problem characteristic of minorities and socially disadvantaged social groups, yet he also sets up a mirror to reflect (on) a more generalized, human tendency to adapt, "out of prudence" and "security" to dominant moral as well as political principles promoted by "societies, parties, opinions" (1982, 26: 20–21) in terms characteristic not only of minorities but of "all Europeans." Thus, he specifies: "As they attain a more advanced age, almost all Europeans confound themselves with their role: they become the victims of their own 'good performance' [...] the role has actually *become* character, and art, nature" (1974, 356:302). Thus reframed, the case of Zelig renders visible a mimetic principle that is characteristic of a thoroughly imitative species qua homo mimeticus endowed with protean capacities for plastic adaptations that, for good and ill, are still forming, transforming, and conforming humans and posthumans today, and will continue to do so in the future as well.[6]

So far, so good. But we might still wonder: if this process of adaptation that dispossesses the ego of its proper identity is first and foremost determined by *social* factors, why does Nietzsche insist on calling it an "instinct," rooting it in nature rather than culture? While the terms may initially sound indicative of essentialist mimetic pathologies that still plagued the past century, tend to be directed against minorities in terms of class, gender, race, and sex, and are far from being dissolved, they may actually pave the way for recent empirical developments in the neurosciences that open an alternative door to the unconscious in the present century—a mimetic unconscious that, as we turn to see, accounts for Zelig's mirroring metamorphoses.

## A Mirroring Case: From Hypnosis to Mirror Neurons

When it comes to offering a medical diagnostic of the origins of Zelig's mimetic pathology, the doctors within the diegesis open up a variety of different perspectives that are comic in their antagonistic possibilities. We are in fact told that "no two [doctors] can agree on a diagnosis": from pathologies that are physiological and "glandular in nature" to a fear of contagion that is cultural in orientation and was "picked up from eating Mexican food," from a "neurological" account of a "brain tumor" to a "poor alignment of the vertebrae," the diagnostics within the film mirror, once again, the scientists' own cultural, disciplinary, and "scientific" prejudices, stretching to ironically reflect their own pathologies as well.

Thus, in a mirroring inversion of perspectives, one of the doctors who diagnosed a "brain tumor" falls victim of the sickness he had unconsciously projected onto the mimetic case—an indication that supports the young female doctor in the background, Dr. Eudora Fletcher (Mia Farrow) who, contra the patriarchal medical orthodoxy, suggests that Zelig might not by suffering from

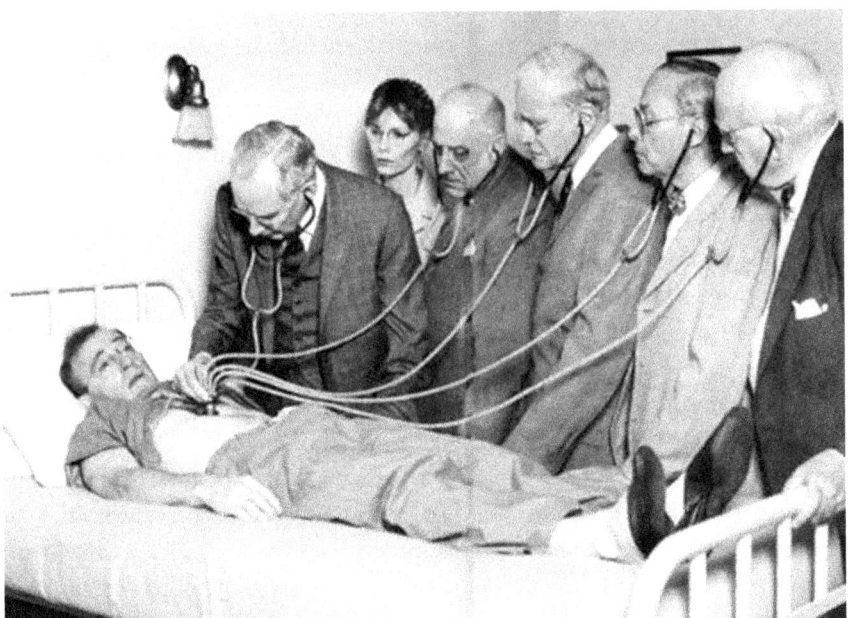

**Figure 9:** Zelig and the doctors (*Zelig*, USA Warner Bros, 1983)

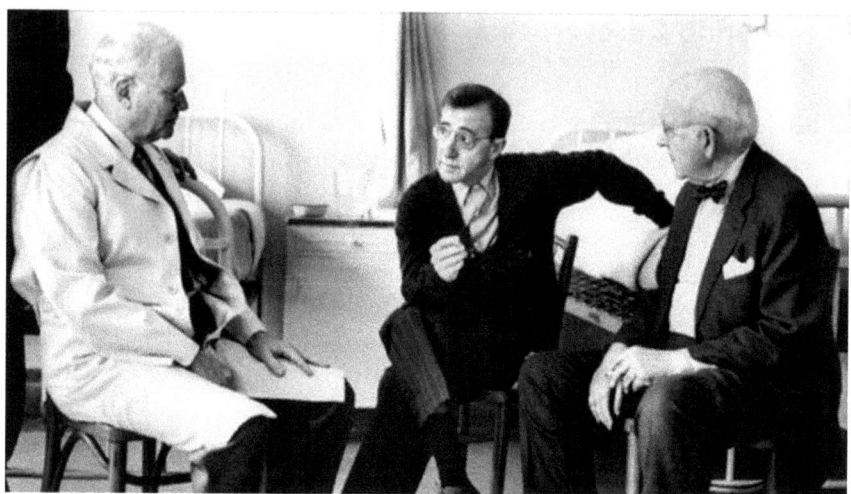

**Figure 10:** "I am a doctor" (*Zelig*, USA Warner Bros, 1983)

"a physiological disorder but from a psychological one," thereby opening a psychological door to his unconscious.

Now, given Woody Allen's well-known predilection for Oedipal scenarios and sexual drives, often shadowed by anxieties about death drives, we could expect that psychoanalysis would provide the master key to unlock the door to Zelig's psychic life. This suspicion is initially suggested by direct allusions to traumatic childhood experiences (childhood beatings) and is subsequently reinforced by Zelig's explicit references to Freudian concepts ("penis envy").[7] Interestingly, such interpretations emerge as Zelig mimics, not without irony, the posture, professional identity, and diagnostics of psychiatrists within the film. An indication that the patient playing the role of the doctor is conforming to diagnostic scripts that were beginning to spread in the 1920s had become dominant in the 1980s—stretching to inform mainstream Hollywood clinical expectations as well.

In a comic film about mirror games, ironies can be double and may not be deprived of patho(-)logical insights that cut both ways. It is, in fact, not only Zelig's histrionics as a patient qua psychoanalyst that is the subject of irony here; in a mirroring inversion, the irony also turns against the psychoanalytical theory the patient effectively mimics. What the therapeutic scene suggests, in fact, is that a dominant theory of the psyche can lead patients to mimetically adopt and conform to the dominant diagnostic categories, perhaps even perform the symptoms the theory expects. This is not only a fictional suggestion. As historian of psychology and early advocate of mimetic studies, Mikkel Borch-Jacobsen convincingly shows "the patients, far from simply submitting to the psychiatric categories imposed upon them, very actively conform to them" (Borch-Jacobsen 2009, 5)—a critique that, he adds, applies to psychic theories from hysteria to depression and casts a long shadow on psychoanalysis as a "chameleon" therapy in particular.[8]

*Zelig*'s ironic warning against this mimetic fallacy suggests to clinically oriented critics not to map diagnostics on the case of Zelig a posteriori in terms that risk mirroring the mimetic principles at play in the patient. If the mirroring dynamic of mimesis blurs the line between patient and doctor, the pathology and the patho-*logy* within the film, the same effects risks affecting the critic outside the film. Hence our goal is not to project a mirroring diagnostic but rather to focus on a patho-*logy* that is already internal to the aesthetics of the film itself. Within the diegesis, for instance, John Morton Blum, author of the fictitious book *Interpreting Zelig*, already tellingly discourages psychoanalytical approaches to the case as he says: "of course, the Freudians had a ball. They could interpret him in any way they pleased." This diagnostic suspicion is even confirmed by the real psychologist that frames the case: Bruno Bettelheim. A child psychologist known for his psychoanalytical approach to autism in the 1980s, Bettelheim initially relies on psychoanalytic categories, as he says: "The question whether Zelig was a psychotic or merely extremely neurotic was a question that was endlessly discussed among us doctors." But then, Bettelheim immediately transgresses this nosological opposition, as he evaluates Zelig as neither "psychotic" nor "neurotic" but, rather, as "normal." As he specifies: "I myself felt that his feelings were really not all that different from the normal maybe what one would call the well-adjusted normal person only carried to an extreme degree, to an extreme extent." Nietzsche would have added that, to some extent, all subjects confound themselves with their role. Somewhat ironically, Bettelheim posthumously attracted a number of charges (from plagiarism to fake credentials) that cast a shadow on his psychological theory, yet mirror the case of Zelig in practice—thereby lending support to the reality of the chameleon tendencies at play in the fictional case he had so effectively framed.

Rather than mapping pathological diagnostics on the human chameleon from the outside in, let us thus continue to treat *Zelig* as an aesthetic source for new mimetic studies to theorize mimesis as a normal human condition from the inside out. This entails taking seriously the young woman doctor, Dr. Fletcher (Mia Farrow) who, contra the patriarchal medical orthodoxy that proposes a cure through "experimental drugs," tries a "new approach": namely, "hypnosis." A prepsychoanalytical method initially used by physicians and psychologists like Jean-Martin Charcot, Hippolyte Bernheim, and Pierre Janet, hypnosis was applied by Freud to his first case (Anna O.) and later rejected in order to develop an interpretative method based on the "talking cure" that became known as psychoanalysis. Hence, hypnosis was far from new in the 1920s. Its "golden age," as historians of psychology have noticed, was the 1880s (Chertok 1993, 23). Hypnosis was also internal to pre-Freudian psychologists like Nietzsche whose diagnostic of mimesis, as we saw, finds a confirmation in "physicians" who "hypnotized" (1974, 361:317) women—a clear allusion to Charcot and his legendary *leçons du mardi* at the Salpêtrière, where hysteric patients were staged in front of male physicians to display symptoms that mimetically conformed to the physician's theory—that is, a theory that considered hypnosis a pathological condition restricted to hysteric patients.

Framed against this psychological background predicated on a mimetic sexism that projects mimetic behavior onto female bodies, we can safely say that *Zelig* is not immune from the pathologies of mimesis. The film, for instance, has been rightly critiqued for its exclusion of women as models for his chameleon-like transformations. At one remove, sexual scandals have also cast a long shadow on Allen in real life, tainting his authorial reputation in the age of #MeToo. At the same time, the film is not deprived of patho-*logical* supplements. It is worth noticing, for instance, that *Zelig* deftly subverts gender power/knowledge relations in clinical practices by inverting the stereotype of the hysteric woman in the hands of male doctors—a suggestion indicating that Zelig's mimetic patho(-)logy cuts across the gender divide, cannot be contained within patriarchal binaries, and has both pathological implications and *logical* potential as well, at least if we follow the doctor's diagnostic of the human chameleon.

After a series of hypnotic failures that only accentuate Zelig's mirroring tendencies to play the role of the doctor, Dr. Fletcher hits on the idea of doubling the mirror game. Paradoxically, she uses a mimetic lie to reveal a mimetic truth: mimicking Zelig's imitation of a doctor, Dr. Fletcher falsely admits that she is actually not a real doctor but only pretends to be one. Interestingly, she finds in Zelig's mimetic sickness (or pathology) a clue to develop a therapy (or patho-*logy*). This mirror game, in fact, has the performative effect of putting Zelig in a double bind: faced with what he believes to be a simulation of a doctor, he is led to mirror his "true" self—that is, the "liar" that he actually is. This entails revealing the truth about who he really is—namely, that there is "nothing" or "nobody" behind the mask. At a loss with himself, Zelig falls into a state of trance (from Latin, *transire*, to pass) in which he is not consciously present to "himself," and is thus, paradoxically, most "himself."

**Figure 11:** Hypnotic trance (*Zelig*, USA Warner Bros, 1983)

Under hypnosis (*hypnos*, sleep), Zelig not only confesses the root of his mimetic drive at the level of the message; he also renders manifest—via the medium of trance—the origin of the unconscious mimicry that plagues him in his waking life.

On the side of the message, Zelig reveals to Dr. Fletcher the psychological defense mechanism Nietzsche had already identified a century before. If the philosopher had rooted human mimicry in "prudence" (Nietzsche 1881, 26:21), Zelig admits that he mirrors others because "it's safe to be like the others." And again like Nietzsche, this prudence is rooted in imitative instincts Dr. Fletcher traces back to the animal mimicry. Dubbing Zelig "the human chameleon," the female psychologist develops—in an anti-mimetic presentation that is up against an audience of skeptical male doctors—the following mimetic hypothesis: namely, that as the lizard "blends in with its immediate surrounding" in order to protect itself "Zelig protects himself by becoming whoever he is around." Dr. Fletcher is neither Freudian nor Lacanian; she is also closer to Nietzsche than to Caillois. In fact, she considers human mimetism a defense mechanism linked to animal mimicry, which Zelig as a Jewish minority renders visually manifest. In this specific diagnostic sense, then, his mimetic pathology is restricted to a specific psychological and cultural case. And yet, what the film *Zelig* also shows is that the human chameleon reveals latent mirroring tendencies that are, to a degree, "normal," and are at play among all humans—which leads to the hypnotic aesthetic medium in question.

On the side of the medium, under hypnosis, *Zelig* foregrounds a paradoxical state of consciousness characteristic of a somnambulistic trance in which he is both himself and not himself, conscious of his identity, which is not one, and suggestible to others, which makes him more than one. This Janus-faced state could be dissociated as follows. On the one hand, it is during the hypnotic trance that Zelig is most "himself," so to speak. Thus, he unashamedly confesses his fears, desires, affects, and says what he really thinks at the level of his speech, going as far as revealing his waking personality to be a coat with nobody inside—"I am nobody, I am nothing," he says when asked who he is. On the other hand, it is during the state of hypnotic dispossession, his arm lifted at the injunction of the doctor, that the medium of cinema makes us see the physiological roots of his mimetic "instinct"—namely, that an unconscious mirroring reflex can be triggered by an external order that is not only perceived but experienced as one's own: ordered to lift his arm, he unconsciously lifts it, as if by reflex. This state of docility that leads the hypnotized patient to follow orders sets up a mirror to the psychic condition of dispossession characteristic of Zelig's waking state. Just as under hypnosis so in his daily life Zelig also unconsciously conforms to the expectations of others, involuntarily mimicking not only gestures but also expressions, accents, opinions, professions, and ultimately thoughts of others, so as to literally become other. In short, while Zelig's linguistic message reveals his "true" self, the spell of the hypnotic medium reveals that his daily life is actually lived, experienced, in a quasi-somnambulistic pathological trance—something the movie within the movie, titled *The Changing Man*, describes, at one additional fictional remove, as a "zombielike" stare.

But Zelig is not the only person vulnerable to hypnotic suggestions. Far from it. Drawing on an established connection between cinema and hypnosis characteristic of classics of the 1920s like *The Cabinet of Dr. Caligari* (Robert Wiene 1920), *Zelig* directs the power of hypnosis outside the screen to make us not only see but also feel this mimetic power on our nerves via a visual medium that transgresses the fiction/reality opposition and affects spectators as well.

Who, then, is "the subject" that is placed under hypnosis here? Not only is our subject position conflated with the subject in question (formal reasons); we are also subjected to the same hypnotic influence that breaks the fourth wall and—if you fix your gaze on that spiraling point for a while—can induce a light psychic trance. Just try it for thirty seconds, and you will begin to feel the spell-*binding* force of a *vita mimetica* Plato was the first to fear (chapter 2). This

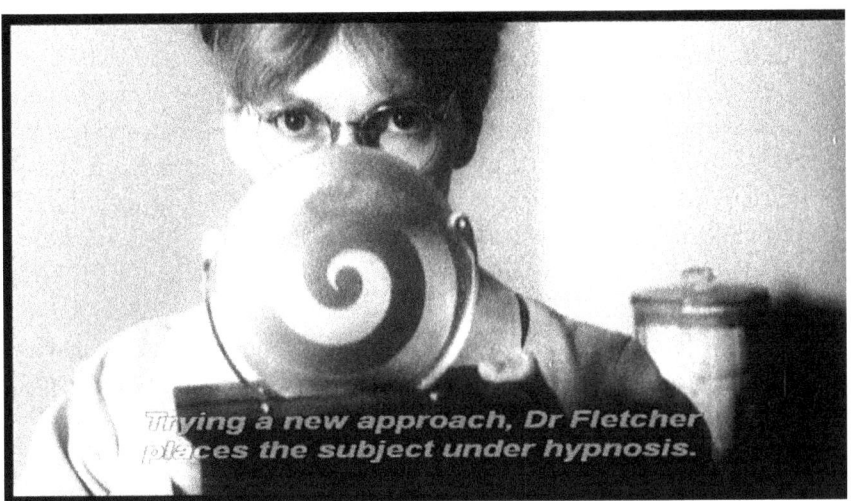

**Figure 12**: Hypnotizing spectators (*Zelig*, USA Warner Bros, 1983)

formal choice is, of course, not accidental. We are in fact given to feel that cinema is a medium that is mimetic not only in the visual sense that it represents images we can safely contemplate from an aesthetic distance; it is also mimetic in the affective, performative sense that it has the power to induce what Edgar Morin calls an "imitation-hypnotic state" (2005, 96) in spectators. In the darkness of the cinema but also watching a screen at home, we can easily fall under the spell of a process of becoming other via an interplay of "projection and identification" (103) that is characteristic of the *vita mimetica*, is constitutive of the magic of cinema, and, as we shall see, via new media reach into the present as well.

Genealogical lenses remind us that the lesson that in a hypnotic state the subject is unconsciously vulnerable to mirroring mechanisms was once well known among philosophical physicians working in fin de siècle Europe. Given their popularity, it is astonishing how quickly this mimetic condition has faded from memory.[9] For our purpose, let us just recall that Hippolyte Bernheim, from the School of Nancy, paved the way for Dr. Fletcher's "new approach," as he relied on hypnosis to cure his patients of what he considered "psychological" problems. Contra his rival already alluded to by Nietzsche, Jean-Martin Charcot of the Salpêtrière, Bernheim, in fact, argued that hypnosis was not a pathological state reserved to hysteric patients—be they psychotic or neurotic, nor was it limited to women or racial minorities. Rather, Bernheim considered hypnosis a normal psychic tendency that affected "a very large majority of people," including, he added, "very intelligent people belonging to the higher grades of society" (1957, 5). And, significantly, he added that via hypnotic suggestion "an idea may originate in the mind through imitation and may give rise to a corresponding sensation" (132). Thus, the sight of someone's smiling or crying not only induces an idea into the self as to why this person is happy or sad, but actually triggers, "through imitation," an unconscious mirroring sensation of the other into the self.

How does this mirroring principle operate? As Bernheim puts it: "The phenomena of automatic activity of the nervous centers may be *instinctive*. Acts occur naturally, without ever having been acquired, by means of the spontaneous, unconscious initiative of the brain," by which he means "imitative acts" (127). For Bernheim, then, just as for Nietzsche before him and Caillois after him, there is a mirroring physio-psychological mechanism in the brain that "may be instinctive" and leads subjects to unconsciously imitate others so profoundly as to feel what the others feel, as if one were other.

We now know why this mirroring mechanism looks familiar. On the shoulders of the same tradition of the mimetic unconscious we have been unearthing and is only now returning to the foreground of the theoretical scene,[10] Dr. Fletcher paves the way for a scientific discovery that accounts for her subject's tendency to mirror others in the first place. Though we shall be careful not to mimic doctors within the film and call it "the scientific medical phenomenon of the age," doctors in real life have not hesitated to call this mirroring reflex "the single most important 'unreported' (or at least unpublicized) story of the decade" (Ramachandran 2000).

The story is now well known, and we have already encountered it, but the case of Zelig allows us to broaden the implications of the discovery of mirror neurons from a perspective that is already double for it is as attentive to aesthetics as it is to politics. On the aesthetic side, Allen's cinematic dramatization of the human chameleon offers an additional confirmation that this discovery is actually a *re*-discovery of a hypnotic principle that was well known in the pre-Freudian period attentive to the physiological fact that humans are wired for imitation. As a consequence, imitation has been returning to the center of a number of studies that cross the boundaries between the sciences and the humanities, stretching to provide new experimental foundations to film studies as well, which have recently being grouped under the rubric of "*experimental aesthetics*" (Gallese and Guerra 2015, 13).[11] Considering aesthetics in its etymological sense of *aisthēsis*, that is, as a "multimodal perception of the world through the body" (13; my trans.), these emerging perspectives on mimetic forms of corporal cognition, or "embodied simulation" (15) find a paradigmatic dramatization in the case of Zelig. If the medical diagnostics within the film are off mark, the film *Zelig* dramatizes embodied, intersubjective, and affective mechanisms that blur the opposition between self and other, the mind and the body, physiology and psychology, but also protagonist and spectators, action seen on the screen and reflex simulated in the body. The lesson is clear: to different degrees, we might all be human chameleons after all.

A key measure of the relevance of the discovery of mirror neurons for our specific case study is the following one. Even skeptics of mirror neurons in theory could not resist the impulse of considering *Zelig* as a dramatic manifestation of the mirror neuron system in practice. As the neuroscientist Gregory Hickok puts it: "You may have noticed that in some social situations people tend to mimic each other's postures and gestures" (2014, 202). Yes, we did. Lest we are ourselves busy mimicking others, it's hard to miss. And then he adds: "Woody Allen turned the phenomenon into his 1983 film, *Zelig*, a mockumentary about a fairly nondescript man who takes on the appearance and characteristics of those who surround him—a kind of human chameleon" (202). This is an interesting avowal for a book titled *The Myth of Mirror Neurons* (2014). As often, mythic fictions are not deprived of theoretical insights on mimesis. Hickok even sets up a mirror to the patho-*logies* that inform our diagnostic. When Bellow says in his framing comments that Zelig "touched a nerve in people," or when Bettelheim says that this case is not that different from the "well-adjusted normal person," they are quite literally (not metaphorically) right.

A decade before the discovery of mirror neurons, *Zelig* had already dramatized the powers of an embodied, relational, and affective mimesis. How? By making manifest at the physiological level a normal mirroring principle invisibly at play at the neurological level. Zelig's mirroring transformations, in other words, register and render visible a mimetic principle that leads humans to unconsciously mirror the movements, gestures, expressions, of others. In so doing, what is mirrored is not only the exterior physical appearance but also an inner psychic pathos: the MNS in humans, in fact, allows for an immediate form of prelinguistic communication that mediates affects, states of mind, but also ideas, opinions, values, and ideologies that may originally belong to the other; yet, via unconscious mirroring reflexes that transgress the self/other opposition, they can be perceived, or rather experienced, as one's own. Hence neuroscientists claim that the "*primary* role" of mirror neurons concerns "understanding the meaning of the actions of others" (Rizzolatti and Sinigaglia 2008, 124).

What *Zelig* adds is that such unconscious mirroring actions do not only generate an understanding of others based on a patho-*logy* that works for the better; they can also generate mirroring reactions that, as Nietzsche was quick to point out and Allen to dramatize, are not deprived of sociocultural pathologies that operate for the worse. Just as the genealogy of homo mimeticus we explored in part 1 paved the way for the aesthetic side of a *vita mimetica* we covered in part 2, so aesthetics begins to take us to the political pathologies of mimesis we will discuss in more detail in part 3, yet *Zelig* allows us to foreground.

## The Politics of Mimesis: From Public Opinion to Fascist Contagion

We have seen that *Zelig* remains our contemporary because it anticipates a scientific discovery that roots mimetic instincts in our brain. This is an important point but an entire modernist tradition of the mimetic unconscious that had hypnosis as a via regia had already paved the way.[12] What we must add is that it also urges critics and theorists to reflect on the broader social and, above all, political implications of collective movements of unconscious imitation that cannot be analyzed within the confines of the lab, yet are at play in social life, have a long history in the twentieth century, and continue to cast a shadow on the present century as well.

*Zelig*'s politics of mimesis is at play at the level of the intersubjective relations the film foregrounds but is equally manifest at the level of the collective behavior that is constantly in the background. Just as Zelig's hypnotic trance reveals, in an exaggerated form, the state of psychic dispossession characteristic of his waking life more generally, so his individual case finds a collective counterpart in the mass behavior that is under the spell of the Zelig phenomenon: from the press to the radio, fashion to public opinion, publicity to propaganda, *Zelig* consistently suggests that the case of the human chameleon is not that exceptional after all. On the contrary, it mirrors wider hypnotic and imitative tendencies that are massively shared in modern social life, if only because they are constitutive of the age of the crowd—which is also an age of the public.

The changing fashions, the sudden shifts in public opinion, the presence of streaming crowds thronging the streets and subjected to the daily flow of newspapers, and the radio broadcasting that radically amplifies mass opinions are not simply background; they mirror, on a larger social scale, the Zelig phenomenon in social life, revealing his mimetic condition as a shared condition, while also

**Figures 13 a, b, c:** Mimetic Disseminations (*Zelig*, USA Warner Bros, 1983)

contributing to disseminating the mimetic behavior they presume to simply represent. Framed against such backgrounds, it is clear that the human chameleon sets up an unrealistic mirror that exaggerates imitative tendencies at play in the *vita mimetica* of modern social behavior tout court.

That unconscious forms of imitation are central to social life is, of course, not an original idea. In many ways, *Zelig* offers a cinematic dramatization of a psycho-sociological principle that was well known in the 1920s—and once again, it's astonishing how quickly it faded from memory. *Zelig*, in fact, dramatizes a thesis articulated by the French sociologist Gabriel Tarde in his classic *The Laws of Imitation* (1890). Drawing on Bernheim's psychological theory of hypnotic suggestion as well as on the untimely physiological realization that "'there is in the human brain an innate tendency to imitate'" (Tarde 2001, 148), now timely confirmed by the neurosciences, Tarde argued that an "*unconscious imitation*" (138) is constitutive of social life and generates states of hypnotic/mirroring dispossession he summarized as follows: "to have only suggested ideas and to believe them to be spontaneous: this is the illusion characteristic of the somnambulist and of social beings" (137). Read against the background of crowd psychology, Zelig's somnambulistic state of trance is thus not only pathological at the individual level; it also reveals a patho-*logy*, or law of imitation, that Tarde considers constitutive of social life tout court.

Closer to home, applying the insights of crowd psychology to the rise of "public relations" in the US in the 1920s, Edward Bernays went as far as claiming in his widely popular *Propaganda* (1928) that "the conscious and intelligent manipulation of the organized habits and opinions of the masses is an important element in a democratic society" (2005, 37) and finds in man's "gregarious" or "herd" nature a vulnerability to "influences which unconsciously control his [*sic*] thoughts" (73). These are uncomfortable reflections on homo mimeticus that are not easy to hear and assimilate. They offer a serious challenge to still dominant conceptions of rational subjectivity qua *Homo sapiens* based on autonomy, self-sufficiency, free will, and conscious presence to selfhood that (mis) informs dominant strands in social theory. Hence, with few exceptions, historically, it has been easier to project mimesis onto gendered, sexual, religious, and colonial minorities, or simply erase it from memory and make a tabula rasa of mimetic drives. Contrary to these rationalist tendencies, this book suggests that we should treat mimesis as a mirror to reflect critically on the aesthetic, and by extension, psychic, social, and political life of homo mimeticus.

The case of Zelig provides such an aesthetic mirror. It reveals that humans are endowed with a tendency to unconsciously imitate the dominant models that surround them, especially if these models address individuals in a crowd, or turn to media that have the power to cast a spell on personal opinions, turning them into shared public opinions. Hence, as the roaring twenties led to the darkening '30s, *Zelig* makes us see that humans' imitative tendencies can no longer be projected onto marginalized others, nor contained solely within the walls of psychiatric institutions. If only because the powers of mimesis were all too visibly exploited by authoritarian leaders who relied on the same hypnotic techniques in order to cast a spell on the masses. Despite its cultural specificity rooted in the US of the 1920s, or rather because of it, as the film speeds to an end, it moves from the US to Europe and back, making clear that the nature of "civilization" *Zelig* reflects is imitative in nature, departs from grand fictional

**Figure 14**: The spell of Nazism (*Zelig*, USA Warner Bros, 1983)

narratives of historical progress, and generates fluxes of affective contagion that infect entire crowds at the heart of western democracies.

After his loss of favor with US public opinion and a period of absence, Zelig is, in fact, identified in Germany. The country and ideology changed, but the mimetic phenomenon is fundamentally the same. Zelig is in fact found among a crowd of supporters that is under the spell of a hypnotizing Nazi leader who casts a long shadow on the history of western "civilization."

The archival image provides a historical confirmation that Zelig's tendency to lift his arm in a state of hypnotic trance to conform to an external order was not only a bizarre individual pathology, after all. As the history of the 1930s teaches us, and the archival footage Zelig relies on makes visible, this hypnotic state was massively reproduced by entire crowds as they fell, in a period of economic crisis and generalized discontent, under the spell of a charismatic leader who consciously relied on hypnotic means in order to induce massive outbreaks of dispossessions. As crowd psychologist Gustave Le Bon, on the shoulders of Bernheim and Tarde, was quick to point out in *The Crowd* (1895):

> an individual immerged for some length of time in a crowd in action soon finds himself [*sic*] [...] in a special state, which much resembles the state of fascination in which the hypnotized individual finds himself in the hands of the hypnotizer (2002, 7).

Hitler was a reader of Le Bon; he relied on the notion of hypnotic "suggestion" to account for his mesmerizing (will to) power over the crowd: he was also quick to turn this mimetic insight to political abuse.[13]

In the end, the fact that Zelig shifts from being a representative of a newly found American individualism to a deplorable assimilation with the fascist and Nazi masses is significant. Within the film, it ultimately allows the framing commentators to "make sense" of this psychic case. Thus, commenting on Zelig's appearance in a Nazi crowd, Saul Bellow has the following diagnostic to offer:

> Then it made all the sense in the world because although he wanted to be loved, craved to be loved, there was also something in him that desired immersion in the mass and anonymity. And Fascism offered Zelig that kind of opportunity, so that he could make something anonymous of himself by belonging to this vast movement.

This diagnostic is certainly in line with the mimetic principles that animate the case of Zelig (the patient). Still, it does not fully unpack the disturbing political implications of the powers of mimesis the case of *Zelig* (the movie) dramatizes. If only because "anonymity," as the film repeatedly suggests, is not a unique property of fascism alone; it is constantly at play in the anonymous and ubiquitous crowds that constitute a silent and largely unnoticed leitmotif in the film. At one remove, commentators in the past century have tended to interpret the protagonist's capitulation to the *Führer* in light of the comic scene that follows, as Zelig wakes up from his trance and interrupts Hitler's 1933 Munich speech in what has been called "one of the most hilarious scenes of the movie" (Nas 1992, 98).

The scene is certainly funny, and the transatlantic flight back to the US neatly conforms to Hollywood standards of closure culminating with a romantic happy ending we have, in a spiraling loop, become mimetically accustomed to in the past century. And yet, at the same time, the comic image of Zelig under the spell of the totalitarian leader is not deprived of patho-*logical* insights into tragic horrors the film urges us to take seriously in the present century. It is, in fact, the ultimate consequence of the process of adaptation to dominant models the film had been warning us against from the very beginning—for politics, as we have seen, provides both the alpha and the omega of the film and, at one remove, of this chapter as well.

From beginning to middle to end, we have repeatedly seen and felt that the theoretical potential internal to this aesthetic case study far exceeds the framing interpretations within the film. *Zelig*'s message is much more radical than any of the public intellectuals interviewed is willing to acknowledge. It suggests that a mimetic immersion in fascist and Nazi movements and the hypnotic dispossessions it entails casts a shadow not only on the historical peoples and governments that officially espoused fascism and Nazism in the 1930s and '40s, most notably Italy and Germany—though "mass anonymity" is certainly a characteristic of fascism (from *fascio*, bundle). It also suggests that the hypnotic drive to dissolve in mass anonymity had been constantly in the background as a shadow cast on the crowds whose opinions could so easily be manipulated throughout the movie. It is thus politically significant that the film initially alludes to racist organizations like the Ku Klux Klan that, as recent theorists of fascism have shown, find striking continuities with Nazi ideology (Stanley 2018, 129–130), a racist ideology that, the same theorists argue, should be taken seriously in light of the recent returns of totalitarian leaders who rely on affectively "contagious" forms of "hypnotic" or "mimetic communication" (Connolly 2017b, 37) in order to aspire to fascism, neofascism, or "(new) fascism" (Lawtoo 2019b).

**Figure 15:** Thoughtless mimetic participation (*Zelig*, USA Warner Bros, 1983)

As historian Timothy Snyder also puts it, in terms that confirm the timeliness of our aesthetic case study, these new fascist leaders have the power to draw constituencies into what he calls a "trance by the hypnotic power of its own propaganda," rendering them "zombified" (2018, 264). This is exactly the same diagnostic of the *vita mimetica* that *Zelig* attempts to make us see and feel. It is also a diagnostic that goes as far back as Plato and orients recent historical accounts that resuscitate "prison walls" that go from *Homo Sapiens* to *Homo Deus*.[14] Our supplement is that *Homo Mimeticus* is central to taking hold of these hypnotic powers, if only because mimesis is the affective force that spellbinds individuals in prison walls that can easily turn into totalitarian walls. Finally, and even more problematic, Zelig's capitulation to Hitler suggests that even the distinction between victim and oppressor, a US subject and a German leader, a Jewish victim and Nazi *Führer* is far from stable in the 1930s. In fact, the film suggests that a culturally oppressed chameleon character can go as far in its dispossession as identifying with the very figure that is responsible for his oppression, mindlessly becoming part of a movement whose deliberate intention is the brutal extermination of the Jewish people.

None of the commentators in the framing interviews venture into this dangerous political territory. Perhaps because they are framing a comedy that is intended to make us laugh, after all (aesthetic reasons). But perhaps also because *Zelig* comes awfully close to what was still a controversial thesis in the 1980s (political reasons): that is, an untimely philosophical thesis concerning the power of totalitarian movements to generate a new type of evil that was unprecedented in its horrific effects; yet it may not have been carried out by monstrous criminals but by seemingly normal, dispossessed, and perhaps "banal" figures responsible for what Hannah Arendt grouped under the controversial rubric of "the banality of evil" (2006). *Eichmann in Jerusalem: A Report on the Banality of Evil* (1963) is, in fact, a book attentive to the psychology of a nondescript figure without proper identity who can express himself only in "clichés that the psychiatrists thought so 'normal'" (48–49). As a Jewish intellectual living in New York, Hannah Arendt would thus have provided an interesting political supplement that was missing to the introductory frames of *Zelig*. Since she died in 1975, prior to the making of the film, she was likely on Allen's mind when he looked for Jewish public intellectuals to frame the film, but unfortunately could not contribute her perspective herself.

I thus take the risk, and thus the responsibility, to add this missing frame along lines inspired by Arendt but in my own name. I place this frame in guise of conclusion, but as I noted at the beginning, it is Arendt that encouraged me to re-evaluate the *vita mimetica* of the film from the beginning.

## The Banality of Mimesis: The Missing Frame

Given the misunderstandings caused by Hannah Arendt's report on the case of Eichmann, it is crucial to stress at the outset that the phrase "the banality of evil" does not apply to the horror of the Holocaust, which Arendt uncompromisingly condemned but to the psychology of Eichmann, a figure that, not unlike Zelig under the spell of Hitler, seemed unable to have thoughts of his own—in ways representative of a mass of Nazi supporters as well. I shall return to Arendt's specific account of Eichmann as a "banal" bureaucrat in more detail in the next chapter for her thesis requires closer attention in light of more recent historical facts that have since come to the foreground. For the moment, let us use her re-evaluation of evil to bring our diagnostic of the human chameleon in *Zelig* to an end, while also using the film to supplement a mimetic perspective embryonic in Arendt's account but not fully spelled out in *Eichmann in Jerusalem*.

At the most general level, Arendt's argument was that the type of evil embodied by the case of Eichmann, a SS bureaucrat responsible for organizing the deportation to concentration camps that led to the extermination of millions of Jews, was not characterized by a radical evil that could be restricted to a few monstrous cases—no matter how unprecedented the horror was. Rather, she considered Eichmann "banal" in the sense that he passively conformed to his bureaucratic role so completely that he could express himself only in clichés, had no opinions of his own, and when confronted with the horror of the Final Solution he so effectively implemented, he was characterized by what appeared during the trial as a total lack of guilt or bad conscience.

Why? How is such a lack of human *sym-pathos*, which we have traced back to the very origins of the birth of consciousness, possible in the first place? The reasons, for Arendt, rest on the details of Eichmann's specific life story, which include a struggle to adapt, conform, and ascend the social ladder in a period of economic crisis Arendt takes the trouble to narrate. As she puts it after a detailed chapter recounting his biography, Eichmann "gave the impression of a typical member of the lower middle classes" but was actually "the *declassé* son of a solid middle-class family" (2006, 31). Not unlike Zelig, all his life Eichmann struggled to fit in. Yet Arendt also specifies that the decisive element in Eichmann's psychological transformation—one of the witnesses' comments on a "personality change" (65) as Eichmann was put in charge of implementing the Final Solution—was that he adapted, chameleonlike, to what was at the time a dominant and massively shared view by millions of people. As Arendt puts it: "German society of eighty million people had been shielded against reality and factuality by exactly the same means, the same self-deception, lies, and stupidity, that had now become engrained in Eichmann's mentality" (52). Eichmann, not unlike Zelig, is not the only subject living a *vita mimetica*.

The link between the banality of evil and a drive to "conform" in terms that rendered Eichmann "in tune with the milieu in which he operated" (Backer 2010, 142) has been noticed before. Still, the specifically *mimetic* psychology responsible for this attunement to the milieu has not been in the foreground of theoretical discussions about the banality of evil so far. This is surprising, for Eichmann comes close to offering a diagnostic of the mimetic nature of his banality himself. As Arendt reports, Eichmann admitted to being "'swallowed up by the Party against all expectations and without previous decision'" (2006, 33). This avowal seems to suggest that the affective force of the Party that swallowed him up by affective contagion, rather than a deliberate ideology or political program (a point we shall have to reconsider), led him to join the Nazi movement. And as the war was lost, Eichmann realized to his dismay that an individual life would prove much more difficult than the imitative life he had been living so far: "'I would have to live a leaderless and difficult individual life, I would receive no directives from anybody, no orders and commands [...] in brief a life never known before lay before me'" (32). One who leads a mimetic life, in other words, can easily follow the orders of a leader that can lead to the banality of evil and unspeakable horrors, but will have difficulties leading an individual life of one's own—if only because it is precisely the experience of individuality that the psychology of mimesis calls fundamentally into question.

What the case of Zelig revisited in the company of Nietzsche makes us see, then, is that mimesis and the hypnotic dispossession of a proper individual identity it entails is constitutive of the banality of evil as Arendt understands it. It also allows us to provide a mimetic supplement to her patho-*logical* diagnostic. It is not simply that Eichmann was driven by an "inability to *think*" (2006, 49)—an enigmatic and misleading phrase we shall have to unpack in more detail in the following chapter. It is rather that he was unable to resist the collective power of a *pathos* constitutive of the long genealogy of homo mimeticus.

The case of Zelig sets up a mirror to the case of Eichmann. And what this mirror reveals is the power of mimetic-hypnotic dispossession to trigger, in specific sociopolitical circumstances, a type of embodied "thoughtlessness" that is difficult to account for in the rational terms of a philosophical *logos* alone. And yet, this banality of thought becomes understandable if we frame it against the *patho*-logical background attentive to the power of affect or pathos to inform an idea, logos, or ideo-*logy* the final scenes of *Zelig* render manifest via aesthetic means. Could it be, then, that a vulnerability to mimetic *pathos* is the primary—I don't what to say reason but—affect in generating the banality of evil as Arendt tried to articulate it?

Perhaps. We shall explore this hypothesis on a type of evil that might be complex in its "banality" in more detail soon. What seems certain for the moment is that for Arendt, just as for Nietzsche, Bernheim, Tarde, Bernays, and, later, Allen, far from being confined to exceptional cases, this suggestibility to the *pathos* of totalitarian leaders can, under specific historical circumstances in which evil becomes the dominant norm, threaten to affect *all* subjects, rendering an entire social body under the spell of a tyrannical head or ideology unable not only to think but also to feel the suffering of the other via a sym-pathos that is equally constitutive of homo mimeticus. Put differently, the *patho*-logy internal to the case of Zelig makes us suspect that the affect (*pathos*) of dispossession may be the cause of the loss of thought (*logos*) that defines the banality of evil. What is most disconcerting is that this mimetic banality, Allen and Arendt seem to agree, again in specific historical milieus, can stretch to cast a spell on the very victims these leaders set out to exterminate. For Arendt, in fact, one of the most harrowing realizations of witnessing the Eichmann trial was that even Jewish organizations turned out to be more complicit with the Nazi horrors than they were ready to acknowledge, thereby adding a still controversial mirroring twist to her account of the case.[15]

At the end of this comic movie, then, as we see Zelig in a hypnotic state of dispossession during Hitler's Munich speech in 1933, we are left to wonder: could it be that underneath the mask of a comic mockumentary, *Zelig* is, among other things, also offering a cinematic dramatization of what was arguably *the* most controversial aspect of Arendt's thesis about the case of Eichmann? Was he relying on the powers of comedy to cast light on the seemingly incomprehensible and tragic dynamic that can lead victims to fall under the spell of their oppressors? This is indeed what our reading of the human chameleon suggests.

If the case of *Zelig* remains our contemporary in an age still under the spell of (new) fascist and totalitarian leaders, it is not only because it reveals an all-too-human tendency, amplified by social disadvantage and oppression, to conform to dominant models; nor solely because it recuperates a psychological tradition that had hypnosis, suggestion, and mirroring reflexes as a via regia to a mimetic unconscious the neurosciences are only now beginning to rediscover—though these are amply sufficient reasons for reopening the case. *Zelig* remains our contemporary also because it puts the aesthetic genre of the mockumentary to critical use to make us see and feel how mirroring tendencies can take possession not only of marginalized individuals but of entire crowds and publics that, under the spell of increasingly effective (new) media of (dis)information that spread propaganda and big lies in massive, algorithmic doses, can easily be rendered suggestible, deprived of the ability to think, or better, rendered thoughtless and thus mindlessly ready to commit horrific actions.

In the wake of the totalitarianism of the past century, Arendt warned future centuries as well. She stresses that "highly cultured people were particularly attracted to mass movements and that, generally, highly differentiated individualism and sophistication did not prevent, indeed sometimes encouraged, the self-abandonment into the mass for which mass movement provided" (1976, 316). *Zelig* not only agrees with this diagnostic. It also makes us see that, since an unconscious will to conform triggers this psychic self-abandonment, the banality of evil should, perhaps, be reframed within a genealogical tradition attentive to what I called here the banality of mimesis. On further thought, this so-called banality might turn out to reveal a plurality of mimetic complexities that rest as much on *pathos* as on *logos* and whose patho-*logic* we set out to diagnose in the next chapter.

Although the case of Zelig concludes with a fictional happy ending, then, his story touched a real nerve in people in the end, perhaps in ways in which people preferred not to be touched. It remains to be seen whether *Zelig*'s diagnostic reflections on the mirroring powers of dispossession can still reach beyond the looking glass, wake up spectators, and contribute to breaking the spell of contemporary thoughtlessness generated via increasingly hypnotizing media back in the hands of (new) fascist and totalitarian leaders.

PART 3

# **POLITICS**
*MIMETIC RE-TURNS*

CHAPTER 7

# BANALITY OF EVIL/ MIMETIC COMPLEXITY

"I would have to live a leaderless and difficult individual life, I would receive no directives from anybody, no orders and commands [...] in brief, a life never known before."

—Adolf Eichmann, in *Eichmann in Jerusalem*

It might not be popular to say it, but a plurality of critical voices is currently warning us that the phantom, or the shadow, of fascism is once again haunting the contemporary scene. Political theorists, historians, and philosophers have recently claimed that the growing popularity of far-right leaders in Europe, the US, the UK, not to mention the authoritarian leaders in Brazil, China, and Russia, should not simply be defined as conservative, right-wing, or populist. Rather, a number of influential scholars across disciplines forcefully argue that populist leaders on the far right may not be identical to fascist leaders like Mussolini and Hitler and should thus not be confused with them.[1] And yet, they reanimate fascist phantoms nonetheless in their rhetoric, bodily affects, propaganda machines, big lies, and tyrannical interventions.

These leaders also manifest characteristics of what Umberto Eco, writing in the 1990s, called "Ur-Fascism." Typical features include "fear of difference," "the appeal to a frustrated middle class," "machismo," "irrationalism," "disagreement is treason," "selective populism," and "contempt for the weak" (Eco 1995). Interestingly, among emerging symptoms of Ur-Fascism, Eco also included a type of TV "newspeak," or "impoverished Internet language," which we are by now accustomed to in the age of social media. It has, in fact, become the lingua franca of politicians with an authoritarian bent who rely on new media to trigger a type of affective contagion that is constitutive of what I call, for lack of a more original term, "(new) fascism."[2] As history shows, the step from fascism, old or new, to totalitarianism tends to be a short one, especially if what is at stake are not democratic but oligarchic countries that have long been subjected to tyrannical leaders. As the horror of war has now reappeared on the European political scene with the Russian invasion of Ukraine in February 2022, triggered by an authoritarian leader of a country without a proper identity who launched a war of imperial expansion that is generating humanitarian horrors,[3] it is urgent to rethink the question of evil in light of the patho(-)logies of homo mimeticus.

Building on emerging genealogies of fascism and tyranny, old and new, and furthering the diagnostic of the actor qua chameleon we encountered via the case of *Zelig*, I now seek to reevaluate the contagious powers of mimesis at play in fascist leaders whose "authoritarian personality" (Adorno et al. 1950) has been studied in the past but require an update for the present. I do so by focusing on imperceptible mimetic and unconscious powers that can deprive otherwise normal people of the ability to think critically, and thus act ethically, generating political pathologies that infect the body politic in the present and, most likely, in the future as well. My starting point consists in revisiting Umberto Eco's untimely observation about an "impoverished vocabulary" that has the power "to limit the instruments for complex and critical reasoning" (Eco 1995)—a symptom characteristic of what he calls "Ur-Fascism," which can be reloaded and amplified via new media that cast a hypnotic spell on users in ways constitutive of (new) fascism as well.

That this linguistic impoverishment is an obstacle to the development of thought, including ethico-political thought, in mediatized ages in which apprentice presidents have the possibility to become masters, is now loud and clear. Less clear is that this symptom, and the mimetic powers that trigger it, might also be at play in less spectacular, more ordinary, but not less dangerous forms: among bureaucrats working for hypernationalist administrations that implement, defend, and promote (new) fascist and totalitarian laws, which should be considered unthinkable in normal circumstances yet, in periods of economic, political, and identity crisis, reawaken fascist phantoms that risk being normalized—a disconcerting phenomenon most visible in the pathological consequence of anti-immigration policies in Europe, child detention camps in the US, deportation of people to Russia, and assaults on the environment globally, all of which should be considered as constitutive of (new) fascist policies.

Due to the paradoxical logic of mimesis, the spread of political pathologies does not prevent the emergence of countering patho-*logies* that generate *sym-pathos* with the oppressed, as the European and world support for Ukrainian refugees fleeing from a horrific invasion is making visible as I write. Still, on the pathological political side, the horror of war also reveals disconcerting racist distinctions predicated on a violent hierarchy between "us" and "them," Europeans and non-Europeans, sameness and difference, the human and the nonhuman, uncovering thought-defying forms of administrative cruelty that warn us about the phantom return of what Hannah Arendt controversially called the "banality of evil" (2006).[4] I say the *phantom of that banality* and not the banality of evil itself to mark an obvious difference between old and (new) fascism, let alone Nazism. While the number of deaths that ensue from anti-immigration laws, for instance, is shockingly high, not often mentioned in the media, and on the increase, these laws are not *intentionally* designed to exterminate people. Children detention camps are thus not Nazi extermination camps, just like anti-immigration laws are not the same as extermination laws. Moreover, the case of Eichmann remains unique in the history of western "civilization," and the horror generated by the Holocaust defies easy comparison.

And yet, this does not mean that humans made much progress on the ethico-political front and that this case no longer speaks to the contemporary condition. Quite the contrary, if we shift perspective from the inhuman *historical* horrors to the all-too-human *psychology* that triggers them and prevents identification with the point of view of the victims, it might be instructive to reopen a juridical case Arendt considered a "veritable gold mine for a psychologist" (2006, 48). This much-discussed case, in fact, allows us to foreground a will to mime, or *pathos*, internal to the banality of evil Arendt intuited, for she compared it to a contagious pathology that "spreads like a fungus on the surface" (2000a, 396). And yet, she did not fully diagnose it, perhaps, because she did not pay sufficient attention to the power of mimetic affects to cast a spell on thought.[5] Building on the diagnostic of the human chameleon we discussed via the case of *Zelig*, this chapter aims not only to close this scholarly gap; it also opens up a precedent for new mimetic studies by addressing both the affective and logical sides of a will to mime that animate Eichmann's patho(-)logy.

Rather than hastening to define the "banality of evil" in terms of Eichmann's "*inability* to think"—a phrase that has caused much confusion and, as we shall see, was *not* originally Arendt's phrase—I shall consider the banality of evil as part of a more general mimetic state of mind that is not entirely inimical to thought as we have repeatedly seen, is highly contagious, and is animated by both *affective* and *rational* patho-logical principles characteristic of actors who play roles so convincingly that they *become* their role. Recent historians who have reopened the Eichmann dossier in light of his Argentina Papers, have, in fact, seriously challenged Arendt's picture of Eichmann as a mediocre bureaucrat who was simply a cog in the Nazi machine. They did so by showing that he remained a "fanatical National Socialist" on "active duty" (Stangneth 2014, xix) till his capture in 1960. Reframing the case in the context of Eichmann's writings before Jerusalem, Bettina Stangneth argues that this self-proclaimed "cog in the machine" turns out to have had a "talent for self-dramatization," which allowed him to play, chameleonlike, "many roles" (xvii) in his career. This mimetic talent characteristic of an actor, or mime, was, in her view, effectively staged during the trial; it allowed Eichmann to reflect, like a "mirror" (367), the expectations of both witnesses and judges—stretching, at one remove, to cast a spell on political theorists intent in understanding this case via the tools of reason or thought.[6]

My approach to the case forges a middle path between these competing philosophical/historical perspectives. On one side, furthering Arendt's account, I pay closer diagnostic attention than she did to the enthusiastic affect, or *pathos*, internal to Eichmann's psychology, a mimetic psychology that made him vulnerable to the will to power of Nazi models, rendering him, if not entirely unable to think, at least disconcertingly thoughtless—subject to what I also call a *patho*-logical state designating the will to power of *affect* to cast a spell on his thought in mimetic terms dramatized by the case of *Zelig*. On the other side, furthering Stangneth, I take seriously the hypothesis that Eichmann's capitulation to the Nazi idea in his youth led him to a "role-play," or "masquerade," during the trial in deceivingly mimetic terms that set up a "mirror" to people's "fears and expectations" (Stangneth 2014, 367) in the 1960s. At one further remove, it might also set up a mirror to contemporary administrators and spokespeople working for (new) fascist and authoritarian leaders who intentionally use old theatrical methods to manipulate people's expectations via new media—what I call patho-*logy* to indicate the power of mimetic *thought* to manipulate affects.

Once joined, we shall be in a position to see and feel that the case of Eichmann does not allow for clear-cut evaluations that simply oppose an inability to think to an ability to act or impersonate a role. The banality of evil is, in fact, triggered by the complexity of mimesis, a complexity based on a dynamic interplay between contagious affects that generate an irrational pathos, on the one hand, and a cold capacity to play a mirroring role from a rational distance, on the other. Or, to put it in our Nietzschean terminology, the pathos of distance constitutive of the case of Eichmann reveals that the banality of evil is ultimately driven by a mimetic will to power, or will to mime, that is as much based on irrational and contagious affects (or Dionysian pathos) as on rational impersonations of a mirroring role (or Apollonian distance). Together, these principles give birth to a complex (rather than banal) chameleon subject. Eichmann is not simply pathological but patho-*logical*, in the double sense that he is animated by the dynamic interplay of affect and thought, pathos and logos constitutive of the *vita mimetica*. In a mirroring move, I also attend to these mimetic principles and urge political theorists to re-evaluate the affective and rational foundations of a type of evil that led to unprecedented political horrors in the past century and—under different masks and dramatic personae—can continue to trigger new horrors in the present century. Hence the urgency of re-evaluating this case for new mimetic studies more generally.

But let us start with Arendt's diagnostic of Eichmann's patho-*logy* first.

## Reopening the Case: Eichmann's Anti-mimetic Patho-*logy*

The reasons that led Arendt to travel to Jerusalem and cover the case of Eichmann in propria persona were manifold and cannot be dissociated from the double Jewish/German identity she experienced in the world of action or *vita activa*, yet these reasons ultimately turned around an unprecedented crime that, for Arendt, posed first and foremost a baffling problem for theory traditionally under the lens of abstract proponents of the *vita contemplativa*. It concerned the emergence of a new type of crime (and criminal) that, in her view, was not only directed against a specific population (the Jews) but against humanity tout court. This crime, she argued, called for new evaluations of what humans, under certain circumstances, can do and, potentially, enact—without being fully aware of the ethico-political implications of what they are doing for patho-logical reasons that eluded Arendt's diagnostic and are constitutive of what I call *vita mimetica*.[7]

Much has been said about Arendt's report on Adolf Eichmann's 1961 trial, published first as articles in *The New Yorker* and then as a book titled *Eichmann in Jerusalem: A Report on the Banality of Evil* (1963), so much so that the juridical case is by now well known and doesn't need to be reiterated in detail.[8] As the report goes, Arendt's presence at the trial in Jerusalem forced her to revisit her previous evaluation of the horror of the Holocaust in the Kantian terms of "radical evil" that still informed *The Origins of Totalitarianism* (1951).

Rather than the "monster" she expected to find on trial as she confronted the *Obersturmbannführer* responsible for meticulously organizing the transportation system that led to the extermination of millions of Jews, she found a "ghost-like" bureaucrat she labeled "banal" in a phrase that was used rarely in the book itself, but provided its subtitle nonetheless.

In the wake of Arendt's publication, the controversy that ensued around this phrase was not without performative, mirroring effects. As Judith Butler notes, due to its reiteration, "the banality of evil" has become a sort of "intellectual cliché" (2011)[9] that is often echoed but perhaps not sufficiently thought through. This also means that those who use it risk redoubling—and thus being complicit with—the type of "banality" the phrase designates and seeks to counter. It is perhaps also due to its iteration that, on both side of the controversy, insufficient attention has been given to the fact that this oxymoronic phrase, which, it should be clear, applies to Eichmann's psychology not to his crime, is animated by a contradictory push-pull between mimetic and anti-mimetic drives that are not only in line with the pathos of distance characteristic of homo mimeticus; they are also in urgent need of diagnostic re-evaluation for genealogical reasons that are both past-oriented and future-oriented and will guide our investigation as we reopen the case.

Reopening the dossier of Eichmann in the twenty-first century from a genealogical perspective attentive to what the Greeks called enigmatically *mimēsis* might surprise. This is especially evident if we consider the number of developments in continental philosophy, critical theory, political theory, and the social sciences that—often in dialogue with the neurosciences—we have been convoking throughout to give transdisciplinary substance to the *telos* of this book: namely, shifting dominant accounts of mimesis as an homogeneous aesthetic category restricted to realistic representation toward a heterogeneous conception of mimesis understood as behavioral (psychic, social, political) imitation that connects or interweaves all the chapters of *Homo Mimeticus*. Thus reframed, "mimesis" covers a wide range of phenomena central to the human and social sciences that punctuated our genealogy. They include imitation and mimicry, adaptation and conformism, but also mirroring reflexes, emotional contagion, identification, unconscious influences, psychic suggestibility, sympathy or *sym-pathos*—all of which share the characteristic of blurring the distinction between self and others, activity and passivity, pathos and distance, introducing affective continuities that cast a spell on the ego, generating phantom egos instead.

In our contemporary sense, then, mimesis has emphatically *not* been considered relevant to understand the case of Eichmann. And rightly so, for a strong anti-mimetic drive is constitutive of the banality of evil as Arendt defined it. It is in fact crucial to recall that for Arendt, Eichmann's so-called banality was not linked to his actions (what he did), which she uncompromisingly condemned, but to his speech (how he spoke), which she tried to understand. Given the unspeakable horror of his actions, the language he used to account for it sounded horrifyingly ordinary, commonplace, and in this sense, banal. Soon after the trial started, Arendt noticed in fact that the "ghostlike" (2006, 8) figure behind the glass booth expressed himself in an impoverished administrative language, or "officialese [*Amtsprache*]'" (48). That is, a language Eichmann considered "'his only language'" (48) and Arendt identified as the main symptom of the banality of evil. As she puts it in an often-quoted passage that attempts to pinpoint what she meant with this enigmatic phrase: "The longer one listened to him, the more obvious it became that his inability to speak was closely connected with his inability to *think*, namely, to think from the standpoint of somebody else" (49). This is, in a nutshell, Arendt's definition of the banality of evil.

At first sight, then, the diagnostic seems clear, rational, and above all, utterly deprived of mimetic elements. Arendt, in fact, considered Eichmann's inability to speak, except in administrative clichés and ready-made Nazi slogans, as symptomatic of his "inability to think" in general, by which she meant a silent Socratic dialogue within the mind in which a duality or contradictions turned toward oneness, or consistency. While we agree with Arendt on the centrality of dialogue for thinking, a mimetic perspective stresses the relational quality of dialogue that does not take place within the mind alone, "between me and myself" (Arendt 2000b, 409),[10] but between self and others instead. Either with self or others, Eichmann seemed especially unable to think, and thus develop a dia-*logos* by taking into consideration the perspective of his victims in particular. He was thus unable to integrate their antithetical point of view in his unitary worldview, let alone *feel* his victims' suffering, or *pathos*, via a mimetic form of sympathy (*sympathos*) or pity (*Mitleid*) in which suffering is at least partially shared.

Language, thought, affect. Arendt is not a Platonic or an idealist thinker, quite the contrary. As we have seen in part 1, she favors the *vita activa* within the cave over and against the solipsistic ideal of the vita *contemplativa* outside of it. And yet, considered closely, an implicit vertical hierarchy haunts her diagnostic of Eichmann nonetheless. In fact, an impoverished language (or *logos*) masks an impoverished thought based on an internal dialogue (or dia-*logos*), which, in turn, blocks the development of a shared affect (or *pathos*) that is constitutive of what I call Eichmann's anti-mimetic patho-*logy*, understood not simply as sickness—for Eichmann in Arendt's view was disquietingly normal—but as a *logos* disability that prevents the development of any shared sym-pathos, or pity. Thus, at a key moment during the trial, Arendt reports the following exchange: "'Mr. Witness, in the negotiations with your superiors, did you express any pity for the Jews and did you say there was room to help them?'" Eichmann's reply: "'I am here under oath and must speak the truth. Not out of mercy did I launch this transaction'" (in Arendt 2006, 25). From this logocentric perspective that privileges thought and language over affects and bodies, *logos* over *pathos*, Eichmann is framed as a cold, sealed-off, autonomous, and disconnected monad who is not able to step outside his shoes in order to "think," or, as Arendt also puts it, drawing on a Kantian aesthetic concept, "imagine"[11] the perspective of the victims he is facing at the trial, let alone step into their shoes and feel their pain in affective terms that would generate "pity," "remorse," or "bad conscience" for the horror of the Holocaust. This, at least, is the dominant image of Eichmann that, in the wake of Arendt's diagnostic, is often repeated.

If we now want to go further into the diagnostic of this psychological case, we might still wonder: what exactly triggered this complete identification with a bureaucratic language, role, and perspective that deprives Eichmann not only of a private language but also of the human capacity to think from the perspective of the other and, at one remove, feel basic human emotions such as pity when put face to face with the perspective of the victims of the atrocities he implemented? As we have seen via Nietzsche (chapter 1), this shared pathos is constitutive of the genealogy of *Homo sapiens* and arguably played a major role in human development, for it allows for the emergence of consciousness and language in the first place. For Arendt, however, Eichmann's inability to think (or patho-*logy*) is generated by a concept that is usually associated with thought—namely, an idea, which is constitutive of Nazi thought (or ideo-*logy*). While Arendt no longer relies on the language of ideology she had used in *The Origins of Totalitarianism*, she stresses time and again that Eichmann is nonetheless driven by what she calls an "idealist" tendency he carries to extremes by blindly adhering to what she calls "an idea." Hence, she defines Eichmann as a "perfect 'idealist'" who "had of course his personal feelings and emotions, but he would never permit them to interfere with his actions if they came into conflict with his 'idea'" (Arendt 2006, 42), no matter how unspeakable or horrifying that idea and the actions it led to, actually was. Hence again, Arendt specifies that Eichmann was "a man who *lived* for his idea [...] and who was prepared to sacrifice for his idea everything and, especially, everybody" (42).

In many ways, then, Stangneth's historical scrutiny of the Argentina Papers might challenge Arendt's evaluation of Eichmann's so-called banality theory;

yet her emphasis on Eichmann as a thoroughgoing "fanatical National Socialist" lends historical confirmation to the fact that he never let go of the Nazi idea in practice. Quite the contrary, he endorsed it to the very end.[12] On this point, then, Arendt and Stangneth provisionally agree: it is was first and foremost because Eichmann was an idealist in the sense that he bowed down to the Nazi idea, and was ready sacrifice everyone and everything to it, that he could enthusiastically contribute to the Holocaust's "unspeakable horror" (Arendt 2006, 54), as Arendt puts it, echoing Joseph Conrad's narrative account of the horror in his famous critique of Belgian colonialism in *Heart of Darkness* (1899).

The narrative echoes are perhaps not accidental, for the case of Kurtz dramatized by Conrad casts a shadow on the case of Eichmann diagnosed by Arendt. As an attentive reader of Conrad, Arendt must have sensed that the "idea" that drives the case of Eichmann to the "unspeakable horror" of the Holocaust is not unlike the "idea" that drives Kurtz to the "unspeakable horror" internal to *Heart of Darkness*. Both cases of genocidal racism are, in fact, based on what Conrad calls, in a phrase that must have made an impression on Arendt, "not a sentimental pretense, but an idea, and an unselfish belief in the idea—something you can set up, and bow down before, and offer a sacrifice to ..." (Conrad 2010, 47). The linguistic echoes between the case of Kurtz and the case of Eichmann who was responsible for the fact that "horror was piled upon horror" (Arendt 2006, 8) confirm this literary genealogy. In *The Origins of Totalitarianism*, Arendt had in fact not only considered *Heart of Darkness* as "the most illuminating work on actual race experience in Africa" (1976, 183); she also used this narrative as a model to frame her account of "Race and Bureaucracy" to give an account of the origins of totalitarianism. Interestingly, what she says via Conrad of the European role in the African genocide ominously applies to the European role in the Jewish genocide and to Eichmann's role in particular: "when European men massacred them, they somewhat where not aware that they had committed murder" (192). There is thus a genealogical connection between hollow European figures at the heart of Africa and hollow men at the heart of Europe, generating mirroring effects revealing that "all Europe contributed to the making of Kurtz" (Conrad 2010, 95) and thus of Eichmann as well—hollow men deprived of the ability to feel the pathos of the other.[13] This, at least, is the *anti*-mimetic diagnostic of the case that emerges from Arendt's detached theoretical account of the disabled *logos* at play in the banality of evil.

And yet, as the Conradian echoes suggest, it is equally important to note that Arendt's report is not only a distanced clinical account of a *juridical* case she sets out to understand with the tools of reason; it is also a political *narrative* that is polemical in nature, ironic in tone, and attentive to both linguistic and emotional elements that are constitutive of the *psychological* case she sets out to dramatize. The theatrical language of dramatization is particularly apt for a reason that is at least double: first because Arendt in *The Human Condition* (1958) famously drew on the theater, which she considered "the political art par excellence [...] [for] it is the only art whose sole subject is man [*sic*] in his relationship to others" (1998, 188) to articulate her relational account of the *vita activa* based on "actors" (rather than spectators) that inject plurality in the sphere of political action; and second, because Arendt notes at the outset of *Eichmann in Jerusalem* that the trial had the elements of a theatrical stage and that theatricality informs her evaluation of the case. As she puts it: "Whoever planned this auditorium had a theater in mind, complete with orchestra and gallery, with proscenium and stage, and with side doors for the actors' entrance" (2006, 4). The auditorium was indeed held in a former theater called "The House of the People of Jerusalem."[14] While the theorist's focus is on understanding, then, the narrative voice suggests that this "theater" or "spectacle" cannot fail to generate "sensational" (6) effects that affected the audience, the witnesses, the jury, and at one remove, continue to animate Arendt's report as well. It does so in terms that are not only conceptual and based on thought but also dramatic and based on affect. As we turn to see, both sides are not deprived of reflections into the patho-logical dynamic of the *vita mimetica* Arendt began to stage in her narrative but did not fully dramatize in her evaluation.

## Restaging the Case: Eichmann's Mimetic *Patho*-Logy

The opening chapter of *Eichmann in Jerusalem*, titled "The House of Justice," narrates a trial that aims to be impartial and objective. And yet, given the theatrical setting it entails, it also sets the stage for mimetic principles internal to the case that might not be explicitly foregrounded at the level of Arendt's thought, but are at play nonetheless at the level of what Adriana Cavarero would call her "relating narrative" (Cavarero 2000).[15] Let's attend to this narrative.

Drawing on a theatrical register that doubles and frames her theoretical report from the outset, Arendt is, in fact, critically sensitive to "the play aspect of the trial" (2006, 8) insofar as it reveals a fundamental structural problem that leads to a narrow focus on one protagonist qua "hero," clear-cut roles, and predictable conclusions. As she puts it:

> A trial resembles a play in that both begin and end with the doer, not with the victim. A show trial needs even more urgently than an ordinary trial a limited and well-defined outline of what was done and how it was done. In the center of a trial can only be the one who did—in this respect, he is like the hero in the play—and if he suffers, he must suffer for what he has done, not for what he has caused others to suffer. (9)

What is true for a classical play is redoubled in a sensational show. The mimetic logic of the spectacle is implicit in Arendt's ironic account and can be schematically summarized as follows: first the focus on the "doer" qua tragic "hero" who, due to a reversal of fortune, is supposed to recognize his fault, relegates the plural voices of the "victims" to the backstage area of the show; second, the logic of the play/show is dependent on a well-defined "outline" that, since Aristotle defined tragedy as a "mimesis of an action" (1987, 37) in the *Poetics* is structured around a conflict, or *agôn*, which is complex in the case of classic tragic plays.[16] Yet, in the case of a "show" like the Eichmann trial that degenerates into what Arendt calls a "comedy of the soul" (2006, 26), the ideological conflict reduces the complexity of tragedy to clear-cut oppositions between a set of simple roles (accuser/accused; victim/doer; high/low characters; good/evil); and third, the simplistic frame of the show cannot possibly do justice to the complexity of a case that could not be focused on a single figure alone, no matter how guilty this figure was, for as Arendt makes clear, it implicated eighty million Germans. Adding to the controversy, Arendt partially implicates the victims and accusers—most notably the Jewish council or *Judenräte*—in the horror they set out to denounce, leading "the play aspect of the trial" to collapse "under the weight of the hair-raising atrocities" (8–9) that blurred the clear-cut oppositions the trial attempted to stage. The scene is thus set in inevitably mimetic terms, but not in the Aristotelian sense that it represents horrific actions structured in a tragic plot that the audience can contemplate from a visual distance, perhaps even with cathartic effects. On the contrary, the scene is mimetic in the Platonic sense in which actors that impersonate a role produce contagious affects on the audience, generating a deplorable dramatic scene with pathological effects on the *vita mimetica* at play in the body politic.[17] A scene Arendt, at one remove, sets out to narrate—beginning, middle, and end—in order to give philosophical substance to this show.

In Arendt's view, taken as a whole, these dramatic elements did not allow for the emergence of an impartial judgment. Instead, they led the trial to degenerate into a "bloody show" of what the presiding judge also called, drawing on a Platonic analogy, "'a rudderless ship tossed about on the waves'" (Arendt 2006, 9). From a critical pathos of distance of the involved observer, Arendt noticed how the trial qua "play" did not live up to an Aristotelian notion of tragedy as an imitation of an action predicated on rational laws of causality and necessity that, due to their universal character, are "more philosophical and more serious than history" (1987, 41); nor did it lead to the *katharsis* of tragic emotions like "pity and fear" (37) in terms Aristotle considers characteristic of complex tragic plays. Rather, the show generated a sensational outbreak of mimetic *pathos* that, as Plato noted in the *Republic*, was far removed from the truth, yet generated mimetic effects nonetheless. In particular it triggered violent contagious affects that spread like a fungus in the audience, led to a sacrificial expulsion of the doer who considered himself a "scapegoat" (a view Arendt disputed), and above all prevented the members of the trial to think through the new type of crime represented by this singular yet exemplary case. Hence, in Arendt's view, the trial was reduced to a show, for it failed to evaluate rationally a new type of evil that, once staged, needed to be understood precisely because it went beyond established moral evaluations.

Given this theatrical frame, then, readers who want to supplement Arendt's theoretical *logos* on the banality of the evil from the angle of a mimetic *pathos* constitutive of theatrical spectacles at play in the *vita mimetica* are led to wonder about the strategies of dramatic impersonation displayed by the protagonist on the scene. Was Eichmann a shallow bureaucratic cog in the machine, fundamentally "unaware" of what he was doing and deprived of the ability "to think"—as Arendt seems to suggest? Or was this image of Eichmann a theatrical mask, or persona, designed to hide a fanatical Nazi who manipulated the image of his personality (from Latin, *persona*, mask worn in the theater) by carefully staging a bureaucratic role—as Stangneth argues? Or perhaps an untidy intermixture of both? Whichever way, while Arendt and Stangneth disagree in theory on their psychic evaluation of the case, they once again agree in practice in drawing from a theatrical, dramatic, and in this sense mimetic register in order to frame the case—an indication that a diagnostic of "mimesis" that roots this concept back to the dramatic practice of the *mimos*, in mime or performance, continues to provide a solid thread to find our way out of the labyrinth of what turns out to be a complex case.

Now, to deepen our diagnostic reevaluation of the case from a genealogical perspective attentive to complex interplay between conscious impersonation and unconscious identification, mirroring speech (*logos*) and contagious affect (*pathos*), which I consider constitutive of the case of Eichmann and, at one remove, of (new) fascist patho(-)logies more generally, a seemingly minor but decisive linguistic fact in Arendt's diagnostic is worth highlighting: namely, that "inability to think" was, strictly speaking, *not* Arendt's original phrase; it was not even the term she wanted to use to define the banality of evil in the first place. "Inability to think" was actually Mary McCarthy's English translation of a rather different German term Arendt initially had in mind and found difficult to translate. This term was not *Unfähigkeit zu Denken* but, rather, *Gedankenlosigkeit*—and this changes things significantly. As Amos Elon makes clear in a footnote to his introduction to *Eichmann in Jerusalem*: Arendt's longtime friend

> Mary McCarthy would soon take [Arendt] to task, and not for the first time vainly, for her use of the word *Gedankenlosigkeit*, which in English didn't mean what it means in German. In English, "thoughtlessness" means forgetfulness or neglect. "Inability to think," McCarthy suggested, "would have been better." (in Arendt 2006, xxiii, n. 7)[18]

But was it really better? Or is it a case of what Italians proverbially call *traduttore traditore*?

In a mirroring linguistic inversion, native German speakers might object that *Gedankenlosigkeit* is not all equivalent to "inability to think." If "inability to think" implies the presence of a thinking subject, or res cogitans, that lacks the skills to develop a rational dialectical thought, or Socratic dia-*logos*, *Gedankenlosigkeit* questions the very presence of a subject that is in a position to take distance from itself and consciously articulate such dual thoughts. Irrespective of its Kantian or Heideggerian origins, which have been debated by scholars,[19] what *Gedankenlosikeit* seems to indicate *for Arendt* is a disconcerting kind of "thoughtlessness" that is not simply a failure to master a rational thought—Eichmann, as Arendt readily noted, could think perfectly within the narrow limits of his bureaucratic role. Rather, it suggests a type of absentmindedness, hypnotic slumber, or half-sleep that gestures toward an altered state of mind we have already seen at play in *Zelig*: here the subject is so under the spell of an other or an idea that, paradoxically, it cannot think outside of its own ideo-*logy*; in this sense this ego that is not one but a is a phantom of the ego cannot develop an independent *logos* that would integrate the perspective of the other. If only because phantom egos are suggestive to the hypnotic spells that generate the "somnambulism" (Tarde's term) characteristic of the *vita mimetica*. This is why Arendt says elsewhere that "unthinking men are like sleepwalkers" (2000b,

413)—yet another confirmation that she could have provided a revealing frame to the case of *Zelig*. Since she couldn't do so, we did it for her. Conversely, the frame of the somnambulistic case of Zelig allows us to cast new light on the case of Eichmann.

Let me now go further in the diagnostic and say that unthinking men are under the spell of mimetic affects. There is, in fact, nothing rational at the origin of this patho-*logy*, for it is driven by an affect or *pathos* that, once shared by a majority, disables one's personal ability to think or develop a *logos*. This *patho*-logical state is psychosomatic in nature and is symptomatic of an affective, subliminal, and quasi-hypnotic psychic dispossession that belongs to what a pre-Freudian tradition of the unconscious called hypnotic "suggestion" and I grouped under the rubric of the mimetic unconscious.[20]

Let us recall that "suggestion" was originally defined as the assumption of an idea that belongs to another into the self so fundamentally that the idea is experienced as one's own and transformed into action. As Hippolyte Bernheim had noted, all subjects are, to a degree, vulnerable to suggestion, including, it is worth repeating it, "very intelligent people" (1957, 5); it is thus not reducible to a pathological condition affecting a few cases. On the contrary, it is part of our all-too-mimetic condition. We had already seen this mirroring strategy dramatized by Zelig, as he voluntarily mimics the doctors diagnosing him; the same patho-*logical* phenomenon seems now dramatized by Eichmann. There might, in fact, be no fundamental contradiction between thought and affect, after all; at least if we rely on a conception of the unconscious that is animated by both dramatic pathos and rational distance, or pathos of distance. The mimetic unconscious is, in fact, distinct from the psychoanalytical variant insofar as it does not set up a clear split or *Spaltung* between consciousness and the unconscious based on a repressive hypothesis to be accessed via the interpretation of dreams. Rather, it is attentive to degrees of consciousness, is relational rather than monadic in nature, and is based on a mimetic hypothesis that manifests itself in suggestive states that permeate everyday life we have already encountered: relational processes like emotional contagion triggered by mimicry, identification, crowd behavior, and involuntary mirroring reflexes the neurosciences currently group under the rubric of mirror neurons are among its most common manifestations.

To be sure, Arendt does not explicitly identify mimetic symptoms as constitutive of Eichmann's psychology at the general level of her anti-mimetic thought, or rational logos. As Stangneth critically puts it: "like all philosophers she wanted to understand" (2014, xxii). Such a will to know did not lead Arendt to consider sufficiently Eichmann's theatrical "talent for self-dramatization" (xvii). Perhaps she was partially blinded by her faith in rational understanding that presupposes a uniqueness at the heart of each individual, which is certainly there but can be more easily dissolved than rationalist trends in western philosophy are willing to acknowledge. This anti-mimetic focus on uniqueness on which Arendt's account of the *vita activa* rests can have blinding effects when it comes to analyzing the imperceptible contagious powers of dispossession at play in what we called *vita mimetica*.

And yet, to be fair to Arendt, she registers the drama of Eichmann's idea implicitly, at the microlevel of her narrative dramatization of Eichmann's mimetic pathos via formulations that require an interpretative effort, or *hermeneia*, to bring them to the fore. We are in fact told, time and again, that the dramatic register of emotions—be they true or false—is constitutive of Eichmann's psychology. Thus, Arendt reports that he was in an "elated state," "in an ebullient mood, full of enthusiasm about this unique opportunity 'to pour forth everything [...]'" (2006, 28). Or again, that he was driven by "changing moods" and "elating stock phrases" (55), "'in an extraordinary state of elation to think that [he] was exiting from the stage this way'" (47), etc. And as the narrative unfolds, it is clear that this emotional state is not restricted to Eichmann alone. Far from it. Thus, Arendt relates that at the Wannsee Conference in 1942, whose aim was nothing less than the coordination and implementation of the Jewish genocide, "The Final Solution was greeted with 'extraordinary enthusiasm' *by all present*" (113; emphasis added).

The notion of "enthusiasm" can thus not be peeled off from the banality of evil; nor can it be confined to the case of Eichmann alone. We shall go further in the affective perspective Arendt opened up but did not pursue by saying that there is a path that leads from enthusiasm to a state of psychic (dis)possession that renders the case in question but not only, *gedankenlos* and thus hypnotically unable to both think and feel from the perspective of the victim—a complex mimetic *patho*-logy that, to different degrees, continues to cast a shadow on the present and should be under the lens of new mimetic studies.

## From the Banality of Evil to the Complexity of Mimesis

We were initially wondering: how does the banality of evil spread rhizomatically, like a fungus? And why is it endowed with contagious powers that induce *Gedankenlosigkeit*? Despite Arendt's supposed devotion to the rational perspective of the "philosopher" (a title she actually rejected), as a political theorist trained in classics, she would have known that "enthusiasm" is a philosophical concept that belongs to the register of affective, dramatic, and thus theatrical mimesis. This is the moment to restage the *vita mimetica* constitutive of the origins of a species sensible to states of psychic dispossession. Let us recall that Plato, in a dialogue titled *Ion* we discussed in part 1, refers to "enthusiasm" to diagnose a reciter of poetry (or rhapsode) specialized in Homer endowed with a strange dramatic power that drives a wedge between the *vita contemplativa* of the philosopher and the *vita activa* of the world of action, for it relies on that specific interplay of pathos and logos constitutive of the *vita mimetica*.

At first sight, if we listen to Socrates, Ion's mastery in recitation and impersonation of Homer does not stem from reason (*logos*) or know-how (*techne*); nor does it participate in the world of political action (*praxis*). Instead, the rhapsode finds himself at play in a sacred collective ritual in which he is not himself but in a state of being *en-theos*, in the god, that is, possessed by a god and dispossessed of its own rational thought. This possession, in turn, triggers an altered state of mind that is not reducible to a dialogue of the mind but is visceral, intoxicating, and highly contagious. As Plato puts it, under the mask of Socrates engaged in dialectical thinking, or dia-*logos*, it generates a form of mimetic communication that does not take place within the mind alone but is truly relational: he compares it to magnetism in which a magnetic stone "imparts to the rings a force enabling them to do the same thing as the stone" (1963a, 536a). And as we have seen in chapter 2, this magnetic force spreads though different vertical "rings," from Apollo to the muses to the poet and rhapsode generating an enthusiastic outbreak of dispossession in the community, which Plato compares to the Dionysian revelers or "worshipping Corybantes" who are "not in their senses" (534a).

What we must add now is that although Arendt does not acknowledge such a genealogy explicitly, there is nonetheless a magnetic, hypnotic, or as Plato will also say, mimetic path that leads from "enthusiasm" to a state of "elation" and enthusiastic dispossession that renders Eichmann *gedankenlos* and thus unable to think his own thoughts—perhaps because he is already possessed by the thoughts of another. Interestingly, this is also the diagnostic that emerges from Stangneth's account of the psychic state in which Eichmann wrote the Argentina Papers. Inferring his emotional state from the manuscripts she consulted, Stangneth paints the following, rather dramatic picture of Eichmann: he "was capable of throwing books against the wall and tearing them to pieces, filling them with aggressive marginalia, insults, and invectives, and covering mountains of paper with commentaries, writing *like a man possessed*" (2014, xix; emphasis added). Indeed, submission to the Nazi idea generated an irrational, violent *pathos* that not only informed Eichmann's ideology as he put it on paper; it also took violent possession of his ego, generating a "ghostly" figure that is a phantom of the ego in real life.

Eichmann's notorious 1957 Sassen interviews in Argentina also corroborate this mimetic point. Addressing "Comrade Sassen"—a Dutch-German journalist and former Nazi collaborator—and a large group of friends assembled for the occasion, Eichmann recites what Stangneth calls an "untimely peroration" imbued with dramatic *pathos*: "I say this. I—and I tell you this as a conclusion to our matters—I, the 'cautions bureaucrat' that was me, yes indeed" (in Stangneth 2014, 303). But then Eichmann specifies, "the 'cautious bureaucrat' was attended by a [...] a fanatic warrior fighting for the freedom of my blood [...] led by inspiration [*inspirierend geleitet*]"— that is, inspired not by a god, but by the "people [*Volk*]" (303; trans. modified). Eichmann considers this dramatic conclusion as an "address" to the future, "for study of some kind" (304). Indeed, his case has been studied. These tapes will now also be in the public domain and, via documentaries, are contributing to shifting public opinion from "the *banality* of evil" thesis to what has been called "the *devil's* confession" (Mozer 2022).[21]

The telos of this shift of emphasis is historically correct and does much to bringing our understanding of Eichmann's case up to date with the reality. It finally unmasks him as the enthusiastic Nazi fanatic that he was to the bitter end. In fact, it disputes once and for all Arendt's claim that Eichmann "was obviously [...] no case of insane hatred of Jews, of fanatical anti-Semitism or indoctrination of any kind" (Arendt 2006, 26). On the contrary, the Sassen Tapes reveal the *Obersturmbannführer* chillingly boasting to his interviewer:

> Eichmann: Every fiber in me resists that we did something wrong. I must tell you honestly, had we put 10.3 million Jews to death, then I would be content and say: Good, we destroyed [*vernichtet*] the enemy... that is the truth. Why should I deny it [...]
> I didn't even care about the Jews that I deported to Auschwitz. I didn't care if they were alive or already dead. There was an order from the *Reichsführer* that said Jews who were fit to work were sent to work. Jews who were unfit to work had to be sent to the Final Solution. Period.
> Sassen: And with that you clearly and openly meant physical extermination?
> Eichmann: If that's what I said, then yes, for sure. (in Kotsonis & Chakrabarty 2022)

The statement could not be clearer and more horrifying: what we see and hear behind the mask of the "cautious bureaucrat" that already made the world uneasy is, indeed, a twentieth-century manifestation of a "fanatical warrior" capable of generating what Conrad in *Heart of Darkness* had called "the horror." Once again, the mimetic fiction had prefigured, via the example of colonial genocide, the historical reality of the Holocaust at the heart of Europe.[22]

At the same time, and without contradiction, if we want to further our understanding of the case from a genealogical perspective attentive to the horror of mimesis, we should not rest content with unilateral evaluations that bring the case to a historical close—no matter how satisfying this closure is. Notice in fact that Eichmann says to Sassen that the "cautious bureaucrat" was not a mask hiding the "fanatic warrior" but "was attended by" it, implying the two coexisted as part of his Janus-faced personality. Let us thus continue to go beyond the banality/devil, bureaucrat/warrior binary in order to account for the *complexity* of a mimetic patho(-)logy that has been urging us to join, rather than divide, philosophical and historical perspectives.

What has so far not been sufficiently diagnosed on either side of the banality/devil opposition is that submission to the Nazi *völkish* idea generated an irrational *pathos* that not only informed Eichmann's fanatical ideology as he put it on paper and tape; it also took possession of his ego, generating a "ghostly" figure that is a phantom of the ego ready to fanatically sacrifice millions of Jews in real life. A lot of symptoms in Arendt's report equally support the hypothesis that Eichmann embodies a case possessed by another and thus dispossessed of a proper self, a subject who is no one, leading a *vita mimetica*: from the clichés Eichmann hypnotically repeats from the beginning of the trial whenever he hears words like "SS," or "career," or "Himmler" which "triggered in him a mechanism that had become completely unalterable" (Arendt 2006, 50) to his chameleonlike "personality change" (65) in which his Nazi role becomes so constitutive of his personality qua theatrical mask that a witness reported: "'I did not know whether I was meeting the same man. So terrible was the change. ... Here I met a man who comported himself as a master of life and death'" (64);[23] from the fact that Eichmann's docile acceptance of the most unspeakable horror induced a shared state in which "he could see no one, no one at all, who actually was against the Final Solution" (116) to his very last words before the execution in which the enthusiastic state of "elation" Arendt staged at the beginning is re-enacted, one last time, in a confusion of identity with others I shall return to in guise of conclusion—from all these symptoms, it is clear that the phantom of affective mimesis had taken possession of Eichmann's ego.

And yet the decisive shortcut to the path that reveals the mimetic, contagious, and rhizomatic foundations of the evil "fungus" stems from the Wannsee Conference reported in the middle, which marks a radical transformation in both Eichmann's career and personality. Arendt reports it in a free indirect speech that mixes her detached third-person diegetic narrative voice with Eichmann's mimetic speech imbued with pathos:

> Now he could see with his own eyes and hear with his own ears that not only Hitler, nor only Heydrich or the "sphinx" Mueller, not just the S. S. or the Party, but the élite of the good old Civil Service were vying and fighting with each other for the honor of taking the lead in these "bloody" matters. "At that moment, I *sensed* a kind of Pontius Pilate feeling, for I *felt* free of all guilt." *Who was he to judge*? Who was he "to have [his] own *thoughts* in this matter"? (114; emphasis added)

Sensing, feeling, thoughts. Notice the overturning of perspective: the hierarchy Arendt had set up in theory is now overhauled in her narrative practice. If Eichmann can't have personal thoughts, can't think for himself, is *gedankenlos* when it comes to the ethical effects of "his" political idea as it is set in practice, it is because he is up to the neck in mimetic affects! He is magnetically-hypnotically-mimetically chained to Nazi models that—from the *Führer* to the Nazi officials to the "élite of the Civil Service"—are eager to implement the Final Solution with much "enthusiasm." Such "enthusiasm," as Nietzsche recognized in *The Birth of Tragedy* (1872), is contagious, disrupts the boundaries of individuation, and reveals a Dionysian flow of unconscious communication that takes possession of the subject, rendering it *en-theos*, elated, uncapable of that "solitary dialogue" within oneself that Arendt, echoing Socrates/Plato, called "thinking"—in a word, he is *gedankenlos*. This is perhaps why Arendt, generalizing Eichmann's state of *Gedankenlosigkeit* and speaking of the Final Solution, specifies: "everyone was fast asleep when it occurred" (2000b, 406).

I signal three steps in this continuous mimetic-hypnotic flow: first, Eichmann who, at this stage, occupies the lowest position within this Nazi vertical hierarchy, feels intimidated and honored to be included, and identifies with the higher officials qua models, most notably Hitler, to whom he is bound by an "'immoderate admiration'" (Arendt 2006, 149)—call this mimetic pathos; second, these figures not only enthusiastically embrace the idea but become engaged in a rivalry to take the lead in such "bloody" matters, generating a competition in which all subjects reach for the same position—call that mimetic rivalry; and third, and more important, due to this affective contagion, the rings in the Nazi chain set the wheels of an impersonal bureaucratic machine into motion that will legalize, mechanize, and routinize the unspeakable horror of the Final Solution, generating a fungus that spreads rhizomatically from self to others in invisible, nonlinguistic, yet nonetheless affective and infective ways—call it mimetic contagion. Arendt lends support to Eichmann's identificatory-mimetic-contagious principles when she recognizes that the decisive factor in his chameleon transformation was the following: "His conscience was indeed set at rest when he saw the zeal and eagerness with which 'good society' everywhere reacted as he did" (2006, 126).

True, Eichmann and the members of the "good society" might have been "banal" in their mindless adherence to what they considered their duty and adherence to the law; yet the mimetic psychology that informs this contagious, conformist adaptation to fanatic Nazi ideo-logy is complex, for it is based on an interplay of thoughtless affects and affective thoughts constitutive of his mimetic patho-logy, a patho-logy that entangles affects and thoughts, pathos and logos, in spiraling interplays of (un)consciousness. Eichmann was, at this stage, already in an enthusiastic state of dispossession, that he was ready, as he himself put it, to give up "his own *thoughts* in this matter." Thus reframed, we cannot say that it was individual "thoughtlessness" that was at the origin of the banality of evil. On the contrary, it is a shared mimetic pathos that induced the presumptive "lack of thought," or better hypnotic slumber, constitutive of the complexity of evil.

A complexity of evil is triggered by the interplay of suggestive forms of affective, contagious, and mimetic communication that spread like a fungus, from self to other, body to mind. In fact, it is only because an affective identification with fascist models leads to a dispossession of the ego, or enthusiasm, that a *Gedankenlosigkeit*, depriving the ego of his own thoughts and Eichmann crucially adds, feelings, ensues, leading him to "*feel* free of all guilt." Put differently, a mimetic pathos takes possession of the ego, or, as Arendt says, puts it "under the spell" (2006, 156) of dominant others; and this mimetic relation with others prevents not only the development of independent thinking (*logos*) and all it entails (responsibility, agency, self-reflection, bad conscience, etc.) but also extinguishes the basic sense of human sympathy, or *sym-pathos*, we saw as deeply rooted in the genealogy of our species. Thus, the shadow of mimesis was cast on Eichmann's ego turning it into a phantom of other egos: the banality of evil is born out of this complex mimetic *patho*-logy.

And yet, let me repeat it: in such a complex case, we should be careful not to offer unilateral evaluations. If a Nazi *patho*-logy took possession of Eichmann's ego as of 1942, this does not mean that at the trial in 1961, almost twenty years later, he was unable to use the tools of refined reason, or patho-*logy* to willfully stage a dramatic performance at the trial where he played only the bureaucratic side of his Janus-faced personality in view of saving his life. On the contrary, since the birth of dramatic theory, actors have been known to oscillate, pendulum-like, from states of enthusiastic dispossessions, in which a role is impersonated unconsciously via forms of bodily (or Dionysian) mimesis, to more conscious forms of dramatization, in which the actor deftly manipulates the affects of the audience via identification with an image or idea based on visual (or Apollonian) mimesis.

This is already at play in the Socratic dialogue *Ion*, a *dia-logos* that may aspire to lead from duality to oneness in abstract theory or *vita contemplativa* yet leaves open contradictory possibilities in dramatic practice, or *vita mimetica*. In fact, this dialogue inaugurates the view of the inspired and dispossessed artist qua actor who mindlessly impersonates a role with the enthusiastic pathos we have considered. At the same time, it also stages—in an aporia "Socrates" is wise *not* to resolve—a much more self-conscious theatrical figure who consciously plays a role to manipulate the audience's emotions from a cold, mirroring distance. Thus, the following dramatic dialogue ensues between Socrates and Ion:

> Socrates: Now then, are you aware that you produce the same effects in most of the spectators too?
> Ion: Yes, indeed, I know it very well. As I look down at them from the stage above, I see them, every time, weeping, casting terrible glances, stricken with amazement at the deeds recounted. In fact, I have to give them very close attention, for if I set them weeping, I myself shall laugh when I get my money, but if they laugh, it is I who have to weep at losing it. (Plato 1963a, 535d–e)

They weep, I laugh; they laugh, I weep: this mirroring inversion is not deprived of ironic distance, yet it generates mimetic affects nonetheless. If we transpose this Socratic dialogue to the mimetic case in question now, we could say that Eichmann is possessed by his Nazi role so as to speak with enthusiastic pathos about the Final Solution in a state of *Gedankenlosigkeit*; at the same time, and without contradiction, he equally takes rational control of his personality (from *persona*, mask worn in the theater) so as to study his public from a visual distance. He sets up a mirroring image that inverts affective perspectives: they weep, he laughs; they laugh, he weeps.[24]

As Nietzsche would be quick to notice, there can be both Dionysian (bodily) and Apollonian (visual) mimetic principles simultaneously at play in dramatic spectacles. This distanced, Apollonian, or mirroring side of Eichmann's dramatic skills is, indeed what Stangneth, contra Arendt, promotes as she claims that there was a "method" to Eichmann's behavior, as he "acted out a new role for every stage of his life, for each new audience and every new aim" (2014, xvii). Being no one in particular, this subject relied on his "talent for self-dramatization" to set up a theatrical "mask" through which, "like a mirror, he reflected people's fears and expectations, whether they were fearing for their own lives or hoping he would confirm a theory of evil" (367). The fact that Eichmann was "possessed," as Stangneth put it, by the Nazi idea, does not entail that he could not methodically play a role on the stage—including the role of the Nazi bureaucrat. On the contrary, it might have been precisely the enthusiasm for the idea that led him, over time and due to his chameleon adaptations, to play that role so effectively and professionally. In sum, a mimetic approach to the case of Eichmann suggests that he relied on both an experiential (Dionysian) pathos and the projection of an (Apollonian) image whose dynamic interplay generated disconcerting mirroring effects in the audience.

The mimetic complexity I have been dramatizing cannot be reduced to an inability to think, as Arendt suggested; nor can it be restricted to a virtuoso play of roles, as Stangneth indicates. It is rather based on a complex interplay between dramatic thoughts and affects, pathos and logos, constitutive of the patho-logy that animates homo mimeticus in general and, once pushed to extremes, of cases like Eichmann in particular. That Eichmann's so-called mirroring performance continued to be in touch with the enthusiastic affects that drove him throughout his life, is confirmed, one last time, by the way he exited the stage, as he faced his execution. Having diagnosed the powers of mimesis at play at the beginning and in the middle of this trial, I turn to this last scene, in guise of conclusion.

## Coda: Exiting the Stage

Insufficiently attentive to the powers of affective mimesis in her political theory, Arendt nonetheless used mimetic principles to structure her account of the trial in her narrative practice: beginning, middle, and end. Thus, she ends her account by narrating the scene of Eichmann's execution in great detail. The scene generates mirroring effects that illustrate both the extremity of this case's mimetic drives while facing the pathos of death on one side, and the extremity of ironic distance Arendt mobilizes to prevent the risk of a tragic identification at the end, on the other. Thus, Arendt specifies that "this horrible gift for consoling himself with clichés did not leave him in the hour of his death" (2006, 55).

The scene of Eichmann exiting the stage is imbued with both tragic pathos and ironic distance constitutive of the two sides, or hands, of the complexity of mimesis we have been delineating. Here is how Arendt dramatizes it:

> Adolf Eichmann went to the gallows with great dignity. He had asked for a bottle of red wine and had drunk half of it. He refused the help of the Protestant minister, the Reverend William Hull, who offered to read the Bible with him: he had only two more hours to live, and therefore no "time to waste." [...] He was in complete command of himself, nay, he was more: he was completely himself. (252)

Arendt's tone is ironically detached, but her account makes us seriously wonder: how can a subject whose defining characteristic is to have a chameleon personality that designates no proper or original self, but only a mask or role, be "*completely* himself"? Wouldn't that entail that Eichmann is most himself when he is completely dispossessed of selfhood, so confused with others that there is, strictly speaking, no one to speak of?

This ironic possibility is indeed the one Arendt pursues, as she continues her dramatization as follows:

> Nothing could have demonstrated this more convincingly than the grotesque silliness of his last words. He began by stating emphatically that he was a *Gottgläubiger*, to express in common Nazi fashion that he was no Christian and did not believe in life after death. He then proceeded: "After a short while, gentlemen, *we shall all meet again*. Such is the fate of all men. Long live Germany, long live Argentina, long live Austria. *I shall not forget them*." In the face of death, he had found the cliché used in funeral oratory. Under the gallows, his memory played him the last trick; he was "elated" and he forgot that his was his own funeral. (252)

To be sure, an enthusiastic state of "elation" haunts the case of Eichmann—beginning, middle, and end—providing him with a tragicomic ending in which it is not clear *who* the subject is that is being hanged. Arendt's framing, in fact, indicates that in the face of the real pathos of death, Eichmann who, after half a bottle of wine has regained the state of elation he displayed at the beginning of the trial show, finds in the phrase used in "funeral oratory" the last cliché that renders him, quite literally, *en-theos*, possessed by another and dispossessed by his proper thoughts. Hence, Eichmann does not realize that he is not in a position "not to forget them [the dead]," if only because it is actually himself who is going to the gallows in a way that—thanks to Arendt, paradoxically—shall not be forgotten. And this mimetic thoughtlessness that leads him to be "completely himself" while being in the position of someone other, for Arendt, sums up the final lesson of the banality of evil: "It was as though in those last minutes he was summing up the lesson that this long course in human wickedness had taught us—the lesson of the fearsome, word-and-thought-defying *banality of evil*" (252).

This lesson, as we indicated, is symptomatic of a *Gedankenlosigkeit* that troubles not only moral conscience, but the ethico-political foundations of consciousness. What we have seen is that this *thought*-defying state cannot be satisfactorily explained in terms of a "faulty memory" or an "inability to think" —for, as I tried to show, purely rational thought is precisely what is defied when confronted with this case. Nor is it the sole effect of a virtuoso "masquerade" that sets up a mirror to what the audience feels or thinks—for there is no theatrical audience to speak of at this stage. Rather, the funerary cliché Eichmann falls back on, and the confusion it entails, mirrors, in a viscerally embodied and unconscious way, the patho-logy that has been at play throughout the entire trial—beginning, middle, and end—and that we finally unmasked as part of disconcertingly horrific case of *vita mimetica*.

That a mimetic *pathos* triggers this state of elated dispossession and the re-enactment of the clichés it entails is clear. Amplified by wine and by the imminence of death, the complexity of mimesis generates a psychosomatic automatism that had been constitutive of Eichmann's personality all along and is partially unconscious in nature. It could be summarized as follows: first, the cliché allows Eichmann to play a role in which the script is given in advance and is part of the "image" he may want to project, if not for others, at least for himself— what Stangneth calls "masquerade"; second, the recitation has a ritual function that allows him to impersonate via a first-person direct speech (*mimesis*) a phrase that he recalls perfectly due to multiple recitals and repetitions, is comforting due to its shared, communal nature, and does not require any individual thought but an affective participation (*methexis*) instead; and third, it is this mimetic speech that leads him to "exit the stage," so to speak, by identifying his position with the dead Nazi others of the past, thereby approximating that position of "being himself" while being tied to a mythic chain of others. Thus, while being "completely himself," he returns to the position of ghost, shadow, or phantom he had been from the beginning of the trial—unconscious that his all-too-mimetic ego is already dead. This state of dispossession is viscerally embodied, and yet can be put on stage to generate dramatic emotions. It is nothing less than the hidden, obscure, and thought-defying complexity of mimesis the case of Eichmann urged us to unmask.

In the end, restaging the case of Eichmann revealed that the complexity of mimesis is implicitly at play in the banality of evil as Arendt attempted to theorize it. By reframing of the much-discussed case of a *vita mimetica* devoted to unspeakable horrors, our goal was to provide a precedent for mimetic studies to prepare for horrors to come. We did so by overturning Arendt's diagnostic of the banality of evil by shifting the focus from an inability to think to an ability to feel, from a deficient logos to an excess of pathos—not for the victims but for the dominant position of the perpetrators. Far from being the original *cause* of the banality of evil, the subject's so-called inability to think is a superficial *consequence* of a less perceptible, more subliminal, and embodied all-too-mimetic ability to feel, characteristic of homo mimeticus.

It is, indeed, Eichmann's excessive receptivity to an enthusiastic pathos triggered by dominant models or examples that induces the state of dispossession, or *Gedankenlosigkeit*, that deprives the ego of feelings first and thoughts after—but not completely. In fact, Eichmann was not deprived of the ability to look in the mirror and think about his mimetic pathology from a critical distance. At times, he is, in fact, perfectly aware that the mirror he sets up at the trial is not only an occasion for the audience to project their evaluations but also an occasion for self-critique. In a move that lends credibility to both the imitative and unconscious foundations of an identity that was not one he realizes after Hitler's fall:

> "I would have to live a leaderless and difficult individual life, I would receive no directives from anybody, no orders and commands would any longer be issued to me, no pertinent ordinances would be there to consult—in brief, a life never known before lay before me." (in Arendt 2006, 32)

An individual life is indeed difficult to maintain, both in mimetic and hypermimetic ages, under fascist regimes and in periods haunted by the shadow of (new) fascist or authoritarian phantoms. The case of Eichmann is, of course, unique;

the unspeakable horror his name is associated with, unprecedented. Yet, as authoritarian leaders who promote (new) fascist policies threaten to spread like a fungus, carried by the surface of new media that should be center stage, let us take Eichmann's words as a warning, but also as an invitation to live an individual life.

The warning concerns the powers of mimesis to generate a shared mimetic pathology that, to different degrees and in different political circumstances, can potentially spread contagiously, like a fungus whose rhizomes reach into the present. The number of spectacular lies performatively announced on mass-media channels that spread propaganda on a daily basis to defend antidemocratic policies on the far right in Europe or in the US and, more aggressively, in authoritarian countries like Russia and China, requires both a commitment to (new) fascist ideas in theory and a conscious ability by bureaucratic minds to mindlessly perform a role scripted by the dominant administration in practice. To be sure, so far these recent cases do not generate a type of evil that is equivalent to the case we considered; yet the banality of the figures in question should not lead us to underestimate the contagious horrors that, in a nuclear age, still threaten to escalate if we do not hasten to come to grips with the complexity of mimesis.

Arendt did not sufficiently stress the mimetic powers at play in the banality of evil, leaving its pathos on the back burner of her attempt to understand Eichmann. She lacked a theory of mimesis to do justice to Eichmann's mimetic patho(-)logy. Arendt's attention to the uniqueness of a plurality of actors in the *vita activa* doubled by her reluctance to think through the powers of emotions cast a shadow on the impersonal magnetic powers of the *vita mimetica*. These are, indeed, the powers *Homo Mimeticus* aims to bring out of the shadows for mimetic studies to consider in the future.

And yet Arendt was quick to recognize that Eichmann's "thoughtlessness," while extreme, should not be confined to his case alone but threatens to spread contagiously via new technologies of communication. As she warned in *The Human Condition* (1958), we risk becoming "thoughtless creatures at the mercy of every gadget which is technically possible, no matter how murderous it is" (1998, 3). The risks have increased exponentially since. Hence the urgency to consider the unconscious powers of mimesis reloaded via new digital media to infect subjects from bodies to minds, affects to thoughts, pathos to logos—and vice versa—so that we can be, not fully immune, but at least on guard against the spread of (new) fascist patho-logies.

But mimesis itself, I hasten to add, goes beyond good and evil. It is not only constitutive of fascism, old and new; it can also be used to fight contra fascism. If it generates evil pathologies that are part of the problem, mimesis can also affirm patho-*logies* that open up a plurality of democratic solutions, which, thanks to inspiring examples, can generate transformations for the better.[25] Therein lies perhaps Eichmann's invitation to future generations: namely, the invitation to lead the individual yet still mimetic life he "himself" failed to live. Interestingly, despite her anti-mimetic focus on individual "uniqueness" (1998, 181), Arendt eventually came to appreciate the powers of mimesis, as she realized that the *logos* of truth cannot be dissociated from imitative practices. As she puts it in a late essay titled, "Truth and Politics": "philosophical truth can become 'practical' and inspire action without violating the rules of the political realms only when it manages to become manifest in the guise of an example" (2000c, 561). And what is an example if not a mimetic model whose powers are first and foremost affective, yet can generate thoughts nonetheless?

After a long struggle with a complex case under the spell of evil, Arendt came to the realization that mimesis can inspire good as well and that mimetic phantoms can be countered via mimetic antidotes. Thus, she concludes her agonistic confrontation with Eichmann with the following insight: "examples teach or persuade by inspiration, so that whenever we try to perform a deed of courage or of goodness it is as though we imitate someone else" (2000c, 561). On this affirmative, perhaps "banal," but certainly mimetic, all-too-mimetic note, I draw this complex case to an end.

CHAPTER 8

# VIBRANT MIMESIS

> A Phantom arose before me with distrustful aspect,
> Terrible in beauty, age, and power.
>
> —Walt Whitman, *Leaves of Grass*

> "What am I to think of that!" said Zarathustra.
> "Am I then a spectre?"
> "But it will have been my shadow. You have surely heard something
> of the Wanderer and his Shadow."
>
> —Friedrich Nietzsche, *Thus Spoke Zarathustra*

An account of the politics of mimesis in the Anthropocene, as Roger Caillois already urged us to consider, cannot be confined to human actions—no matter how mimetic those actions continue to be in the twenty-first century. It also needs to consider the agentic power of nonhuman forces that retroact on humans via a spiraling loop that turnvibrant matters into mimetic matters—and vice versa. This loop, whose paradoxical shape we have encountered in the multiple iterations on the ancient, modern and contemporary avatars of mimesis that compose this book, encourages us to redraw the *subject* matter these nonhuman and human perspectives might share, or have in common.

That vibrant and mimetic matters are two hands of the same drawing of homo mimeticus we have been sketching from the beginning can initially surprise. After all, the "new" internal to recent theoretical approaches, such as new materialism, that go beyond the nature/culture divide suggests an original aspiration apparently at odds with an old concept such as "mimesis." And this difference is subsequently redoubled if we recall that the nonhuman turn advocated by object-oriented ontologies casts a shadow on long-standing anthropocentric tendencies in western thought that single out human subjectivity as a privileged object, or rather, subject of inquiry—including diagonal inquiries into the all-too-human tendency to imitate exemplary models. And yet, it is precisely the problematic of the mimetic subject that was necessarily suspended at the dawn of object-oriented turns beyond the human that now *re*-turns to question, trouble, perhaps even haunt, phantom-like, the nonhuman turn, urging new generations of theorists to re-evaluate the contagious, affective, and highly suggestive powers of mimesis. If modern romantic figures called these powers "sympathy," this book continues to build a diagonal bridge between the moderns, the ancients, and the contemporaries by grouping the same powers under the protean rubric of mimetic *pathos*.

By now, we have had ample evidence that mimesis is an untranslatable concept we should refrain from automatically restricting to a stabilizing mirror, a realistic image, or a transparent representation of realty—if only because stability, realism, and representation are only the most reassuring sides of a protean concept that changes form and color to adapt, chameleonlike, to different periods and environments, reaching into nonhuman environments as well. While mimesis appears to vanish during a romantic period haunted by anxieties of originality, influential case studies in the twentieth century reveal this phantom concept didn't vanish at all. On the contrary, it animates contagious influences that cast a spell on the rational ideal of a unique, autonomous, and self-sufficient subject, self, or ego that continues to cast a political shadow on the West and planet Earth more generally.

These mimetic influences, as we have seen, are heterogeneous in nature; they include mimicry, identification, affective contagion, hypnosis, suggestion, trance, mirroring reflexes, and other destabilizing affects whose distinctive characteristics are at least double: on the well-known, dominant side, mimesis blurs the boundary dividing truth and lies, originals and copies, realities and shadows, or phantoms of reality in line with a vertical idealist and transcendental ontology, which is far removed from the materiality of life, yet already in Plato's thought, cannot be fully dissociated from it; on the minor, lesser-known, yet not less important side, we have seen time and again that mimesis blurs the very boundaries of individuation, introducing horizontal continuities between self and others, mind and body, conscious actions and unconscious reactions that take possession of an ego that is not one but double or multiple, generating a phantom ego that is deeply in touch with the materiality of life. It is this second, immanent, affective, and materialist tradition, which is currently generating a mimetic turn, or *re*-turn of attention to the vitalist side of homo mimeticus in new materialist strands of political theory previously attentive to vibrant matters and now entangled in vibrant mimesis as well. This, at least, is what our encounter with the North American political theorist, environmental thinker, and advocate of new materialism Jane Bennett suggests.[1]

After "suspending" the problematic of the subject in an influential book for new materialism titled *Vibrant Matter* (2010), Bennett's new book *Influx & Efflux* (2020) joins forces with a life-affirmative genealogy of homo mimeticus to further the mimetic turn or *re*-turn. From different but entangled perspectives, we both promote the vital powers of subliminal influences that cut across dualistic boundaries (self/other, mind/body, human/nonhuman) in order to affirm the possibility of mimetic transformations for the better. In the process, Bennett draws on an heterogeneous tradition at the crossroads of process philosophy, political theory, modern literature, and mimetic studies to affirm, with Walt Whitman as a main investigative lens, the positive, agentic, and nonanthropocentric vibrancy of matter via an emerging conception of a subject that is not singular but plural, not autonomous but relational, not solid but plastic and phantasmal—thereby opening up the ego to nonhuman influences that give a new and timely vibrancy to the increasingly protean manifestations of what I had called, with Nietzsche as a main source of inspiration, *The Phantom of the Ego* (2013).

My aim in this chapter is thus to continue building a diagonal bridge between new materialism and mimetic studies we started with Nietzsche and Caillois, in the company of Bennett's recent mimetic turn of attention toward relational, affective, sometimes anxious, but always contagious and vibrant influences. This bridge is located between what we could call, to simplify things somewhat, a new materialist turn attentive to "thing-power" (Bennett 2010, 3) that distributes agency across nonhuman actants central to *Vibrant Matter*, on the one hand, and a *re*-turn of attention to the protean powers of mimesis that cut across the human/nonhuman divide as a manifestation of what Nietzsche called the "will to power," and I have been grouping under the rubric of "mimetic pathos," on the other hand. As we turn to see and feel, these two entangled perspectives converge on a porous, impersonal, and relational conception of the self, ego, or phantom of the ego, that is now animating shadow-like the affective and material flows streaming through what Bennett, echoing Whitman, calls "influx and efflux."

To be sure, a bridge is a precarious in-between space that allows for the possibility of encounters that are as material as they are affective, are as much based on thing-power as on the power of sympathy. Let us thus recall at the outset that, for the theoretical voices Bennett invokes in *Influx & Efflux*, especially Walt Whitman but also Henry Thoreau, Alfred Whitehead, Roger Caillois, Gilles Deleuze, and Harold Bloom, not unlike for the modernist voices I lean on, primarily Nietzsche but also D. H. Lawrence, Joseph Conrad, Georges Bataille, Roger Caillois, and Philippe Lacoue-Labarthe, for these figures, sympathy means first and foremost "feeling with rather than feeling for" (Lawrence 2002, 158)—designating a *sym*-pathos, or shared pathos, constitutive of a multiple and permeable ego that is open to the outside. As Bennett also puts it: "What prompts any deliberate pathos of sympathy, then, is this apersonal mimesis always already in play" (2020, 97). This is, indeed, the same apersonal mimesis we have been drawing and redrawing in this book.

At one remove, then, this pathos is also theoretically shared, for it gives both affective and material vibrations to what I call *homo mimeticus*, just as much as it injects mimesis into what Bennett calls *influx and efflux*. While we establish a genealogical bridge between two mimetic/materialist traditions in theory, it is thus important for genealogists to register that mimetic fluxes flow in writing because material encounters have already taken place in reality—leaving traces behind.[2] Thinking, we have stressed from the beginning, is not an abstract mental or conceptual process restricted to a *vita contemplativa* out of touch with the materiality of bodily pathos, if only because those immanent material powers are constitutive of the *vita mimetica* as we defined in (chapter 2). As Bennett also puts it, commenting on the "sympathies" at play in Whitman's verses, the thinking subject

> is traversed by ambient sounds, smells, textures, words, ideas, and erotic and other currents, all of which commingle with previously internalized immigrants and become "touched" by them, until some of the incorporated and no-longer-quite-alien materials are "breathed" out as positions, dispositions, claims, and verse. (2020, xiii)

This process of breathing in and breathing out, constitutive of influx and efflux internal to the nonhuman turn, already animated the pathos of distance at play in the mimetic turn. It rests on what Bennet calls "an older definition of sympathy as a physics of attraction (and antipathies) between porous bodies" (32), or a "feeling-with that respects the distance" (36). In this feeling at a distance, or pathos of distance, mimetic subjects are caught in material, embodied, and contagious processes of becoming other. We shall thus remain true to one of the key methodological principles internal to our theory of homo mimeticus by paying attention to both the pathos of encounters and to the distance of genealogy (from Greek *genea*, generation, descent; *logos*, discourse, theory, from *legin*, to speak, tell); that is, a *logos* on a vibrant mimesis that goes beyond human and nonhuman binaries to account for entangled subject matters vital to both the materialist and mimetic turn, or *re*-turn.

My wager, then, is that by explicitly bridging these two genealogically related perspectives, a vibrant conception of mimesis continues to emerge from two drawing hands that now blur the shadow-line dividing the human and the nonhuman, subject-oriented and object-oriented ontologies, the pathos of sympathy and the distance of patho-*logies*. In the process, this bridge casts a new, vital, and perhaps even original light on the dynamic flows that continue opening subjectivity to influences that are both affective and material; they are not only volitional and conscious but also automatic and unconscious, both open to debilitating human pathologies that threaten to dissolve the boundaries of individuation and receptive to vital nonhuman processes constitutive of a new materialist poetics—a mimetic poetics attentive to the influx and efflux of a shared pathos, or *sym-pathos*.

## Mimetic Influx & Efflux: Encounters

*Influx & Efflux* is, in many ways, a personal, subjective, perhaps even intimate, and experiential book that marks a new turn in Jane Bennett's thought and writing. This is not simply because she now foregrounds the question of the "I" or "self," which had been "bracketed" in *Vibrant Matter* in order to attune her political theory to imperceptible, subliminal, yet powerful influences that flow through the self and are "experienced as most local, most personal" (Bennett 2020, xii)—though these political influences, as we shall see, require an aesthetic touch and genealogical sensibility to be registered. Nor is this book personal solely because Bennett now focuses primarily on the American poet Walt Whitman, who made the self and the multitudes it contains his privileged focus of experimentation via a type of poetic writing, which, as he wrote in a letter Bennett quotes at the outset, "'is personal, confessional, a *variegated* product'" (xvi)—though this description, as we shall see, applies at one remove to *Influx & Efflux* as well. Both subjective and poetic perspectives are visibly constitutive of the personal, experiential, at times confessional and existential dimension of this untimely book and find variegated expression in different chapters.

But to immediately foreground the less obvious, but not less powerful driving force that, like an invisible undercurrent, flows through all the chapters in order to carry forth a porous, plastic, and permeable self, I, or ego, open to outside (non)human influences, it is necessary to pay diagnostic attention to the following genealogical question: what do concepts like "sympathy," but also "influence," "nervous mimicry, spirituo-sexual magnetism, neuromimesis" (29), a mimetic communication between mind and body called "pathognomy" (19), or "an automatic biomimesis working to destroy individuation" (xvii) and related notions have in common? As the key term "sympathy" already suggests, they share a concern with a type of mimetic *pathos* that is at the foundations of our theory of mimesis, is impersonal or apersonal insofar as it blurs the boundaries that divide self and others, the human and the nonhuman, often "below conscious awareness" (xvii) operating on what we call the mimetic unconscious. In the process, it *trans*-forms—that is, forms via a trance that "alter[s] states of mind" (xv)—an untimely conception of mimesis that has mirroring influences as a *via regia* to subject formations and plastic transformations. If we saw these subject matters as central to the long genealogy of homo mimeticus that goes from antiquity to modernity, reaching into the present, they now stretch to animate new materialism as well.

Bennett's conception of sympathy that gives shape to a porous, plastic, and dilated "I" differs from dominant nineteenth-century understandings of the term in two significant ways in line with the mimetic turn. First, she makes clear we should not translate the flows of *sym-pathos* in Whitman's poetry, as well as in the writings of Thoreau and others, as a feeling *for* the suffering, or pathos, of the other in terms of personal or religious moral sentiments that find in Christianity—what Nietzsche dubbed "the religion of pity"—a moral and transcendental imperative. Thus, Bennett writes that "Whitman is developing an I who, while still imitating Christ's love for the poor and weak, appears not so much to be performing a voluntary act of pity as to be physically 'possess'd' by the circuit of pain" (2020, 31). She also specifies that Whitman is much closer to modernists like D. H. Lawrence who, echoing Nietzsche, also articulates a nonmoralistic notion of *sym-pathos* predicated on an oxymoronic tension or oscillation toward/away from the pathos of the other Bennett describes as follows: "Lawrence affirms, for example, a Whitmanian sympathy that appears not as a merging without remainder [...] but as a feeling-with that respects the distance, and preserves the differences, between each being" (36). Nietzsche, as we saw time and again, calls this hovering vibration between feeling and distance the *pathos of distance*, identifying an oscillation between mimetic pathos and critical distance central to D. H. Lawrence in particular and to modernist studies more generally.³ Second, the Whitmanian sympathy Bennett posits at the heart of democratic (American) pluralism should not be hastily conflated with major voices in romanticism, if only because it does not rest on the transcendental powers of what (British) romantic poets grouped under the category of an organic or primary "imagination"—that is, a poetic faculty, which, as we have seen, in its Kantian version played a role in Arendt's political (mis)interpretation of Eichmann's inability to think.

The imagination, as theorized by thinkers and dramatized by poets is animated instead by a contradictory push-pull toward/away from mimesis. In fact, if it was expressed in the anti-mimetic figure of the romantic genius who may spontaneously "overflow with powerful feelings" (Wordsworth 2005, 490), the romantic imagination remains nonetheless based on a "repetition" of an "eternal" creative power that finds expression in the imitation of an "infinite *I am*" (Coleridge 3005, 504). Such an imaginative "I" expresses beautiful and sublime sentiments central to romantic poetics that shine from the inside out like a "lamp," to borrow M. H. Abrams's anti-mimetic metaphor in the *Mirror and the Lamp* (1953).⁴ It also give rise to "anxieties of influence" that lead poets in search of originality to "repress some of [influence] and remember others" (Bloom 1989, 332), as Harold Bloom noted in his perhaps still Oedipal account of poetic creation out of an agonistic struggle with predecessors, a romantic agonism that, as I have discussed elsewhere, stretches to inform accounts of mimetic desires still entangled in the "novelistic lie [*mensonge romantique*]" of autonomous originality (Girard 1965).⁵ This also means that this romantic I or ego is less horizontally inclined to acknowledge impressions from others, be they human or nonhuman, with the power to generate mirroring reflexes in a multiple, yet finite, embodied, and phantom ego in touch with the materiality of life. Its power of creation, Bennett would say, is closer to the sovereign autonomy of Zeus than to democratic nonchalance of a democratically inclined I.

This *différend* with dominant romantic accounts of sympathy, be they moral or poetic, mimetic or anti-mimetic, is directly in line with our genealogy of homo mimeticus. It presupposes the specific, immanent, and unconscious dynamic of a pathos that transgresses the boundaries of individuation, is immediately shared, while also allowing for some distance to emerge from the liminal space between I and not-I. Bennett does not convoke British poets, for her focus is primarily on American poets and thinkers, but she notes that influential theorists of moral sympathy who precede them rely on the romantic category of the imagination to mediate the *pathos* of the other, which is only a partially shared or *sym-pathos*. Adam Smith, who in *The Theory of Moral Sentiments* (1759) famously defined sympathy as "our fellow-feeling with any passion whatever" (2002, 13), is a case in point. Smith, in fact, posits that face-to-face encounters with the pathos of the other person tend to be mediated by a mental "representation" or "idea" he locates in the faculty of the imagination. As he puts it:

> By the imagination we place ourselves in his [*sic*] situation, we conceive ourselves enduring all the same torments, we enter as it were into his body become in some measure the same person with him, and thence form some idea of his sensation, and even feel something which, though weaker in degree, is not altogether unlike them (12).

There is indeed a Platonism haunting this theory of moral sentiments. For Smith, an idea or representation appears to be required to feel, at some remove, the pathos of the other. Commenting on this passage, Bennett rightly stresses that the "as it were" dimension of this mimetic experience presupposes a detour via an interior (or reflective) subjectivity to partially access the (embodied) pathos of the exterior other. As she critically puts it, for Smith "only by way of a detour through one's own reflective interior is it possible to 'enter into' the feelings of another—and then only '*as it were*'" (Bennett 2020, 28). Indeed, this "as if" experience is mimetic not so much because it leads to an immediately shared pathos with the other but because it rests on a rational mediation predicated on an idea or mental representation mediated from a distance.

There is thus a pathos of *distance* internal to this romantic theory of *sym*-pathos. Smith confirms this point as he continues a bit later: "If the very appearances of grief and joy inspire us with some degree of the like emotions, it is because they suggest to us the general idea of some good or bad person that has befallen the person in whom we observe them" (Smith 2002, 14). This is still an influential theory of how we access the minds of others that had an impact on a number of philosophers attentive to sympathy, compassion, or *Mitleid*.[6] It is safe to say that, to this day, ideas of representation continue to dominate theories of mind in the analytic tradition but not only. Its fundamental assumption is that a mediated knowledge or rational distance based on an idea of the reasons of suffering decides whether a pathos will actually be allowed to flow or not from self to others in order to become a shared pathos. A rational mediation based on a representation in a volitional, rational subject, in short, keeps the powers of mimetic pathos at a safe rational distance.

Now, contra mediated conceptions of sympathy that presuppose the interiority of an autonomous I still dominant in analytic strands of theory of mind and political theory, Bennett joins forces with the genealogy of homo mimeticus we have been pursuing from the beginning attentive instead to less-mediated, more embodied, and unconscious influences constitutive of the relational dynamic of mimetic pathos. As she puts it: "What it means to be a sympathizer is to partake, both consciously and unconsciously, in an atmospheric of mimetic inflection" (33). She does so, among other things, by registering in the compressed, "processes-oriented syntax" (xv) of Whitman's poetic lines a type of "direct affective transfer" (30) rooted in a sympathy with the power to infiltrate a poetic/mimetic I that is porous, relational, and characterized by an "unusually sensitive cuticle" (74), a dilatable cuticle that leads Whitman to express with pathos the following impression: "'I am possess'd! / Embody all presences outlaw'd or suffering, / See myself in prison shaped like another man'" (31). For Whitman, then, as for Schopenhauer, Nietzsche, and other advocates of the mimetic unconscious, the experience of *sym-pathos* is not mediated by an idea or representation modeled on a transcendental I, or ego; yet his inner/outer experience oscillates, pendulum-like, between the immediacy of bodily pathos and the mediation of visual distance. In fact, while Whitman's speaker emphasizes vision as a privileged sense that leads him to be "shaped *like* another man," it also stresses that the expressive force of a possession is "embodied." Body and mind are thus entangled in a physio-psychological experience that is not under the full control of consciousness and is animated by a more immanent, relational, and embodied unconscious we have already encountered.

To account for the "affective transfer" of sympathetic influences that flow from self to others, Bennett does not explicitly convoke the Freudian conception of the unconscious that finds in Oedipal dreams a via regia. Yet this does not mean that an alternative, pre-Freudian conception of the unconscious rooted in a physio-psychological forms of magnetic dispossessions is not internal to her diagnostic of a porous self. Bennett, in fact, makes clear that the dynamic of sympathy goes "beyond 'imaginative projection' or psychological 'identification'" (2020, 42), suggesting that the concepts constitutive of Freud's metapsychology do not fully capture the impersonal flows of mesmeric influence that dilate the self or ego to the point of (dis)possession. And rightly so, for a genealogy of the unconscious attentive to the pre-history of psychoanalysis convincingly demonstrated that, despite all appearances, these Freudian concepts continue to implicitly presuppose a traditional philosophical category of the "subject."[7]

Bennett implicitly concurs with this tradition. Hence, while she notes that the influence she is concerned with "is often unconscious" (2020, 29), she does not lean on a repressive hypothesis to the unconscious based on an Oedipal myth. Instead, she aligns her diagnostic with a pre-Freudian but also post-Freudian mimetic hypothesis attentive to altered states of consciousness that are as psychological as they are psychological, for they are physio-psychological. "Mesmerism," suggestive "influences," "automatic" reactions, "altered states," and other relational processes Bennett convokes to account for the dynamic of *sym-pathos* cut across dualistic boundaries that simply oppose mind and body, self and others, consciousness and the unconscious, generating imitative dispositions that operate at the juncture of "physiognomy" and "physiology"—what she calls "phyz" (1)— and inflect psychology as well. What we can add is that such physio-psychological processes were not only well known in the nineteenth century; they were also constitutive of the discovery of the unconscious. After a century dominated by the "Freudian legend," genealogists of the psyche uncovered a pre-Freudian, embodied, and relational unconscious, which, as the historian of psychology Henri Ellenberger has convincingly shown in *The Discovery of the Unconscious* (1970), has a long and complicated history that goes from mesmerism to hypnosis, suggestion to influence. As we have seen in preceding chapters, this mimetic unconscious is animating the genealogy of homo mimeticus as well.

Jane Bennett draws on and furthers the genealogical tradition of an embodied, relational, and mimetic unconscious that accounts for a dilated, porous, and suggestive phantom ego. She does so by paying attention to involuntary reactions that trouble volitional accounts of human agency and that she groups under the rubric of "nervous mimicry, spirituo-sexual magnetism, neuromimesis" (2020, 29), but also "influence," "eroticism" and other flows of apersonal affect that generates movements or "attractions and repetitions" (97), are mimetic in the immanent sense that they are contagious, blur the boundaries between human self and (non)human others, and rest on an all-too-human openness to contagious powers that render the subject susceptible to plastic impressions from within but also receptive to mirroring expression from without. Thus, in different chapters, Bennett explores the ramified powers of this shared pathos via Henry Thoreau's take on "natural sympathy" and the awareness of the "effort it takes to maintain the boundaries of individuation" (93); Alfred Whitehead's diagnostic of the "physiology of affective tone," which is "*not* sensed" for it operates on the "visceral" level (53); Caillois's surrealist diagnostic of a "animal mimicry" that, as we have seen in chapter 5, induces a human "*dissolution* of self" (78) that Pierre Janet diagnosed as "legendary psychasthenia." In the process, she establishes bridges with some of the most recent empirical confirmations of homo mimeticus—namely, "mirror neurons" and brain "plasticity"—while also stretching to include a critical self-reflection on the process of creative writing itself via practices of "misprison" of predecessors Harold Bloom grouped under the rubric of "anxiety of influence" (82)—an anxiety of indebtedness, Bennett specifies contra Bloom, that could be "operating in the unconscious (or perhaps even Whitehead's 'viscera')" (85).

Bennett and I could not agree more: it is on the basis of a genealogy of a mimetic unconscious open to *sym-pathos* that a dilated phantom I, is born. In a characteristic personal tone imbued with the pathos of self-recognition, Whitman identifies this phantom as follows: "Myself effusing and fluid, a phantom curiously floating, now here / absorb'd and arrested" (in Bennett 2020, 111). And brining this phantomlike figure into theoretical focus Bennett outlines its shape as follows: "An 'I' existentially open to outsides is both a profoundly *relational* being suffused with apersonal 'affections' and a profoundly *fragile* being susceptible to an anxious attempt to close its pores" (64). Since this "I" is embedded in a plurality of human and nonhuman influences the discontinuous efforts at human closure is a legitimate attempt to set up a distance in the continuous flow of impersonal pathos that threatens to overwhelm the subject. It also calls for a negotiation between the contradictory push-pull of a pathos of distance out of which a different, less anthropocentric, and more relational political consciousness, in favorable circumstances, could emerge.

Taken together, the phantom I that emerges from *Influx & Efflux* entails a reconsideration not only of the I but of the multiplicity of others that are intrinsically related to it from a perspective that is at least double. First, what was true for Whitman then remains true for Bennett now: a deeply divided country calls for pluralist efforts to inflect or incline individual physiology—and thus psychology—away from an increasingly self-absorbed ego toward the plurality of immigrant others constitutive of a pluralist and aspirational view of the American self. In the wake of (new) fascist phantoms, this self is still desperately in need of "identifications across the color-line" to go beyond its racist history that is still part of political realities. Such a "*democratic* disposition" (Bennett 2020, 8) is all the more vital to affirm collectively in periods plagued by antidemocratic and racist positions, as the spread of Black Lives Matter movements demonstrated during the COVID-19 pandemic, in the US and globally. Second, what is true for the mimetic turn in new materialism is also true for the re-*turn* of mimesis in the different patho-*logies* informing homo mimeticus. In fact, both object-oriented and subject-oriented perspectives converge toward the same fragile conception of the phantom I, whose multiple (ideological, digital, conspiratorial etc.) dispossessions needs to be seriously revisited in the digital age. The flows of influence internal to this account of a porous, dilated, and relational ego suggests that the turn internal to Bennett's new book supplements, among other things—for this book is variegated and contains multiplicities—a new voice to the heterogeneous chorus opening up the diagonal field of new mimetic studies.

And yet, if the return to the question of the self is predicated on a *re*-turn to the question of mimesis, it does not mean that this mimetic turn in new materialism is deprived of original theoretical insights. Quite the contrary. As a long genealogy of modern and contemporary thinkers of mimesis we have been engaging with—from Plato to Nietzsche, Derrida to Girard, Arendt to Cavarero, Caillois to Lacoue-Labarthe to Malabou, among others—have repeatedly confirmed, mimesis tends to generate repetitions with a difference. Jane Bennett is no exception. Her contribution to the mimetic turn, or *re*-turn, is at least double, for it concerns as much the content of her thought or logos as it does the form through which she mediates it with pathos, a mimetic pathos whose distinctive characteristic is that it does not limit the experience of mimesis to the human but, as anticipated, includes nonhuman influences as well. Let us take a closer look at both sides.

## Erotic *Logos* & Nonhuman *Pathos*

Vibrant mimesis emerges from the liminal space between the vibrations of matter and the vibration of the self, whose (non)human resonances I take to be Jane Bennett's distinctive theoretical contribution to the mimetic turn, or *re*-turn. As she makes clear from the outset, the *sym-pathos* that flows through the veins of the poetic lines of *The Leaves of Grass* opens up the already dilated phantom I beyond human influences. And it does so to affirm a "cosmic dimension of the self" (2020, xii) that is "*a more-than human atmospheric force* that greatly interested Whitman" (27) as well as the other materialist thinkers she convokes.

Attuned to "'magical traditions'" that favored embodied forms of affective participation as constitutive of mimesis, Bennett contributes to putting contemporary theorists back in touch with the "more-than-human consistency of the

I" (48). She does so by foregrounding nonhuman forces that have the mimetic power to take possession of the human ego precisely because they are more than human. On the shoulders of Whitman, in fact, the boundaries of *sym-pathos* keep dilating from "sympathy as moral sentiment to a more naturalistic, not-exclusively-human kind of affectivity" (40) that animates Whitman's verses. This inner/outer experience, then, allows the I to contain nonhuman multitudes as well as it "begins to 'spread' into what it 'touches,' becoming the breast of another, a trickle of sap, a fibre of wheat, a generous sun, a sweaty brook, a lusty wind" (36). Whitman puts it performatively as follows: "Breast that presses against other breasts it shall be you!/ Trickling sap of maple, fibre of manly wheat, it shall be you! Sun so generous it shall be you!" (in 35). There is thus, between the lines, a touch of eroticism at play in Whitmanian *sym-pathos* that resonates with transgressive experiences characteristic of modernists like Oscar Wilde and D. H. Lawrence, Roger Caillois and Georges Bataille, generating a push-pull between the fusion of erotic pathos and the distance of individuation. As Bennett notes: "The figure of erotic sympathy highlights the powerful allure of oneness and the thrill of letting go of the efforts required to maintain the perimeter of a self" (36). In erotic possession there is indeed an alluring power of dispossession that puts not only lovers in touch but also opens them up to apersonal forces, animating a creative, generative, and cosmic nature, or *natura naturans*.

What was true of mimetic pathos remains true of erotic sympathy: a negotiation of proximity and distance is in order to preserve the boundaries of individuation while remaining in touch with the other. For instance, in what appears to be a philosophical echo to the American poet who lies "in the grass," in a section of *Thus Spoke Zarathustra* titled "On the Poets," Nietzsche, under the mask of Zarathustra, speaks the following lines from Alpine vistas:

> But this all powers believe: that whoever lies in the grass or on lonely slopes and pricks up his [*sic*] ears will discover somewhat of the things that are between Heaven and earth. / And if tender emotions should come to them, the poets always think that Nature herself is in love with them. (2005, 111)

Across romantic and modernist traditions, there is thus a shared sense that not only a mimetic but also an erotic pathos troubles the boundaries of individuation opening up channels of communication "only the poets have let themselves dream" (111). If Zarathustra is somewhat suspicious of the poets' attraction to heavenly dreams, Nietzsche himself is not immune to their charms while attempting to negotiate his distant proximity to the inner experience of pathos. Or, as Graham Parkes puts it: "The hydrodynamics of Zarathustrian generosity depend on keeping the boundaries of the self-permeable and the channels clear for a continuous influx and outflow" (1994, 153).

Riding the influx and efflux of Whitman's prose, Bennett puts us back in touch with erotic/mimetic forms of (non)human communication with the power to dispossess the ego. I say "back in touch" because a Nietzschean strand in political theory never lost touch with the realization that mimesis goes "beyond nature and culture,"[8] and this lesson applies to our genealogical tradition as well. At least two distinguished precursors—one ancient, the other modern(ist)—need to be mentioned to continue deepening our genealogy of the nonhuman powers of vibrant mimesis beyond all-too-human affects. This will allow us not only to continue circumventing influential accounts of mimesis as a false copy of an ideal reality but also to better evaluate Bennett's distinctive (new) materialist contribution to the mimetic turn.

We have already noted that the language of possession and dispossession is constitutive of Whitman's poetics of a phantom I, who has no trouble expressing, with pathos, "I am possess'd." What we must add now is that this type of poetic (dis)possession comes close to the ancient Greek sources of *pathos* (πάθος), this time understood not in the romantic sense of feeling with or for but in the Greek sense. That is, as an impersonal and uncontrollable force that takes possession of the I, leading to frightening forms of dispossessions that are as physical as they are psychic, as human as they are nonhuman. As E. R. Dodds makes clear in *The Greeks and the Irrational* (1951):

> The Greek had always felt the experience of passion as something mysterious and frightening, the experience of a force that was in him [*sic*], possessing him, rather than possessed by him. The very word *păthos* testifies to that: like its Latin equivalent, *passio*, it means something that "happens to" a man [*sic*], something of which he is the passive victim (1973, 185).[9]

This something, as the Greeks well knew, can be tied to a human force that found in *eros* a privileged human medium of (dis)possession. In a recent dialogue, for instance, Jean-Luc Nancy also notes that "Eros – the erotic impulse [*élan*], the impulse of desire – is thus the energy of participation [*methexis*]" (Nancy and Lawtoo 2022, 26). Nancy and I agree that an emotional participation provides the power or pathos animating a "sharing [*partage*]" of voices and affects in which mimesis is not opposed to desire. On the contrary, it blurs the artificial boundaries between desire and mimesis that psychoanalysis split in two distinct ties to form a familial triangle but that the experience *of sym-pathos* joins in an influx and efflux that opens the ego to others—including nonhuman others.

In many ways, then, the realization that mimesis goes beyond nature and culture is already constitutive of the birth of mimetic studies. Plato, as we noted at the outset, is notoriously biased contra representations or "phantoms" at "three removes from nature" (1963c, 597e) for metaphysical and epistemic reasons that inaugurate an idealist, transcendental, and still dominant tendency in western thought that, to this day, casts a shadow on mimetic theories. Yet, at the same time, and without contraction, we have seen that he is equally attentive the dramatic, hypnotic, and mesmeric powers of the actor or mime to induce a mirroring contagion with the phantom power to take possession of an enthusiastic theatrical audience in immanent, embodied, and psychosomatic terms characteristic of the *vita mimetica*. What we must add now is that Plato, under the mask of Socrates, also broadens the scope of the powers of mimesis beyond the human, as he asks his interlocutor in book 3 of the *Republic* the following rhetorical but rather revealing question:

> Socrates: Well, then, neighing horses and lowing bulls, and the noise of rivers and the roar of the sea and the thunder and everything of that kind—they [the guardians] imitate these?
> Adimantus: Nay, they have been forbidden, he said, to be mad or liken themselves to madmen. (1963c, 396b)

The question is, of course, rhetorical. Plato will make clear that forms of dramatic impersonation that lead actors, and at one remove, spectators, to be magnetically possessed by a fictional figure and are thus deprived of their proper identity should be banned from the city as a pathological form of intoxicating madness. And yet, the question is also revealing, for it indicates that already for Plato the powers of mimesis were not restricted to impersonations of human figures with the power to impress the malleable souls of children and adults he compares to the plasticity of clay or, to update the metaphor, to the plasticity of Play-Doh, as we have seen in chapter 4. On the contrary, they stretched to nonhuman expressions that go from horses to bulls, rivers to thunders, with the electrifying power to shake, destabilize, and take possession of homo mimeticus disrupting the very boundary that divides humans and nature. If at the dawn of philosophy, Plato feared these nonhuman forces for the destabilizing powers they had on a precarious city, or polis, at the twilight of the Anthropocene, we should perhaps attune ourselves to nonhuman mimesis to better sense the agentic power of nature with which we are, nolens volens, already mimetically entangled, part of what William Connolly calls "entangled humanism" (2017)—which leads us to the second, modernist precursor.

It is true that representational theories of mimesis dominant in the twentieth century accustomed generations of critics to restrict mimesis to realistic plots or transparent images that cast a shadow on this nonhuman inclination at the origins of mimetic studies; but it is equally true that, for more nuanced theorists, the human faculty to imitate remains rooted in (human) nature. Walter Benjamin, for instance, opens his essay "On the Mimetic Faculty" (1933) with the assertion that not only humans but rather "nature creates similarities" (2007, 333). And paving the way for Caillois's diagnostic of continuities between human and animal mimicry, Benjamin establishes a bridge between natural mimesis, animal "mimicry," and a "magical" animistic tradition attentive to the all-too-human compulsion visible in childhood but still present in adulthood "to become and behave like something else" (333): from windmills to trains (Benjamin's examples), bears to tigers (my children's examples). These are all forms of embodied, material, and sensuous similarities that can still be heard in onomatopoeic words and continue to animate, albeit less tangibly, nonsensuous similarities that operate below the register of conscious awareness and are in this sense unconscious—which brings us back to Bennett's diagnostic of influence.

When Bennett calls attention to the powers of sympathy to transgress the boundaries dividing humans and nonhumans, she encourages scholars to go beyond tired nature/culture binaries that no longer hold in the age of the Anthropocene. She does so via a conception of an I that is, as she puts it, "possessed by possessions, irradiated by sunlight, caught by the sympathies of pine needles, intoxicated by drops, and is a mass of thawing clay" (2020, 117). When she dramatizes these mimetic things, Bennett can be seen as revitalizing an ancient, mesmerizing, perhaps magical, yet nonetheless immanent and material genealogy that never lost touch with the nonhuman powers of mimesis. Or as she also puts it, she "mingles with predecessors already on the page" (ix). And yet, as this tradition also taught us, sitting on precursors and mingling with them, whether consciously or unconsciously, does not preclude the possibility of innovation. On the contrary, it is the necessary but not sufficient genealogical condition to push mimetic studies further. Thus, Bennett's qualifications to the mimetic powers of nature applies to her ancient/modernist predecessors as well, as she specifies—"*and yet* I make a difference" (117). This difference, as we turn to see, concerns not only the content (*logos*) of her materialist theory of a phantom I but animates the formal diction (*lexis*) that mediates it in the first place. What she says of doodling, in fact, equally applies to her new materialist take on mimesis—she seems to add something to the process, which takes me to the formal qualities of the mimetic poetics that is taking shape.

## Doodling Poetics: "Lo a Shape!"

As any theorist of mimesis worth their salt has by now learned to appreciate, an account of the powers of imitation cannot operate only at the level of philosophical content or *logos*; it must pay equal attention to form, diction, or *lexis*. The process of mimetic influx and efflux is, in fact, already at play in the doodles that provide an elegant cover, or dress, to the book and punctuate it throughout. They are no simple decorations or representations to be seen from a distance. On the contrary, they trace unconscious emerging processes that are not the expression of a volitional ego but, rather, have the power to induce subliminal impressions, or influences. And these mimetic influences are equally at play in the style of "writing up" that in-form this book and trans-forms this self.

Suspended in the space between a passive disposition for receptivity to impressions and an active position of agentic expression, possessed and dispossessed at once, open to the influx of mimetic pathos and distant from affective influences, forming and giving form, there is a sense in which Bennett's style of writing up mimes, so to speak, the stylistic movement of her doodling. She does so not to simply copy, reproduce, or mimic their external form in writing; rather, the goal is to embody, through writing, an inner disposition that is as receptive to the influx as it is to the efflux she strives to capture. How? By performatively reproducing the effects of this movement outside the page for the readers to feel. What Bennett says of doodling in the epigraph that opens the book equally applies to the style of writing up she practices throughout: "Lines flow down arm, fingers, length of pencil, to exit at graphite tip and mingle with predecessors already on the page. 'Lo, a shape!' I say to myself (quoting Whitman) as it emerges" (2020, ix)—and in the process an epigraph stylistically crafted at the in-between juncture of activity and passivity, impression and expression, influx and efflux, has taken shape as well.

Notice that this stylistic effect is subliminal, imperceptible, and easy to miss, especially for readers primarily attentive to the content, thought, or logos of writing. And yet, the epigraph suggests that any reader who wants to capture the mimetic powers of influx and efflux Bennett performatively describes in her political theory should begin by paying attention to the poetic, and thus aesthetic, influences at play in her stylistic register, mimetic influences the epigraph attunes us to, and the rest of the book pursues via an alternation of concepts to be mediated from a distance and drawings to be immediately experienced with pathos. I consider this pathos of distance that generates movements of "attractions and repetitions" (2020, 97) with both logical and affective powers that blur the human/nonhuman divide as Bennett's distinctive contribution to the mimetic turn.

As the epigraph suggests, and the whole book confirms, this contribution calls for a poetic voice that is not the property of a volitional subject, or I. Rather, it relies on verbs in the middle voice (to partake, to inflect, to sympathize) in order to hover in the space between impression and expression, activity and passivity, conscious actions and unconscious reactions, opening up an in-between space of articulation that goes beyond static dualities in view of fostering mimetic processes of becoming instead. It is in fact no accident that such a hovering space Bennett locates in the "and" connecting/disconnecting influx "and" efflux has its physio-psychological counterpart in altered states of consciousness in which the ego experiences itself as both located in the mind and in the body, active and passive, inside and outside, present and absent, conscious and unconscious, in touch with pathos and distant, being mostly herself while being someone else—in short a middle state of pathos of distance that is the defining disposition of homo mimeticus.

The style, then, redoubles the content, to bring us back to the palpitating heart of what I take to be the distinctive characteristic of vibrant mimesis. As Bennett puts it, it is a style that is "simultaneously descriptive and performative" (32), echoing Whitman's poetics in prompting "the reader to take on, to mimetically reenact, the nonchalance of earth" (10). We are thus not dealing with a type of writing that is mimetic in the narrow sense that it realistically describes or represents external shapes or forms already crystallized in the materiality of the world and, at one remove, in the immaterial sphere of ideas. On the contrary, the style is mimetic in the ancient, rhetorical, yet also increasingly contemporary performative sense: a performativity that not only does things with words, as poststructuralism taught us, but also does things through bodies, as genealogists of mimesis remind us. That is, via imitative bodies that register unconscious influences that are not simply visible from a stabilizing rational distance but are felt vibrating with the immediacy of bodily pathos—stretching to potentially affect and inflect readers' dispositions as well.

Once again, what Bennett says of the mimetic powers of Whitman's poetry applies to her poetic theory as well: readers are in fact encouraged to "mimetically reproduce in their own bodies protoversions of the stance described" (2020, 11). Writing-up does not entail writing and reading only; it has performative properties built in it that encourage affective and bodily dispositions constitutive of what we called, *vita mimetica*. If we saw that the mimetic inclinations we traced back to the Platonic cave had pathological political effects on the subjects in the polis, this does not mean that magnetic influences cannot be turned to patho-*logical* political use, for the same phantom I is vulnerable to both good and bad influences. It is, in fact, on the basis of a vibrant receptivity to mimetic pathos that has the disconcerting power to take possession of the ego, turning into a phantom ego who can cast a spell on others, that Bennett's "distinctive model of the I" is born. As she puts it, this I is constituted as "a porous and susceptible shape that rides and imbibes waves of influx-and-efflux but also contributes an 'influence' of its own" (xi). There is thus a paradox of influence at the heart of the realization that "I alters and is altered" (xii) that mirrors a mimetic paradox we have already encountered via the problematic of a plastic subject: both are simultaneously susceptible to impressions and to expression, active and passive, receptive to being shaped and to giving shape via a process-oriented, unconscious, and plastic conception of a phantom I located at the paradoxical juncture of the *both-and* rather than of the *either/or*.[10]

Indeed, the line dividing impressions and expressions, activity and passivity, giving shape and being shaped is progressively blurred as an ancient paradox of mimesis circulates through the channels of (non)human sympathetic influences. If we traced in chapter 4 a plasticity of the mimetic subject whose genealogy goes from contemporary mimetic theorists (Malabou, Lacoue-Labarthe) back to modernist theorists (Nietzsche, Hegel) to find a privileged locus of emergence in ancient theorists (Plato), Bennett inscribes her theory in the same paradox that turns passivity into activity, receptivity to impressions to propensity for creative expressions, receiving shape and giving shape. Thus, she recognizes that the so-called materiality of the soul, or "'clay' has some impressive agency of its own" (2020, 18). It is indeed the conversion of restricted to general mimesis precursors like Lacoue-Labarthe (via Diderot) had located at the center of the paradox of the actor, Malabou (via Hegel) subsequently translated into the paradox plasticity, and as I argued (via Nietzsche) is constitutive a genealogy of a homo mimeticus that turns passivity into activity, pathologies into patho-*logies*.

From different perspectives, then, creative accounts on the powers of mimetic pathos have the performative effect to generate a shared, theoretical sym-pathos that is now gaining traction in the heterogeneous field of new mimetic studies. Having heard powerful vibrations of mimesis in the flows of influx and efflux, it is thus with affirmative nonchalance that I join paradox to encounter to extend the rings of what is already a long chain. We can thus add a vibrant new voice to our genealogy of mimetic thinkers, who (via Whitman) sing of the powers of (non)human sympathy to generate a phantom I suspended between impressions and expressions, giving shape and being shaped, as it "alters and is altered" (xiii). How? By partaking from body to soul, soul to body in mimetic waves of expression, "some mine, some yours, some apersonal" (xxiv).

Animating the human and nonhuman pathos of sympathy, but also mimicry, eroticism, magnetism, contagion, plasticity, dispossessions and other manifestations of vibrant mimesis from within, this paradox is the product of "encounters" that are already double-faced, for they are as theoretical as they are experiential, as based on reason or logos as they are based on affect or pathos, as generative of mimetic pathologies that threaten to dissolve an anxious and perhaps still romantic conception of the influenced self that echoes Bloom, as they are of genealogies that open up this self to the vital network of human and nonhuman influences, as Bennett writes up with Whitman. Both sides are as constitutive of nonhuman turns as they are to mimetic *re*-turns; they invite back-and-forth oscillations that are as theoretical as they are affective and require a change of stylistic perspective in order to be foregrounded.

## Mirroring Influences in the Anthropocene

Riding the waves of mimetic influx and efflux imbibes the reader with unpredictable influences, for the seas have been polluted and the multitudes we contain are as patho-logical as they are pathological, flowing both from human and nonhuman life. Especially in her chapter on Caillois but also in subtle allusions to the dangers of (new) fascism, the pathologies of racial discriminations, and the reality of viral pandemics that plague an already vulnerable, precarious, and increasingly fragile planet, Bennett's diagnostic of influences remains indeed attentive to what William Connolly calls "the fragility of things" (2013). And rightly so, for we live in a world increasingly dominated by influences that have the contagious power to dissolve the human ego against an environment that still sustains us.

For the moment, at least. Due to rapid anthropogenic climate change, the agentic powers of the earth responding to all-too-human actions are now displacing a plurality of subjects, threatening in the long run to dissolve us against an increasingly warming environment, as Caillois prefigured. If we then recall that we live in an age that can easily fall under the spell of (new) fascist and tyrannical leaders who rely on the old strategies of the actor now supplemented by new digital media powered by algorithms that amplify the powers of influence and propaganda to unprecedented degrees, while also reactivating the phantom of nuclear escalations, it is indeed politically urgent to come to grips with the realization that the all-too-human "ego" is far from the ideal of a rational, autonomous, and logical *Homo sapiens* that still informs dominant strands of political theory. A minor transdisciplinary tradition that goes from Nietzsche to Bataille, Caillois to Girard, Deleuze to Derrida, Lacoue-Labarthe to Nancy, Cavarero to Miller, Connolly to Bennett, Borch-Jacobsen to Morin, among other contributors to homo mimeticus, have been taking the powers of mimesis seriously along with the unconscious processes that cast a spell on egos and crowds, democracies and autocracies, especially in an age characterized by global pandemics, nuclear threats, and rapid climate change that threaten to literally erase *Homo sapiens* from the surface of the earth. Hence the urgency to reload the ancient realization that humans are—and I say this without narcissistic anthropocentric bias—perhaps still the most mimetic creatures in order to counter human and nonhuman influences that generate contagious pathologies generating dispositions for the worse.

And yet, without contradiction, the same tradition attentive to humans' imitative nature has equally been calling attention to the metamorphic power of transformation that influence us for the better. *Influx & Efflux* is a strong recent ally in this immanent tradition. It draws on a minor, perhaps eccentric and heterogeneous, yet deterritorializing and quickly proliferating mimetic tradition that "tends to float between genres—part political theory, part mythmaking, part poetry, part speculative philosophy, part political and existential diagnosis" (Bennett 2020, xxi). And it does so to affirm a conception of the subject that tends to fall through the cracks of disciplinary boundaries, yet is central to the transdisciplinary theory of imitation that affirms the transformative potential of a porous, relational, plastic, and sympathetic I open to human and nonhuman influences; it also mimetically performs this metamorphic power in order to influence new dispositions at the level of style, a style that performs the duplicity of influence, with the uncertainties, anxieties, and possibilities it entails in view of affirming new metamorphoses of homo mimeticus for the future.

In the end, then, following the pathognomonic movements of Bennett's pen, revolves us back to the problematic of a phantom of the ego with which our new theory of imitation started. Such a phantom is, in fact, the genealogical point where Whitman's multiple self and Nietzsche's multiple soul momentarily touch in an immanent instant of mimetic vibration—or vibrant mimesis. This instant is but a fleeting vibratory interval located in genealogical spaces between the lines and can easily be missed or misread. Yet, in the process of patiently reconstructing it in the spirit of the "egalitarian generosity" (2020, 35) that Bennett encourages us to pursue, a vital bridge between the nonhuman turn and the mimetic turn, an object-oriented "pathognomy" and a subject-oriented patho-*logy* has progressively taken shape.

Provisionally joined in the vibratory space between the human and the non-human, Bennett and I fundamentally agree that the self is not self-contained, autonomous, and disconnected from others, including nonhuman others. On the contrary, it is precisely because the I is, from the very beginning, mimetically entangled with the other, through the other, in a relation of material and affective dependency with the other that our disposition is to remain inclined toward others. We are porous, relational, embodied subjects open to human and non-human influences that operate below the register of consciousness of a phantom subject caught in the process of becoming other. Who knows? Perhaps in the future such subjects can also paradoxically serve as "models" not to be simply reproduced but to inspire a plurality of different creative influences in others to further new explorations of homo mimeticus in the twenty-first century.

Bridging mimetic studies and new materialism via the in-between medium of influx and efflux is, in the end, a natural-cultural process. While the bridge is a work in process and calls for subsequent back-and-forth movements across a (non)human divide that is not one for it is plural, it also rests on encounters that have already taken place in this world, generating oscillations between pathos and distance that are now internal to the affective reverberations of vibrant mimesis as well, giving it a moving shape. Since genealogy, in the Nietzschean tradition, is not deprived of personal confessions, let me conclude with an experiential observation about what influenced me to write this chapter in the first place. At the end of reading *Influx & Efflux*, I had the vibrant impression, or perhaps expression, that this timely book breathed an ego in and breathed a phantom out—with nonchalance. I can thus only mime the original voice that gives this untimely book an identity that is not one but double, or multiple, and echo:

"I am integral with you; I too am one phase and of all phases.
Partaker of influx and efflux I" (Whitman 1990, 46).

CHAPTER 9

# THE AGE OF VIRAL REPRODUCTION

The coronavirus, like all viruses, is mimetic in the biological sense that it reproduces itself through other living beings. But what is the link between the concept of *mimēsis*, viral contagion, and immunity? And if a link there is, as recent developments in posthuman studies suggest,[1] how can an apparently unoriginal concept often translated as "imitation," or "representation," help us reflect critically, philosophically, and thus diagnostically, on contagious cultural pathologies such as crowd behavior and conspiracy theories that do not simply misrepresent the truth about the virus online but also cast an affective shadow that undermines immunization and amplifies the spread of viral contagion offline?

As we bring our drawing of homo mimeticus closer to its conclusion, and thus to contemporary preoccupations, it is time to show that new mimetic studies can indeed continue to provide, if not a magical immunization, at least a long-standing genealogical perspective to reflect critically on cultural pathologies that, in times of pandemic crisis but not only, are in urgent need of transdisciplinary diagnostics attentive to the all-too-human tendency to imitate others in a plurality of ways: with their brains and bodies, gestures and expressions, individually and collectively, consciously and unconsciously, offline and online, among other variants of a type of mimesis that goes viral on a plurality of levels and concerns the humanities as well.

After the speed with which virologists produced medical vaccines, or *pharmaka*, to contain and hopefully eventually immunize the world population against the coronavirus pandemic started in 2020, the problem of equal vaccine distribution in an increasingly uncertain world—plagued by social inequality, racist and sexist discrimination, (new) fascist leaders, and conspiracy theories—made clear that an epidemic may generate a contagious undifferentiation in the general sense that all humans are equally vulnerable to infection in theory; yet a number of differentiating factors render some humans more vulnerable than others in practice. As the SARS-CoV-2 virus keeps mutating via genetic differentiations that increase the speed of contamination at the viral level, the coronavirus pandemic made visible a plurality of cultural differences that are equally slowing down immunization in complex or interwoven ways, urging cultural theorists and philosophers to stress what should have been clear from the beginning: namely, that a pandemic belongs to the diagonal category of what Marcel Mauss called "'total' social phenomena" (1966, 76). Hence, it concerns not only virologists, immunologists, medical experts, and health care workers fighting the virus on the front lines; it also infects and affects all aspects of social life, from economy to politics, education to media communication, polices of immunization to vaccine distribution and sensibilization that are fully constitutive of a pandemic crisis. As Edgar Morin puts, it in the spirit of Mauss but relying on a specific mimetic terminology, the coronavirus pandemic sets up a "magnifying glass to social inequalities" (2020, 39), a trope that will be used by Jean-Luc Nancy as well in his account of an "all too human virus" (2020).

If we then also consider that a significant segment of the population is composed of pandemic deniers, anti-lockdown protesters, and vaccine skeptics who have fallen prey to conspiracy theories that have gone viral online before retroacting on the population offline in pathological ways that amplify viral infection, we can indeed contribute to developing patho-*logies* relevant for a pandemic crisis for at least two reasons. First, because the ancient definition of mimesis as a false representation of reality is still relevant to account for epistemic and ontological concerns with truth and lies in an age that we were perhaps too quick to dub "post-truth." And second, because the powers of the false also have political, ethical, pedagogical, affective, and medical consequences that are constitutive of what we have been calling the patho(-)logies of mimesis, understood as both mimetic cultural pathologies that spread by mobilizing the register of affect (*pathos*) and critical discourses (*logoi*) that give a rational account of this pathos (or patho-*logy*).

Since cultural forms of affective contagion are not simply added to viral contagion, but amplify the latter's reach and power of infection, they cannot be considered as external from it, in an old-fashioned two-cultures opposition that is clearly inadequate to account for complex, transdisciplinary problems. On the contrary, a pandemic crisis calls for a plurality of patho-*logical* supplements to account for the joint problematic of contagion and immunization, both at the viral and affective levels, in a spirit of transdisciplinary collaboration. My hypothesis is that, to account for the complex relation between viral pathologies and cultural pathologies, as well as their respective practices of contagion and immunization, it is useful, perhaps even urgent, to remember that it is not only the nonhuman virus that is contagious; humans' imitative tendencies are imbued with affective properties that spread contagiously as well, from self to others—for good and ill.

Despite optimistic futuristic accounts of *Homo Sapiens* qua *Homo Deus*, arguing that "epidemics are far smaller threat to human health today than in previous millennia" (Harari 2017, 2),[2] genealogical lenses put us in a position to see at the same time that viral contagion in an age still haunted by pandemics sets up a magnifying mirror to an all-too-human tendency to imitate characteristic of homo mimeticus. What both *sapiens* and *mimeticus* have in common is the disconcerting ability to fall under the pathological spell of emotional contagion in physical crowds offline and conspiracies theories in virtual publics online, which call for heterogeneous forms of cultural immunization in critical practice.

## The Patho(-)Logies of Homo Mimeticus

While the coronavirus pandemic generated a viral contagion that was immediately placed under the lens of epidemiologists and virologists to effectively develop a plurality of vaccines, it has also made clear that a viral pandemic infects and affects the totality of human activities in complex ways that involve the humanities and social sciences as well. In particular, it made visible on a global scale what philosophers from Plato and Aristotle onward considered to be one of humans' defining characteristics, for which there is no single effective immunization: namely, that *homo sapiens* is an extremely mimetic species, not only in the aesthetic sense that humans represent the world via realistic media like painting, theater, cinema, TV, and now a proliferation of new media with the potential to represent realities that are epistemically false—though in the digital age we continue to do that well and with alarming efficacy. Humans are also imitative in the psychological, sociological, anthropological, and political sense that we imitate, often unconsciously, other people, be they real or fictional, embodied or represented, including their emotions, habits, and beliefs, which go viral online and spread "contagiously," from self to others, offline as well.[3]

The metaphor of going viral is not accidental. Rethinking mimesis in the age of the return of viral pandemics makes us see that imitation turns out to share some important characteristics with viruses: it is linked to a type of reproduction that is not limited to representation but affects and infects human bodies; it does so in ways that operate via microimitations that are imperceptible to the naked eye; it renders bodies vulnerable to a type of contagion that is amplified by proximity with others; and last but not least, it generates effects that go beyond clear-cut categories of good and evil, health and sickness, and cannot be contained within unilateral, universal, and transhistorical diagnostics.

For instance, on the one hand, scientifically informed models of behavior based on a rational knowledge, or *logos*, can be amplified affectively by public personalities (presidents, celebrities, actors) who have the power to turn to social media to promote therapeutic or patho-*logical* forms of prevention like social distancing, mask-wearing, and vaccination; on the other hand, the proliferation of pathological cultural models among the same categories of "exemplary" personalities can also spread irrational sentiments that have nothing to do with the *logos* of science but are animated by a resentful *pathos* that promotes pandemic denial, mask protests, vaccine hesitancy, and conspiracy theories, among other cultural pathologies infecting *Homo sapiens*. The latter "go viral" in the metaphorical sense that they reproduce, like a virus, at impressive speed in the virtual world of Internet simulations. They also go viral in the sense that they retroact, via spiraling feedback loops, to affect and infect social practices offline in ways that literally disseminate viral contagion among homo mimeticus.

This structural ambivalence entails therapeutic insights that provide a humanistic supplement to the medical sciences. If the virus can, in the weakened and genetically modified form of a vaccine, provide a therapeutic immunity to the viral infection, mimesis as we have seen in part 1, is equally endowed with double pharmaceutical properties. Since classical antiquity, in fact, the all-too-human propensity to imitate others (be they real or fictional) has been considered as both pathological and therapeutic. Already Plato, in fact, considered mimesis as a "*pharmakon*," that is, as Derrida famously noted, both "medicine and/or poison" (1981b, 70). Or, to put it in our diagnostic language, if the coronavirus generated a form of mimetic contagion that spread a multiplicity of contagious *pathologies* that affected *Homo sapiens* on a plurality of levels—biological, psychological, sociological, anthropological, political, economic, etc.—it can also serve as a therapeutic and reflective mirror that provides the necessary balancing distance to mobilize different discourses or *logoi* to account for the dynamic of mimetic affects or *pathoi*—what I called, "patho-*logies*" to emphasize the transdisciplinary discourses or *logoi* internal to a theory of homo mimeticus attentive to the contagious power of *pathos*.

Disseminated by globalization, indifferent to national borders, favored by political inefficiency, and obsessively followed by (new) media, true and false, a pandemic is indeed a "total social fact" insofar as this heterogeneous phenomenon is at "once legal, economic, religious, aesthetic, morphological and so on" (Mauss 1966, 76). It thus escapes cultural generalizations that aim to contain the proliferating effects of viral and affective contagion within unitary theoretical diagnostics that may still have worked in a relatively secure nation state in the postwar period but are no longer adequate for a present interconnected and increasingly precarious world. In the wake of the differentiated reality of the coronavirus pandemic and the future pandemics that will continue to haunt an increasingly interconnected world, the reality of viral contagion leads us to correct unifying theories of mimetic contagion that were still dominant in the past century in order to continue furthering a different theory of imitation for the present century.

We already encountered this precursor in part 1 in the context of structuralist controversies in theory, but it is now the moment to revisit his mimetic theory in light of the reality of contagion in practice. In the 1970s the French literary theorist René Girard rightly noticed important similarities between the viral contagion internal to epidemics and the affective contagion that follows it, shadow-like. He did so via hermeneutical analyses of renderings of "the plague in literature" that uncovered what he considered a referential "mimetic crisis" (1974, 834) hiding behind literary representations of epidemic crises—from Sophocles to Shakespeare, Dostoevsky to Thomas Mann, among others. As Girard puts it: "Between the plague and social disorder there is a reciprocal affinity" (834) based on the fact that both are "contagious" in nature; he adds: "The appropriateness of the metaphor comes, obviously, from this contagious character" (836). If the plague is contagious in the viral or literal sense, violence is indeed contagious in the affective or metaphorical sense. This remains a timely observation.

And yet it is not how Girard intends the metaphor to work. In a striking mirroring inversion of perspective, Girard overturns the relation between reality and metaphor, as he claims that the plague in literature does not literally represent the contagious reality of viral contagion. On the contrary, viral contagion, as he puts it, "becomes a transparent metaphor for a certain reciprocal violence that spreads, literally, like the plague" (836). In this metaphorical overturning, it is the contagious nature of violence, not of the plague, that should be taken literally for Girard. Put differently, the plague as represented in literature turns out to be a mere "transparent metaphor" for the mimetic violence that is the center of Girard's own theory of violence and the sacred. Contagious violence is thus rendered literal whereas the plague is metaphorical, which does not mean that this interpretation of the plague renders us immune to viruses.

Girard's hermeneutical move might be in line with his mimetic theory but is invalidated by viral realities in a way that is at least double. First, writing from the position of a still relatively immune nation state, in an optimistic period of capitalist expansion, Girard downplayed the danger of viral contagion. Like Harari after him, he argues, for instance, that we "live in a world less and less threatened by real epidemics" (1974, 845). And in a striking rewriting of the historical horrors the plague and viral infections generated, from the Black Death in medieval Europe to the Spanish flu that went global 1918, Girard adds:

> This fact looks less surprising now, as we come to realize that the properly medical aspects of the plague never were essential; in themselves, they always played a minor role, serving mostly as a disguise for an even more terrible threat that no science as ever been able to conquer. (845)

What applies to theories in general applies to mimetic theories as well: they may aspire to universal ideas characteristic of the *vita contemplativa*, but the historical reality of the *vita activa* now redoubled by a *vita mimetica* allows us to put the theory to the test. Unfortunately for humans, even recent history shows that Girard's theory did not withstand the test of time: from the plague of HIV to the COVID-19 pandemic, we have been living in an increasingly precarious world open to infections that are likely to literally, rather than metaphorically, plague an increasingly interconnected and interdependent humanity in the future as well. To his merit, in his last writings Girard corrected his diagnostic and recognized the danger of pandemic contagion.[4] Still, his revisions did not go far enough. He retained the category of crisis of differences to account for the dynamic of the pandemic, encouraging theorists of imitation of the future to supplement his diagnostic to account for the differences a pandemic generates—which takes us to the next invalidation.

Second, Girard claims that both viral and affective contagion generate a state of "undifferentiation" (2010, 24) that affects all subjects equally, generating what he often calls "mimetic crisis" or "crisis of differences." What he suggests is that individual, social, economic, political, national, and other differences are erased by the double dynamic of mimetic contagion, be it literal or metaphorical, in transhistorical ways Girard considers constitutive of "the eternal ethos of the plague" (1974, 834). While humans are indeed all vulnerable to both forms of medical/affective contagion that erase differences in the sense that all are equally vulnerable to infection in abstract theory, the coronavirus pandemic taught us that the opposite is true in clinical and cultural practice. In fact, both viral and social contagion generate an exacerbation of a plurality of medical, social, cultural, and political differences that need to be considered. It is not simply that certain social categories (the elderly, patients with pre-existing conditions, exposed workers) are more vulnerable than others. The toll of viral infections, in fact, manifests itself radically differently across the world, depending on age, ethnic group, class, nationality, economic status, and so on.

Differences were also radically amplified by the politics of each national countries and the social and economic inequalities that differentiated the levels of infection significantly. Countries like Brazil and India, populations like African Americans in the US, and undocumented migrants in Europe and other parts of the world made these differences strikingly visible, and the unequal rollout of vaccines across the globe subsequently confirmed it. Rather than "undifferentiation," then, the coronavirus pandemic magnified the differentiation caused by sociopolitical pathologies like systemic racism that plague what Frantz Fanon called "the wretched of the Earth" while also revealing class inequality, systemic racism, and sexism that continues to structure white nationalist patriarchal structures, not to speak of the violent divide between the Global North and Global South that deprives silent majorities of what Achille Mbembe calls "the universal right to breathe" (2020).[5]

From the contemporary perspective of new mimetic studies attentive to a plurality of differences, then, we can say that violence is not only physical but manifests itself in a number of structural and systemically pervasive forms of oppression; and precisely for this reason, it is crucial to account for the interplay between two different, entangled, and quite literal and all-too-real pathologies such as viral reproduction and sociopolitical mimesis. If Girard's mimetic theory still accounts for the scapegoating mechanisms internal to ritual crises that routinely direct violence against minorities, it no longer adequately reflects the complex reality of a pandemic crisis, which now calls for patho-*logical* supplements. For future-oriented thinkers of mimesis concerned with the real and rather differentiated implications of a pandemic crisis, the coronavirus pandemic gives us a timely occasion to rethink mimesis and theorize contagion again to prepare for crises to come. Rather than a hermeneutic that uncovers a sameness hidden behind an epidemic plague treated metaphorically, then, genealogical lenses propose a diagnostic of the multiplicity of differences that emerge from the patho(-)logical interplay of social contagion and viral contagion, both constitutive of homo mimeticus.

A genealogy of mimesis that looks back to the past in order to cast light on the patho(-)logies of the present does not provide a unitary answer, universal structure, or transhistorical theoretical system to frame a constantly changing phenomenon. Instead of taking its starting point in a triangulation of mimetic desire still of Oedipal inspiration, it foregrounds an all-too-human vulnerability to what I have been calling mimetic *pathos* (both good and bad) and the critical *distance* that can potentially ensue if we step further back to a longer genealogy of precursors. This paradoxical double movement between mimetic pathos and critical distance, or "pathos of distance," is indeed the defining dynamic of our new theory of imitation. A central concept in Nietzsche's genealogy of morality that unmasks a magical faith in other worlds "behind the world [*Hinterwelt*]" (1996a, 5), Nietzsche informs my genealogy of viral mimesis as well, urging us to remain faithful to this world. On the shoulder of Nietzsche but also of the long chain of thinkers we have encountered so far, I take three genealogical steps in this immanent direction to outline a diagnostic of mimetic patho(-)logies in the age of pandemic contagion. I take two steps back to re-evaluate the relation between mimesis and contagion for the ancients in Plato's philosophy and for the moderns in crowd psychology. These steps back will then allow me to leap ahead toward the challenge of immunization in an age dominated by conspiracy theories that reload the contagious powers of false shadows for a digital age constitutive of the *vita mimetica*.

## *Vita Mimetica*: Ancient Shadows, New Simulations

First step. Origins, we have learned, are never simply pure and singular. Yet given the dominant translation of "mimesis" as representation or copy of an original model, it might still be useful to briefly step back to the one of the most influential thinkers who introduced this concept in western thought.[6] According to Plato's philosophical logos, mimesis, pathos, and cultural pathologies cannot easily be dissociated.

Let us in fact briefly recall that when the concept of *mimēsis* first appears on the philosophical scene in books 2 and 3 of the *Republic*, Plato does not introduce an ontological concept that reduces the phenomenal world to a visual copy, shadow, or "phantom [*phantasma*]" of transcendental ideas, turning artistic representations into phantoms of phantoms "at three removes" (1963c, 597e) from the metaphysical world of intelligible Forms. We will have to wait until book 10 for this famous critique of mimesis qua ontological mirror based on the logic of visual likeness, adequation, and representation to appear, a metaphysical and epistemic critique Plato also theorized via the example of the painter and continues to cast a shadow on contemporary limitations of mimesis to the sphere of realistic aesthetics.

Instead, as we have insisted since the beginning, in the *Republic* mimesis is first introduced as a theatrical, dramatic concept in line with its etymological origins—from *mimos*, actor as well as performance—linked to theatrical impersonations that concern first and foremost the education (*paideia*) of youth in the Greek city (*polis*) in a period still partially dominated by an oral culture. As Eric Havelock argues in *Preface to Plato* (1963), Plato's critique of mimesis must be understood in the context of what he calls an "oral state of mind" (1963, 41), in which the actor or reciter of poetry (rhapsode) speaks in mimetic (first-person) rather diegetic (third-person) speech, has "the power to make his audience identify almost pathologically and certainly sympathetically with the content of what he is saying" (45). Both at the level of diction (*lexis*) and content (*logos*) of mimetic spectacles, dramatic impersonations of the *Iliad*, the *Theogony*, or the tragedies and comedies, Plato says, under the mask of Socrates, have a pathological effect on the public not only because they do not represent the truth about the gods (epistemic reasons) but also because the public participates emotionally in these spectacles by sym-pathos (feeling with) endowed with contagious affective properties that, as we have seen in the preceding chapters, are currently returning to the forefront of the theoretical scene (political reasons).

Reframed within the political context of the city or polis, the famous Allegory of the Cave in book 7 of the *Republic* is brought closer to home in this period of seclusion within our private caves, reduced freedom of movement, and intensified mediatized exposure to (mis)representations that shadow reality and spellbind us to a plurality of screens. Remember that in the Platonic myth, the chained prisoners are spellbound by a "puppet show," projected by carriers of simulacra walking in front of a fire generating "shadows cast from the fire on the wall that fronted them [the prisoners]."[7] The prisoners mistake the shadows for reality because they lack the critical distance of the philosopher who, with the help of a guide, can take rational steps back from the illusory sphere of sensorial perception, break the chain that ties him to these projections, and start the steep, ascending path of thought characteristic of the *vita contemplativa*—as a metaphysical tradition that goes from Plato to Heidegger suggests.[8] And yet, depending on how we interpret those shadows projected in the cave, we have also seen and felt that the myth is open to alternative, more immanent and embodied perspectives. In particular, it welcomes interpretations attentive to the imperceptible dynamic of affective contagion, or pathos, within a cave haunted by the powers of phantasmal simulations that have spellbinding, hypnotic, and magnetic effects—a psychological perspective attentive to what we called *vita mimetica*.

If we now further this genealogy of mimesis from our contemporary problematic, the old myth still helps us to reflect critically on new (social) media that, perhaps more than ever, cast a magnetic, contagious, and intoxicating spell on the human imagination. As film critics from André Bazin onward routinely noted, the Allegory of the Cave anticipates the affective powers of cinema to induce spellbinding effects that magnetized human chameleons in the past century and continue to magnetize homo mimeticus in the present century. As Edgar Morin puts it: "Our needs, our aspirations, our desires, our obsessions, our fears, project themselves not only into the void as dreams and imaginings, but onto all things and all beings" (2005, 85). While cinema reproduces the Platonic scenario of the cave in the twentieth century, in the digital age the "imitation-hypnotic" (96) effects of moving shadows continue to operate on a variety of smaller screens, which, from TV to computers, tablets to smartphones, intensify the power of images to cast a spell generating an intoxicating psychic dispossession of the ego via black mirrors that are haunting the twenty-first century.[9]

What was true for the Platonic prisoners remains true for contemporary spectators and digital users: if phantoms of reality disseminated via new media online are often rightly stressed in contemporary discussions of the powers of lies in the age of "post-truth," it is equally crucial to stress the affective (Dionysian) receptivity of the phantom of the ego that makes homo mimeticus vulnerable to (Apollonian) illusions in the first place. These contagious illusions are particularly virulent in periods of crisis, like a pandemic crisis or a war, and can lead to collective intoxications that manifest themselves in political pathologies (pandemic denial, antimask protests, conspiracy theories, etc.) that amplify exponentially the reach of the viral pathology via hypermimetic media constitutive of our process of becoming posthuman.[10]

Thus reframed, we are in a better position to re-evaluate the relevance of mimesis in the age of viral reproduction. Plato's allegory reaches into the present, as it foreshadows a world of simulation that postmodern critics were perhaps too quick to disconnect from the problematic of mimesis. Contra Plato, Jean Baudrillard, for instance, diagnosed a hyperreal world of simulacra and simulation that no longer rests on the logic of "imitation" but, as he puts it, "liquidates all referents" insofar as the hyperreal, "substitutes the real with signs of the real" (1981, 11; my trans.). Influential at the twilight of the last century, this postmodern diagnostic of simulation is of loose Nietzschean inspiration. Yet it does not account for the all-too-human effects generated by a hyperreal world of simulacra, which, while no longer resting on the logic of mimesis as representation, continues to cast a material (Dionysian) shadow on this world, generating not only phantoms of reality but phantoms of egos in the twenty-first century.

The inversion of perspective from mimetic phantoms to mimetic egos that already informed Nietzsche's critique of Platonism is now redoubled by our critique of postmodernism. We have seen that in light of the discovery of mirror neurons in the 1990s, the neurosciences provide an empirical confirmation that visual representations, no matter how far removed or disconnected from reality, have the performative power to generate contagious reflexes; images seen from a visual distance can trigger neurological discharges that generate mimetic pathos via an immediate form of communication that is not necessarily mediated by consciousness but generated "embodied simulations" (Gallese 2005) nonetheless. In light of humans' confirmed receptivity to mirroring reflexes caused by perception of movements (real or represented, true or false), it is thus urgent to provide a mimetic supplement to postmodern diagnostics of hyperreality prominent at the twilight of the last century that no longer account for the catastrophic realities of the present century. In fact, hyperreal simulations disconnected from the logic of representation have the performative power to retroact on the plastic brains and porous bodies of homo mimeticus via feedback loops that blur the line between truth and lies, origins and copies, facts and alternative facts, digital simulations and embodied imitations, generating shadows that are far removed from reality indeed; and yet, they can also performatively induce deeply felt, false, and intoxicating beliefs that trigger contagious actions that are socially pathological and are endowed with the immanent power to amplify viral contagion in real life. I call this looping effect whereby hyperreal simulations retroact on mirroring reflexes *hypermimesis*. I do so to stress that the hyperreal may no longer be subordinated to the logic of representation but continues to be rooted in the all-too-real laws of imitation to be revisited from the transdisciplinary angle of new mimetic studies.

Now that we have reloaded this ancient myth on the contagious powers of mimesis whose intention was to dispel artistic lies as shadows in the past, let us continue to uncover the truth on the contagious power of hypermimetic simulations in the present. As a significant section of the world population was holed up in private caves during multiple lockdowns in what was the first world pandemic to be simultaneously shadowed and redoubled by digital media, practices of social distancing in privileged countries protected *Homo sapiens* from the epidemic contagion and the viral pathology it spread. Still, homo mimeticus was far from immune from affective contagion and the social pathologies a *vita mimetica* also entails. On the contrary, chained to the continuous flow of daily news on a plurality of digital devices that amplified the pathos—especially in its link to *penthos*, suffering—generated by the still growing number of victims, a contradictory double movement well familiar to genealogists of mimesis began to take shape.

With some critical distance, increased by the growing number of theoretical reflections on the systemic and highly differentiated implications of the pandemic crisis, this double movement allows us to return to our driving question whereby we started in more specific diagnostic terms. I reframe it as follows: in the case of the coronavirus pandemic, we are indeed facing a hybrid viral/virtual phenomenon in which the viral pandemic is shadowed by an obsessive media focus on the spread of the virus that not only generates pathos for the real victims; the pandemic also generates a multiplicity of conspiracies theories that challenge the logos of science and disseminate magical causal explanations that reload the mimetic faculty in the age of the Internet. It does so by directing responsibility for complex systemic problems toward simple imaginary scapegoats (from Bill Gates and 5G to Corona beer) that made a significant part of *sapiens* lose the sense of the reality of the pandemic itself.

Given the systemic complexity of the pandemic, even among philosophically informed perspectives, some wondered: did rational *Homo sapiens* driven by the pathos of homo mimeticus lose sight of the proportions between the mass-mediatized phenomenon and the pandemic itself—as the Italian philosopher Giorgio Agamben controversially claimed at the outset of the pandemic, as he compared COVID-19 to a "normal flu" and condemned the Italian government's "disproportionate response" qua "state of exception" (2020) from a philosophical distance?[11] Alternatively, and considered from the other end of the spectrum, is the coronavirus pandemic a symptom that humanity has reached a tipping point and that we are now a facing an epochal transformation that is likely to generate even more catastrophes—as Slovenian philosopher Slavoj Žižek writes with pathos in *Pandemic!*, when he claims that the virus will "destroy the foundations of our lives" (2020). Or should we rather forge a complex middle path between pathos and distance, as our genealogical lenses have encouraged us to do, beginning, middle, and end?

Before finding this middle path, the patho(-)logies of contagion remind us that the (new) media are certainly not a transparent window onto the world but should be framed within the long history of mimesis, which I schematically and partially reconstruct as follows:

1) at the dawn of philosophy, Plato (in)famously introduced the trope of the "mirror" to account for different ontological degrees of reality predicated on a philosophical *logos* that denounces mimesis as a phantom of a phantom;
2) at the twilight of metaphysics, writing with and contra Plato, Nietzsche overturned the diagnostic by relying on the logic of pathos, or patho-*logy*, to unmask the power of phantoms to take possession of the modern ego;
3) jump-starting mimetic theory from a romantic source of inspiration, Girard diagnosed mimesis as a state of undifferentiation predicated on the Dionysian logic of violent pathos (with Nietzsche), while framing this logic in an ideal triangular form that culminates in a scapegoating mechanism that (with Plato) operates as a *pharmakos*;
4) at the end of metaphysical spectrum, Baudrillard, with Nietzsche, contra Plato, rejected the doubling logic of the mirror at the twilight of realism by introducing a hyperreal world of simulation that has nothing to do with imitation.

This is a schematic and rather partial genealogical account that does not do justice to the complex genealogy of homo mimeticus we selectively reconstructed in this book. Still, it allows us to see some of the shoulders on which we provisionally stand to look further ahead.

Now, pushing with and against this genealogy, I convoke the trope of the magnifying glass we have seen both Morin and Nancy also use to diagnose pathological phenomena rooted in material process of viral and affective reproduction infecting homo mimeticus in differentiated ways. Once doubled by a heterogeneous media landscape, attention to the duplicity of mimetic patho(-)logies reveals how new media, while not having access to a stabilizing essence of truth can nonetheless either faithfully reproduce a scientific *logos* to inform the population or, alternatively, spread pathological lies via the power of mimetic *pathos* to deform and, in the case of conspiracy theories, dissolve the contours of reality. Both true and false forms of communication can in turn generate hypermimetic processes that do not simply mirror an ideal immutable theory—for the *logos* on the virus evolves as scientific knowledge does; nor do they reveal a metaphorical truth hidden at the foundation of the world—for viral and affective contagion operate on two different but related and equally real levels of contamination. Rather, they generate spiraling feedback loops between the pathology of viral contagion and affective contagion whereby the latter is not simply an effect of viral contagion but also a cause of it. This dynamic looping effect can in turn lead to pathological effects (as in the case of pandemic denial) and patho-*logical* affects (as in the case of legitimate fear), depending on the message communicated to human faculties that are as sapient as they are mimetic faculties.

Narratives of linear progress based on the *logos* of science give us hope that the vaccine rollout will eventually put this pandemic to a global stop, though a complete elimination of a protean virus seems increasingly unlikely. At the same time, this *logos* should not underestimate the looping effects of false accounts of realty that convince by drawing on the intoxicating *pathos* of contagion to work contra immunization in insidious ways critical theorists can analyze from a patho-*logical* distance. At its very minimum, a critical *logos* on mimetic *pathos* can be put to use to dispel one of the greatest myths that should have been unmasked by the horrors of the twentieth century but still informs "scientific" approaches to the human in the twenty-first century: namely, the ideal of a fully rational, autonomous, and self-sufficient creature characteristic of the subject of *Aufklärung* fails to account for a *vita mimetica* that was already at play in the classical period, makes a massive comeback in the modern period, and is now casting a long shadow on the present and future as well.

## Modern Contagion: Microbes, Crowds, Publics

Second step. The connection between mimesis and affective contagion became central to sociological reflections in the last decades of nineteenth century, which saw unprecedented numbers of people assembled in cities. The phenomenon of the "crowd" (*foule, Masse, folla*) gave rise to transnational theories of crowd behavior that after a period of massive implementation in the 1920s and 30s, were somewhat neglected in the second half of the twentieth century yet are currently returning to the forefront of critical attention in the present century in the context of political crises.[12] This mimetic, or rather, hypermimetic phenomenon deserves to be revisited in the context of pandemic crises as well.

Founding figures of crowd psychology—like Gustave Le Bon and Gabriel Tarde in France, Wilfred Trotter and William McDougall in England, and, later, Sigmund Freud and Elias Canetti in Austria—noted that when people are assembled in a physical crowd or, at one remove, become part of a virtual public, while reading newspapers for instance—and today, Twitter, Facebook, YouTube, etc.—emotions are transmitted from self to other in an irrational, unconscious, and as they would say, "contagious" way. As Le Bon puts it in his widely popular *The Crowd* (1895): "In a crowd every sentiment and act is contagious, and contagious to such a degree that an individual readily sacrifices his personal interest to the collective interest" (2002, 7). Already prior to Le Bon, Gabriel Tarde had expanded the diagnostic from the crowd to account for the social bond tout court by considering society in terms of flows of imitation. Thus, he asks in *The Laws of Imitation* (1890): "And this similitude [in opinions and emotions] is it not due to a flow of imitation which can be accounted for by needs and ideas disseminated by previous imitative contagions [*contagions imitatives*]?" (2001, 50; my trans.).[13] Well before Girard, then, both Le Bon and Tarde pave the way for mimetic studies by using the term "contagion" metaphorically to indicate an invisible transmission of emotions that spread, viruslike, from self to others, blurring the porous line between inside and outside while generating an affective contagion that, we should add, has spiraling systemic implications for viral contagion as well.

Despite the numerous and still underexplored analogies between crowd psychology and mimetic theory, it is important to stress that the metaphorical use of *contagion* in crowd psychology differs significantly from Girard's theory—and in this difference lie additional foundations for furthering a new theory of homo mimeticus. If Girard interpreted the plague in literature as a metaphor for a more fundamental dynamic of contagious violence, crowd psychologists inverse the perspective and draw inspiration from the reality of medical contagion to metaphorically account for the psychosocial dynamic of affective contagion. The benefits of this inversion are plural: first, the metaphorical use of the term "contagion" does not dispute the danger or reality of bacterial or viral contagion; on the contrary, it draws on the language of medical contagion to account for the disconcerting capacity of emotions in a crowd to spread invisibly, from self to others, like a microbe or virus. Writing in fin de siècle France, both Le Bon and Tarde borrowed the concept of *la contagion* directly from Louis Pasteur's then relatively new discovery of microbes to account for diseases like cholera and rabies.

Second, confronted with the disconcerting emotional suggestibility of urban crowds, social theorists applied the concept of contagion to the collective psyche to account for the unconscious relation, or hypnotic rapport, between self and others, a mirroring relation that leads the ego to reproduce the affects of others in potentially exponential ways that go beyond familial triangles and provide alternative theoretical foundations. Crowd psychology, in fact, proposes a dyadic/rhizomatic rather triangular/familial structure at the origins of a type of contagion that resembled much more the dynamic of viral infection. In fact, a subject driven not only by mimetic desire but by a mimetic pathos that includes desire and other affects as well, good and bad, has the power to contaminate others with the same pathos in ways that can expand exponentially to affect and infect the entire mass or crowd. The metaphor of contagion is thus well chosen to account for a dynamic of transmission that operates not only at the intersubjective level but also at the broader social and collective level. Last but not least, this metaphorical use is relevant for our diagnostic, for it shows that the social logos on affective contagion and the scientific logos on viral contagion are genealogically linked, encouraging contemporary theorists to think more about the spiraling interplay between viral and social pathologies.

How does affective contagion operate? Via a mirroring principle that belongs to a pre-Freudian tradition of the unconscious that was marginalized in the past century; yet, as we have had numerous occasions to see, genealogical lenses are bringing this tradition back to account for contagious phenomena for the present century. Both Le Bon and Tarde, in fact, like Nietzsche before them, relied on the model of hypnosis or hypnotic suggestion to account for the contagious dynamic of emotions. For Le Bon, contagion and suggestion are two sides of the same mimetic phenomenon. As he put it:

> When defining crowds, we said that one of their general characteristics was an excessive suggestibility, and we have shown to what an extent suggestions are contagious in every human agglomeration; a fact which explains the rapid turning of the sentiments of a crowd in a definite direction. (2002, 14)

It is because subjects who are part of a crowd are in a psychic state of light hypnosis, or suggestion, that they are prone to mirroring the emotions of others, going potentially as far as turning the idea of others into an action, which is the very definition of suggestion. Tarde confirms this point, as he zooms in on the neuronal mimetic principles that account for this contagious process: "the action at a distance from brain to brain that I call imitation, is assimilable to hypnotic suggestion [*suggestion hypnotique*]" (2001, 257 n. 1); he specifies that this mirroring/contagious mechanism via theories of hypnotic suggestion that already in the late nineteenth century assume (rightly, we now know) that in humans "nerves imitate nerves, brains imitate brains" (264). If this mirroring principle was discovered in the 1990s and attributed to "mirror neurons," genealogical lenses confirm once again that it is more accurate to speak of a *re*-discovery of unconscious mirroring mechanisms already advocated by untimely figures in mimetic studies in the 1890s.

What we must add is that this psychological tradition of the mimetic unconscious, which is attentive to mirroring reflexes, intersubjective bonds, altered states of consciousness, porous selves, psychic influences, and contagious emotional dynamics, provides a sociopolitical supplement to account for the interplay between viral and affective contagion. After all, leaders like Mussolini and Hitler were quick to put Le Bon's lessons on how to cast a hypnotic spell on the crowd to fascist use. There is little evidence that authoritarian leaders in periods of pandemic, economic, or national crisis do not use the same affective strategies to come to power, remain in power, and in certain cases, downplay the pandemic crisis, thereby undermining immunization and amplifying its power of infection. The dynamic interplay between viral contagion and affective contagion in an age haunted by the shadow of what we called "(new) fascism" amplify the viral pathology via pathological political responses. Antidemocratic leaders like Donald Trump in the US and Jair Bolsonaro in Brazil, for example, revealed the plurality of ways in which a pathological politics based on antimask stance and pandemic denialism that follows conspiracy theories rather than scientific facts aggravated the viral pathology in these countries. They contributed to amplifying the number of casualties in criminal ways that, along with climate change denial, should be considered as constitutive of the politics of (new) fascism in the twenty-first century.

And yet, at the same time, pathological political responses to the epidemic also had the paradoxical effect to generate liberating and positive patho-*logical* forms of antifascist contagion. The *pathos* generated by systemic racial oppression, for instance, ignited antiracist protests that, under the banner of "Black Lives Matter," also spread contagiously during periods of confinement, this time generating life-affirmative, nonviolent sympathy not only in the US but across the world. Similarly, in the UK protests against systemic violence directed against women sparked solidarity across nations to oppose sexist patriarchal societies, which, as recent studies show, render women's lives, just like minorities and illegal immigrants, much more vulnerable and precarious in periods of pandemic crisis.

To move toward our last step, what we must add is that the same (new) fascist rhetoric that privileges use of images rather than thoughts, emotion, or *pathos*, rather than reason, or *logos*, is effective in spreading illusory legends among a suggestible crowd, which reach unprecedented proportions in the digital age. As Le Bon had already warned in a passage that is worth quoting at length:

> The creation of the legends which so easily obtain circulation in crowds is not solely the consequence of their extreme credulity. It is also the result of the prodigious perversions [*déformations*] that events

undergo in the imagination of a throng. The simplest event that comes under the observation of a crowd is soon totally transformed [*défiguré*]. A crowd thinks in images, and the image itself immediately calls up a series of other images, having no logical connection with the first. We can easily conceive this state by thinking of the fantastic succession of ideas to which we are sometimes led by calling up in our minds any fact. Our reason shows us the incoherence there is in these images, but a crowd is almost blind to this truth, and confuses with the real event what the deforming action of its imagination has superimposed thereon. A crowd scarcely distinguishes between the subjective and the objective. It accepts as real the images evoked in its mind, though they most often have only a very distant relation with the observed fact. (2002, 15)

Credulity, disregard of contradictions, blind belief in false images, fantastic succession of ideas, suggestibility to repetitions, among other tendencies at play in the *vita mimetica*, have, indeed, the magnetic power to render a crowd dangerously vulnerable to legends. Fictions not only drive the coordinating abilities of *Homo sapiens* for the better; they also cast a magnetic spell on homo mimeticus for the worse. This is, after all, an old story. If we already saw it at play in *Zelig* (chapter 6) it harkens back to the origins of philosophy (chapter 2).

Yet the diagnostic gains new traction in a modern age (dis)informed by hypermimetic media that are mechanically reproduced on a massive scale and generate what Tarde calls a "public." What Le Bon says of the "era of crowds [*ère des foules*]" is, in fact, amplified in what Tarde calls the "era of the public [*ère du public*]" (1901, 11; my trans.): that is, a "virtual crowd [*foule virtuelle*]" he considers already in 1901 the "social group of the future" (13). The public is in fact physically dispersed yet mentally connected by a simultaneous exposure to media that generates a "suggestion at a distance" (5). Taking the readership of newspapers as a paradigmatic example of a public, Tarde speaks of a mutual suggestion between readers at a distance that generates the "unconscious illusion that our sentiment was commonly shared with a great number of others" (4). Furthering this diagnostic of contagion on the shoulders of Tarde for the digital age, we might add that this suggestibility is aggravated by conspiracy theories that have no relation to facts whatsoever. And yet they operate on the mimetic unconscious nonetheless by going viral online and generating contagious behavior offline, posing a serious hypermimetic threat via cultural pathologies that still require diagnostic investigations and with which I would like to conclude.

## Conspiracy Theories: The Patho-*logies* of Immunization

Two steps back to the ancient and modern foundations of philosophy allow us to make a last step—or maybe jump—ahead to present conspiracy theories that cast a shadow on the future of new mimetic studies as well. Isolated by lockdowns, exposed to a plurality of new media that rely on algorithms to amplify already held beliefs, *homo sapiens* can easily let go of a tenuous grip on rational *logos* to be driven by an irrational *pathos*, shot through by anxiety, fear, and resentment, but also poverty, dispossession, and lack of education. Overwhelmed by conflicting (dis)information, a growing number of the world population is increasingly threatened by the spread of conspiracy theories that go viral online, and, in a spiraling hypermimetic loop, generate contagious pathological effects offline, contaminating a phantom subject chained to a multiplicity of new media programmed to amplify exponentially the mimetic faculty in the digital age.

Conspiracy theories provide a new name for an ancient mimetic phenomenon. As Karl Popper made clear in *The Open Society and Its Enemies* (1945), they can be traced back to a collectivist, magical, or as he calls it, "tribal" or "closed society," animated by the mimetic faculty and dominated by poetic figures that already worried Plato at the dawn of western civilization. Of course, Popper considers Plato's theory of justice to be tyrannical and antithetical to what he calls the "open society;" and for good reason, given the explicit antidemocratic stance of the author of the *Republic*. Thus, Popper spends considerable energy in critiquing "the spell of Plato" in the first part of his Magnus opus of political theory predicated on the thesis that "totalitarianism belongs to a tradition which is just as old or just as young as our civilization itself" (Popper 2020, xlii). Plato's political solution to posit a philosopher-king who imposes the *techne* of the *logos* from the top down to censor the *pathos* of poets is indeed complicit with mimetic pathologies that will be put to devastating fascist practice in the twentieth century. That is, the century from which Popper's critique of the close society in general and magical or mimetic thinking in particular is launched, since he wrote the book during World War II.

And yet, with respect to Popper's specific diagnostic of the contagious powers of mimesis, this agonistic relation with Plato might not be as clear cut as it first appears to be. Popper, in fact, acknowledges Plato's "overwhelming intellectual achievement" (xli) in terms that convey admiration for what he calls "Plato's power of diagnosis" (2020, 163). As in the case of Nietzsche but for different reasons, Popper's oppositions to Plato may be yet another instance of *mimetic agonism*, for he fights his exemplary opponent with some of Plato's diagnostic moves.[14] Taking the paradigmatic example from Plato's critique of mimesis in book 3 of *Republic* with which we started, Popper notes that in Homer's *Iliad* the human vicissitudes during the Trojan war were seen as "enforced by a supernatural will," driven by the god's decisions located in an Olympic and magical afterworld, to use Nietzsche's phrase. As Popper puts it: "The belief in the Homeric gods whose conspiracies explain the history of the Trojan War is gone. The gods are abandoned. But their place is filled by powerful men or groups" (306) that, to this day, continue to cast a spell on homo mimeticus in this world. The mimetic faculty, as we have seen, is open to influences for the best but also tends to presuppose a magical individual intention to account for big systemic events for the worse. As Popper specifies: "whatever happens in society—especially happenings such as war, unemployment, poverty, shortages, which people as a rule dislike—is the result of direct design by some powerful individuals and groups" (306). Tribalism, magic, and irrational associations between great historical events in this world and great transcendental causes animated by powerful forces in other worlds are characteristic of a closed society, which as Plato foresaw, is under the magnetic spell of powerful myths.

But Popper goes further. He foresees that these mimetic powers can resurface with a vengeance in what he calls an "abstract society." That is, a technology-mediated, (new) media-dependent, modern society in which people "have no, or extremely few, intimate personal contacts, who live in anonymity and isolation, and consequently in unhappiness" (2020, 166). Popper's avowedly exaggerated thought experiment in the 1940s became a reality in the 2020s and should now ring a bell:

> We could conceive of a society in which men [*sic*] practically never meet face to face—in which all business is conducted by individuals in isolation who communicate by typed letters or by telegrams, and who go about in closed motor-cars. (166)

Needless to say, this has been the very condition of good part of the world population during the first global lockdown in the digital age during the COVID-19 pandemic. The abstract society is now our actual, individualistic, atomistic and hypermediated society. Given the complexity of an event such as a pandemic, simple intentional explanations have gone viral online: from considering the virus as a biological weapon to linking the vaccine to microchip implants, from blaming 5G technology to scapegoating Bill Gates and considering the pandemic a hoax, the conspiracies are many in what has been called "*an ocean of misinformation*" (Stein et al. 2021, 1). And given the lonely, isolated, and suggestible status of homo mimeticus whose genealogy we have traced, no wonder that the mimetic faculty predicated on the *pathos* of magical thinking was reloaded in a period of crisis—with a vengeance.

What defines conspiracy theories from antiquity to the present is that they provide a simple, unifying, direct, and often grand causal explanation for complex systemic problems that defy singular explanations. As Umberto Eco notes, commenting on Popper, conspiracy theories "purport to offer explanations in ways that appeal to people who feel they've been denied important information" (Eco 2014). More recently, in an authoritative collection on the subject, Michael Butter and Pieter Knight group conspiracy theories under the heading of "nothing happens by accident; nothing is at it seems; and everything is connected" (2020, 1). They then summarize the main characteristics of conspiracy theories as follows:

> they assume that everything has been planned and nothing happens by coincidence; they divide the world strictly into the evil conspirators and the innocent victims of their plot; and they claim that the conspiracy works in secret and does not reveal itself even after it has reached its goals. (Butter and Knight 2020, 1)[15]

Paradoxically, then, as conspiracy theories proliferate online, the public is encouraged to play the role of "master of suspicion" (Ricoeur's phrase), supplementing Marx, Nietzsche, and Freud in uncovering latent truths behind manifest scientific contents that are, for an increasing number of believers in conspiracies, deemed too factual to be true. No training in hermeneutics is of course presupposed. Consequently, the "master of suspicion" quickly turns into the slave of conspiracies that appeal to an all-too-human, and now posthuman, suggestibility to a will to mime whose magical-magnetic-mirroring-unconscious powers our genealogy of homo mimeticus has been urging to take seriously for some time.

In theory, unmasking the falsity of conspiracies is not difficult for researchers given the former's lack of empirical foundations. And yet, since they generate a magical hypermimetic pathos that operates on the mimetic faculty in practice, effectively countering them via a rational *logos* alone is not sufficient—for the power of *logos* is precisely what the *pathos* of conspiracies defy altogether. If we agree with Popper that conspiracy theories are as old as Homer at the level of the message, we should add that (new) media rely on algorithms that amplify the powers of the mimetic unconscious by feeding users' misinformation that reinforces already held beliefs (or confirmation bias), generating bubbles that create, via social media and Internet channels (Facebook, Twitter, YouTube...), alternative or parallel worlds that can all-too-easily be mistaken for the "real" world. This challenge is especially visible with respect to the plurality of conspiracies that deny the danger of a pandemic (or the reality of a war for that matter) in a period of general crisis, isolation, and hyperconnectivity to a multiplicity of contradictory information, both true and false.

Conspiracies not only generate false theories but also pathological practices. They lead homo mimeticus to deny the danger of the pandemic, counter safety measures, and spread vaccine hesitancy during an already complex and bumpy vaccine rollout that, in addition to medical, political, and economic hurdles, finds it is undermined by conspiracies about vaccines. As Butter and Knight confirm: "psychologists have shown that belief in conspiracy theories about vaccines or global warming leads to a refusal to vaccinate oneself or one's children, or an unwillingness to reduce one's carbon dioxide footprint" (2020, 6).[16] The proliferation of conspiracies on social media supplemented by increasingly professional-looking documentaries to spread them, have performative hypermimetic effects that reach massive proportions in periods of crisis, like a pandemic crisis, in which everyone is susceptible to pathos.

This is not a minor problem that can be solved from the angle of a scientific *logos* alone, for rational knowledge and empirical methods are precisely what are undermined by conspiracy theories, nor can conspiracies easily be censored. Although some prohibitions are in place (with respect to Holocaust denial, for instance), the right to free speech in an open, hyperconnected, and abstract society escapes censoring mechanisms that, already at the time of Plato's relatively closed society, could only be imagined in theory. As my genealogy of mimesis from antiquity to modernity, now reaching into the present, tried to show from different perspectives, conspiracy theories call for balancing diagnostic operations that accounts for the role of *pathos* in reloading the mimetic faculty in the digital age. Conversely, it turns the mimetic faculty to patho-*logical* use by relying on the power of positive models or examples to promote the importance of vaccination via both logical and affective means.[17]

In the end, an awareness of the complex interplay of reason and emotions, pathos and distance, in the digital age is not only essential to viral immunization during a pandemic crisis. It is equally vital to confront crises to come, including the return of wars that put the loop of hypermimesis to devastating political use.[18] This includes the shadow of nuclear threats that many thought relegated to the past and now turns out to be a still possible destination for the future—or lack thereof. If we then also consider that conspiracy theories contribute to spreading climate change denial in the epoch of the Anthropocene while also promoting imaginary migrations to other planets beyond our planet, then we have no choice but to heed Zarathustra's warning: "*stay true to the Earth* and do not believe those who talk of over-earthly hopes!" (2005, 12)

For all humans, be they *sapiens* or *faber, economicus* or *deus, ludens* or *mimeticus*, there is no alternative choice. Hence the urgency to join the powers of *logos* and *pathos* to affirm a metamorphosis of the spirit vital for facing crises of the future that already cast a long shadow on the present.

CODA

# THE COMPLEXITY OF MIMESIS: A DIALOGUE WITH EDGAR MORIN

As we have seen time and again from three different but deeply interwoven philosophical, aesthetic, and political perspectives, mimesis is far from the stable representational concept a dominant western tradition long depicted it to be. On the contrary, the recent *re*-turn of attention to the ancient realization that humans are, for better and worse, imitative animals reveals a destabilizing, protean, and complex emergent phenomenon each generation needs to rethink anew. Multidisciplinary thinking is thus necessary to apprehend the numerous manifestations of homo mimeticus in its process of metamorphic transformation. From the origins of communication in prehistoric times to philosophical exclusions of the *vita mimetica* in classical times, from the discovery of the unconscious in the pre-Freudian period to the linguistic turn in more recent periods, from the rise of fascism in the 1920s and '30s to (new) fascist insurrections or global pandemics in the 2020s now reawakening the specter of world war as well, we have seen that mimesis exceeds unitary definitions, transgresses disciplinary boundaries between "two cultures," including the opposition nature/culture, and manifests itself via plurality of registers constitutive of the drawing of homo mimeticus we have been outlining.

From birth to death, from the individual psyche to the social body, from the birth of consciousness to the birth of language, from the origins of art to the invention of cinema and now new media, multiple manifestations of our behavior are animated, in direct and indirect ways, consciously or, more often, unconsciously, by the all-too-human tendency toward imitation. Hence the need to join forces with a multiplicity of scholars working in different disciplines to inaugurate a diagonal and pluralist field of studies I proposed to call *new mimetic studies*. Contrary to dominant translations of mimesis as reproduction of the same, this is a protean concept whose identity is indeed not one but plural: mimetism, identification, affective participation, sympathy, contagion, imprinting, projection, mirror neurons, plasticity, trance, influence, possession, hypnosis, mass behavior, simulation and many other conceptual masks at play in the complexity of mimesis unmask it as a protean slippery phenomenon that often operates below conscious awareness and, for better or worse, connects self to others, the human to the nonhuman, contributing to shaping or dissolving our bonds with society, nature, and the earth.

To bring this study to a provisional conclusion, I turn the mimetic genre of the dialogue to productive use to open up future-oriented explorations for new mimetic studies. A number of candidates presented themselves. During the years devoted to the *Homo Mimeticus* project (2016–2022) I have benefited from friendly alliances with influential figures in political theory (William Connolly), literary theory (J. Hillis Miller), continental philosophy (Jean-Luc Nancy), feminist philosophy (Adriana Cavarero), anthropology (Christoph Wulf), posthuman studies (Katherine Hayles), philosophy of sport (Gunter Gebauer), history of psychology (Mikkel Borch-Jacobsen), among other voices that are currently contributing to the *re*-turn of mimesis.[1] To bring this genealogy to a provisional open end, I turned to an unclassifiable thinker, whose centenary genealogy traverses most of the twentieth century and helps us enter deeper in the twenty-first century as well: the French sociologist, philosopher, and transdisciplinary thinker Edgar Morin (1921–).

Morin provides a far-reaching perspective on the contemporary relevance of the "complexity of mimesis" that resonates with the fundamental assumptions of the study at hand. Director Emeritus of Research at the French National Center for Scientific Research (CNRS), codirector of the Center for Interdisciplinary Studies at the École des Hautes Études en Sciences Sociales between 1973 and 1989, founder of the Association pour la pensée complexe (Association for Complex Thought), and doctor honoris causa of over forty universities around the world, Edgar Morin is at the origin of a transdisciplinary, original, and groundbreaking thought he calls "complex thought [*pensée complexe*]" whose paradoxical movements have been at play since the beginning of this study.

This thought invites new generations of teachers, researchers, and students to overcome disciplinary strictures that all too often still oppose empirical sciences and human sciences, nature and culture, body and soul, or even brain and psyche in antagonistic fields. Morin's methodological assumption is that "the hyperspecialization of the human sciences disintegrates the notion of the human" (2004, 87).² Hence, he calls for a transdisciplinary method that goes beyond Cartesian dualisms to integrate different perspectives and develop a multidimensional account of human complexities located at the juncture of the both-and, rather than at the disjunction of the either-or. A complex subject can, in fact, be both active and passive, subject and object, forming and being formed, with hands drawing while being drawn, as M. C. Escher taught us from the beginning.

Morin's complex thought joins contradictory perspectives without sublating the polarities that compose them via a perspectivism that resonates with the study at hand—unsurprisingly so, since the theory of imitation we proposed nourished itself from a genealogy that, within the confines of this book, started with Nietzsche, stepped back to Plato, leaped ahead to Caillois, Girard, Derrida, Arendt and other contemporary thinkers and artists, and ends with Morin. Thus, *homo complexus*, as he understands it, is both subject and object, rational and irrational, *sapiens* and *demens*, prone to violence and altruism, but also both individual and social, since individuals create a society that in turn create the individual, generating feedback loops in which the cause turns into an effect, in a paradoxical movement that animates Morin's thought. As we have seen, there is a similar paradox that I found at the palpitating heart of *homo mimeticus*: humans are a species particularly prone to mimesis, and this imitation is constitutive of human originality; similarly, mimesis makes subjects prone to cultural pathologies, and for this reason, we are paradoxically capable of developing patho-*logies*.³ Morin is indeed an untimely thinker, in the Nietzschean sense, which means that his *gay savoir* was well ahead of his time and thus remained marginalized for a long time.

Perhaps due to its transdisciplinary nature, perhaps due to an increasingly specialized academic world, perhaps due to Morin's marginal position within the hierarchical French academic *grandes écoles*, perhaps due to the dominance of structuralist theories in the 1960s and '70s that sparked interest in a younger generation of thinkers including the well-known names of Michel Foucault, Pierre Bourdieu, and Jacques Derrida, perhaps due to his personal preference for Latin American countries where he is widely known, or perhaps simply due to the few available English translations of his works⁴—all these reasons are complexly entangled—Edgar Morin is still very little known in the anglophone world. This neglect is nonetheless surprising and somewhat embarrassing. Morin, who recently turned one hundred and is still actively publishing—four new books in 2020, two in 2021—is a "century man [*homme siècle*]," as the current French president called him during a national commemoration for his centenary birthday at the Palais de l'Élysée.⁵

The reasons to finally discover Morin's thought in the anglophone world are many, and the field of new mimetic studies is well placed to pave the way. The last of a generation of thinkers who actively joined the French Resistance in the 1940s, Morin traveled to Berlin to record the aftermath of the Nazi capitulation in his first book, *L'An zéro de l'Allemagne* (1946). A close friend of figures like Marguerite Duras and Roland Barthes, pioneer of film studies with now canonical books like *Cinema: or The Imaginary Man* (1956) and *The Stars* (1957), inspiration with Jean Rouch of cinema verité in a film/documentary *Chronique d'un été* (1960), Edgar Morin also coauthored a number of books with Jean Baudrillard, Claude Lefort, and Cornelius Castoriadis, among other influential figures. One of the first European thinkers to incorporate the insights of cybernetics during a stay at the Salk Institute of Biological Studies in La Jolla in 1969, while also going beyond artificial machines, Morin sounded the alarm on climate change as early as in 1972. As he warned: "degrading the ecosystem is equivalent to degrading humanity for humans, like all animals, nourish themselves not only of energy but also, as Schrödinger put it, of neganthropy, that is of order and complexity" ([1972] 2020, 25–26; my trans.).[6] More recently, Morin continued to notice that "university and pedagogic structures make it impossible to include ecology, which is by nature multidisciplinary and complex, into teaching" (2020, 9), thereby encouraging new generations of independent thinkers to go beyond dominant oppositions that divide nature and culture, mind and body, self and others, the human and the nonhuman.

To go beyond these binaries and the compartmentalized disciplinary approaches that preserve them, Morin developed an immense oeuvre (more than eighty books) addressing complex phenomena as diverse as the anthropology of death, cinema, sociology of media, ecology, aesthetics, education, as well as the encyclopedic *La Méthode* (in six volumes), which invites us to rethink the epistemic foundations of knowledge.[7] From the Spanish flu pandemic that had an influence on his birth in 1921 as he narrates in his autobiographical memoire, *Les Souvenirs viennent à ma rencontre* (2020), to the COVID-19 pandemic of 2021, Morin is indeed a century man who encourages humanity to change course, or *changer de voie*, in order to avoid catastrophe.

Morin never devoted a single book to mimesis in particular, but this complex phenomenon traverses his entire oeuvre, providing affective and conceptual principles that animate it from within. From his first book, *L'Homme et la mort* (1951), where he engages the question of the magical power of the shadow and the double, to his more recent book *Sur l'esthétique* (2016), where Morin considers the power of mimetic participation in the cave paintings at the origin of art, through his pioneering analyses of cinema stars, sociology of media, the critique of totalitarianisms, as well as the different volumes of *La Méthode*, mimesis is a key—and until now mostly neglected—problematic that is constitutive of the emergence of his complex thought. As Morin puts it in volume 3 of *La Méthode*: "Humans are not chameleons but they dispose of extremely diverse mimetic possibilities" (1986, 146). What Morin says about the complexity of human life in general applies to a multifaceted concept like mimesis specifically, a complex phenomenon that is "at the same time, biological, psychic, social, affective, and rational" (1999, 42). At stake in mimesis then is a "physico-bio-anthropo-social" complex central to a "humanistic culture" that encourages new generations of researchers to go beyond the "simplifying paradigm of disjunction/reduction" (1991, 71) dominant today and reconnect knowledge instead—a gesture that, as Morin never tires to stress, is inherent to the very definition of complexity: from *complexus*, tied or woven together.

In this dialogue, I take mimesis as a guiding thread within the labyrinth of Morin's complex thought in order to further delineate the plural identity of homo mimeticus, a Janus-faced figure animated by fundamental tensions and contradictions that do not allow for harmonious syntheses and, as we have seen, reach into the present. Morin is sensitive to what I designated as the patho(-)logies of mimesis to call attention to both its rational and irrational sides, stressing both the pathos and the logos constitutive of *homo mimeticus*. Hence, throughout his corpus, he reminds us that humans are not only *homo sapiens* but also *homo demens*, not only *homo economicus* or *homo faber* but also homo *homo sacer* and *homo ludens* (1999, 69). The aim of this dialogue is to begin to show that mimesis, as both Morin and I understand it, lies at the heart of the contradictions that animate the complexity of living through the multiple crises of the twentieth and twenty-first centuries—a vital concept to urgently rethink to face crises that are yet to come.[8]

## The Heart of the Matter

**Nidesh Lawtoo [NL]:** Having had the pleasure of reading your inspiring transdisciplinary work over the years, I could not help but notice that although you never devoted a single work explicitly to mimesis, this complex concept can perhaps serve as a thread to orient oneself in the labyrinthine thought on complexity. Let us thus go straight to the heart of the matter, to *Le Vif du sujet* (1969), to echo the title of one of your most autobiographical early books, and start from a subjective, lived, and hence experiential and affective point of view.

I propose to begin with a personal paradox, since, for you, the object of thinking is inseparable from the subject who thinks. I could perhaps formulate it as follows: imitation is constitutive of the birth of the subject, since, especially in childhood and adolescence, although not only then, imitation directs the self toward models which, good or bad, consciously or unconsciously, have the effect of "imprinting" our formation. Extending Konrad Lorenz's ethological observation to culture, you note: "Cultural imprinting marks humans since birth with the seal of familial culture first, then with primary school, which is then continued by the university or the profession" (1999, 31).

In light of this ancient insight, I noted a paradox in your autobiographical writings: you deem yourself as not too marked by the cultural imprinting of dominant institutional models (family, school, university), and, in this sense, you apparently identify as an anti-mimetic subject; at the same time, you say that you have been very open to imitating models outside dominant frames (heroes from novels and cinema but also friends, masters, fellow resistants). Is there a dialogic link between these two seemingly contradictory perspectives? And if so, how does it reflect your understanding of complexity?

**Edgar Morin [EM]**: I think these two aspects are linked. Since I have no truth in me, as soon as anyone formulates a truth, I can find it convincing in some respects and unconvincing in others. I could thus go from one truth to another. This is not really mimetism; it is more the absence of strong dogmatic systems so as to withstand the most contradictory truths. This has made me sensitive to systems of contradictions.

I first felt the mimetic side in me, and I say this in my book on aesthetics, when I was young, especially as a student. I used to make sketches, caricatures of people who were close to me—comrades, friends, teachers. It amazed me that I could make portraits resemble the person without looking at them. Whenever I tried to draw by looking at the person, in an analytic way, focusing on the forehead, the nose etc. ... the sketch did not resemble them.[9] The resemblance came more from a mimetic capacity. This is why I think that, at the origin of art, those who made prehistoric paintings in the dark, narrow caves of Chauvet and Lascaux, without seeing the animals, must have had in them a mimetic power.

We all have, since childhood, a mimetism that not only makes us learn words and language but also makes us integrate certain facial expressions, the manners of laughing and speaking of people who influenced and mark us, usually our parents. I have seen this mimetic character in my close friends. At any given moment, one of them would laugh as I do, and I would laugh as he or she does. There are minimal unconscious mimetisms throughout all our lives. This is how I see mimesis. Even as I grow older, I have seen young collaborators who unconsciously imitate my manner of speaking and I myself, unconsciously, reproduce certain expressions that I like.

**NL**: One of my methodological assumptions is that in order to really understand mimesis one must grasp it from the outside as well as from the inside: that is, with a critical distance that aims to be as objective as possible but also via an affective participation that draws on what Georges Bataille (a figure you knew personally) called "inner experience [*expérience intérieure*]." Since mimesis is a Janus-faced concept, it would thus be necessary to adopt a double perspective to apprehend both sides: a logic-rational side through disciplines like philosophy, the social sciences, and neurosciences, as well as a *patho*-logical side, in the sense that this rational discourse or logos must attend to the affect or pathos at play on the side of arts and literature, as well as in a lived individual and collective experiences.

In light of this Janus-faced approach, do you think mimesis is a faculty proper to all humans? What else have you learned about imitation while imitating with pathos, besides what you already knew from the various academic discourses you draw on, be it anthropology, sociology, or film studies among other disciplines? Can you give us any examples?

**EM**: Each person has, potentially, a mimetic aptitude. The theory of mirror neurons is perhaps one of the discoveries that, at least at the level of the brain, allows us to understand the conditions of mimesis. I think that the mimetic capacity depends in every case on the individual person: those with very rigid, determined personalities have an underdeveloped mimetic capacity; those with a more open personality, one more sensitive to the presence of others, have developed it more. While studying movie stars, for instance, I recognized something that I had always experienced. Early on, since I was ten years old, after my mother died, cinema became my home. As happens to every spectator during the screening, I experienced mimetically what my favorite characters experienced.

One film that particularly impressed me is *The Sailors of Kronstadt* (directed by Efim Dzigan, 1936). In this film, a political commissar goes by boat to stir the sailors of Kronstadt so that they resist the attack of the White Army during the [Russian] Revolution of 1917. This commissar impressed me. He had a meditative, silent attitude and wore a leather jacket. When I joined the resistance during the German occupation, I got myself a secondhand leather jacket. I often enjoyed putting on the meditative air of a political leader. I think this genre of mimesis diminishes as one becomes an adult, but it is very strong during infancy, adolescence, and youth.

## Anthropology of the Double

**NL:** We will return to cinema, a mimetic art which not only represents reality from a distance but also affects spectators with pathos in ways that are performative, as you just indicated. But to proceed in the chronological order of your books, let me change disciplinary perspective. Although literature and film played a formative role in your life, your starting point to think about mimesis is not aesthetic in the sense of a reproduction or a representation of reality as one finds it, for example, in realism or photography.

At the beginning of your career, you were interested in a more general anthropological conception of mimesis understood as an affective participation that ties humans to other people, but also to the animal world, the natural, and the supernatural. In *L'Homme et la mort*, you write: "Man mimes everything, it is the mimetic animal par excellence. Mimetism is the faculty of resonating with the environment, an opening to the world, participation itself, the possibility of being in confusion with the other" (1970, 99). This definition of mimesis as participation or *methexis* recalls the theories of magic found in Lucien Lévy-Bruhl and Roger Caillois, as well as Georges Bataille, who you often quote, although these writers have become more marginal in the postwar period.

Contrary to structuralist thought founded on a linguistic binary model that opposes nature to culture and has dominated the human sciences since the 1950s, these anthropologists have been attentive to experiences of communication or affective participation that are not solely linguistic and transgress, diagonally, oppositions such as nature/culture, but also the imaginary and the symbolic, the self and the other, the body and the mind. This might be also one of the reasons why, since you did not embrace the structuralist and poststructuralist fashions that were so successful in the United States, few of your books have been translated into English so far, while they have been translated in more than twenty other languages. And for this reason, relying on this prestructuralist anthropological tradition, you already offered an account of humans that is not anthropocentric, goes beyond the opposition between culture and nature, and allows us to think of humans in mimetic relation with other humans but also the nonhuman.

These insights have been making a comeback now that the structuralist fashion has been overcome. What do you think is the bio-socio-anthropological need of this mimesis of affective participation within archaic societies? And how has mimesis contributed to the birth of *Homo sapiens*?

**EM:** No doubt it must play a role in the birth of language and poetry. I am thinking in particular of the imitation of birdsong, for example. Ever since we attained the glottic possibility, the internal cavity that permits multiplying sounds and especially singing, the mimetic capacity became very large. Our hunting ancestors could imitate animal cries very easily. The vocal mimetic capacity of the human being is very large, and I think that it played a very important role in the development of language, as well as gestures and customs. One must recall that, for millennia, humanity did not have schools. Learning occurred through mimesis, influence, reproduction.

In the animal world, it is evident that certain animals practice a physical mimesis or mimetism. Certain insects imitate tree leaves, the chameleon imitates the colors of its environment, for example. In other words, mimesis is not originally human. In nature, there is a mimetic capacity for both defense and ornament. However, this capacity is evident in a creativity that is manifested at the moment of reproduction, the site par excellence of mutations and transformations. For us, this mimetic capacity happens at the level of our brain, our mind—above all, of our culture.

Yet, to retake those elements of truth of earlier theories that were abandoned with Lévi-Strauss but that remain interesting today, in what was called totemism, there was a common ancestor who could be an animal. People identified themselves with animals. "The Bororos are araras," according to the famous phrase, means that Bororos are also parrots besides being human. We can consider ourselves as relatives of a different animal species if we consider it as our ancestor. I have never done it systematically, but it would be interesting to study in a systematic manner the role that mimetism plays in this phenomenon.

**NL:** It would certainly be a fascinating subject of a transdisciplinary PhD in new mimetic studies. In your own work, the tropes of the shadow and of the double are some of the main cultural manifestations of mimesis. In both cases, it is not only a copy or a representation that is at stake, but a participatory mimesis that gives life or soul to humans, while placing them in the proximity of death, phantoms, or ancestors. You specify that "the double is not a copy, an image [representation] of the living which, at the origin, survives death, but its own reality, an *ego alter*. The ego alter is truly Rimbaud's 'I' is another [*Je est un autre*]'" (Morin 1970, 153). You also write elsewhere that "most often, we ignore that we are possessed" (2005, 91).

Here we find the idea that mimesis transforms us, takes possession of us; it turns us into someone other, according to a logic that is, once again, paradoxical: on the one hand, at play in the shadow is a dispossession of the ego and a loss of one's proper identity, which is tied to the loss of the self, the dissolution of the ego, and *death*; on the other hand, the shadow is not the ego itself but its double, which animates and therefore gives *life* to the ego, giving it a soul, so to speak. Could you explain the dialogic relation between death and life, possession and dispossession that you see at work in the anthropology of the double and the shadow?

**EM:** Yes, the double is an experience that comes from shadows, reflections, and dreams. When one dreams, one knows that one has done things during sleep. So, the double is an experience of the living. Each one of us is "accompanied," more or less unconsciously, by a double that appears when, for example, we look in the mirror. This double survives as a spectral, immaterial being, whereas the body decomposes. This is not exactly mimetism; it is more a projection of the image of the self that one identifies with, while preserving a certain alterity. It is an alter ego, or an ego alter, if you want.

## Cinema and New Media

**NL:** Your books on cinema, *The Cinema, or the Imaginary Man* (1956) and *The Stars* (1957), are among your few books translated into English so far and have long been considered pioneers and classics of film studies. In these books, you transpose, in a transdisciplinary and original manner, the anthropology of mimesis (doubles and shadows) you explored in your work on death to the domain of aesthetics at play in film (cinematic shadows, movie stars). We go from physical rituals to imaginary rituals, but the mimetic capacity of projecting/identifying with nonhuman (animal, technological) shadows and phantoms remains the same. It is even amplified by the technology of projection and by the embodied situation of the spectator in cinema: that is, the semihypnotic relaxation produced by sitting in a dark room which, like a cave, assembles spectators in a collective ritual. How is it that the identification with a fictional shadow can be stronger than the identification with real persons? And that a state of physical passivity can make us psychically active?

**EM**: Before cinema, we must remember that we also have the capacity of identifying with characters in novels. We also have it in the theater. It is above all on the issue of theater that Aristotle talks about this mimesis that allows for catharsis. In the cinema, it is more intense. Why? Because we are in a semihypnotic situation, in a dark hall with magnified images. One sees close-ups of faces that have an extraordinary psychic and suggestive power, a very strong presence of a different nature than that of the theater actor who is physically present. It has another intensity. During the spectacle, there is a mimesis at play when we associate the actress, who is a star, and her character. Once we have seen her, we remain attached to the star that we love. This happened to me with Brigitte Helme, the German star of *Queen of Atlantis* (directed by George Wilhelm Pabst, 1932). Cinema, reinforced by music, allows for the psychic participation of the spectator in this mimetic and semihypnotic state.

**NL**: It is a commonplace to remark that the dispositive of cinema recalls a mythical scene that very much resembles the cave described by Plato in book 7 of the *Republic*. Plato emphasizes the illusory dimension of shadows, which are twice removed from the world of ideas and thus from what he consider true, but he is also conscious of the affective power that these shadows have to imprison the spectators in what I call the *vita mimetica* of the Greek city, or *polis*. Prisoners are, in fact, chained; they are forced to watch these shadows that move and appear to speak (there is "an echo" in the cave, Plato says) as magnetized or hypnotized by them. This critical tradition of the power of subjugation of cinema continues until the twentieth century with thinkers of the Frankfurt School such as Theodor Adorno and Max Horkheimer, for example, who emphasize the imprisoning, ideological side of the cultural industries. You are of course familiar with this tradition you helped introduce in France via your journal *Arguments*, but in your books, you put the accent on the emancipatory, and magical side of cinema—a gesture that reminds us that mimesis is always double and that it cannot be enclosed within one-sided perspectives.

From the perspective of this constitutive duality between catharsis and contagion, let us cast a critical glance at the power of mimesis in the twenty-first century.

A great transformation is taking place with the digital revolution. We live in a society that is no longer that of (analog) cinema but that of the Internet, the iPhone, and the new (digital) media, which multiply screens as well as the duration of the immersion in another, parallel, perhaps a more ideal world (in Plato's sense), but not necessarily closer to the material reality of immanent life (in Nietzsche's sense).

The advantages of the diffusion of information, of a more egalitarian access to education, and the speed of communications are, of course, immense. I tried to contact you back in 2006 with a letter that you probably never received. It is thanks to the Internet, to email, that I could reach you in the first place and make this interview available for others on YouTube and now in a book in print but also available electronically. This is fantastic! At the same time, since mimesis is double and Janus-faced, it is remarkable that the dominant models in cinema, TV shows, video games, Internet, etc., are often violent and that this imaginary violence, instead of having cathartic effects, risks reproducing violence or at least rendering us insensitive to it, perhaps creating pathological dependences toward them, according to a patho-*logy* of contagion that I call "hypermimetic," since it links the virtual or hyperreal world to the real one. Recently, as part of the *Homo Mimeticus* project, I traced the genealogy of the ancient problematic of media violence reloaded by the digital age.[10] What are your current reflections on the catharsis/contagion debate with respect to the violence represented in new media?

**EM:** This problem had already been stated with respect to cinema in the early thirties, especially in the United States. There were already a number of films characterized by a certain violence, such as gangster films, or Westerns. This violence, it is true, was not as strong as today's but was present nonetheless. The idea was to know if cinema played a role in juvenile violence. Afterwards, the question was posed with respect to comics as well, due to parents' anxieties. The studies in fact demonstrated that the influence was minor. These images taught above all certain gestures, certain ways of using a shotgun or breaking into buildings, but this was not a powerful incitation to violence.

Now, today, the violent stimuli that you mention are multiple and omnipresent. Does it have a bigger impact? There is total ambivalence. To retake the example of cinema, at that time, for the majority of adult spectators who led a tranquil, bourgeois, ritualized, and chronometrized life, these violent adventures entailed not so much a catharsis but a way of exempting their violent desires through dreaming. It is not a catharsis at all but rather a psychosis, if you like.

Today, there is a conjunction of factors that are directly connected. First of all, the formation of a relatively autonomous adolescence within our societies, which did not exist in this way before, since a great part of youths lived between the cocoon of infancy and the integration into adult life, which brings larger aspirations, turbulence, and revolt. What you say is therefore true. I lived the development of the French rock generation, with Johnny Hallyday and others. It was interesting. There was a manifestation [at the Place de la Nation], which at first was completely pacific. Yet the youths who gathered there started breaking everything. Next to that you have today's social conditions, the diminished authority of teachers, the freedom given to youths ... All of this can enable the irruption of violence but can also enable ceremonies where liberation takes place in fervor and dance, as in rock concerts.

Within all these factors, the imitation of images plays a role. I could not quantify this role; I think it would be hard to do, but I don't think this is an issue. The question is to know in what respect imitation eases off some people and, on the contrary, excites other people, a minority. To take another example, consider the Brazilian favelas, where it is above all the breakup of families, social misery, the grip that the mafia and drugs have over the population, that turns four-year-olds into delinquents, even criminals. The principal factor is not mediatic, but sociologic. Consider Medellin, which was a city with a large crime rate among children. Barbet Schroeder even made a film about it. In Medellin, a municipality managed to create, with the help of sponsors, a large training school for these lost children. They were taught the basics, but also dance, music, computing. They became socially recognized. As long as this school worked, there was a total cessation of violence. So, you have to see where the biggest responsibilities are.

**NL**: With respect to the relation between mimesis and violence, René Girard has become one of the major theorists of mimesis since the 1960s, attending primarily to its psycho-anthropological side. I believe early in your careers, your paths intersected. What is your position with respect to his mimetic theory, according to which mimetic desire necessarily leads to rivalry and to a contagious violence that can only be interrupted with another violent act, notably a sacrifice?

**EM**: René Girard has overvalued an aspect of the problem of mimesis. He has a tendency to reduce mimesis to rivalry. It is very interesting to reflect on mimetic desire after *Deceit, Desire and the Novel* (1961). It is very convincing but only with regards to these novels, theater pieces, and works of art. One cannot universalize his thesis. I also believe his idea that Jesus is the end of sacrifice to be false. On the contrary, it is the perpetuation of human sacrifice that is restarted at every Mass.

## Ethics and the Ecology of Action

**NL**: In many ways, my theory of imitation is intended as a correction or alternative to Girard's overemphasis on rivalry. It aims to consider both the violent and empathic sides not of mimetic desire alone but of mimetic *pathos*. On the patho-*logical* side, the question of *sym-pathos*, or sympathy, opens the way for a rethinking of ethical relationship with others who, given the human reflex for mirroring forms of affective participation with human and nonhuman influences, are not simply exterior to the ego but are constitutive of it—what I call, following Pierre Janet, a *socius* (Lawtoo 2013, 260–283).

At the same time, this ethical relation, as you emphasize, must be understood within the frame of an "ecology of action" that escapes the intention of the subject and which, taken within systemic feedback loops of action and retroaction, can lead to results that go against the initial intentions. As you put in the last volume of *La Méthode*, devoted to ethics: "the effects of an action depend not only on the intentions of the actors, but also of the specific conditions internal to the milieu where this action unfolds" (2004, 47). A well-intentioned relation of identification or affective sympathy with the other, for instance, depending on the specificity of the context in which it is performed, can involuntarily generate unintended negative ethical consequences. I was wondering if mimesis plays a role within this ecology of action?

**EM**: I don't think it does a priori. The idea of the ecology of action is, first, to realize that every decision is a wager; second, [it is] to realize that action within a given milieu elevates the reactions and the contradictions of the milieu and risks escaping the will of the decider. So, it is a matter of developing a strategy. But I do not see a direct relation with mimesis.

**NL**: Let me provide more context to better frame my question. The ethics that emerges from your account of the ecology of action is not founded upon universal moral imperatives that can be applied a priori across different contexts. You do not think as a Kantian on ethical issues. On the contrary, you like to recall Hegel's phrase that "one cannot reduce the criminal to her crime." In the processes of analyzing some of Joseph Conrad's nautical tales in which a crime is committed on board a ship, your concept of "ecology of action" made me think of the feedback loops that entangle human and environmental actions in unpredictable ways that call for a re-evaluation of what is good and evil, depending on the context (Lawtoo 2016, 59–85). Could there be feedback loops within relations of compassion and sympathy, for instance, where well-intentioned actions produce retroactions in humans or nonhumans that are contagious, and in this sense mimetic, with harmful ethical effects at the systemic and social level?

**EM**: That is an example of phenomena of good will that produce contrary effects. There is misplaced sympathy. Perhaps I could, through mimetic sympathy, feel confident about someone based on a face that I like and realize later that he stabbed me in the back. Thus, with respect to Hegel's phrase that "one cannot reduce a criminal to her crime," I recently saw the film by Jacques Audiard, *The Sisters Brothers* (2018)—it is extraordinary. Two brothers, two brutes, two killers are charged by a cynical commodore of having killed someone in Texas. All the film follows the brothers, and, almost at the end, one gradually discovers the humanity of one of the two characters. It is a virtue of great works, such as [Fyodor] Dostoyevsky's *Crime and Punishment* (1866), to show how killers were pushed into their situations. In Audiard's film, we learn that their father was an alcoholic, that the younger brother has killed the father because he was violent. We realize there is a terrible background that has determined their situation. We also see that one of the brothers is attached to the one who is a killer in order to protect him, thus out of love.

This, I think, is complex thought: discovering the potential for regret and transformation in human beings. This is the truth that Hegel's phrase expresses. Cinema makes us capable of empathy. In *The Birdman of Alcatraz* (John Frankenheimer, 1962), we sympathize with people who commit crimes or have committed crimes because we are shown aspects of their humanity. What is interesting is that, as much as watching a film we become insightful and intelligent and understand the characters; even though we are in a semihypnotic state, we become closed and obtuse again as soon as we leave the cinema. This is the tragedy.

## Mimesis, Society, and Politics

**NL**: Let us thus enter the tragedy of twentieth- and twenty-first-century history. Your impressive and admirable life spans most of the twentieth century. You were engaged in the resistance in the 1940s, and you have seen the power of dominant ideologies (communism, Stalinism, fascism, and Nazism) as well as the horrors and blindness generated by these totalitarianisms. You speak about this in many autobiographical texts, notably *Autocritique* (1959) and *Mes Démons* (1994). You hold that social imitation plays a role in the diffusion of totalitarianisms. In an analogy that I also found in Gabriel Tarde, for example, you say that totalitarianisms have the power of inducing mimetic effects of "somnambulism," of hypnosis, which manifest themselves above all in the masses and that are amplified by the mass media: radio, newspapers, and TV in the twentieth century.

With the rise of new digital media in the twenty-first century, the hypnotic power seems to have intensified; many, including myself, fear a return of fascist or neofascist regimes. A return not of the same fascism of the last century but perhaps of its "phantom"—what I call "(new) fascism." As I see it, (new) fascist leaders amplify the pathological powers of mimesis through new media (Twitter, Facebook, etc.) that spread lies or conspiracies that deny facts and accelerate what you call the race "toward the abyss [*abîme*]" What political lessons do you draw from the double face of mimesis (sympathy and identification but also somnambulism, hypnosis) throughout the twentieth century? And what must be retained to avoid the worst in the twenty-first?

**EM**: There are two things. To begin with, the fact that communism has been a religion. A religion of earthly, not heavenly salvation anymore. It is a religion in all its aspects: the struggle of good against evil, the promise of a better world, of an ideal world, the final apocalypse; even the proletariat was seen as the figure of the savior, of the messiah. As in all great religions, it was a factory of martyrs, tormentors, saints, or monsters. These are profoundly religious phenomena. Communism has imposed an absolute truth, and even those who did not believe were forced to obey. But even if communism was a universal religion like Christianity, Nazism was the religion of a superior race, which reinforced itself in the conscience of being this Aryan race. At the same time, nations, and above all nationalisms, are based on a religious cult of the nation for which one must kill or be killed, as in any good religion. So, there has been this religious side of a superior nation, called on to guide humanity.

In addition to that, Nazism relied on the charismatic personality of Hitler. Hitler entered a "post-shamanic" state of trance, a hysterical trance, which had an extraordinary effect in galvanizing his German listeners. In a certain way, Goebbels also had this oratorical gift. Stalin did not have it, but his myth, his image and cult, made up for his failure as an orator. These phenomena are profound religious phenomena which have engendered a crazy hope, and which ran aground: one to military defeat, the other to the autocollapse of the system in a situation of international competition. After this, the older religions have returned. The lesson is that we need to maintain a balance between the idea of individual autonomy on the one hand, and a profound relation to community, on the other. This is the equilibrium that must be retained, a difficult one.

**NL**: I could not agree more. This oscillation between communal pathos and individual distance, or pathos of distance, is in many ways, the soul of my theory of imitation. Furthering this dialogic view, against a still current academic tendency that tends to place knowledge in two rival cultures (the humanities and the empirical science), under the impulse of cybernetics but already before it, you worked early on toward relinking these two fields, relying on the humanities to give a conscience to the sciences, and employing science to provide empirical foundations for the humanities. With respect to imitation, the discovery of mirror neurons in the 1990s, found first in primates and then in humans, provides an empirical basis for the human tendency toward imitation, a tendency that has long been recognized at least since Plato and Aristotle and animates aesthetic spectacles that go from the theater and cinema to new media.

This discovery has also generated controversies given its broader cultural, social, and philosophical implications. It offers, in fact, an empirical explanation for the intersubjective aspects of communication based on automatic and unconscious reflex mechanisms, which, figures like Giacomo Rizzolatti and Vittorio Gallese argue, play a role in understanding others as well as in sympathy or empathy. This discovery has also been criticized in the humanities, perhaps because it complicates the dominant notions of free will, intentionality, autonomy, and rational control that characterize idealizations of *Homo sapiens*. What do you think about the contributions of the neurosciences for an understanding of a homo mimeticus that is open to reason and unreason, to consciousness and unconsciousness?

**EM**: The phenomenon of mirror neurons does not diminish autonomy. It is a phenomenon that manifests itself almost unconsciously. We are not conscious that we incorporate mimetically what our interlocutor says, but this unconscious process does not diminish our capacity to control the situation. So, the neurosciences, or better, the sciences of the brain, have some very important contributions.[11] Besides mirror neurons, Antonio Damasio's insight on reason and emotion is very important as well. Why? Because from the moment we know that emotion is always present, even in a rational moment, we have a more interesting vision of our relationships with others.

## Aesthetics and Homo Mimeticus

**NL:** As your engagement with cinema already indicated, your conception of aesthetics is based on a complex understanding of mimesis that grounds art in the social, spiritual, and affective life of human beings. As you put it, cinema entails a "mimetic power" that "generates conducts, opinions, actions" (2018, 132), and rightly so, for humans' aesthetic drives are rooted in the senses, and from the very beginning.

In particular, in your book *Sur l'esthétique* (2016), you link anthropology and art, the figure of the shaman and that of the artist, and propose a mimesis of affective participation, of semipossession or trance at the origin of art. At stake is always a mimesis of magical participation that, I agree with you, characterizes our imaginary conception of death, our relationship to theater, cinema and art in general, and which you see already at play at the very origin of aesthetic representations in prehistoric cave paintings. Regarding the impressive paintings at Lascaux and, even earlier, at Chauvet, you speak of the "psychic mimetic capacity" to "create resemblance with animals without seeing the model" (2016, 42; my trans.). The ability of the shaman/artist to enter into a trancelike state of identification with the animal, according to your hypothesis, enables the analogic representation in the darkness of the caves. From the dawn of art to the sketches of your friends you mentioned at the beginning, affective mimesis not only seems to precede but enables realistic representations. Does this mean that an affective participation gives birth to a technique of reproduction and so that artistic capacity is an effect and not a cause of mimesis?

**EM:** The way in which this is produced is hard to detail. Still, the idea of representing animals must have emerged at a given moment in the shamanic artist. The fact that this idea presented itself many times, in caves or elsewhere, shows that there is a mimetic relationship that exists in nature between hunters and the animals they hunt. This relation was notoriously affective, and it is very strong with shamans who are able to identify with animals. Without a doubt, it is out of this experience in the heart of nature—probably during sacred ceremonies—that shamans experienced the need to represent animals. Once this idea appeared, shamans searched for the means to realize it with colors and instruments. What is extraordinary is that once they had this idea, they worked it out in an extraordinarily realistic manner.

**NL:** With respect to more recent arts, such as the novel, poetry, cinema, and new media, your approach stands apart from other dominant formalist tendencies on the autonomy of art because you emphasize the cognitive potential of art for life more generally. For example, with respect to the novel, you underline a complex and qualitative attention to affective life that supplements the reductionist and quantitative tendencies of the social sciences. What can art in general and mimetic studies in particular contribute to *Homo sapiens* in the twenty-first century?

**EM:** I think we do not have enough awareness of our mimetic capacities and that we must become conscious of them. They work without our being aware of them. However, we also have certain mimetic capacities that we could be capable of developing voluntarily. At bottom, what interests me is that these capacities require a certain subjective state of trance, which can be frenetic or soft. These secondary, particular, poetic states are very important for us, because they are very present in our lives, and we often do not realize it. Mimesis manifests itself in a state of trance, more or less soft, more or less strong. There are no precise words for these trances: they could be cases of what is called possession, or of hysteria, or of similar terms. These states, which are very frequent in our lives, should interest us more. We ignore them too much.

**NL:** Yes, indeed, mimesis, like water, tends to be imperceptible, and yet it's the water in which we swim and has such an influence over the course of our lives. To conclude, we have seen how complex thought illustrates the many bio-psycho-anthropo-sociologic aspects of mimesis and how this mode of thinking can account for paradoxes that go across periods, disciplines, and different experiences. In a mirror-reflex movement, could you sum up how mimesis illustrates complex thought and the pertinence of new mimetic studies for the twenty-first century?

**EM:** Mimesis is integrated into the complex vision of humanity. It is thus true that to the notions of *homo sapiens, demens, faber*, or *economicus*, we can add the term *homo mimeticus*.

# NOTES

### Introduction: Drawing Mimetic Studies

1. Dates in parenthesis following the title refer throughout to the original date of publication, or in this case, creation.
2. Contributors to the mimetic turn include J. Hillis Miller, Jean-Luc Nancy, William Connolly, Adriana Cavarero, Jane Bennett, Edgar Morin, Christoph Wulf, Gunter Gebauer, Katherine Hayles, among other influential figures. For a representative sample of dialogic encounters, see Miller and Lawtoo 2020, Nancy and Lawtoo 2022, Connolly and Lawtoo 2021, Cavarero and Lawtoo 2021, Bennett 2017, Hayles and Lawtoo 2022, as well as the special issue of *MLN* 132.5 (2017), *CounterText* 8:1 (2022), and *Journal of Posthumanism* 2:2 (2022).
3. As the classicist Gerald Else argues, mimesis was still a "rare word in the fifth century [BC]"; the "first and most obvious thing about *mimeisthai*, whatever its meaning, is that it is a denominative verb based on *mîmos*" (Else 1958, 74). Else specifies: "It can hardly be doubted that Aristotle [in the *Poetics*] is alluding to *mimoi*," which is "the name of a Sicilian dramatic genre" (76) and entails "a miming or mimicking of the external appearance, utterances, and/or movements of an animal or a human being by a human being." (78) For an informed overview of the history of mimesis as a "*conditio humana*" that starts with *mîmos* and goes from Plato to poststructuralism, see Gebauer and Wulf 1995; for a recent study of the image from the angle of mimesis qua performativity, see also Wulf 2022.
4. For a special issue on the "mimetic condition" in post-literary culture, see Lawtoo 2022a.
5. Mimetic studies would include mimetic theory as defined by René Girard but will not be reduced to it, as it rests on a more dynamic conception of homo mimeticus whose general contours we sketch here. For an assimilation of mimetic theory in new mimetic studies, see Borch 2019, Lawtoo 2023a, 2023b.
6. This is the case of the present book that was written thanks to funding from the European Research Council (ERC) and benefited from a transdisciplinary seminar that cut across the philosophy/arts binary, titled *Homo Mimeticus Seminar* (2017–).
7. See also Lacoue-Labarthe 2012b.
8. See *Lesser Hippias*, Plato 1963d.
9. See Lawtoo 2023a, 149–164.
10. For his analysis of *Drawing Hands*, see Hofstadter, 1999, 689–692.
11. Shorter versions appeared in the following journals: chapter 1 in *CounterText* 8.1 (2022): 61–87; chapter 3 in *Modern Language Notes* 134.5 (2019): 898–909; chapter 4 in *Modern Language Notes* 132.5 (2017): 1201–1224; chapter 5 in *Effects* 3 (2022): 20–33; chapter 6 in *Film-Philosophy* 25.3 (2021): 272–295; chapter 7 in *Political Research Quarterly* 74.2 (2021): 479–490. I am very grateful to all these journals for allowing me to reproduce, revise, and expand these articles to form a perspectival whole on homo mimeticus. Other articles not included here on mimetic perspectives that go from Bataille to D.H. Lawrence, *Avatar* to *Black Mirror*, conspiracy theories to the posthuman, can be found at http://www.homomimeticus.eu/publications/

12  For a philosophically informed genealogy of Lacan's theory of the imaginary as a "twenty-first century Platonism," see Borch-Jacobsen 1991, 64, 43-71..
13  For seminal studies that dramatize the (im)propriety of mimesis and of the mimetic subject, see Agacinski et al. 1975, Deleuze 1969, 292–324, Derrida 1981ab, Lacoue-Labarthe 1986, 1989, and Borch-Jacobsen 1988, 1993.
14  On sexual mimicry, see Irigaray 1977; on racial mimicry, see Bhabha 1994, 121–131; on gender imitation, see Butler 1991; for an overview on mimesis and subjectivity, see Potolsky, 2006, 115–135.
15  On "mimetic racism and sexism," see Lawtoo 2013, 108–131; on mimesis and "(new) fascism," see Connolly 2017b and Lawtoo 2019b.
16  For an early engagement with gendered/racial mimesis, see Lawtoo 2006. My engagement with postcolonial mimesis took two major figures in modernist and postcolonial literature, respectively, as paradigmatic examples—namely, Joseph Conrad and Chinua Achebe. See Lawtoo 2016, 129–209.
17  For Cavarero's feminist critique of *Homo erectus*, see also Cavarero 2016a. A more specific genealogy of gendered forms of mimetic inclinations focusing on Cavarero, Malabou, and Butler is currently ongoing in a project I lead, titled *Gender Mimesis*; it supplements a gendered perspective to voices already internal to *Homo Mimeticus* that deserve to be developed further.
18  In addition to the rich studies by Gebauer and Wulf and Potolsky already mentioned, for informed accounts of mimesis up to deconstruction, see also IJsseling 1990, Spariosu ed. 1984, and Melberg 2008.
19  I cannot fully address posthumanism here. For a special issue on "posthuman mimesis," see Lawtoo 2022b.
20  Jacque Derrida's insight is that, since Plato, "mimesis is lined up alongside truth," either "it hinders the unveiling of the thing itself by substituting a copy or double for what is" or by revealing it via the logic of "resemblance (*homoiōsis*)" (1981a, 187). Part of a deconstruction of Plato's vertical metaphysics that reduces writing to a copy of speech, this foundational Derridean move nonetheless preserves the traditional metaphysical conception of mimesis as a copy, representation, or adequation. Between the lines Derrida also points to the hypnotizing powers of "sorcerers" or "magicians (*pharmakeus*)" (1981b, 117–119) and to a theatrical "Mime [who] imitates nothing" (1981a, 194), which he left for others to explore further. On mimesis as mime "without proper identity," see Lacoue-Labarthe 1989, 248–266. For a discussion on the role mimesis plays in deconstruction, see also Miller and Lawtoo 2020.
21  I articulate the fundamental differences between my theory of homo mimeticus and Girard's mimetic theory, including his unavowed debt to Freud in Lawtoo 2013, 281-305, and 2023a, 33–80.
22  For an influential account of philosophy as "creation of concepts," see Deleuze and Guattari 1994, 8–10.
23  On the contagious, rather than cathartic properties of (new) media violence, see Lawtoo 2023b.
24  For seminal studies in media studies that resonate strongly with the oral tradition internal to mimetic studies, see McLuhan 1962, 1964; for a more recent guide to digital reason attentive to imitative processes, see Baetens, de Graef, Mandolessi 2020.

## Chapter 1: Birth of Homo Mimeticus

1. For an informed, overarching account of the history of mimesis from Plato to Derrida, see Gebauer and Wulf 1995; for a recent post-Derridean/Girardian supplement on the "mimetic condition," see *CounterText* 8.1 (2022).
2. Interesting in their own right, they have already received attention in the past century; see, for instance, Aarselff 1982.
3. For a genealogy of violence that furthers the mimetic turn and finds in Nietzsche a main representative, see Lawtoo 2023a, 2023b
4. References to Nietzsche's aphoristic works will give the aphorism's number followed by page number; in case of works divided into parts, references will be to part and section number, followed by page number. To minimally contextualize the phrase, it is Nietzsche's mirroring reply contra positivism, which reads as follows: "Against positivism, which halts at phenomena—'There are only *facts*—I would say: No, facts is precisely what there is not, only interpretations'" (1968, 481:267). For an informed account of perspectivism, see Alloa 2020; for a contextualization of Nietzsche's take on metaphor in relation to consciousness and the body, see Emden 2005; on Nietzsche and the origins of language, see also Mangion 2012. What follows foregrounds the centrality of mimesis in Nietzsche's genealogy of *logos* (both reason and language) out of mimetic *pathos*.
5. I trace in detail Nietzsche's mimetic patho(-)logies at play in phantom egos in Lawtoo 2013, 27–83. This chapter extends the diagnostic back in time. For other studies attentive to mimesis in Nietzsche's corpus, see also Lacoue-Labarthe 1986; Parkes 1994; Siemens 2021.
6. For a penetrating analysis of the tensions internal to Nietzsche physio-psychology, see Staten 1990 and Pearson 2022; for a vitalist reading beyond nature/culture binary in Nietzsche, see Bennett and Connolly 2002; for an account of biopower attentive to Nietzsche patho(-)logical evaluation of mimetic infection and immunization, see Esposito 2004, 79–114.
7. This is arguably the source of inspiration for Roger Caillois's analogy between animal mimicry and a human psychopathology called "legendary psychasthenia," whereby the patient feels like "dissolving in space" (1938, 86–122). Nietzsche considers mimicry as an evolutionary mechanism for survival, whereas Caillois sees in it a loss of individuation akin to a psychic death. Still, Caillois's specific attention to the link between human mimetism, animal mimicry, and death is in line with Nietzsche's insight that via the "chromatic function" many animals "pretend to be dead or assume the forms and colours of another animal or of sand, leaves, lichen, fungus (what English researchers designate 'mimicry')" (Nietzsche 1982, 26:20). I shall return to Caillois in more detail in chapters 5, 6, and 7.
8. For a Girardian evolutionary supplement see Antonello and Gifford; for a genealogical reconsideration of Girard's Freudian epistemic foundations and the development of a Nietzschean alternative, see Lawtoo 2023a.
9. For an incisive and creative contestation of the nature/culture binary in Nietzsche, see Bennett and Connolly 2002. I will return to both Bennett's and Connolly's contribution to the mimetic turn in chapter 5 and 7 respectively.
10. Nicolas Lema Habash is particularly attentive to the political implications of the "language without logos" internal to this section, see Habash 211–215.
11. I first gave an account of the mimetic unconscious in Lawtoo 2013; see also Lawtoo 2019a, 2023b.

12  The passage specifies: "All that the philosopher asserts about humanity, however, is basically nothing more than testimony about the human being of a *very restricted* stretch of time" (Nietzsche 1997, 2:16).
13  See Lawtoo 2019a, 48–50.
14  For an initial account of maternal forms of nonlinguistic communication, see Lawtoo 2013, 40–43, 272–276, and Cavarero and Lawtoo 2021, 192–196.
15  See also Baetens, de Graef, and Mandolessi 2020, 30–36
16  On maternal sympathetic instincts, see also Hrdy 1999.
17  See, for instance, Corballis 2002; Wulf 2004, 183–198; Armstrong and Wilcox 2007; Tomlinson 2015, 71; Staten 2019, 77–78. All these studies support Nietzsche's mimetic hypothesis from different perspectives.

### Chapter 2: *Vita Mimetica* in the Cave

1  Yuval Harari revitalizes an ancient idea, as he stresses "that belief in shared myths" is central to building "astounding networks of mass cooperation" (2014, 117, 115). This is a central historical insight still in need of a philosophical supplement. Unlike Plato, and later Nietzsche, Harari does not focus on myth's primary medium of mass communication: namely, mimesis. Hence the need to complement the history of *Sapiens* with a genealogy of homo mimeticus.
2  I trace a genealogy of the phantom of the ego in Nietzsche's thought in Lawtoo 2013.
3  For admirable deconstructive readings of Plato's mimetic practice, see Derrida 1981b and Lacoue-Labarthe 1989, 43–138.
4  If the *vita contemplativa* starting with Plato is clearly *anti*-mimetic in its theoretical orientation away from both sensible and aesthetic phenomena, the *vita activa* for Arendt is not less anti-mimetic. As she puts it, overturning Plato but echoing him as well, the *vita activa* is rooted in the uniqueness of plural individuals who are not "endlessly reproducible repetitions of the same model whose nature or essence was the same for all" (Arendt 1998, 8).
5  In the *Republic*, Plato is critical of mimesis at the level of his *logos*, yet in *Phaedrus* he aligns philosophy with different forms of madness (*mania*) that include poetic and thus mimetic madness; see Plato 1961b, 244a–252a.
6  For a perceptive reframing of Plato's critique of mimesis from the angle of techne or "knowledge-based action" that is "incompatible with the general idealizing trend of Platonic thought" and is sensitive to an immanent transmission of crafts via imitation of examples, see Staten 2019, 47–61.
7  Translations of Nancy's *Le Partage des voix* are my own.
8  This chapter picks up a connection between Plato's *Ion* and Nietzsche's *The Birth of Tragedy* I first noted in Lawtoo 2013, 64–66. For a rich and foundational oral corrective to a devocalization of the Logos in western philosophy this chapter aims to further, see also Cavarero 2005.
9  A feminist precursor like Luce Irigaray called attention to the cave's "theatrical artifice" shot through both vertical (phallic) symbols and a womb-like "theatrical pregnant enclosure [*enceinte*]" that destabilizes the metaphysics of the same via specular mirroring effects characteristic of a "topographic mime [*mime topographique*]" (Irigaray 1974, 302–304, my trans.). See also 301–320.

10   See Burckhardt, 1998, 160–213. I first developed the productive, patho-*logical* dynamic of mimetic agonism via Nietzsche in Lawtoo 2013: 27–81 and then more systematically in Lawtoo 2023a, 45–57. For an informed study on Nietzsche's agonistic philosophy that resonates with the study at hand, see also Siemens 2021.

11   For a selection of his writings on mimesis, see Lacoue-Labarthe 1989, 1986, and chapter 4 in this volume.

12   On mimesis and methexis, see also Nancy 2016.

13   The full passage establishes a link between hermeneutics and rhapsody via the link of a "'knowledgeable' [*savante*] mimesis" (Nancy 1982, 78) and reads as follows: "*Hermeneia* is *mimesis*, but an active *mimesis*, creative or re-creative, or again it is a mimetic creation, but effectuated by a mimesis that proceeds from *methexis*, of a participation itself due to enthusiasm—unless mimesis is not the condition of this participation" (71). Cavarero's avowed proximity to Nancy on the *partage des voix* is thus also implicitly a proximity to Lacoue-Labarthe, which is redoubled by their shared attention to "echoes" and the "song of the muses." See Lacoue-Labarthe 1989, 139–207, and 2005. For Nancy's reflections on his shared thought and life with Lacoue-Labarthe, see Girard and Nancy 2015, 12–64, and Nancy and Lawtoo 2021, 151–157. I shall return to the Nancy-Lacoue shared interest in mimesis in more detail elsewhere.

14   Registering the hypnotic spell of the "contagious delirium, descend[ing] from the Muse to the audience" (2002, 51) in magnetic terms that recall the chain in the "Allegory of the Cave," Cavarero's interpretation struggles with this specific central question: "why do the poets-charlatans in Plato's depiction of the cave use artifices involving sight rather than the sweet sound of verse?" (2002) Our answers share a focus on orality, embodiment, and affect. A minor difference, as I see it, is that Plato's emphasis on vision is not only a philosophical trick to displace orality—though it is that, and the trope of the mirror in book 10 will eventually succeed in tricking metaphysically inclined minds for millennia. Vision, in fact, is also part of artistic powers that resound with the oral tradition of mimos qua performance. If I stress this, it is less for philological reasons that are past oriented and more for theoretical concerns with the amplifying effects of both visual/oral mimetic powers in urgent need of diagnostics in a present and future oriented digital age.

15   In their dialogue on the Aristotelian concept of scene (*opsis*), Nancy reminds us that the "dialogue is the matrix form [*forme matricielle*] of philosophy" (2013, 73), and Lacoue-Labarthe follows up with a detailed account of the "sharing of voices [*partage des voix*]" (76) generated by the *lexis mimētikē* of the dialogue—yet another confirmation that Nancy's account of the sharing of voices cannot be disentangled from the problematic of mimesis as Lacoue-Labarthe understands it. On their voices in common, see also Lawtoo and Nancy 2021, 151–158.

16   Nancy confirms this point even with respect to *Ion*: "It is in Ion's enthusiasm that Homer's enthusiasm is interpreted, staged and not only to hear but also to see [*à voir*]" (1982, 74).

17   See Heidegger 1977.

18   Even a sophisticated phenomenological interpreter of mimesis like Samuel IJsseling falls into this epistemological trap, as he writes, commenting on the same lines: "The biggest problem here is that the actors do not speak in their own name, do not mean what they say and therefore do not consider themselves responsible for what they say" (1997, 12). Thus, the "how" is subordinated by the "what." But actors are not philosophers; they do not go onstage to mean what they say and be responsible for a *logos*; they go onstage to reanimate

ancient myths via the power of *pathos*—as Plato was the first to know, yet a chain of philosophers seems to have forgotten. For an important exception, see Havelock 1963.

19  I discuss the hypnotic effects of new media via the TV series *Black Mirror* in Lawtoo 2021.

## Chapter 3: Sameness and Difference Replayed

1  From 2013 to 2016, I held a position as visiting scholar at the Humanities Center, where I decided to apply for an ERC grant on homo mimeticus, out of which this book was born. I thank Paola Marrati and Hent de Vries for inviting me back in 2017 for a symposium titled The Structuralist Controversy and Its Legacy 50 Years Later; William (Bill) Connolly and Jane Bennett for numerous conversations on and around mimesis; and Richard (Dick) Macksey for sharing stories about the original symposium in his mythic home library. I could not have hoped for a more inspiring genealogical context for this chapter.

2  For an informed deconstructive account of Girard's theory that establishes genealogical connections—via Heidegger and Nietzsche—that go back to Plato's *Republic*, see Lacoue-Labarthe 1989, 102–121.

3  I offer a genealogical story of the birth of Girard's mimetic theory out of the 1966 structuralist controversy in Lawtoo 2023a, 57–67.

4  See Lawtoo 2013, 234–247, 284–295, 2018b, and 2023a, 33–80.

5  For a discussion with J. Hillis Miller on the role mimesis plays in "Mimique" and deconstruction more generally, see Lawtoo and Miller 2020.

6  McKenna sets out to "explicate Derrida and Girard via each other" in view of offering an anthropological supplement to deconstruction by "grounding" (1992, 24) the latter's (linguistic) concerns with signifiers in referential (sacrificial) practices. I suggest that the agon cuts both ways, for Girard is also indebted to Derrida, though more than one influence is at play.

7  What Girard says of Derrida's take on Socrates's rivalrous relation to the sophists is not deprived of strangely revealing mirroring effects that cast a shadow on Girard and Derrida as well: "he [Derrida] demonstrates that between Socrates and the Sophists, the structure of the opposition belies not the difference that Plato would like to establish but rather the reciprocity that is suggested by the recourse to one and the same word. All difference in doctrines and attitudes is dissolved in violent reciprocity, is secretly undermined by the symmetry of the facts and by the strangely revealing, even somewhat naïve use of *pharmakon*. This use polarizes the maleficent violence on a double, who is arbitrarily expelled from the philosophic community. From Plato right down to Nietzsche [and, we should add, Derrida and Girard] […] the philosophical tradition has piously reaffirmed this absolute difference" (Girard 1977, 296). Perhaps. Mimetic agonism, in any case, breaks with this violent tradition of expulsion, as it underscores both similarities and differences, or better, traces the emergence of sameness and difference.

8  I discuss romantic agonism in more detail in Lawtoo 2023a, 54–57.

9  I cannot address the mimetic relation between Bataille and Girard here. For starting points see Lawtoo 2013, 284–394, and Lawtoo 2019b.

10  I develop a genealogy of the Oedipal unconscious in Lawtoo 2023a.

11  See the sibling project to *Homo Mimeticus* titled *Gendered Mimesis*, http://www.homomimeticus.eu/gendered-mimesis-c1/

12  For important precursors, see Salomé 2001 and Irigaray 1991.

13   In addition to furthering chapter 1, this section deepens a genealogy of the mimetic unconscious started in Lawtoo 2013, and 2019a.
14   As Roberto Esposito rightly recognizes, "birth, procreation, pregnancy constitute perhaps the most symbolically charged figure of Nietzschean philosophy—itself qualified by the author as a painful childbirth" (Esposito 2004, 113; my trans.).
15   See, for instance, Borch 2019, Lawtoo 2023ab.
16   See Hurley and Chater 2005.
17   See Garrels 2011.
18   Culturally informed neuroscientists are careful to inscribe their discovery in a longer genealogy of mimetic insights in the humanities they treat with respect. Thus, Rizzolatti and Sinigaglia open *Mirrors in the Brain* with a reference to the theatrical director Peter Brook, who quipped that "with the discovery of mirror neurons, neuroscience had finally started to understand what has long been common knowledge in the theater" (2008, ix). Similarly, Gallese in an interview quotes Dante to show how "art can anticipate science" and goes as far as positing "the superiority of art with respect to science" (Wojciehowski, 2011) when it comes to insights into interpersonal mimetic relations. On the relation between mirror neurons and violence see also Iacoboni 2008 and Lawtoo 2023b; on mirror neuros and cultural evolution see Ramachandran 2011 and chapter 1. Nietzsche and the genealogy of mimetic thinkers I convoke fundamentally agree with these insights.
19   I borrow the concept of "*socius*" from the French psychologist and philosopher Pierre Janet, whose intersubjective psychology is constitutive of my theory of mimesis. See Lawtoo 2013, 266–280.
20   As the neuroscientist V. S. Ramachandran puts it, commenting on Meltzoff's work: "It has not been proven whether mirror neurons are responsible for these earliest imitative behaviors, but it's a fair bet. The ability would depend on mapping the visual appearance of the mother's protruding tongue or smile onto the child's own motor maps, controlling a finely adjusted sequence of facial muscle twitches" (2011, 127).

## Chapter 4: The Plasticity of Mimesis

1   Derrida's essay is, to my knowledge, still the most penetrating introduction to Lacoue-Labarthe's theory of mimesis. For book-length introductions to his thought in general, see Martis 2006 and Mckeane 2015; for special issues that foreground mimesis in particular, see *MLN* 132.5 (2017), where a first version of this chapter appeared, as well as *L'Esprit Créateur* 57.4 (2017) and *CounterText* 8.1 (2022).
2   Malabou delineates the "double meaning" this "speculative word" has for Hegel in Malabou 1996, 19–27.
3   See Lacoue-Labarthe 1993, 99–115, Girard 1977, 169–21, and Borch-Jacobsen 1988, 1992. For a historian of psychology that inherited via Borch-Jacobsen this mimetic genealogy and is mentioned by Malabou, see Leys 2000.
4   This collective volume played a key role, at least in France, in shifting mimesis from an ontology of sameness to one of difference. Lacoue-Labarthe's intervention in particular (the longest in the volume) started a focus on mimetic subjectivity the *Homo Mimeticus* project aimed to further almost half a century later.
5   Lacoue-Labarthe's agonistic relation with Heidegger, especially the latter's refusal to engage with the question of mimesis and Nazism, looms large in his mimetology. Yet, as Derrida

also recognized, "what he [Lacoue-Labarthe] does remains entirely different [from Heidegger]" (Derrida 1989, 28). It is this difference I find productive to further a theory of homo mimeticus in the twenty-first century.

6   See Harari 2011, 2017.
7   The conference was hosted by The Humanities Center on February 18–19, 2016.
8   For Lacoue-Labarthe's critique of Nazi mimetology see Lacoue-Labarthe 1987, Lacoue-Labarthe and Nancy 1990; I further this critique of fascist psychology for the mimetic turn in Lawtoo 2013 and 2019b.
9   In the context of a discussion of "the fabulous plasticity of humans," the ethologist Boris Cyrulnik gives a definition of culture that echoes Lacoue-Labarthe's definition of mimesis, as he states: "As for culture, its plasticity is so great that we could say that its only permanent trait is change!" (Cyrulnik 2010, 198; my trans.)
10  *L'Imitation des modernes*, in my opinion Lacoue-Labarthe's best book on the subject of mimesis, has regretfully still not been translated into English in its complete form. Selected chapters, including the essay on Diderot, have been translated and included in Lacoue-Labarthe 1989. When available, I will refer to Christopher Fynsk's English translation; otherwise, I will quote and translate from Lacoue-Labarthe 1986.
11  I discuss the mimetic agon between Plato and Aristotle via the catharsis and contagion hypothesis in Lawtoo 2023a, 2023b.
12  Compare Derrida's claim that the *pharmakon* of writing has "no 'proper' characteristics" (1981b, 125) or that "The Mime imitates nothing" (1981a 194); see also chapter 3.
13  On mimesis as an improper "supplement" that serves as structural inspiration for Lacoue-Labarthe's "mimetology," see Derrida 1967, 289–297 and 1981ab. While this dangerous supplement goes from the moderns all the way back to the ancients, the structural matrix of this paradox emerges at the juncture of "savage" and "structuralist" thought and can be traced further back to Lévi-Strauss's account of the Polynesian *mana*. As Lévi-Strauss puts it, outlining the "symbolic content *supplementarity*" *mana* is a "simple form" with "zero symbolic value [*valeur symbolique zéro*]" "capable of becoming charged with any sort of symbolic content whatever" (qtd. in Derrida 1972, 261; Derrida's emphasis). Once again, the traces lead us back to the 1966 Structuralist Controversy conferences discussed in chapter 3.
14  I am thankful to Jane for accepting my invitation to engage Lacoue-Labarthe's thought back at Johns Hopkins in 2016, for numerous friendly conversations, and for joining forces in entangling the new materialist turn with the mimetic turn I shall discuss in chapter 8.
15  Despite its inversion of Platonism, Diderot's mimetology remains of Platonic inspiration. Thus, he compares the mimetic actor to the Platonic trope of the "looking-glass" that represents a "perfect type" or "vast specter [*grand fantôme*]" the actor "copies," or "imagines," as an "unmoved disinterested onlooker" (Diderot 1992, 366). Plato's Ion would not have disagreed (see chapter 2).
16  For Lacoue-Labarthe's full commentary of this passage and its relation to Nietzsche's account of history, see Lacoue-Labarthe 1986, 97–101; see also Didi-Huberman 2000, 59–64.
17  On the relation between eroticism, transgression, and mimesis in Bataille, see Lawtoo 2018a.
18  The mimetic language of "impression" and "figure" is central to "Typography" but also to Lacoue-Labarthe's critique of Nazism and Heidegger; see Lacoue-Labarthe and Nancy 1990 and Lacoue-Labarthe 1987; on mimesis as rhythm, see "The Echo of the Subject" in Lacoue-Labarthe 1989, 139–207.

Notes    329

19   "[W]e are today on the eve of Platonism," writes Derrida, and he adds: "Which can also, naturally, be thought of as the morning after Hegelianism" (1981b, 107–108).

## Chapter 5: On Animal and Human Mimicry

1   For an informed collection on Bataille's influence on the linguistic turn that barely mentions Caillois, see Botting and Wilson 1997; on Bataille's contribution to the mimetic turn making preliminary connections with Caillois, see Lawtoo 2013, 209–280, and 2018a.
2   For a good selection of English translations of Caillois's work, see Frank 2003; for French readers a comprehensive selection can be found in Caillois 2008. What follows refers to both while including other books as well.
3   On the relevance of Bataille's critique of (new) fascism at the College, see Lawtoo 2019, 53–128. On Caillois's ambivalent evaluation of the sacred and the hierarchy it entails, see Hollier 1993, 56–59. As I finalize this book in the spring of 2022 Russia is currently invading Ukraine, resuscitating the horror of war in Europe and the threat of nuclear escalation globally.
4   For an informed introduction to Caillois see Frank 2003, 1–53; see also Hollier 1993, 55–71.
5   For a journal special issue on *Mimicries* devoted to Caillois where an abridged version of this chapter was published, see Stuker and Tumlir 2022; for an informed discussion of Caillois in the context of posthuman mimesis, see Wolf 2022.
6   On new materialism and mimesis, see Bennett 2017; on the recuperation of Caillois's materialist theory of mimetism for democratic pluralism, see Bennett 2020, 74–78, 86–88. These genealogical entanglements are rooted in real encounters that took place during my appointment at Johns Hopkins from 2013 to 2016: if I invited Jane to engage Lacoue-Labarthe's work, she reciprocated by inviting me to introduce Caillois's work. Our exchange, as chapter 8 makes clear, is ongoing.
7   In what follows I translate Caillois's *mimétisme* as "mimetism" and will retain "mimicry" for the instances in which Caillois uses the English term and for animal mimicry.
8   On his brief but informed discussion of Caillois's theory of mimetism, see Potolsky 2006, 142–143.
9   As Caillois also puts it in a related essay on the praying mantis that sets up continuities between sexuality and death in the world of insects and humans: "from insect behavior to human consciousness, in this homogeneous universe, the path is continuous" (1938, 72; my trans.).
10  I share with Brennan not only the insight that the ego is porous to affect and thus prone to becoming a phantom ego but also that judgment is internal to unconscious transmissions of pathos from a distance, or pathos of distance. I thank Stephanie Erev for calling my attention to Brennan's work.
11  Caillois was a competitive candidate for the prestigious Collège de France, but the position went to Claude Lévi-Strauss. He eventually settled for an administrative position at UNESCO that allowed him to continue writing. He was elected to the Académie Française in 1971.
12  The two sections that follow significantly expand an embryonic account of Caillois first initiated in Lawtoo 2016, 223–227 and subsequently expanded in the journal *Effects*, Stuker and Tumlir 2022, 20–35.

13  For an English translation I follow, unless indicated otherwise, see Caillois 1984.
14  For precursors on sympathetic magic, see Frazer 1952, chapter 3; Mauss 1995, chapter 1; and Lévy-Bruhl 2010.
15  As Frank notes, important agonistic differences will later emerge between Bataille and Caillois; on the notion of expenditure, however, Caillois stresses mirroring continuities in line with the logic of mimetic agonism: "Between Bataille and myself there was a very unusual communion of minds, a kind of osmosis with respect to basic issues—so much so that our respective contributions were often difficult to tell apart" (Caillois 2003b, 144).
16  On Janet's influence on the Collège, especially on Bataille, see Lawtoo 2013, 260–282.
17  For a historical re-evaluation of the role of Janet in the discovery of the unconscious, see Ellenberger 1970, 331–418. Furthering Ellenberger, more recent historians of psychoanalysis re-evaluate this mimetic and agonistic relations as follows: "What was good in psychoanalysis was not new, and stemmed from Janet's work. What was new was not good and could be safely left to Freud" (Borch-Jacobsen and Shamdasani 2012, 75).
18  For Janet's detailed account of over three hundred case studies of psychasthenic patients whose symptoms range from obsessive ideas to indecision, intimidation to fatigue, amnesia to indifference, to other symptoms indicative of a loss of psychic tension, see Janet 1903, 260–397.
19  For the first philosophical commentary of Lacan's psychic theory, see Lacoue-Labarthe and Nancy 1992; for an incisive account of Lacan's complex relation with mimesis in the mirror stage in particular, see Borch-Jacobsen 1991, 43–71.
20  Primatologists have since shown that chimpanzees recognize their image in the mirror.
21  In a review of Minkowsky's *Le Temps vécu*, Lacan will once again stress the importance of Caillois's diagnostic, albeit indirectly, as he states that "the most original form of intuition of this book, although it is barely broached, at the end, [is] that of another space besides geometrical space, namely, the *dark space* of groping, hallucination and music, which is the opposite of clear space, the framework of objectivity. We think that we can safely say that this takes us into the 'night of the senses,' that is, the 'obscure night' of the mystic" (qtd. in Frank 2003, 90).
22  Before Girard, Caillois, Bataille, and the members of the Collège were indeed concerned with the power of mimesis to induce a crisis of difference. As Denis Hollier points out: due to mimetism an organism "renounces to this distinction, gives up on difference" (1993, 67), which in the context of the rise of fascism, led Caillois and the members of the Collège to "revitalize difference between difference and indifference" (68).
23  For a productive recuperation of both Caillois and Huizinga in the context of "*Homo ludens 2.0*" that resonates with homo mimeticus in its diagonal attention to aesthetics, games, and politics and the mimetization qua "ludification of contemporary culture it entails," see Frissen et al. 2015, 15.

### Chapter 6: The Human Chameleon

1  As critics pointed out, this formal device led initial viewers to believe in the historical existence of Zelig. See Stam and Shoat 1987, 192 n. 7, and Nas 1992, 99.
2  On Zelig as a "metaphor for ethnic assimilation," see Johnston 2007; on Zelig as a "metaphor for intertextuality" predicated on "poststructuralist mimesis," which reproduces other

cinematic texts, see Nas 1992, 95; on Zelig as representative of the performative dimension of Jewish identity in the 1980s, see Stratton, 2001, 152–154.

3   See Golomb and Wistrich 2002.
4   See Lawtoo 2013, 76–83.
5   On Nietzsche's vulnerability to affect in general, see Staten1990; on Nietzsche's mimetic relation to Wagner, see Girard 1978, 61–83. More recently Roberto Esposito also recognizes that "the more Nietzsche multiplies efforts to fight the immunity syndrome" characteristic of what he condemns as slaves or the herd, "the more he falls back on the semantic of infection and contamination" (2004, 100; my trans.). This paradox goes to the heart of Nietzsche's diagnostic of modernity. My supplement is that the problematic of mimesis is at the center of this paradox in Nietzsche's thought and modernism more generally. On the paradoxical mimetic logic that turns Nietzsche's contagious pathology into an immunizing patho-*logy*, and vice versa, see Lawtoo 2013, 45–83.
6   First steps for a theory of posthuman mimesis can be found in Lawtoo ed. 2022b.
7   Given the film's release in the 1980s psychoanalytical approaches to *Zelig* were informed by structuralist/linguistic recuperations of Freud. On Zelig as a case of psychic "*méconnaisance*" responsible for the "dissolution of personality," see Feldstein 1985. Given the influence of Roger Caillois on Lacan's "mirror stage" and his focus on the continuities between animal and human mimicry, it is surprising Caillois is not usually mentioned in discussions of *Zelig* in particular and mimetic aesthetic phenomena in general. The diagnostic that follows both benefits from and furthers Caillois's (Nietzschean) account of mimetism we considered in chapter 5.
8   For an incisive critique of Freud that paints a "portrait of the psychoanalyst as a chameleon," see Borch-Jacobsen 2006, 173–182. For a recent reevaluation of hysteria as a mimetic performance at play in discourses on contemporary movements, from Black Lives Matter to COVID-19, see Braun ed. 2020.
9   For an informed historical account of the role of "hypnosis" in the discovery of the unconscious, see Ellenberger 1970.
10  On the return of hypnosis in critical and social theory, see Borch ed. 2019; on the centrality of the "Bernheim effect" for psychic theories, see Borch-Jacobsen 2009, 109–125.
11  On the role of embodiment in cinema that confirms the importance of the MNS system, see also Coëgnarts and Kravanja 2015.
12  In addition to Nietzsche and Caillois, this modernist aesthetic tradition includes figures like Oscar Wilde, Joseph Conrad, D. H. Lawrence, Georges Bataille, among others. See Lawtoo 2013, 2016.
13  For recent returns of attention to crowd psychology and its politics, see Borch 2012; Connolly 2017b; Lawtoo 2013, 2019b.
14  Harari 2011, 126–133, 2017, 167–178.
15  As Arendt puts it: "Without Jewish help in administrative and police work […] there would have been either complete chaos or an impossibly sever drain on German manpower." She adds: "To a Jew this role of the Jewish leaders in the destruction of their own people is undoubtedly the darkest chapter of the whole dark story" (2006, 117).

## Chapter 7: Banality of Evil/Mimetic Complexity

1   See Snyder 2017; Stanley 2018; Albright 2018; Connolly 2017b.
2   See Lawtoo 2019b.

3     As I finalize the manuscript, Russia has attacked Ukraine in a horrific war that is currently still ongoing, displacing populations (over six million so far), and brutally exterminating civilians, including women and children. The type of evil I explore in this chapter finds in a Nazi figure its most extreme paradigmatic case study, but the psychology of evil is widespread and reaches into the present. For an informed historical starting point on this "road to unfreedom" specifically attentive to the case of Russia, see Snyder 2018.

4     Elsewhere, Arendt also spoke of bureaucracy as a form of "domination," characterized by the "rule of Nobody" in which it is "impossible to localize responsibility and identify the enemy" (1970, 38–39).

5     As William Connolly notes, Arendt's thought involved a "depreciation of the body in ethics and politics" (Connolly 1997, 15), a depreciation that affected her evaluation of the mimetic side of the banality of evil, as we shall see.

6     For a recent documentary not yet available as I write (except for the trailer) that integrates the Argentina Papers and Tapes to make the case, with Stangneth, contra Arendt, that Eichmann was a Nazi "devil" rather than a "banal" bureaucrat, see Mozer 2022.

7     On the classical sources of the *vita mimetica* see chapter 2.

8     For a representative sample of studies, see Bergen 1998; Mack 2009; Villa 1999, 39–60; Berkowitz, Katz, and Keenan 2010, 131–160; Bernstein 1996, 137–178; Felman 2001; Benhabib 1996.

9     As Richard Bernstein also puts it: "We still have not fully appreciated or assimilated Arendt's insights about the banality of evil. There is an enormous temptation to think about good and evil in the most simplistic and crass ways [...] We need to understand how ordinary people can be complicit with evil deeds, including genocide" (2010, 135).

10     In a chapter of *The Life of the Mind* (1977) that picks up the relation "between evil and lack of thought," Arendt clarifies that the origins of her conception of thinking are modeled on the example of Socrates, as she states: "It is this *duality* of myself with myself that makes thinking a true activity, in which I am both the one who asks and the one who answers" (2000b, 408). And she specifies: "In brief, the specifically human actualization of consciousness in the thinking dialogue between me and myself suggests that difference and otherness [...] are the very conditions for the existence of man's mental ego as well, for this ego actually exist only in duality" (409). I shall reframe this rational Socratic ideal in the context of an ego who is but a phantom of the ego in dialogue not with herself only but with others below.

11     Arendt puts here the Kantian aesthetic notion of "imagination" to use to mediate between the particular and the universal in the context of ethics. This focus on a Romantic anti-mimetic concept might have contributed to overshadow the mimetic side of Eichmann I aim to uncover.

12     See especially Stangneth's account of the so-called "Sassen Interview" for historical support (Stangneth 2014, 183–310).

13     For a diagnostic of the mimetic pathologies at play in *Heart of Darkness* that prefigure Nazi horrors, see Lawtoo 2010, 2016, 129–171, and Lacoue-Labarthe 2012a. For an Arendtian essay on *Heart of Darkness* and the horror of the Holocaust, see Cavarero 2016b.

14     See the documentary, *The Adolf Eichmann Trial* (Prazan 2011).

15     For an account of Eichmann's trial that stresses Arendt's appreciation for "storytelling as a way of combating the violence theory does to human experience" and for the theater as a "guide in her effort to understand what meaningful action might be like," see also Swift

2009, 38, 41, 74–85. What follows supplements a mimetic perspective to Arendt's narrative dramatization of the trial.

16  Commenting on the *Poetics*, Arendt specifies that "the specific revelatory quality of action and speech [...] can be represented and 'reified' only through a kind of repetition, the imitation or *mimēsis*, which according to Aristotle prevails in all arts but is actually appropriate only to the *drama*, whose very name (from the Greek verb *dran*, 'to act') indicates that play-acting actually is an imitation of acting" (1998, 187).

17  I reframe Aristotle's theory of catharsis and Plato's theory of contagion in relation to media violence for new mimetic studies in Lawtoo 2023a, 2023b.

18  Elon's source is likely a June 9, 1971 letter Mary McCarthy wrote to Arendt in response to the lecture, "Thinking and Moral Considerations." McCarthy writes: "I have one objection to your vocabulary here. 'Thoughtlessness.' It doesn't mean what you want it to mean in English, not any more [...] My suggestion would be to find [...] substitutes. E.g., in one instance you yourself, page 2, come up with a synonym, which to me is preferable, 'inability to think'" (Arendt and McCarthy 1995, 296). I am grateful to *PRQ*'s external reader for this philological insight.

19  On Arendt and Heidegger, see Wolin 2014; on Arendt and Kant, see Benhabib 2014. It is true that Kant's "reflective judgment" is the major philosophical frame for Arendt's conception of thinking from the point of view of the other; equally true is that Arendt is inspired by Heidegger's claim that "thoughtlessness [*Gedankenlosigkeit*]" is characteristic of a technocratic "calculative thinking" that "goes everywhere in today's world" (Heidegger 1966, 45). The prolonged exchange between Benahbib and Wolin (five articles in total), two established Arendt scholars, dramatizes the all-too-human difficulties in adopting the perspective of the other in such a politicized debate—but they both have a point: both Kant and Heidegger inform Arendt's take on *Gedankenlosigkeit*. My genealogical supplement consists in reframing this concept in the specific conceptual and narrative context of Arendt's own diagnostic of Eichmann, a political diagnostic predicated on a Socratic conception of dia-logic thinking, which cannot be detached from the problematic of dramatic mimesis. That is, a problematic that neither Kant nor Heidegger, and perhaps not even Arendt herself, fully thought through—yet haunts the case of Eichmann nonetheless, rendering the banality of evil mimetically complex.

20  For a recent rehabilitation of "suggestion" as a key category for social thought, see Borch ed. 2019; on the mimetic unconscious, see Lawtoo 2013, 2019a, 2023b.

21  As noted, as I write the full documentary is not yet available. For an informed radio interview with both Mozer and Stangneth that includes excerpts, see Kotsonis and Chakrabarty 2022.

22  This is the thesis both Lacoue-Labarthe and I develop in Lawtoo 2010, and Lacoue-Labarthe 2012a.

23  Arendt adds: "Prosecution and judges were in agreement that Eichmann underwent a genuine and lasting personality change when he was promoted to a post with executive powers" (2006, 64–65).

24  The classical text on the psychology of the actor deprived of sensibility who can impersonate all roles without emotion and affect the public is Denis Diderot, "The Paradox of Acting"; see Diderot 1992 and chapter 4. Furthering Lacoue-Labarthe from a psychological perspective, this view is recently supported by Mikkel Borch-Jacobsen who, in a detailed re-evaluation of Bernheim's theory of suggestion, also argues that the suggestible subject "observes

the scene that one has him play, he reflects upon his state" (2009, 113). If this insight already applies to Ion, the discovery of the Eichmann tapes based on the Sassen interview in Argentina indicates that it applies to Eichmann as well; see Mozer 2022.

25  For an emerging mimetic turn—or *re*-turn of mimesis—in contemporary political theory that, in current dialogue with homo mimeticus, emphasizes the democratic/pluralist potential of the powers of mimesis under the different rubrics of the "politics of swarming," "influx and efflux," and "surging democracy" see, respectively, Connolly 2017a; Bennett 2020; and Cavarero 2020.

## Chapter 8: Vibrant Mimesis

1  This encounter, I should specify, took place in the material world, as I held a visiting appointment at Johns Hopkins University from 2013 to 2016. It started informally in conversations that took place in a vibrant reading group, and materialized in publications that now entangle new materialism and mimetic studies in friendly collaborations.

2  For a sample of written traces of such encounters already partially registered in chapters 5 and 7, see Lawtoo (ed.) 2017, Bennett 2017, Connolly 2017b, Lawtoo 2019c, and now Bennett 2020.

3  On sympathy qua shared *pathos* from a distance in both Lawrence and Nietzsche, see Lawtoo 2013, 3–6, 30–45, 150–162, and Lawtoo 2020.

4  If Abrams uses the mirror/lamp distinction to indicate a shift from realism (mirror) to romanticism (lamp) (Abrams 1953), I overturn the image to indicate a *re*-turn to mimesis via mirroring reflexes that are not confined to a realistic mirror but affect the poetic I instead.

5  As both the notion of "repression" Bloom convokes and the triangulation with paternal figures and desires internal to both Bloom and Girard confirms, both models remain indebted to a Freudian tradition of the unconscious they attempt overturn via a romantic agonism that erases traces of influences—a romantic move at odds with a modernist genealogy based on mimetic agonism (see Lawtoo 2023a, 45–57).

6  For instance, Schopenhauer's mediated theory of sympathy is indebted to Smith but also paves the way for a more immediate theory of *Mitleid* Nietzsche will echo (see Lawtoo 2013, 40–45), which is in line with Whitman too. Interestingly, even Smith leaves open a more direct mimetic possibility as he writes: "Upon some occasions sympathy may seem to arise merely from a view of a certain emotion in another person. The passions, upon some occasions, may seem to be transfused from one man to another, instantaneously, and antecedent to any knowledge of what excited them in the person principally concerned. Grief and joy, for example, strongly expressed in the look and gestures of any one, at once affect the spectator with some degree of a like painful or agreeable emotion. A smiling face is, to every body that sees it, a cheerful object; as a sorrowful countenance, on the other hand, is a melancholy one" (2002, 13).

7  See Borch-Jacobsen 1988, 1992; Lawtoo 2013, 2019a.

8  See Bennett and Connolly 2020.

9  E. R. Dodds specifies: "Aristotle compares the man [*sic*] in a state of passion to men asleep, insane or drunk: his reason, like theirs, is in suspense" (1973, 185). Before Aristotle, Plato had already specified that this suspension of reason, whereby the subject is possessed, is not deprived of enthusiastic, magnetic, and electrifying properties characteristic of a type of po-

etic inspiration akin to intoxication, eroticism, and madness or *mania*, which Nietzsche will later group under the rubric of Dionysian mimesis. See chapter 2.

10   The encounter that sealed this additional genealogical connection can be traced back to Bennett 2017 and Lawtoo 2017.

## Chapter 9: The Age of Viral Reproduction

1   In her contribution to the mimetic turn in posthuman studies, Katherine Hayles relies on her biological training "to consider what mimesis may signify in the nonhuman realm" (2021, 777) by zooming in on processes of "microbiomimesis" that allows bacteria to "defend themselves against viral attacks" (778). Taking mimesis beyond the humans in ways that recognize "the mimetic theories of Roger Caillois" (777) we have already considered as constitutive of homo mimeticus, Hayles uses nonhuman mimesis as a mirror to expand "sympathy" beyond the human realm. Given the slow progress on sympathy when it comes to human "others," I still focus on this all-too-human problem here. On posthuman mimesis, see Hayles and Lawtoo 2022.

2   As we saw, Yuval Harari has perceptive insights on the contemporary dangers haunting *Sapiens*—from climate change to AI—that resonate with *Homo Mimeticus*, but history corrected him on pandemics seen from the fictional point of view of *Homo Deus*. New mimetic studies does not claim prophetic powers on the history of the future but noted early on that in an "increasingly globalized, permeable, and precarious world, the shadow of epidemics looms large on the horizon" (Lawtoo 2016, 92).

3   As Christoph Wulf and Gunter Gebauer put it, "the relevance of mimesis is not restricted to the aesthetic […] its effects press outward into the social world, taking root, as Plato saw it, in individual behavior like a contagion." (1995, 309).

4   Correcting his diagnostic, the late Girard, confronted with the reality of the H5N1 influenza, acknowledged that it is a "pandemic that could cause hundreds of deaths in a few days and is a phenomenon typical of the undifferentiation now coursing across the planet" (2010, 24). It is of course easy to critique Girard's youthful metaphorical blunder in 2022. I thus note that my first concerns with the "contemporary pandemics that, every year, threaten to contaminate an increasingly globalized, permeable, and precarious world" led me to state, in 2016, that "the shadow of epidemics looms large on the horizon" (Lawtoo 2016, 92; see also 91–125). For an account of the coronavirus from the angle of mimesis that is less critical of Girard but also emphasizes social differences and power relations in pandemics, see Gebauer 2022.

5   On gender inequality and the pandemic, see Ali et al. 2020.

6   For a more detailed discussion of Plato, see chapter 2.

7   Plato, *Republic*, 514b–515a, 747.

8   See Heidegger 1977.

9   For the hypnotic effects of new media via the TV series *Black Mirror*, see Lawtoo 2021.

10  On posthuman (hyper)mimesis and hypermimesis see Lawtoo 2022b.

11  See also Agamben 2021

12  For this recent revival of interest, see Borch 2012, 2020; Gebauer and Rücker 2019; Lawtoo 2013, 2019b.

13  On the contemporary relevance of Tarde's theory of imitation, see Brighenti 2010, and Borch 2020.

14  As Popper says in a precise definition of mimetic agonism: "it is obvious that we must try to appreciate the strength of an opponent if we wish to fight him successfully" (xlii).
15  This is a rich, transdisciplinary collection that opens up multiple perspectives to conspiracy theories—from historical to psychological, semiotic to political, literary to philosophical, among others—and to which this chapter supplements a mimetic perspective.
16  For an historical genealogy of "antivax" conspiracies in relation to the Internet, see also Stano 2020.
17  In addition to scientists and politicians, actors and celebrities play a key mimetic role in pro-vaccination campaigns, as an identification with them is already in place.
18  See Lawtoo 2022b.

## Coda: The Complexity of Mimesis: A Dialogue with Edgar Morin

1  Recordings of these voices are available via video interviews or HOM Videos: https://www.youtube.com/channel/UCJQy0y0qCxzP4QImG2YWqpw.
2  On the limits of hyperspecialization to account for homo mimeticus, among other subjects, see Lawtoo 2023a, 149–163.
3  If I first identified this patho(-)logical paradox via Nietzsche's perspectivism (see Lawtoo 2013, 3–8, 27–83), I'm delighted to see it confirmed by Morin's complexity theory.
4  For the English translations available, good places to start are Morin 2008; Morin and Kern 1999; Morin 2001.
5  Cérémonie du centième anniversaire d'Edgar Morin, https://www.youtube.com/watch?v=Wmav5ZsY-Bo.
6  All translations from French are the mine.
7  For a bibliography, see https://en.wikipedia.org/wiki/Edgar_Morin.
8  This dialogue was recorded at Morin's home in Montpellier in the fall of 2018. I am grateful to Daniel Villegas Vélez for translating the oral version on which the written version is based. I warmly thank Edgar Morin for his friendly exchange during my memorable visit, his inspiring example, and for continuing to discuss plans for metamorphoses of the future.
9  Elsewhere Morin, speaking of his drive to imitate his teacher and friend the sociologist Georges Friedmann, who had invited him to work at the CNRS, specifies: "in imitating his voice I would think like him, I was him, while barely remaining myself" (2017, 136; see also 1986, 146).
10  See Lawtoo 2023a and 2023b.
11  If Morin has been attentive to the discovery of mirror neurons, conversely, neuroscientists developing an experimental aesthetics, like Vittorio Gallese, have been drawing a genealogical connection with Morin's work on the mimetic "symbiosis" at play in cinema (see Gallese and Guerra 2015, 119–121).

# BIBLIOGRAPHY

Aarsleff, Hans (1982). *From Locke to Saussure: Essays on the Study of Language and Intellectual History*. London: Athlone.
Abrams, M. H. (1953). *The Mirror and the Lamp: Romantic Theory and the Critical Tradition*. Oxford: Oxford University Press.
Adorno, Theodor, Else Frenkel-Brunswik, Daniel Levinson, Nevitt Sanford (eds.) (1950). *The Authoritarian Personality*. New York: Harper and Brothers.
Agacinski, Silviane, Jacques Derrida, Sarah Kofman, Philippe Lacoue-Labarthe, Jean-Luc Nancy, Bernard Pautrat (1975). *Mimesis: Des articulations*. Paris: Aubier-Flammarion.
Agamben, Giorgio (2005). *Homo sacer: Il potere sovrano e la nuda vita*. Torino: Einaudi.
⸺ (2020). "L'Invenzione di un'epidemia, Quodlibet, https://www.quodlibet.it/giorgio-agamben-l-invenzione-di-un-epidemia
⸺ (2021). *A che punto stiamo? L'epidemia come politica*. Macerata: Quodlibet.
Albright, Madeleine (2018). *Fascism: A Warning*. New York: HarperCollins.
Ali, Kecia, Julia-Watts Belser, Grace Y. Kao, Shively T. J. Smith (2020). "Living It Out: Feminism During Covid 19." *Journal of Feminist Studies in Religion* 36.2, 107–116.
Allen, Woody (dir.) (1983). *Zelig*. Orion Pictures, Warner Bros.
Alloa, Emmanuel (2020). *Partages de la perspective*. Paris: Fayard.
Antonello, Pierpaolo, and Paul Gifford (eds.) (2015). *How We Became Human: Mimetic Theory and the Science of Evolutionary Origins*. East Lansing: Michigan State University Press.
Arendt, Hannah (1970). *On Violence*. New York: Harvest Book, 1970.
⸺ (1976). *The Origins of Totalitarianism*. New York: Harvest Book.
⸺ (1998). *The Human Condition*. Chicago: University of Chicago Press.
⸺ (2000a). "'A Daughter of Our People': A Response to Gershom Scholem," in *The Portable Hannah Arendt*, ed. Peter Baher. New York: Penguin, 391–396.
⸺ (2000b). "The Answer of Socrates," in *The Portable Hannah Arendt*, 397–407.
⸺ (2000c). "Truth and Politics," in *The Portable Hannah Arendt*, 545–575.
⸺ (2006). *Eichmann in Jerusalem: A Report on the Banality of Evil*. New York: Penguin Books.
Arendt, Hannah, and Mary McCarthy (1995). *Between Friends: The Correspondence of Hannah Arendt and Mary McCarthy 1949–1975*. New York: Houghton Mifflin Harcourt.
Aristotle (1984). *Physics*, in *The Complete Works of Aristotle*, ed. Jonathan Barnes. Princeton: Princeton University Press, 315-445.
⸺ (1987). *The Poetics of Aristotle*, trans. Stephen Halliwell. Chapel Hill: University of North Carolina Press.
Armstrong, David F., and Sherman E. Wilcox (2007). *The Gestural Origins of Language*. Oxford: Oxford University Press.
Auerbach, Erich (2003). *Mimesis: The Representation of Reality in Western Literature*, trans. Willard R. Trask. Princeton: Princeton University Press.

Backer, Peter (2010). "Banality and Cleverness: *Eichmann in Jerusalem* Revisited," in *Thinking in Dark Times: Hannah Arendt on Ethics and Politics*, eds. Roger Berkowitz, Jeffrey Katz, Thomas Keenan. New York: Fordham University Press, 139–142.
Baetens, Jan, Ortwin de Graef, and Silvana Mandolessi (2020). *Digital Reason: A Guide to Meaning, Medium and Community in a Modern World*. Leuven: Leuven University Press.
Barthes, Roland (1971). "The Structuralist Activity," in *Critical Theory since Plato*, ed. Hazard Adams. London: Harcourt Brace Jovanovich, Inc., 1196–1199.
—— (1972a). *Mythologies,* trans. Annette Lavers. New York: Noonday Press, 1972.
—— (1972b). "To Write: An Intransitive Verb," in *The Structuralist Controversy: The Languages of Criticism and the Sciences of Man*, eds. Richard Macksey and Eugenio Donato. Baltimore: Johns Hopkins University Press, 134–144.
Bataille, Georges (1988). *Inner Experience*, trans. Leslie Anne Boldt. Albany: State Universityof New York Press.
—— (1986). "The Notion of Expenditure," in *Critical Theory Since Plato (Revised Edition)*, ed. Hazard Adams. London: Hacourt Brace Jovanovich, Inc., 856–864.
Baudrillard, Jean (1981). *Simulacres et Simulation*. Paris: Galilée.
Benhabib, Seyla (1996). *The Reluctant Modernism of Hannah Arendt*. London: SAGE Publications, 1996.
—— (2014). "Who Is on Trial? Eichmann or Arendt." *The New York Times*, https://opinionator.blogs.nytimes.com/2014/09/21/whos-on-trial-eichmann-or-anrendt/.
Benjamin, Walter (1986). "On the Mimetic Faculty," in *Reflections: Essays, Aphorisms, Autobiographical Writings*, trans. Edmund Jephcott, ed. Peter Demetz. New York: Schocken Books.
Bennett, Jane (2010). *Vibrant Matter: A Political Ecology of Things*. Durham, NC: Duke-University Press.
—— (2017). "Mimesis: Paradox or Encounter." *Modern Language Notes* 132.5, 1186–1200.
—— (2020). *Influx & Efflux: Writing Up with Walt Whitman*. Durham, NC: Duke UniversityPress.
Bennett, Jane, and William E. Connolly (2002). "Contesting Nature/Culture: The Creative Character of Thinking." *Journal of Nietzsche Studies* 24, 148–163.
Bergen, Bernard J. (1998). *The Banality of Evil: Hannah Arendt and 'The Final Solution.'* New York: Rowman & Littlefield, 1998.
Berkowitz, Roger, Jeffrey Katz, and Thomas Keenan (eds.) (2010). *Thinking in Dark Times: Hannah Arendt on Ethics and Politics*. New York: Fordham University Press.
Bernays, Edward (2005). *Propaganda*. Brooklyn: Ig Publishing.
Bernheim, Hippolyte (1957). *Suggestive Therapeutics: A Treatise on the Nature and Uses of Hypnosis*, trans. Christian A. Herter. Westport, CT: Associated Booksellers.
Bernstein, Richard J. (1996). *Hannah Arendt and the Jewish Question*. Cambridge: Polity Press.
—— (2010). "Is Evil Banal? A Misleading Question," in *Thinking in Dark Times*, 131–136.
Bhabha, Homi (1994). *The Location of Culture*. New York: Routledge.
Bloom, Harold (1989). "Poetry, Revisionism, Repression," in *Critical Theory since 1965*, eds. Hazard Adams and Leroy Searle. Tallahassee: Florida State University Press, 331–343.

Borch, Christian (2012). *The Politics of Crowds: An Alternative History of Sociology*. Cambridge: Cambridge University Press.
—— (2020). *Social Avalanche: Crowds, Cities and Financial Markets*. Cambridge: Cambridge University Press.
Borch, Christian (ed.) (2019). *Imitation, Contagion, Suggestion: On Mimesis and Society*. New York: Routledge.
Borch-Jacobsen, Mikkel (1988). *The Freudian Subject*, trans. Catherine Porter. Stanford: Stanford University Press.
—— (1991). *Lacan: The Absolute Master*, trans. Douglas Brick. Stanford: Stanford University Press.
—— (1992). *The Emotional Tie: Psychoanalysis, Mimesis, and Affect*, trans. Douglas Brick et al. Stanford: Stanford University Press.
—— (2009). *Making Madness: from Hysteria to Depression*. Cambridge: Cambridge University Press.
Borch-Jacobsen, Mikkel, and Sonu Shamdasani (2012). *The Freud Files: An Inquiry into the History of Psychoanalysis*. Cambridge: Cambridge University Press.
Botting, Fred, and Scott Wilson (eds.) (1997). *Bataille: A Critical Reader*. Oxford: Blackwell.
Braun, Johanna (ed.) (2020). *Performing Hysteria: Images and Imaginations of Hysteria*. Leuven: Leuven University Press.
Brennan, Teresa (2004). *The Transmission of Affect*. Ithaca: Cornell University Press.
Brighenti, Andrea Mubi (2010). "Tarde, Canetti, and Deleuze on Crowds and Packs." *Journal of Classical Sociology* 10.4, 291–314.
Burckhardt, Jacob (1998). *The Greeks and Greek Civilization*. London: Harper Collins.
Butler, Judith (1991). "Imitation and Gender Insubordination," in *Inside/Out: Lesbian Theories, Gay Theories*, ed. Diana Fuss. New York: Routledge.
—— (2011) "Hannah Arendt's Challenge to Adolf Eichmann." *The Guardian*, https://www.theguardian.com/commentisfree/2011/aug/29/hannah-arendt-adolf-eichmann-banality-of-evil.
Butter Michael, and Pieter Knight (eds.) (2020). *Routledge Handbook of Conspiracy Theories*. New York: Routledge.
Caillois, Roger (1938). "Mimétisme et psychasthénie légendaire," in *Le Mythe et l'homme*. Paris: Gallimard, 86–122.
—— (1961). *Man, Play, and Games*, trans. Meyer Barash. New York: Free Press of Glencoe, Inc.
—— "Mimicry and Legendary Psychasthenia," trans. John Shepley. *October* 31, 16–32.
—— (2003a). "A New Plea for Diagonal Science," in *The Edge of Surrealism: A Roger Caillois Reader*, 343–347.
—— (2003b). "Interview with Gilles Lapouge, June 1970," in *The Edge of Surrealism: A Roger Caillois Reader*, 142–146.
—— (2008). *Oeuvres*. Paris: Quarto Gallimard.
—— (2008a). *Cases d'un échiquier*, in *Oeuvres*, 559–618.
Cavarero, Adriana (2000). *Relating Narratives: Storytelling and Selfhood*, trans. Paul A. Cottman. London: Routledge.

—— (2002). "The Envied Muse: Plato versus Homer," in *Cultivating the Muse: Struggles for Power and Inspiration in Classical Literature*, eds. Efrossini Spentzou and Don Fowler. Oxford: Oxford University Press.

—— (2005). *For More than One Voice: Toward a Philosophy of Vocal Expression*, trans. Paul A Kottman. Stanford: Stanford University Press.

—— (2016a). *Inclinations: A Critique of Rectitude*, trans. Amanda Minervini and Adam Sitze. Stanford: Stanford University Press.

—— (2016b). "The Soundscape of Darkness." *Conradiana* 48.2–3, 117–118.

—— (2021). *Surging Democracy: Notes on Hannah Arendt's Political Thought*, trans. Matthew Gervase. Stanford: Stanford University Press.

Cavarero, Adriana, and Nidesh Lawtoo (2021). "Mimetic Inclinations: A Dialogue with Adriana Cavarero," in *Contemporary Italian Women Philosophers: Stretching the Art of Thinking*, eds. Silvia Benso and Elvira Roncalli. Albany: State University of New York Press, 183–199.

Changeux, Jean-Pierre (1997). *Neuronal Man: The Biology of the Mind*, trans. Laurence Garey. Princeton: Princeton University Press.

Chertok, Léon (1993). *Hypnose et suggéstion*. Paris: Presses Universitaires de France.

Coëgnarts, Maarten, and Peter Kravanja (eds.) (2015). *Embodied Cognition and Cinema*. Leuven: Leuven University Press.

Coleridge, Samuel (2005). *Biographia Literaria*, in *Critical Theory Since Plato 3rd ed.*, eds. Hazard Adams and Leroy Searle. Boston: Thomson Wadsworth, 501–508.

Connolly, William E. (1997). "A Critique of Pure Politics." *Philosophy & Social Criticism*, 23.5,1–26.

—— (2013). *The Fragility of Things: Self-Organizing Processes, Neoliberal Fantasies and Democratic Activism*. Durham, NC: Duke University Press.

—— (2017a). *Facing the Planetary: Entangled Humanism and the Politics of Swarming*. Durham,NC: Duke University Press.

—— (2017b). *Aspirational Fascism: The Struggle for Multifaceted Democracy under Trumpism*. Minneapolis: University of Minnesota Press.

Connolly, William E., and Nidesh Lawtoo (2021). "Planetary Conrad: William Connolly and Nidesh Lawtoo in Dialogue." *The Conradian* 46.2, 144–170.

Conrad, Joseph. (2010). *Heart of Darkness. Youth, Heart of Darkness, The End of the Tether*, ed. Owen Knowles. Cambridge: Cambridge University Press.

Corballis, Michael C. (2002). *From Hand to Mouth: The Origins of Language*. Princeton: Princeton University Press.

Crutzen, Paul J., and Stoermer Eugene F. (2000). "The 'Anthropocene.'" *Global Change Newsletter* 41, 17–18.

Cyrulnik, Boris (2010). *Sous le signe du lien: une histoire naturelle de l'attachement*. Paris: Pluriel.

Darwin, Charles (1970). *The Descent of Man. Darwin: A Norton Critical Edition*, ed. Philip Appleman. New York: W. W. Norton & Company, 132–208.

Deleuze, Gilles (1969). *Logique du sens*. Paris: Les Éditions de Minuit.

Deleuze, Gilles, and Félix Guattari (1994). *What Is Philosophy?*, trans. Hugh Tomlinson and Graham Burchell. New York: Columbia University Press.

Derrida, Jacques (1967). *De la grammatologie*. Paris: Les Éditions de Minuit.

—— (1989). "Introduction: Desistance," in *Typography: Mimesis, Philosophy, Politics*, 3–42.
—— (1972). "Structure, Sign, and Play in the Discourse of the Human Sciences," in *The Structuralist Controversy*, 247–272.
—— (1981a)."The Double Session," in *Dissemination*, trans. Barbara Johnson. Chicago:University of Chicago Press, 173–285.
—— (1981b). "Plato's Pharmacy," in *Dissemination*, 61–171.
Diderot, Denis (1992). "The Paradox of Acting," in *Critical Theory Since Plato (Revised Edition)*, 365–373.
—— (1981). *Paradoxe sur le comédien*, précédé *des Entretiens sur le fils Naturel*. Paris: Flammarion.
Didi-Huberman, Georges (2000). "Plasticité du devenir et fractures dans l'histoire: Warburg avec Nietzsche," in *Plasticité*, ed. Catherine Malabou. Paris: Léo Scheer, 58–69.
Dodds, E. R. (1973). *The Greeks and the Irrational*. Berkeley: University of California Press.
Doidge, Norman (2007). *The Brain That Changes Itself: Stories of Personal Triumph from the Frontiers of Brain Science*. London: Penguin.
Eco, Umberto (1995). "Ur-Fascism." *The New York Review of Books*. http://www.nybooks.com/articles/1995/06/22/ur-fascism/.
—— (2014). "A Theory of Conspiracies," *Mint*. https://www.livemint.com/Opinion/5l-hODHqqZHUCqwOZcw2liL/Umberto-Eco--A-theory-of-conspiracies.html.
Ellenberger, Henri (1970). *The Discovery of the Unconscious: The History and Evolution of Dynamic Psychiatry*. New York: Basic Books.
Else, Gerald F. (1958). "'Imitation' in the Fifth Century. *Classical Philology* 53.2, 73–90.
Emden, Christian J. (2005). *Nietzsche on Language, Consciousness and the Body*. Champaign: University of Illinois Press.
Esposito, Roberto (2004). *Bíos: Biopolitca e filosofia*. Torino: Einaudi.
Feldstein, Richard (1985). "The Dissolution of the Self in Zelig." *Literature/Film Quarterly* 13.3, 155–160.
Felman, Shoshana (2001). "Theaters of Justice: Arendt in Jerusalem, the Eichmann Trial, and the Redefinition of Legal Meaning in the Wake of the Holocaust." *Critical Inquiry* 27.2, 201–238.
Foucault, Michel (1977). "Nietzsche, Genealogy, History," in *Language, Counter-Memory, Practice: Selected Essays and Interviews*, ed. Donald F. Bouchard, trans. Donald F. Bouchard and Sherry Simon. Ithaca, NY: Cornell University Press, 139–164.
—— (2004). "La culture de soi," in *Philosophie: Anthologie*, eds. Arnold I. Davidson and Frédéric Gros. Paris: Gallimard, 735–771.
Frank, Claudine (ed.) (2003). *The Edge of Surrealism: A Roger Caillois Reader*, trans. Claudine Frank and Camille Naish. Durham, NC: Duke University Press.
Frazer, James (1954). *The Golden Bough: A Study in Magic and Religion*, vol. 1. New York: Macmillan.
Freud, Sigmund (1940). *Totem and Taboo*. Harmondsworth: Penguin.
Frissen, Valerie, Sybille Lammes, Michiel de Lange, Jos de Mul, and Joost Raessens (2015). *Playful Identities: The Ludification of Digital Media Cultures*. Amsterdam: Amsterdam University Press.
Fumaroli, Marc (2001). *Les Abeilles et les araignées*, in *La Querelle des anciens et des modernes*, ed. Anne-Marie Lecoq. Paris: Gallimard, 7–218.

Gallese, Vittorio (2011). "The Two Sides of Mimesis: Mimetic Theory, Embodied Simulation, and Social Identification," in *Mimesis and Science: Empirical Research on Imitation and the Mimetic Theory of Culture and Religion*, 87–108.
—— (2005). "Embodied Simulation: From Neurons to Phenomenal Experience." *Phenomenology and the Cognitive Sciences* 4, 23–48.
Gallese, Vittorio, and Michele Guerra (2015). *Lo schermo empatico: cinema e neuroscienze*. Milan: Raffaello Cortina.
Garrels, Scott R., (ed.) (2011). *Mimesis and Science: Empirical Research on Imitation and the Mimetic Theory of Culture and Religion*. East Lansing: Michigan State University Press.
Gebauer, Gunter (2017). *Wittgenstein's Anthropological Philosophy*. London: Palgrave.
—— (2022). "The Undifferentiation of Mimetic Violence: From Oedipus to COVID-19." *CounterText* 8. 1, 88–102.
Gebauer, Gunter, and Christoph Wulf (1995 [1992]). *Mimesis: Culture, Art, Society*, trans. Don Reneau. Berkeley: University of California Press.
Gebauer, Gunter, and Sven Rücker (2019). *Vom Sog der Massen und der neuen Macht der Einzelnen*. Deutsche Verlags-Anstalt.
Girard, René (1965 [1961]). *Deceit, Desire and the Novel: Self and Other in Literary Structure*, trans. Yvonne Freccero. Baltimore: The Johns Hopkins University Press.
—— (1974). "The Plague in Literature." *Texas Studies in Literature and Language* 15.5, 833–850.
—— (1977 [1972]). *Violence and the Sacred*, trans. Patrick Gregory. Baltimore: The Johns Hopkins University Press.
—— (1972). "Tiresias and the Critic," in *The Structuralist Controversy*, 15–21.
—— (1978). *To Double Business Bound: Essays on Literature, Mimesis, and Anthropology*. Baltimore: The Johns Hopkins University Press.
—— (2010). *Battling to the End: Conversations with Benoît Chantre*, trans. Mary Baker. East Lansing: Michigan State University Press.
Girard, Mathilde, and Jean-Luc Nancy (2015). *Proprement dit: entretiens sur le mythe*. Fécamp Lignes.
Golomb, Jacob, and Robert S. Wistrich (eds.) (2002). *Nietzsche, Godfather of Fascism? On the Uses and Abuses of a Philosophy*. Princeton: Princeton University Press.
Habash, Nicolas Lema (2019). "Agon and Politics in Nietzsche's Early Writings on Language," in *Conflict and Contest in Nietzsche's Philosophy*, eds. James Pearson and Herman Siemens. London: Bloomsbury, 211–233.
Harari, Yuval Noah (2014). *Sapiens: A Brief History of Humankind*. London: Vintage Books.
—— (2017). *Homo Deus: A Brief History of Tomorrow*. New York: Harper Collins Publisher.
Harris, Stephen P. (1992). "Fear of the Dark." *Iron Maiden*. Barnyard, EMI.
Harrison, Jane (1913). *Ancient Art and Ritual*. London: Williams and Norgate.
Havelock, Eric A. (1963). *Preface to Plato*. Cambridge, MA: Harvard University Press.
Hayles, Katherine N. (2021). "Microbiomimesis: Bacteria, Our Cognitive Collaborators." *Critical Inquiry* 47, 777–787.

Hayles, Katherine N., and Nidesh Lawtoo (2022). "Posthuman Mimesis II—Connections: A Dialogue between Nidesh Lawtoo and Kathrine Hayles." *Journal of Posthumanism* 2.2, 181–191.

Heidegger, Martin (1966). *Discourse on Thinking*, trans. John M. Anderson and E. Hans Freund. New York: Harper & Row.

—— (1977). "On the Essence of Truth," in *Basic Writings*, ed. David Farrell Krell. San Francisco: Harper Collins, 113–141.

Hickok, Gregory (2014). *The Myth of Mirror Neurons: The Real Neuroscience of Communication and Cognition*. New York: W. W. Norton & Company.

Hofstadter, Douglas R (1999). *Gödel, Escher, Bach: An Eternal Golden Braid*. New York: Basic Books.

Hollier, Denis (1993). *Les Dépossédées (Bataille, Caillois, Leiris, Malraux, Sartre)*. Paris: Les Éditions de Minuit.

Hollier, Denis (ed.) (1995). *Le Collège de Sociologie, 1937–1939*. Paris: Gallimard.

—— (1998). *The College of Sociology*, ed. Denis Hollier. Minneapolis: University of Minnesota Press.

Homer (1991). *The Odyssey*, trans. E. V. Rieu. London: Penguin Group.

Hrdy, Sarah Blaffer (1999). *Mother Nature: Maternal Instincts and How they Shape the Human Species*. New York: Ballantine Books.

—— (2011). *Mothers and Others: The Evolutionary Origins of Mutual Understanding*. Cambridge, MA: Harvard University Press.

Huizinga, Johan (2016). *Homo Ludens: A Study of the Play-Element in Culture*. Kettering, OH: Angelico Press.

Hurley, Susan, and Nick Chater (eds.) (2005). *Perspectives of Imitation: From Neuroscience to Social Science*, vol. 1 & 2. Cambridge, MA: MIT Press.

Iacoboni, Marco (2008). *Mirroring People: The New Science of How We Connect with Others*. New York: Ferrar, Straus and Giroux.

Irigaray, Luce (1974). *Marine Lover of Friedrich Nietzsche*, trans. Gillian C. Gill. New York: Columbia University Press.

—— (1974). *Speculum de l'autre femme*. Paris: Les Éditions de Minuit.

—— (1977). *Ce Sexe qui n'en est pas un*. Paris: Les Éditions de Minuit.

IJsseling, Samuel (1990). *Mimesis: On Appearing and Being*. Kampen: Pharos.

Kotsonis, Stefano, and Meghna Chakrabarty (2022). "The Eichmann Tapes and the Comforting Myth of the 'Banality of Evil.'" *On Point, NPR Radio*.

Janet, Pierre (1903). *Les Obsessions et la psychasthénie*. Paris: Félix Alcan.

Johnston, Ruth D. (2007). "Ethnic and Discursive Drag in Woody Allen's *Zelig*." *Quarterly Review of Film and Video* 24.3, 297–306.

Lacan, Jacques (1977). "The Mirror Stage as Formative to the Function of the I as Revealed in Psychoanalytical Experience," in *Écrits: A Selection*, trans. Alan Sheridan. Paris: Seuil, 1–7.

—— (1972). "Of Structure as an Inmixing of an Otherness Prerequisite to any Subject Whatever," in *The Structuralist Controversy*, 186–194.

Lacoue-Labarthe, Philippe (1986). *L'Imitation des modernes*. Paris: Gallimard.

—— (1989). *Typography: Mimesis, Philosophy, Politics*, ed. Christopher Fynsk. Cambridge, MA: Harvard University Press, 1989.

—— (1987). *La Fiction du politique: Heidegger, l'art, et la politique*. Paris: Christian Bourgois.
—— (1993). *The Subject of Philosophy*, ed. Thomas Trezise, trans. Thomas Trezise et al. Minneapolis: University of Minnesota Press.
—— (2000). *Phrase*. Paris: Christian Bourgeois.
—— (2005). *Le Chant des muses*. Paris: Bayard.
—— (2012a). "The Horror of the West," in *Conrad's Heart of Darkness and Contemporary Thought: Revisiting the Horror with Lacoue-Labarthe*, trans. Nidesh Lawtoo and Hannes Opelz, ed. Nidesh Lawtoo. London: Bloomsbury, 111–122.
—— (2012b). "La Réponse d'Ulysee," in *La Réponse d'Ulysse et autres textes sur l'Occident*, ed. Aristide Bianchi et Leonid Kharlamov. Lignes/IMEC.
Lacoue-Labarthe, Philippe, and Jean-Luc Nancy (1990). "The Nazi Myth," trans. Brian Holmes, *Critical Inquiry* 16:2, 291–312.
—— (1992). *The Title of the Letter: A Reading of Lacan*, trans. François Raffoul and David Pettigrew. Albany: State University of New York Press.
—— *Scène*. Paris: Christian Bourgois, 2013.
Lawrence, D. H. (2002). *Studies in Classical American Literature*, ed. Ezra Greenspan, Lindeth Vasey, and John Worthen. Cambridge: Cambridge University Press.
Lawtoo, Nidesh (2006). "This Sex Which Is Not One: Dissident Voices in Luce Irigaray's *This Sex Which is Not One* and Richard Rodriguez's *Hunger of Memory*." *Texas Studies of Language and Literature* 48.3, 220–249.
—— (2010). "The Horror of Mimesis: 'Enthusiastic Outbreak[s]' in *Heart of Darkness*." *Conradiana* 42.1-2: 45–74
—— (2013). *The Phantom of the Ego: Modernism and the Mimetic Unconscious*. East Lansing: Michigan State University Press.
—— (2016). *Conrad's Shadow: Catastrophe, Mimesis, Theory*. East Lansing: Michigan State University Press.
—— (2017). "The Plasticity of Mimesis." *Modern Language Notes* 132.5, 1201–1224.
—— (2018a). "Bataille and the Homology of Heterology." *Theory, Culture & Society* 35.4-5, 41–68.
—— (2018b). "Violence and the Unconscious (Part One). The Cathartic Hypothesis: Aristotle, Freud, Girard." *Contagion* 25, 159–192.
—— (2019a). "The Mimetic Unconscious: A Mirror for Genealogical Reflections," in *Imitation, Contagion, Suggestion: Rethinking the Social*, 37–53.
—— (2019b). *(New) Fascism: Contagion, Community, Myth*. East Lansing: Michigan State University Press.
—— (2019c). "The Powers of Mimesis: Simulation, Encounters, Comic Fascism." *Theory & Event* 22.3, 722–746.
—— (2020). "Lawrence *Contra* (New) Fascism." *College Literature* 47.2, 287–317.
—— (2021). "Black Mirrors: Reflecting (on) Hypermimesis." *Philosophy Today* 65.3, 523–547.
—— (2022a). "The Mimetic Condition: Theory and Concepts." *CounterText* 8.1, 1–22.
—— (2022b). "Posthumanism and Mimesis: An Introduction." *Journal of Posthumanism* 2.2, 87–100.
—— (2023a). *Violence and the Oedipal Unconscious: vol. 1 The Catharsis Hypothesis*. East Lansing: Michigan State University Press.

——— (2023b). *Violence and the Mimetic Unconscious: vol. 2 The Affective Hypothesis*. East Lansing: Michigan State University Press.
Lawtoo, Nidesh (ed.) (2017). *Poetics and Politics: with Lacoue-Labarthe*. Modern Language Notes 132.5.
——— (2022a). *The Mimetic Condition*. CounterText 8:1.
——— (2022b). *Posthuman Mimesis*. Journal of Posthumanism 2:2.
Lawtoo, Nidesh, and J. Hillis Miller (2020). "The Critic and the Mime: J. Hillis Miller in Dialogue with Nidesh Lawtoo." *The Minnesota Review* 95, 93–119.
Le Bon, Gustave (2002). *The Crowd: A Study of the Popular Mind*. New York: Dover Publications, Inc.
Leroi-Gourhan, André (1964). *Le Geste et la parole: I Technique et langage*. Paris: Albin Michel.
——— (1965). *Le Geste et la parole: II La mémoire et les rythmes*. Paris: Albin Michel.
Lévy-Bruhl, Lucien (2010). *La Mentalité primitive*. Paris: Flammarion.
Leys, Ruth (2000). *Trauma: A Genealogy*. Chicago: University of Chicago Press.
Lury, Celia, Rachel Fensham, Alexandra Heller-Nicholas, Sybille Lammes, Angela Last, Mike Michael, and Emma Uprichard (eds.) (2018). *Routledge Handbook of Interdisciplinary Research Methods*. London: Routledge.
Mbembe, Achille (2020). "The Universal Right to Breathe," trans. Carolyne Shread. *Critical Inquiry* (*In the Moment*) https://critinq.wordpress.com/2020/04/13/the-universal-right-to-breathe/.
Mack, Michael (2009). "The Holocaust and Hannah Arendt's Philosophical Critique of Philosophy: *Eichmann in Jerusalem*." *New German Critique* 106, 35–60.
Macksey, Richard (1972). "The Space Between—1971," in *The Structural Controversy*, 15–21.
Macksey, Richard, René Girard, and Jean Hyppolite (1972), "Concluding Remarks," in *The Structuralist Controversy*, 319–322.
Malabou, Catherine (1996). *L'Avenir de Hegel: Plasticité, temporalité, dialectique*. Paris: Libraire Philosophique J. Vrin.
——— (2008). *What Should We Do with Our Brain?*, trans. Sebastian Rand. New York: Fordham University Press, 2008.
——— (2010). *Plasticity at the Dusk of Writing: Dialectic, Destruction, Deconstruction*, trans. Carolyn Sheared. New York: Columbia University Press.
——— (2012). *The New Wounded: From Neurosis to Brain Damage*, trans. Stephen Miller. New York: Fordham University Press.
——— (2015a). "Will Sovereignty Ever Be Deconstructed?," in *Plastic Materialities: Politics, Legality, and Metamorphosis in the Work of Catherine Malabou*, eds. Brenna Bhandar and Jonathan Goldberg-Hiller. Duke University Press, 35–46.
——— (2015b). "From the Overman to the Posthuman: How Many Ends?," in *Plastic Materialities*, 61–72.
Malabou, Catherine, (ed.) (2000). *Plasticité*. Paris: Editions Léo Scheer.
Malabou, Catherine, and Vahanian Noëlle (2008). "A Conversation with Catherine Malabou." *JCRT* 9.1, 1–13.
Mangion, Claude (2012). "A Critical Commentary on Nietzsche's 'On the Origins of Language.'" *New Nietzsche Studies* 8, 3–4, 35–45.

Martis, John S. J. (2006). *Philippe Lacoue-Labarthe: Representation and the Loss of the Subject*. New York: Fordham University Press.
Mauss, Marcel (1995). *Sociologie et anthropologie*. Paris: Presses Universitaires de France.
—— (1966). *The Gift: Forms and Functions of Exchange in Archaic Societies*. London: Cohen & West, 1966.
Mckeane, John (2015). *Philippe Lacoue-Labarthe: (Un)Timely Meditations*. London: Legenda.
McKenna, Andrew (1992). *Violence and Difference: Girard, Derrida, and Deconstruction*. Urbana: University of Illinois Press.
McLuhan, Marshall (1962). *The Gutenberg Galaxy: The Making of Typographic Man*. Toronto: University of Toronto.
—— (1964). *Understanding Media: The Extension of Man*. New York: New American Library.
Melberg, Arne (2008). *Theories of Mimesis*. Cambridge: Cambridge University Press.
Melzoff, Andrew N. (2011). "Out of the Mouths of Babes: Imitation, Gaze, and Intentions in Infant Research—the 'Like Me' Framework," in *Mimesis and Science: Empirical Research on Imitation and the Mimetic Theory of Culture and Religion*, 55–74.
Morin, Edgar (1970). *L'Homme et la mort*. Paris: Seuil.
—— (1973). *Le Paradigme perdu: la nature humaine*. Paris: Seuil.
—— (1986). *La Méthode: 3. La Connaissance de la connaissance*. Paris: Seuil.
—— (1991). *La Méthode: 4. Les Idées, leur habitat, leur vie, leurs meurs, leur organisation*. Paris: Seuil.
—— (1999). *Les Sept savoirs nécessaires à l'éducation de l'humanité*. Paris: Seuil.
—— (2001). *La Méthode: 5 L'humanité de l'humanité*. Paris: Seuil.
—— (2004). *La Méthode: 6. Ethique*. Paris: Seuil.
—— (2005). *The Cinema, or the Imaginary Man*, trans. Lorraine Mortimer. Minneapolis: University of Minnesota Press.
—— (2016). *Sur l'esthétique*. Paris: Robert Laffont.
—— (2018). *Le Cinéma: Un Art de la complexité*. Eds. Monique Peyrière et Chiara Simonigh.
—— (2020). *L'entrée dans l'ère écologique*. Editions de l'Aube.
—— (2020) *Changeons de voie: les leçons du coronavirus* (with Sabah Abouessalam). Paris:Denoël.
Mozer, Yariv (dir.) (2022). *The Devil's Confession: The Lost Eichmann Tapes*. Israel/United States: MGM & Tadmor Entertainment.
Mukamel, Roy, Arne D. Ekstrom, Jonas Kaplan, Marco Iacoboni, and Itzhak Fried (2010). "Single-Neuron Responses in Humans during Execution and Observation of Actions." *Current Biology* 20, 750–756.
Nancy, Jean-Luc (1982). *Le Partage des voix*. Paris: Galilée.
—— (2008). "D'une 'mimesis sans modèle' (interview avec Philippe Choulet)." *L'Animal: Littératures, Arts & Philosophies* 19–20, 107–114.
—— (2016). "The Image: Mimesis and Methexis," in *Nancy and Visual Culture*, eds. Carrie Giunta and Adrienne Janus. Edinburgh: Edinburgh University Press.
—— (2020). *Un Trop humain virus*. Paris: Bayard.
Nancy, Jean-Luc, and Nidesh Lawtoo (2022). "Mimesis: A Singular-Plural Concept." *CounterText* 8.1, 23–45.

Nas, Loes (1992). "The Unreel in Woody Allen's *Zelig*." *Literator* 13.3, 93–100.
Nietzsche, Friedrich (1967–1977). *Sämtliche Werke: Kritische Studienausgabe*, 15 vols., eds. Giorgio Colli and Mazzino Montinari. Berlin: De Gruyter.
—— (1954). *The Twilight of the Idols*, in *The Portable Nietzsche*, ed. and trans. Walter Kaufman. New York: Penguin Books, 463–563.
—— (1968). *The Will to Power*, trans. Walter Kaufmann. New York: Vintage.
—— (1974). *The Gay Science*, trans. Walter Kaufmann. New York: Vintage.
—— (1982). *Daybreak*, trans. R. J. Hollingdale. Cambridge: Cambridge University Press.
—— (1990). *Beyond Good and Evil*, trans. R. J. Hollingdale. New York: Penguin Books, 1990.
—— (1992). "Truth and Falsity in an Ultramoral Sense," in *Critical Theory since Plato (Revised Edition)*, 634–639.
—— (1995). *Human, All Too Human*, trans. Gary Handwerk. Stanford: Stanford University Press.
—— (1996a). *On the Genealogy of Morals*, trans. Douglass Smith. Oxford: Oxford University Press.
—— (1996b). "Homer's Contest," trans. and ed. Christa Davis Acampora. *Nietzscheana* 5, 1–8.
—— (2003). *Beyond Good and Evil*, trans. R. J. Hollingdale. London: Penguin.
—— (2005). *Thus Spoke Zarathustra*, trans. Graham Parkes. Oxford: Oxford University Press.
—— (2007) *Untimely Meditations*, ed. Daniel Breazeale, trans. R. J. Hollingdale. Cambridge: Cambridge University Press.
Parkes, Graham (1994). *Composing the Soul: Reaches of Nietzsche's Psychology*. Chicago: University of Chicago Press.
Pascual-Leone, Alvaro, Amir Amedi, Felipe Fregni, and Lotfi B. Merabet (2005). "The Plastic Human Brain Cortex." *Annual Review of Neuroscience* 28, 377–401.
Plato (1963a). *Ion*, in *The Collected Dialogues of Plato*, trans. Lane Cooper, eds. E. Hamilton and H. Cairns. Princeton: Princeton University Press, 215–228.
—— (1963b). *Phaedrus*, in *The Collected Dialogues of Plato*, trans. R. Hackforth, 475–525.
—— (1963c). *Republic*, in *The Collected Dialogues of Plato*, trans. Paul Shorey, 575–853.
—— (1963d). *Lesser Hippias*, in *The Collected Dialogues of Plato*, trans. Benjamin Jowett, 200–214.
Popper, Karl (2020). *The Open Society and Its Enemies*. Princeton: Princeton University Press.
Potolsky, Matthew. *Mimesis*. New York: Routledge, 2006.
Poulet, Georges (1972). "Criticism and the Experience of Interiority," in *The Structuralist Controversy*, 56–72.
Prazan, Michaël (dir.) (2011). *The Adolf Eichmann Trial*. Kuiv.
Ramachandran, V. S. (2011). *The Tell-Tale Brain: A Neuroscientist's Quest for What Makes Us Human*. New York: W. W. Norton & Company.
—— (2000). "Mirror Neurons and Imitative Learning as the Driving Force Behind the Great Leap Forward in Human Evolution," *Edge*. https://www.edge.org/conversation/mirror-neurons-and-imitation-learning-as-the-driving-force-behind-the-great-leap-forward-in-human-evolution.

Rizzolatti, Giacomo, and Antonio Gnoli (2016). *In the mi specchio: per una scienza dell'empatia*. Milan: Rizzoli.
Rizzolatti, Giacomo, and Corrado Sinigaglia (2008). *Mirrors in the Brain—How Our Minds Share Actions and Emotions*. Oxford: Oxford University Press.
Rose, Nikolas, and Joelle M. Abi-Rached (2013). *Neuro: The New Brain Sciences and the Management of the Mind*. Princeton: Princeton University Press.
Rosolato, Guy (1972). "The Voice and the Literary Myth," in *The Structuralist Controversy*, 201–214.
Salome, Lou (2001). *Nietzsche*, trans. and ed. Siegried Mandel. Chicago: University of Illinois Press.
Siemens, Herman (2001). "Agonal Configurations in the *Unzeitgemässe Betrachtungen*: Identity, Mimesis and the *Übertragung* of Cultures in Nietzsche's Early Thought." *Nietzsche-Studien* 30, 80–106.
—— (2021). *Agonal Perspectives on Nietzsche's Philosophy of Critical Transvaluation*. Berlin: De Gruyter.
Smith, Adam (2002). *The Theory of Moral Sentiments*, ed. Knud Haakonssen. Cambridge: Cambridge University Press.
Sophocles (1959). *Oedipus the King*. *The Complete Greek Tragedies* vol. II, trans. David Grene, eds. David Grene and Richmond Lattimore. Chicago: University of Chicago Press, 11–76.
Snyder, Timothy (2017). *On Tyranny: Twenty Lessons from the Twentieth Century*. New York: Tim Duggan Books.
—— (2018). *The Road to Unfreedom: Russia, Europe, America*. London: Bodley Head.
Sariosu, Mihai (1984). *Mimesis in Contemporary Theory: An Interdisciplinary Approach. Vol. 1 The Literary and Philosophical Debate*. Amsterdam: John Benjamins Publishing Company.
Stam, Robert, and Ella Shoat (1987). "*Zelig* and Contemporary Theory: Meditation on the Chameleon Text." *Enclitic* 9, 176–193.
Stangneth, Bettina (2014). *Eichmann before Jerusalem: The Unexamined Life of a Mass Murderer*. London: Vintage.
Stanley, Jason (2018). *How Fascism Works: The Politics of Us and Them*. New York: Random House.
Stano, Simona (2020). "The Internet and the Spread of Conspiracies," in *Routledge Handbook of Conspiracy Theories*, 483–496.
Staten, Henry (1990). *Nietzsche's Voice*. Ithaca, NY: Cornell University Press.
—— (2019). *Techne Theory: A New Language for Art*. New York: Bloomsbury.
Stein, Richard A., Oana Ometa, Sarah Pachtman Shetty, Adi Katz, Mircea Ionut Popitiu, andRobert Brotherton (2021). "Conspiracy Theories in the Era of Covid-19: A Tale of Two Pandemics." *The International Journal of Clinical Practice* 75, 1–5.
Stiegler, Bernard (1998). *Technics and Time 1: The Fault of Epimetheus*, trans. Richard Beardsworth and George Collins. Stanford: Stanford University Press.
Stratton, Jon (2001). "Not Really White—Again: Performing Jewish Difference in Hollywood Films since the 1980s." *Screen* 42.2, 152–166.
Stuker, Jeffrey and Jan Tumlir (eds.) (2022). *Mimicries*. *Effects* 3.
Swift, Simon (2009). *Hannah Arendt*. London: Routledge.
Tarde, Gabriel (1901). *L'Opinion et la foule*. Paris: Félix Alcan.

——— (2001). *Les Lois de l'imitation*. Paris: Seuil.
Tattersall, Ian (2022). "Homo Sapiens." *Encylopedia Britannica*. https://www.britannica.com/topic/Homo-sapiens.
Tomlinson, Gary (2015). *A Million Years of Music: The Emergence of Modern Humanity*. New York: Zone Books.
Tomasello, Michael (2010). *Origins of Human Communication*. Cambridge, MA: MIT Press.
Vernant, Jean-Pierre (1972). "Greek Tragedy: Problems of Interpretation," in *The Structuralist Controversy*, 273–288.
——— *Myth and Society in Ancient Greece*, trans. Janet Lloyd. Sussex: Haverster Press, 1980.
Villa, Dana R. (1999). *Politics, Philosophy, Terror: Essays on the Thought of Hannah Arendt*. Princeton: Princeton University Press.
Whitman, Walt (1990). *Leaves of Grass*, ed. Jerome Loving. Oxford: Oxford University Press.
Wolf, Philipp (2022). "Posthuman Mimétisme: Caillois, Adorno and an Aesthetics of Mimesis." *Journal of Posthumanism* 2.2, 101–114.
Wolin, Richard (2014). "The Banality of Evil: The Demise of a Legend." *Jewish Review of Books*. https://jewishreviewofbooks.com/articles/1106/the-banality-of-evil-the-demise-of-a-legend.
Wordsworth, William (2005). "Preface to the Second Edition of *Lyrical Ballads*," in *Critical Theory Since Plato 3rd ed.*, eds. Hazard Adams and Leroy Searle. Boston: Thomson Wadsworth, 482–492.
Wojciehowski, Hannah Chapelle (2011). "Interview with Vittorio Gallese." California Italian Studies 2.1. https://escholarship.org/uc/item/56f8v9bv
Wulf, Christoph (2004). *Anthropology: A Continental Perspective*, trans. Deirdre Winter et al. Chicago: University of Chicago Press.
——— (2022). *Human Beings and Their Images: Imagination, Mimesis, Performativity*, trans. Elizabeth Hamilton and Deirdre Winter. London: Bloomsbury.
Žižek, Slavoj (2020). *Pandemic! COVID-19 Shakes the World*. New York: Polity Press.

# INDEX

**A**

Abi-Rached, Joelle, 131
Abrams, M. H., 261
actor, 137-138, 144-148, 152, 184, 192, 198, 199-205. *See also* mime, mimesis
aesthetics, 188, 199, 318-319. *See also* mimesis
affect. *See* pathos, contagion
Agamben, Giorgio, 111, 288
Allen, Woody: *Zelig*, 30, 192-224
*Anciens/Modernes* (*querelle*), 25, 145-146
androcentrism, 25, 72. *See also* mimetic sexism
animal mimicry, 48-49, 161, 163, 167, 171-176, 201-205, 209, 309. *See also* mimicry
animation, 87-90
Anthropocene, 22, 31, 67, 98, 161, 164-166, 186-189, 255, 270, 274-277, 299, 322
anthropocentrism, 25, 161, 163-164, 166, 175, 186, 187
Arendt, Hannah, 74, 114; and banality of evil, 192-193, 220-224, 229-253; and inability to think, 238-241, 246, 250, 332 (n. 10), 333 (n. 18, n. 19); and *vita activa/contemplativa*, 74-76, 86-88, 93, 113, 181, 231, 233, 324 (n. 4), 333 (n. 16)
Aristotle: *Poetics*, 12-14, 48, 100, 145-146, 148, 150, 161, 237-238, 311, 317, 321 (n. 3), 333 (n. 16)
assimilation: cultural, 195, 197-198, 217; environmental, 165, 188
Audiard, Jacques, 315
Auerbach, Erich, 28

**B**

Bach-y-Rita, Paul, 149
Barthes, Roland, 95, 96, 136
Bataille, Georges, 111, 136, 142, 150, 188, 307; and Caillois, 157-160, 169, 172, 308, 330 (n. 15)
Baudrillard, Jean, 39, 286
Bellow, Saul, 196, 213, 217
Benjamin, Walter, 34, 47, 159, 165-166, 70-171, 270
Bennett, Jane, 147, 162, 257, 329 (n. 6); *Influx & Efflux*, 257-276
Bernays, Edward, 215-216
Bernheim, Hippolyte, 184-185, 208, 211-212, 215, 240, 334 (n. 24)
Bettelheim, Bruno, 195-196, 207, 213
birth, 20, 23, 31-32; of consciousness, 43-67; of the subject, 112-120
Black Lives Matter, 31, 265, 293. *See also* mimetic racism
Bloom, Harold: anxiety of influence, 109, 261, 265, 274, 334 (n. 5)
Borch-Jacobsen, Mikkel, 135, 182, 207, 330 (n. 17), 334 (n. 24)
brain, 131-132, 146-148. *See also* plasticity, mirror neurons
Brennan, Teresa, 168, 329 (n. 10)
Breton, André, 157
Burckhardt, Jacob, 81-82
Butler, Judith, 232, 322 (n. 17)
Butter, Michael, 297-298

**C**

Caillois, Roger, 24, 28, 49, 157-188, 198, 203, 255, 323 (n. 7); and College of Sociology, 159-160; and diagonal science, 165-171, 186; and Lacan 158, 162-163, 179-182
Cavarero, Adriana, 31, 64, 74, 77-79, 80, 84, 114, 236, 325 (n. 14); *Inclinations*, 71-73. *See also* mimetic inclinations
Changeux, Jean-Pierre, 132, 153-154

351

Charcot, Jean-Martin, 208, 211
Chertok, Léon, 208
cinema, 208, 304, 310-311, 315, 318. *See also* Allen
class, 196-197
complexity, 18-19, 301-304. *See also* Morin
conformism, 123, 157, 192-193, 195-196, 203-204, 206. *See also* mimicry, mimetism
Connolly, William E., 164-165, 218, 270, 274, 275, 302, 332 (n. 5)
Conrad, Joseph, 235, 244
consciousness: origins of, 43, 51-67; and birth, 115-119
conspiracy theories, 295-299
contagion: affective 21, 29, 33, 66-67, 77, 80, 88, 130, 152, 159, 160, 168, 170, 182-186, 238, 252, 280-283; viral, 277-284, 290-295
COVID-19, 31, 265, 277-279. *See also* contagion
critical race theory, 29-30
crowd. *See* mass
crowd psychology, 74, 168, 185, 215, 217, 290-295. *See also* hypnosis
Crutzen, Paul, 164

**D**

Darwin, Charles, 44, 50-51, 62, 201
deconstruction, 28-29, 34, 53, 97, 101-107, 147. *See also* Derrida, Lacoue-Labarthe
Derrida, Jacques, 28, 44, 66, 280, 322 (n. 20); and Girard, 97-112, 326 (n. 7); and interpretation, 101-102; and Malabou, 134-135, 152-153; *Of Grammatology*, 103-104
desire, 33, 34, 36-37, 66, 97. *See also* mimetic desire, Girard
deterritorialization, 30-31, 94, 275
Diderot, Denis, 147, 328 (n. 15)
Dionysus, 78, 79, 81, 86-88, 157, 173; and Apollo, 79, 86, 114, 178-179, 231, 246-248
Dodds, E. R., 268, 335 (n. 9)
Doidge, Norman, 131-132

doodle, 271-272
double, 180, 310
Dumézil, Georges, 169
Dzigam, Efim, 307

**E**

ecology of action, 314-315
Eco, Umberto, 227-228, 297
echo, 86-90
Eichmann, Adolf, 30, 220-224, 231-253. *See also* Arendt
Ellenberger, Henri, 177, 264
Else, Gerald, 321 (n. 3)
Elon, Amos, 239
embodied simulation, 212-213, 287. *See also* mirror neurons
empathy 56, 63, 188, 315, 317. *See also* sympathy, pathos
enthusiasm, 77-78, 132, 241-242, 245-246, 325 (n. 13), 325 (n. 16); poetic, 77-80, 147
envy (*Eris*): good/bad, 80, 84, 111. *See also* mimetic agonism
epidemic. *See* COVID-19
Escher, M. C.: *Drawing Hands*, 9-12, 19, 21-22, 25, 26, 27, 31, 37, 40, 303
Esposito, Roberto, 203, 327 (n. 14), 331 (n. 5)
Euripides, 77, 78
evil (banality of). *See* Arendt, Eichmann

**F**

fascism, 29, 73, 182, 184, 193, 205, 209, 227-228; and (new) fascism, 193, 218, 228, 252, 293, 315-316; and Ur-fascism, 227-228. *See also* Nazism
Farrow, Mia, 205, 207-208
feedback loop, 12, 18-19, 21, 22, 38, 39, 164, 187, 280, 287, 289, 303, 314-315. *See also* patho-*logy*
Fitzgerald, Scott F., 196
form: give/receive, 132, 134-135, 137-144, 146
Foucault, Michel, 26, 67
Frank, Claudine, 169
Frankfurt School, 311

Freud, Sigmund, 50, 100-101, 108, 111, 115, 166, 177, 181, 183, 206-208, 264, 330 (n. 17)
Fumaroli, Marc, 146

## G

Gallese, Vittorio, 55, 118, 212-213, 287
genealogy, 14, 15, 26-32, 36-37, 43, 45-46, 86-87, 95, 105, 107-110; of homo mimeticus, 43-67, 98, 114-117. *See also* Nietzsche
genius, 50, 58, 123, 150-151, 170, 261
Girard, René, 33, 35, 44, 66, 135, 261, 313; and Derrida, 97-112; and Freud, 36, 50, 100-101, 108, 321 (n. 5); and Oedipus, 99-101, 105; and pandemic, 281-283, 291, 335 (n. 4); and structuralism, 98-101
Gebauer, Gunter, 302, 321 (n. 3), 335 (n. 3)
Guerra, Michele, 212

## H

Harari, Yuval, 20, 70, 92, 279, 324 (n. 1), 335 (n. 2)
Harris, Steve, 179
Harrison, Jane, 82-83
Havelock, Eric, 78, 131, 138, 285
Hayles, Katherine N., 335 (n. 1)
Hegel, Georg Wilhelm Friedrich, 133-134
Helme, Brigitte, 311
*hermeneia*, 83, 88-89
Hickok, Gregory, 122, 213
Hofstadter, Douglas, 21
Holocaust, 220, 229. *See also* Nazism
Hollier, Denis, 159, 168, 172-173
Homer, 12, 76-81, 170, 242, 297; *Odyssey*, 17-18; vs. Plato, 80-90; *Iliad*, 90-91, 296
*homo ludens*, 19-20, 82, 183, 305, 330 (n. 23)
*homo plasticus*, 150-155. *See also* plasticity
*Homo sapiens*, 11, 20, 23, 25-26, 34, 92, 124; ontogenesis, 115-121

origins of language/consciousness, 43-67; pre-historical evolution of, 39, 43, 164; great leap forward, 59-61; phylogenesis, 43-67, 121
Huizinga, Johan, 19-20, 82, 183. *See also homo ludens*
hypermimesis, 34, 39-40, 70, 187, 287, 298
hyperreal, 39-40, 286-287, 298, 312. *See also* hypermimesis
hyperspecialization, 169-170, 186, 302-303
hypnosis, 205-214, 217, 239-240. *See also* suggestion
Hrdy, Sarah Blaffer, 63-64, 72, 118, 121
hysteria, 207, 319

## I

identification, 17, 33, 64, 83, 100-101, 131, 135, 138, 144, 180-181, 183, 211, 229, 232, 234, 238, 240, 245-249, 249, 263, 265, 311, 314, 318. *See also* mimesis, imitation
IJsseling, Samuel, 325-326 (n. 18)
*imago*, 28, 32, 46, 163. *See also* Lacan
imprinting, 306
immunization, 203, 277-279, 284, 290, 293, 295, 298, 393 (n. 6)
influence, 71, 123-124, 162-164, 210. 215-216, 232, 256, 259, 261, 263-266, 270-273. *See also* hypnosis, suggestion
instinct, 46, 48-52, 66, 200-202, 204-205, 209-210, 212, 214. *See also* nature/culture
interdisciplinarity, 16, 24, 47, 118, 120, 124-125, 166, 301-303
Irigaray, Luce, 324-325 (n. 9)

## J

Janet, Pierre, 177-179, 181, 183, 208, 314, 330 (n. 18)

## K

Knight, Pieter, 297-298

## L

Lacan, Jacques, 96, 158, 330 (n. 21); mirror stage, 28, 123, 162-163, 179-182, 331 (n. 7)

Lacoue-Labarthe, Philippe, 130-132, 135, 147-152; *L'Imitation des modernes*, 15, 129-130, 145-150, 328 (n. 10); and Nancy, 82, 85, 144, 325 (n. 13, 15); and typography, 137-144. *See also* plasticity

Laertes, Diogenes, 139-140

Lawrence, D. H., 258, 260-261

Lawtoo, Michaela, 189

Le Bon, Gustave, 217, 290-294. *See also* crowd psychology

Leroi-Gourhan, André, 59-60,

Lévi-Strauss, Claude, 103, 309, 328 (n. 13). *See also* structuralist controversy

Linaeus, Carl, 25

*logos*, 17, 53, 57-58, 64, 67, 70, 74-75, 81, 85, 87, 92, 104, 113, 116, 122, 134, 200, 202; and *lexis* 89-91. *See also* patho-*logy*

## M

Macksey, Richard, 94, 96, 326 (n. 1)

magic, 159, 164, 171-172, 178, 185, 266, 270

magnetism, 77-78, 83, 242, 260. *See also* enthusiasm, hypnosis

Malabou, Catherine, 130-135, 143-144, 150-155, 273

mask, 131, 183-184, 202

mass, 73, 74, 136, 142, 148, 152, 182-186, 193, 196, 198, 200, 214-215, 217-218, 220, 223, 290, 292-294. *See also* contagion, crowd psychology

Mauss, Marcel, 278, 281

Mbembe, Achille, 283

McCarthy, Mary, 239, 33 (n. 18)

McKenna, Andrew, 104, 326 (n. 6)

McLuhan, Marshall, 89

media violence, 312-313

medium/message, 79, 89, 91, 194-195, 209-211

metaphor, 45-46, 52, 77, 100, 114, 115, 169, 197, 198, 203, 213, 269, 279, 280-283, 289, 291-292

metamorphosis, 28, 67, 124-125, 149, 166, 184, 186, 188-189, 192, 199, 203, 204, 275, 299

*methexis* (participation), 82-83, 250, 268, 308, 325 (n. 13)

#MeToo, 31, 208. *See also* mimetic sexism

mime (*mimos*), 13, 29, 76, 81-82, 96, 117, 138, 139, 201, 285, 321 (n. 3), 238.

mimesis: and "Allegory of the Cave," 17, 71, 74-91, 93, 137, 285, 286, 325 (n. 14); and Aristotle, 12-14, 19, 38, 48, 145-146, 148, 161, 237-238, 311, 321 (n. 3); complexity of, 18-19, 301-304; deconstruction of, 28-29, 34, 101-105; and education, 17-18, 87, 140-141; and examples, 61, 90, 117, 185, 244, 251, 253; genealogy of, 27-33; and Homer, 17-18, 76-78, 80, 90-91; and imitation, 15-16, 18, 20, 25, 32-33; and Jews, 200-205; and mimos, 13, 29, 76, 82-83, 138; oral vs. visual, 84-90; and plasticity, 129-155, 203; performance, 14, 17, 29, 271-272; and Plato, 13, 16, 28, 38, 71-74, 104-106, 122-123, 134, 136-155, 180, 210; quarrel (philosophy and art), 15-19, 69-91; and realism, 9-10, 28; restricted/general, 141-147; ritual, 13-14; and sameness, 25, 34, 73-74; structuralist controversy, 95-97; and theater, 85, 236-237; and writing, 103-104

mimetic agonism, 12, 33, 92, 98, 169, 325 (n. 10); Girard and Derrida, 97-112, 326 (n. 7); Malabou and Derrida, 135; and mimetic rivalry 36, 50, 80-90; Plato and Aristotle, 12-13, 38, 145; Plato and Homer, 17-18, 76-77, 79, 80-90, 170

mimetic communication, 48, 50-56, 65-66, 120-122

mimetic criticism, 98-112

mimetic desire, 36-37, 66, 99, 108. *See also* Girard
mimetic inclinations, 31, 71-74, 77-78, 114. *See also* Cavarero
mimetic pathos, 14, 37-38, 53-54, 57, 64-65, 67, 89-90, 92, 114, 154, 222, 229, 238, 241, 246, 250, 257, 260-261, 263, 267, 284, 289-290, 314; and Allegory of the Cave, 73-74, 81, 83, 89, 93
mimetic racism, 29-31, 72, 195, 201
mimetic rivalry, 50, 80, 99, 101, 108. *See also* mimetic agonism
mimetic sexism, 29-31, 72, 200-201
mimetic studies, 11-40, 43, 57, 61, 64, 70, 76, 81, 92-95, 97, 104-105, 111, 114, 116-117, 120-125, 160, 301-302, 321 (n. 5); and paradox, 17, 21
mimetic turn, 12, 19, 33, 50-51, 130, 131, 137, 157, 162, 165, 186, 321 (n. 2); *re*-tun 12, 16, 44, 56-57, 63, 104-105, 154, 257-259, 266; and structuralism, 95-97; and plasticity, 130, 136, 154; and new materialism, 257, 259, 276, 334 (n. 25)
mimetic unconscious, 15, 30-31, 37, 36, 47, 54-56, 65-66, 112, 113, 115-121, 123-124, 155, 162, 168, 183, 192, 204, 212-215, 240, 264-265, 293, 294, 298, 324 (n. 11). *See also* suggestion, hypnosis, mirror neurons
mimetism, 14, 49, 69, 72, 123, 138, 142, 157-158, 162-163, 165-168, 170-174, 176-184, 186-188, 195, 203, 209, 306-308, 309-310, 323 (n. 7). *See also* mimesis, mimicry
mimicry, 28-31, 33, 38, 46, 49, 50, 54, 60-62, 64, 157-159, 161, 163, 165, 167, 170-178, 180-183, 185-188, 195, 200-205, 209, 260, 322 (n. 14), 323 (n. 7). *See also* animal mimicry, mimesis, mimetism
mirror neurons, 33, 36, 54-55, 118-119, 122, 191-192, 205, 212-215, 240, 265, 287, 292, 302, 307, 317, 327 (n. 18, n. 20); and human evolution, 61-62. *See also* mimetic unconscious, Rizzolatti, Gallese
Morin, Edgar, 18-19, 51, 211, 278, 301-319
mother, 31-32, 46, 63-64, 72-73, 111, 113-115, 118, 121; stereotype of, 72-73, 121. *See also* birth
Muse, 77-80, 84-85, 125. *See also* enthusiasm
myth, 12, 17, 18, 20, 26, 33, 50, 65, 69, 70, 285, 287, 290, 296; and *logos*, 16-17, 21, 23, 81

N
Nancy, Jean-Luc, 77, 268, 278; and Lacoue-Labarthe, 82, 85, 137; and *Partage des voix*, 80, 81, 83-84
nature/culture, 51, 202-205, 268, 301, 308
Nazism, 159, 185, 193, 196, 200, 216-224, 315-317. *See also* Arendt, Eichmann
new media, 15, 34, 65, 70, 182, 187, 191, 194, 211, 223, 228, 230, 252, 279, 282, 286, 288, 295-297, 301, 320. *See also* hypermimesis
new materialism, 147, 255-257. *See also* Bennett
Nietzsche, Friedrich, 31-32, 36-38, 44-67, 71, 75-76, 88, 148, 245, 248, 257, 267-268, 284, 299; and actor, 199-205; and birth, 114-119; and *Daybreak*, 48-49, 55-57, 173; and *Gay Science*, 47-52, 57, 65-66, 123, 125; and *Genealogy of Morals*, 26, 27, 45-46, 98, 105, 136; *Human, All Too Human*, 53; "Homer's Contest," 80-81; and interpretation, 45-46, 323 (n. 4); and Jews, 200-205; and origins of language/consciousness, 45-67; and (animal) and mimicry, 48-49, 120-121, 161, 173, 204-205; and perspectivism, 46, 58; and *Will to Power*, 35-36, 45; and will to power, 53, 57, 200
nomadism, 30-31, 35, 38, 149

## O

Oedipal unconscious, 111-112, 118, 206, 264
originality, 9, 32-33, 47, 62, 81, 109, 113, 124, 170, 256, 261, 303

## P

Pabst, Wilhelm George, 311
pandemic. *See* COVID-19
Parkes, Graham, 268
Pascual-Leon, Alvaro, 131, 149, 153
pathology, 38, 49-50, 74, 109, 153, 177, 181, 193, 205, 207-209, 229, 246, 251, 282. *See also* contagion, patho(-)logy
patho-*logy*, 21, 31, 34, 144, 167, 200-205, 207-208, 246-247, 289; and Arendt, 236-241; and Nietzsche, 38, 49, 54, 62, 67, 148; and Plato, 75, 80, 91; and pandemic 277, 280. *See also* mimetic agon, patho(-)logy
patho(-)logy, 38, 40, 70, 132, 208, 229, 244, 252-253, 278; and Plato, 73, 76; and Nietzsche, 200-205
*pathos*, 37-38, 52-54, 57-58, 70-71, 73-75, 135, 145, 147, 152, 153, 155, 184, 185, 200, 202, 222, 229, 230-231, 233, 239, 243, 268; and *logos*, 46, 76, 79, 81, 234, 240, 246. *See also* mimetic pathos, patho-*logy*
pathos of distance, 37-38, 40, 57, 83, 85, 230, 232, 240, 258-259, 261, 262, 265, 272, 284, 317
phantom of the ego, 15, 32, 34, 35, 37, 46, 71, 123, 147, 161, 181, 203, 239, 243, 244, 257, 275, 286
*pharmakon* (poison/remedy), 44, 65, 102-112, 116, 153, 155, 277, 280, 326 (n. 7). *See also* patho(-)logy
*pharmakos* (scapegoat), 44, 65, 96, 102-112, 116, 289
Plato, 13, 16, 28, 38, 69-91, 289; "Allegory of the Cave," 74-76, 84-90, 137, 284-286, 311; and echo, 86-90; *Ion*, 76-78, 81-84, 242, 247; logos/lexis, 85, 89-90; and metaphysics, 70-71, 75, 86; and pathos 12, 17, 53; and plasticity, 137-144; and quarrel with poetry (Homer), 69-91; and representation, 12, 14, 28, 43; *Republic*, 12, 16-17, 28, 69-70, 75, 137-138, 141, 269
plasticity, 129-130, 133; vs. flexibility, 132, 151; genealogy of, 133-134, 138-139; and neuroplasticity, 131-132, 149; and Plato, 137-144; and Nietzsche 148; and Play-Doh, 140, 143; and paradox, 145, 203; and subjectivity, 133, 137-144. *See also* Lacoue-Labarthe, Malabou
play, 20, 183-184. See also *homo ludens*
Popper, Karl, 295-297, 336 (n. 14)
posthumanism, 34, 277, 286, 321-322 (n. 12)
poststructuralism, 34, 45, 60, 94, 96, 105. *See also* deconstruction, structuralism
post-truth, 39, 286
possession, 34, 71-72, 184, 242-243; poetic, 74, 77, 81
Poulet, Georges, 96

## Q

quarrel: philosophy and literature, 15-19, 69-80; Plato vs. Homer, 69-91. *See also* mimetic agon

## R

Ramachandran, V. S., 61-62, 212, 327 (n. 20)
Rizzolatti, Giacomo, 55, 62, 118, 119, 120, 213, 327 (n. 18). *See also* mirror neurons
romantic agonism, 109, 143, 261, 326 (n. 8), 334 (n. 5). *See also* mimetic agonism
Rose, Nikolas, 131
Rosolato, Guy, 96

## S

Sassen, Willem, 243
scapegoat, 50, 66, 92. *See also pharmakos*
Serres, Michel, 24

simulation, 38-39, 76, 286-287; in the cave, 88-89. *See also* hyperreal, hypermimesis
Sinigaglia, Corrado, 55, 119, 120, 213
Smith, Adam, 262, 334 (n. 6)
Snyder, Timothy, 193, 219, 332 (n. 3)
*socius*, 121, 314, 327 (n. 19)
Socrates. *See* Plato
spectacle (*opsis*), 85
Stangneth, Bettina, 230, 234-235, 238, 240, 242-243, 248, 250. *See also* Arendt, Eichmann
Stanley, Jason, 218
Staten, Henry, 324 (n. 7)
structuralism, 28, 94-96, 98, 101, 105, 157, 159, 186, 308
subject, 21, 96, 142; of *Aufklärung* 32, 33, 48, 160; mimetic, 10, 18, 22, 27-29, 82, 106, 114, 135, 137, 140, 142, 145, 146, 149, 154, 163, 203, 239, 256, 259, 273, 306. *See also* birth, phantom of the ego
suggestion, 11, 183-185, 206, 208, 210, 212, 215, 217, 223, 240, 256, 264, 292, 294. *See also* hypnosis, crowd psychology
surrealism, 158, 165, 172
sympathy, 21, 37, 57, 113, 114, 162, 232-233, 246, 256, 258-264, 267, 274, 314-315, 334 (n. 6). *See also* mimetic pathos

**T**
Tarde, Gabriel, 215, 217, 239, 291-292, 294, 316.
techne, 80, 83, 92, 242, 295, 324 (n. 6)

Tomasello, Michael, 62-64
trance, 175, 185, 208, 210, 214, 219, 260, 316, 319. *See also* hypnosis, possession
two-culture, 19, 54, 120, 186, 239, 278, 301

**U**
Ukraine (war), 191, 228, 332 (n. 3)

**V**
Vernant, Jean-Pierre, 81, 96, 110-112
*vita mimetica*, 17, 18, 26, 30, 40, 37, 93, 95, 160, 179, 199, 210-211, 215, 219, 220-221, 244, 250-252, 269, 273, 284-288, 301, 311; and "Allegory of the Cave," 71-79, 85-91; and evil, 231, 237, 233, 239, 236-238, 241-242, 247, 251; and vita *activa/contemplativa*, 74-76, 86-88, 93, 113, 152, 181, 258, 282

**W**
Wagner, Richard, 200
Whitman, Walt, 257, 258, 260, 263, 267
Wiene, Robert, 210
will to mime, 30, 51, 54, 57-58, 61-62, 66, 71, 90, 199, 202, 229, 231, 297
Wittgenstein, Ludwig, 62-63
Wulf, Christoph, 302, 321 (n. 3), 335 (n. 3)

**Z**
*Zelig*. *See* Allen
Žižek, Slavoj, 288